BLAIR KLING

# SOCIAL ANTHROPOLOGY OF PILGRIMAGE

# SOCIAL ANTHROPOLOGY
# OF PILGRIMAGE

*Edited by*

## MAKHAN JHA

# INTER-INDIA PUBLICATIONS
D-17 RAJA GARDEN EXTN.  NEW DELHI-110015 (INDIA)

**Cataloging in Publication Data—DK**

Social anthropology of pilgrimage / edited by
    Makhan Jha.

    Includes index.

    1. Hindu pilgrims and pilgrimages—India - Congresses.
    2. Ethnology—India --Congresses.    I. Jha, Makhan, 1941-


ISBN 81-210--0265-6

First Published in India in 1991

© Makhan Jha 1990
    **Makhan Jha** (*b*. 1941-    )


Published in India by:
M.C. Mittal
INTER-INDIA PUBLICATIONS
D-17, RAJA GARDEN EXTN.,
NEW DELHI-110015 (INDIA)
PHONE : 5413145


*Printed in India at :*
DEVENDRA PRINTERS
Hari Nagar
New Delhi-110064

# Acknowledgements

I am grateful to Professor Maver and Professor Rudan, the President and General Secretary respectively of the 12th ICAES, who so kindly approved the theme of this symposium and then extended all possible help in organising it at Zagreb.

Thanks are due to all my colleagues who took pains to write their papers, attended the symposium at Zagreb and, thereafter, have submitted the revised draft of their papers for publication. This volume, I believe, would not have come out without the kind cooperation of these colleagues and, therefore, I express my gratefulness to all of them.

My publisher friend, Shri M.C. Mittal, Inter-India Publications, New Delhi, has taken pains to publish it on priority basis for which I am very much thankful to him.

MAKHAN JHA

# Preface

DURING the fourth quarter of this century the inter-disciplinary researches on various aspects of the institution of pilgrimage have been much accelerated all over the world. During this period an important world conference on *Pilgrimage : the Human Quest* was held at Pittsburgh, U.S.A., in 1981, jointly sponsored by the Simon Frazer University, Canada, and the Department of Comparative Religion, University of Pittsburgh, U.S.A., in which nearly a hundred delegates, belonging to different disciplines, besides anthropologists, participated and emphasised upon the need to study the institution of pilgrimage from different angles to understand the networks of relations and complexities of the system, its growing importance in the ultra-modern age of scientific development, its continuity and change, its textual and contextual dimensions etc.

However, this successful world conference on Pilgrimage was followed by an international symposium on *Pilgrimage*, organised and chaired by me in 1983 at Vancouver, Canada, which took place on the occasion of Eleventh International Congress of Anthropological and Ethnological Sciences. Here again an inter-disciplinary approach was emphasised and the proceedings of that international symposium came out in the form of a book *Dimensions of Pilgrimage* (Jha : 1985), which has been received and reviewed all over the world.

In July, 1988, on the occasion of Twelfth International Congress of Anthropological and Ethnological sciences, and international symposium on *Social Anthropology of Pilgrimage* was organised and chaired by me at Zagreb, Yugoslavia, in which a large number of Anthropologists, Sociologists, Geographers, Historians, Linguists, Theologists and scholars of Comparative Religion participated and presented their papers on the varying issues and themes of pilgrimage. The scholars of different disciplines met at a common academic platform to exchange their views and notes to strengthen the common cause of studying the institution of pilgrimage of different societies of the world. The present volume, is based on the proceedings of that world symposium.

There are altogether twenty chapters in this volume. The first chapter of the volume begins with the *Grammatical and Notational Models of Indian Pilgrimage* written by the eminent anthropologist, Professor Agehanand Bharti, of the Syracuse University, New York. I have discussed the *History, Patronage and Social Organisation* of the Kamakhya Temple of Assam, an important Sakta pilgrimage centre in India, in the second chapter. Professor Lars Kjaerholm, a famous anthropologist from Denmark, who has done significant works in South India, has discussed the *Aiyanar and Aiyappan in Tamil Nadu : Change and Continuity in South Indian Hinduism* in the third chapter.

Professor S.M. Bhardwaj, who is a Professor of Geography, Kent State University, Ohio, U.S.A. has thrown light on *Hindu Pilgrimage in America* in the fourth chapter. In the fifth chapter Professor Edward J. Jay, who is known for his work in Indian anthropology has described the *Pañc Kosi Yatra : A Sub-Regional Pilgrimage of Southern Chhatisgarh*, India. Dr. Karma Oraon has thrown light on the *Impact of Hindu Pilgrimage on Tribal Life* in the sixth chapter. Dr. Balanand Sinha, a Psychologist, has studied the *Musicians of a Pilgrimage Centre in India : A Case Study*, which he discusses in the seventh chapter of this volume.

The eighth and ninth chapters have been jointly written by a group of anthropologists of the Department of Social Anthropology, Shri Venkateshwar University, Tirupati. While Dr. V. Narayana Reddy and Professor A. Munirathnam Reddy have contributed a long paper on the *History and Patronage of Tirumala-Tirupathi Devesthanam*, Dr. Vijay Kumar and Professor M. Suryanarayana have jointly discussed *Srisailam : A Shaivite Pilgrimage Centre, Andhra Pradesh, India.*

I have discussed the *Sacred Complex of Kathmandu* with special reference to the Pashupatinath Temple in the tenth chapter, while Dr. Dinesh Kumar has described the *Sacred Complex af Badrinath*, a famous Himalayan *Tirtha* of the Hindus, in the eleventh chapter. Mrs. Sabita Acharya of the

Department of Anthropology, Utkal University, has discussed about *Puri : A Centre of Pilgrimage of Eclectic Shrine* in the twelfth chapter.

Dr. Jitendra Singh and Dr. J.C. Das of the Anthropological Survey of India have contributed two papers for this volume. Their joint papers on the *Traditions of Kumbha : A Study in Continuity and Change* and the *Concept of Tirtha and Traditions of Tirtha-Yatra in the Himalayas* have been accommodated in fourteenth and fifteenth chapter respectively. Another scholar from the Anthropological Survey of India, **Dr.** Asim Maitra, has written on the *Parasuram Kund—A Hindu Centre of Pilgrimage in North-East India,* which he describes in the sixteenth chapter.

Professor Leslie Ellen Straub, O.P., is a famous lady anthropologist of America and she makes analysis of the *Formal Replication in Costa Rican Pilgrimage* in the seventeenth chapter. Professor Rene Gothoni of the Department of Comparative Religion, University of Helsinki, Finland, has studied the *Progress of Pilgrimage on the Holy Mountain of Athos,* which he describes in the eighteenth chapter. Professor **D.J.** Davies of the University of Nottingham, U.K., is both an anthropologist and theologist and his analysis of *Pilgrimage in Mormon Culture* finds expression in the nineteenth chapter. The twentieth chapter is on *Intensification Rituals of Revitalization of Sacred Stages in North-West Mexico and North-West Peru* by Professor N. Ross Crumrine, University of Victoria, Canada.

MAKHAN JHA

# Contents

# List of Contributors

AGEHANANDA BHARATI

Professor of Anthropology, Department of Anthropology, Syracuse University, New York, U.S.A.

A. MUNIRATHNAM REDDY

Professor of Anthropology, Department of Social Anthropology, Shri Venkateshwar University, Tirupati.

ASIM MAITRA

Assistant Anthropologist, Anthropological Survey of India, Shillong, Meghalaya, India.

BALANAND SINHA

Lecturer in Psychology, Bhagalpur University, Bhagalpur.

CHANDRA MAULI JHA

Lecturer in Anthropology, Mandar College, Ranchi University, Ranchi.

DINESH KUMAR

Lecturer in Anthropology, S.S.J.S. Namdhari College, Garhwa, Palamau (Ranchi University).

D.J. DAVIES

Senior Lecturer, Department of Theology, The University of Nottingham, England.

EDWARD J. JAY

Professor of Anthropology, California State University, Hayward, California, U.S.A.

JAGDISH CHANDRA DAS

Anthropologist, Anthropological Survey of India, North India Station, Dehradun, India.

JITENDRA SINGH

Anthropologist, Anthropological Survey of India, North India Station, Dehradun, India.

LARS KJAERHOLM

Professor of Anthropology, Department of Anthropology, Aarhus University, Denmark.

KARMA ORAON

Reader and Head, Department of Anthropology, Ranchi College, Ranchi University, Ranchi, India.

LESLIE ELLEN STRAUB, O.P.

Professor of Anthropology and Director of Anthropology Programme, Providence College, Providence, U.S.A.

MAKHAN JHA

Professor of Anthropology, U.G.C. Centre of Advanced Study, Department of Anthropology, Ranchi University, Ranchi, India.

M. SURYANARAYANA

Reader in Anthropology, Department of Social Anthropology, Shri Venkateshwar, University, Tirupati.

N. ROSS CRUMRINE

Professor of Anthropology, University of Victoria, Canada.

RENE GOTHONI

Professor of Comparative Religion, Department of Comparative Religion, University of Helsinki, Finland.

SABITA ACHARYA

Lecturer in Anthropology, Department of Anthropology, Utkal University, Bhubneshwar, India.

SURINDER MOHAN BHARDWAJ

Professor of Geography, Department of Geography, Kent State University, Kent Ohio, U.S.A.

V. NARAYANA REDDY

Lecturer in Anthropology, Department of Social Anthropology, Shri Venkateshwar University, Tirupati, Andhra Pradesh, India.

VIJAY KUMAR

Chief Public Relations Officer, Tirumala-Tirupati Devesthanam, Tirupati, Andhra Pradesh, India.

# List of Tables

# List of Illustrations

1. Girl with *irumudi* at start of journey for Sabari Malai
2. An Aiyappan altar
3. Main Entrance—Kamakhya Temple, Assam
4. Goat Sacrifice – Kamakhya Temple Assam
5. A distant view of Badridham
6. Author with the Kaulacharya of Kamakhya Temple
7. Indian delegates at the 12th ICAES at Zagreb
8. Indian participants at the symposium
9. A session in progress
10. Sathagoparamaniya group waiting to receive the Raja of Pandalam
11. Gorakhnath Temple at Mrigendra-Van, Nepal
12. Pashupati Temple with river Bagmati in foreground
13. The author with Prof. Rene Gothoni
14. Main Entrance—Badrinath Temple

# List of Figures

# 1

# Grammatical and Notational Models of Indian Pilgrimage

### Agehananda Bharati

In the polarization between idiography and nomothetics, the latter has emerged as a clear winner in the social sciences. The nagging question still remains, however, whether all cultural behaviour, all specialized human activities are amenable to nomothetic analysis and, even if they are, whether a purely nomothetic approach is heuristically productive. In Hinduism, attempts at generalization and cross-cultural comparison, viz. at a global nomothetic, turn out to be less than helpful. The late Victor Turner, a reference key figure in pilgrimage studies as well as one meriting reference, said many things about pilgrimages and pilgrimage. His theses of the liminoid, liminality, of anti-structure, of *communitas* had nomothetic intent. That it does not, or does not quite work for the subcontinent, can be gleaned not only from straight criticism in some studies, but also from the often reluctant effort to accommodate his insights somehow. A highly complex and culture specific template like Hindu pilgrimage, both as precept and performance, mandates a mix of idiographic and nomothetic query. The former is represented by indologists, the latter by social scientists. Recently, however, a bridge has been built between the two. Inspired by Habermas and Gadamer, anthropologists have seriously begun to acquire indological, read philological skills. Clifford Geertz's "thick description" combines elements of all of these in addition to his specific kind of symbol analysis, very different again from Turner's uses of "symbol" as well as from the Jungian and Eliadean overkill by historians of religion.

The seminal conference at Pittsburgh in 1981 started if all those incipient efforts of the participants kept maturing and growing in size, and we may look at this panel as a continuation. Some of my fellow presenters here are no doubt friends or purveyors of *communitas* or of its denial respectively, who look for structure and antistructure. All of these provide resonant counterpoints like in a good symphonic composition.

In the analysis of Indian pilgrimage, Durkheim no longer remains canonical. His axiomatic sacred-profane dichotomy is quite counterproductive for the understanding of Hindu pilgrimage, as well as of Hinduism in general. Jesus evicted the traders and shopkeepers from the temple; much more recently, the Srilanka government converted Kataragama into *sudhanagare* "pure city", legislating shops, drinks, and fun out of the area, to the detriment of the place and the alienation of pilgrims. Durkheim might have looked back to Jerusalem and ahead to Colombo, where latter-day leaders have no doubt been inspired and informed by a western, puritanical, alien notion of the sacred and the profane. Quite recently, and with some mirth, I observed a pilgrim taking the holiest of all possible baths at the Daśāsvamedha Ghāṭ in Varanasi, holding his transistor radio to his ear to monitor the cricket test match against the West Indies broadcast from Calcutta. Neither the anthropologist nor any of the other pilgrims thought this improper—only the tour guide from the Clarks Hotel haranguing a group of American tourists in a boat did.

At Pittsburgh, I suggested the term *patology* and *patetic* (from Greek *pat-ein* "to walk, move", as in peri-patetic) to characterize the infrastructure of all pilgrimage, cutting across emic-etic boundaries without threatening to go anemic and emetic in G.D. Berreman's terms. Patogenesis englobes kinesics, the style of motion and locomotion, the pilgrims' compartment, his or her total demeanour *in situ* as well as *ante situm* and *post situ*. The pathological frame should be a constant in the behavioural rather than the textual study of pilgrimage. The textualists will, and should go their own way, the social scientist needs their input, editions and translations, commentary, apparatus, and all of the *sathalapurānas*, of pamphlets and touting literature, and of the written word in so far as it prompts and promotes pilgrimages. Ideally, scholars should do both, but that is too much to ask from people, and there are limits to polymathy.

Whether appraisals are pathological, patogenic, or other, the uniqueness of Hindu pilgrimage stands out. It is manifest wherever Hindu pilgrims go, on the subcontinent, in the Subramania caves near Kuala Lumpur, in Srilanka, Pittsburgh or Flushing, New York. There is an ostentive element in it, clearer perhaps than even the best analyses; it is a case of Wittgensteinian *das zeigt sich-das ist das Mystische*. Once this has been recognized as the *modus operandi*, other clusters constituting Indian pilgrimage fall in line. In the first place, there is *darśana*, sight, encounter with the deity both as motivation and consummation. *Darśana* is the patological centre piece. Stated intentions, petitions, precations both pragmatic and salvific can be seen as the structure atop the patetic infrastructure; the aesthetic-sensuous corollaries, the quasi-tourist aspects, the shopping and spending, the fun and games are the superstructure. *Darśana* is a bilateral vision of the deity—it is the pilgrim viewing divinity and the divine viewing the pilgrim, in token of which it returns to the pilgrim the blessed food and gifts as *praśada*.

F.J. Staal[1] has produced a seminal model for the analysis of ritual, the Vedic ritual in particular, i.e., as a norm-controlled, grammar-like template. Extrapolating this attempt to pilgrimage and amplifying it, I will show how pilgrimage—Hindu pilgrimage providing my empirical base—can indeed be read as sets of grammar-like rules. Since grammars signify or constitute largely unconscious processes of normative control, and since pilgrimage in its genesis and perpetuation is a conscious process —its creators might be mythical in emic perception, but must have been actual persons—they are to pilgrimage what creative grammarians (like Panini) are to grammar. I will show in this chapter that such an approach may well explain, among other things that have worried anthropologists observing pilgrimage, why pilgrims tend to be quite indifferent, nonenthusiastic, or even blaze about the ritualistic acts they perform or are made

to perform by the specialists. Let me demonstrate the merit of
this syntactic model. Up to this time several anthropologists
have been struggling with the problem of tourism as part of the
pilgrimage template. Now short of some sort of phenomenological, intentionalistic speculation about tourist-pilgrims or
pilgrim-tourists states of mind overlapping, about shared numi-
nous feelings, I have found no attempt at a formal analysis
that would cover tourism and pilgrimage as a new dual paradigm. This model fits rather elegantly. The tourists' movement,
like the pilgrims movement, consists, of course, of travel from
home to marked points and back—here we have a syntagmatic
situation in both cases. The tourist and the pilgrim stop for
sites and sights, where they do certain stereotyped things with
guides, specialists, cameras, children, shopkeepers and themselves—this is the paradigmatic element. Now when personal
things and events coincide between tourists and pilgrims, and
where the travel targets coincide by inclusion, we have a true
tourist-pilgrim paradigm. This notwithstanding the likely fact
that the tourist to a larger, the pilgrim to a lesser extent will
also visit other places en route, and enter other stationary
interactions—they may see such secular sites like a waterfall,
museum, a place to eat, a movie. These visits do not disturb
the syntactic model at all, just as, in the Saussurean linguistic
original, any number of added on clauses in the sentence do not
change the paradigmatic-syntagmatic structure, although they
enlarge the surface structure. Let me illustrate this by a simple
diagrammatic notation :

Pilgrim     A.B.C.D.     $\supset$ x,y,z, + F.G.N.   $\supset$ u,v,w,-n
tourist     A.B.C.D.     $\supset$ x,y,z + H.I.N.    $\supset$ r,s,t,-n

where the capital letters to the left of the + represent the
stationary, paradigmatic "stops", the small letters to the left of
the + the travel routes and targets; the capital letters to the
right of the + represent the "extras" by way of stationary acts
and encounters (paradigmatic), the small letters to the right of
the + the "extra" travelling routes. Where the values on the
left coincide, we have tourist-pilgrims, regardless of overlap or
dissimilarities on the right. Where the terms on the left do not
coincide, we have pilgrims and tourists as separate entities,
implying sheer pilgrimage or sheer tourism.

Let me rephrase this somewhat more impressionistically. In any specific sentence in a natural language, terms of the form X=a, b, c, . . . . n are paradigmatic, terms of the form X →Y are syntagmatic, or for those of you here who may not be familiar with that thesis, "Zagreb is the second largest city of Yugoslavia and it contains many beautiful people and sights" is a paradigmatic sentence, "Anthropologists from all over the world travelled to Zagreb last week" is sytagmatic. Analogously, those elements in a pilgrimage sequence which are fixed, stationary, and focal, are paradigmatic segments of the pilgrimage, like the shrines, the pandits, the ritual utensils. The movement of the pilgrims from home to the site, from key point to key point at the site and back home is syntagmatic. Easy enough, but what does it do for the analysis of pilgrimage ? Like all models, it does something, but not very much, or rather, something rather specific and nothing world shaking. It helps us in analytically distinguishing norms of place from norms of movement. What the priests, *paṇḍas*, and other specialists do vis-a-vis the pilgrim, and what he or she does by way of interacting with the specialist, follows a set of norms quite different from the norms controlling the pilgrims' decision-making, their itinerary, and the patetic sequence of the pilgrimage itself. Rather than muse about moods and feelings somehow spread along the route and their relation to feelings and moods at the place of ritual and worship, and rather than having to conflate processes of ritual with processes of getting there and away from it, we can attack these two separate structures with different tools. We can marshall indological texts including *sthalapurāṇas*, priestly manuals for the stationary rituals, and we can marshall tourist guides time tables, expense accounts, fiscal planning and layout, health care and pilgrims fun talk en route for the motion sequences of the pilgrimage.

Quoting from Obeyeskere's magnum opus *Pattini*, Staal writes "the hand may go wrong and the mouth may go wrong". These are the *kapurāla's* (Srilankan religious specialists) words when he asks the gods forgiveness for a mispronounced text or a wrong ritual movement. Staal elaborates that the clear emphasis here is no form, performance, not on meaning. Now this is of statutory importance not only for the study of pilgrimage, but in fact for all ritualistic acts misunderstood by

virtually all modernized Hindus and Buddhists. I have heard
dozens of modern Hindus, by no means only Arya Samajists,
complaining about the priests not knowing the meaning of the
text, not being able to explain it. This whole neo-Hindu and
neo-Buddhist idiom is one big dead alley. Meaning is important in one branch of religious thought and science in India,
i.e., in speculative abstraction and *Śāstrārtha* or doctrinal
disputation. It is not only not important, but quite irrelevant to
ritual. In South India, with its much greater sacerdotal sophistication than in the North, there is a social as well as a cognitive distinction between the *purohita*, the ritualist and the
*śāstrī*, the scholar, and no one who is knowledgeable would
charge the one with the necessary shortcoming of the other. It
is the performative aspect that counts. I have pointed this out
many times. St. Tambiah's piece about it is seminal and should
be made mandatory graduate reading.[2]

I shall now reapply these insights to pilgrimage. Quite
simply, a pilgrimage is emically successful when it has been
properly performed, not when the chants and prayers used by
pandits and other functionaries have been understood, nor
when it has "shown results" just exactly as in the case of a
wedding—its successful, *i.e.*, valid, when mantras have been
chanted, the right movements carried out (*pradakṣiṇa, saptapadī
aśmāroha*, etc.) not when the texts have been understood by the
priest or explained by him. Now in the case of weddings no
one ever even doubts the binding validity of the ritual, regardless of the pandits' prowess—in fact, as my North Indian
colleagues here well know, pandits are often urged to hurry up
with the recitation to leave more time for food, reception, and
other more conspicuous display. In talking about pilgrimage,
however, Hindu commentary tends to exhaust itself in complaining about priestly greed (actual and imagined). Priest and client,
however thorough the physical and recitation sequences prescribed, their feelings, attitudes, and degrees of faith, or numi-
nous involvement are totally irrelevant. In fore or hindsight,
the pilgrim and his kinsfolks talk, and probably think in terms
of *bhakti* humility, nearness to the deity, etc., but none of this
is necessarily present during the paradigmatic and little if anything during the syntagmatic phases of the pilgrimage. As the
Hindu pilgrim travels or walks from site to site, he may indeed

entertain properly religious sentiments but at the actual occur-rence of the ritual exchange for the duration of these actions and transactions properly "religious" thoughts, if they are maintained at all, are at best marginal in the minds of both the pilgrim and the practitioner. Performers, it should be known as a matter of general knowledge, must not and do not perform in a specific artistic or aesthetic mood –if they did, the result would be disastrous; just ask Pavarotti or Domingo what they think or feel when they produce the Rodolfo's High C—they will tell you they think and feel nothing, they just activate a particular skill. Staal's article contains a very subtle discussion with the work of Geertz, Tambiah, and Obeyesekerse, as well as with the lesser known Hoykaas, a Dutch scholar critical of Geertz's work on Bali religion.

Pilgrimage is not performed by a set of ideas, beliefs, reli-gious doctrines. These act only in the planning stage. Rather, it is based on a set of actions and interactions which follow a norm that is most like a syntactical rule. To use correct syntax, the speaker does not put himself into some sort of a linguistic or syntactic mood—he just performs speech on the basis of his lingui-stic competence, in line with Chomsky's original diction. The correct use of syntactical rules can best be observed in syntac-tical default, in linguistic errors of performance. Analogously, the norms controlling the process of pilgrimage can best be seen by default, i.e., in some erroneous performance. Every Hindu circumambulates a religious object clockwise—if he or she started moving counter clockwise, the norm would be spelt out in such statements as "it isn't done" or "hey you there, what are you doing." This is not the case with most Tibetan Buddhists, who circumambulate a *stupa*, etc., in either direction apparently without any preference.

In an excellent recent publication, I.M. Lewis[3] pointed out that there isn't a whole lot of difference between the discarded diffusionist notions of earlier anthropological days and some of the bases of structuralism given almost ritualistic importance by many anthropologists. In what he calls a "splendidly egoistic passage". Lewis quotes Strauss from *Mythologiques* "It is immaterial whether the thought processes of the South American Indians take shape through the medium of my thought, or whether mine take place through the medium of

theirs." Wrong, unless you want to write a novel. If I, not as
a pilgrim but as in anthropologist, buttonhole a bright looking
pilgrim along the Amarnath trek, keeping him company for
four days and nights, and if I tell him about deep structures
and surface structures, in simpler words and in Hindi, and if
I enthusiastically talk to him about my reading pilgrimage in a
deep structure-surface structure fashion, chances are that my
informant the pilgrim will "see the light" and feed back to me
structuralist ideas—his ideas, he thinks and I avidly agree.
When I then extrapolate what transpired, quoting my informant
as representing emic pilgrimage talk, I cheat myself, him and
you. This sort of marvellous informant is no informant at all. I
think this applies to some famous anthropologists and their
informants, *e.g.*, Turner's Muchona among the Ndembu[4] or
Griaule's Ogotommeli among the Dogon.[5] In my books, they
disqualify as informants, even though they qualify well enough
as fellow-dialecticians, human beings, sages and saints or what
have you.

   In other words, the actors (here the pilgrims) and more
generally, the informants' speculation about the ideas behind a
ritualistic set do not tell us much that is analytically important.
Pilgrims' ideas about the meaning of their pilgrimage, or about
pilgrimage in general, do not tell us much about the structure
of pilgrimage. We must look for another, more radical model.
In Marvin Harris' terms, we must do some etic anthropology
after being done with emics.

   Romantic sloppiness passing as analysis stands in need of
sober correction. When involved pilgrims also report as
scholars, the extra effort they must put into avoiding advocacy
may be considerable, but it is essential. Edith Turner and the
late Victor Turner writing about Roman Catholic pilgrimage
in which they were involved seemed to imply that their analysis
applied to pilgrims in general. It doesn't. When you look up
the "pilgrimage" entry in the ancient *Encyclopedia of Religion
and Ethics*, close to a century old, you will see that there is
no overarching introduction at all. It starts right away with
specific pilgrimage, Muslim, Christian, Buddhist, etc. In the
new *Encyclopedia of Religion* under the general editorship of
that late Eliade (1987)[6], there is an "overview" by Edith
Turner, rich on advocacy and thin on analysis. She and her

late husband created the term *communitas,* a shared feeling of closeness, a kind of temporary bonding between the pilgrims, a suspension of hierarchies. She quotes (it doesn't say from whom) "here is the only possible classless society." The next subheading is "spiritual magnetism of pilgrimage", an emic persuasive phrase etically intended I suppose. She then speaks of "prototypical pilgrimage" pilgrimage created by some hierophant. *Nihil obstat* to her final two headings "high period pilgrimage" and "modern pilgrimage" (1987, Vol. XII, 328). But let me read her concluding remarks : "Pilgrimage is a process (correct), a fluid and changing phenomenon (partly correct), spontaneous (wrong), initially unstructured and out-side the bonds of religious orthodoxy (wrong outside Roman Catholic settings). It is primarily a popular rite of passage (yes; but isn't everything in religious praxis ?); a venture into religious experience rather than a transition to higher status" (correct, but vacuous if meant as analysis; eloquent if meant as advocacy).

The question then arises whether one should continue the way the old *Encyclopedia of Religion and Ethics* did, *i.e.,* assuming there are no general, analytically helpful patterns underlying pilgrimage by avoiding a general "overview." I think not, but the common base must be a model which is not generated by any kind of apologetic or advocacy. To wit—there is no communitas, no classless society, no spontaneous decision, there are no unstructured phenomena outside the bonds of religious orthodoxy at least in Hindu pilgrimage, and I doubt whether there are in some or all forms of Muslim and Buddhist pilgrimage. Others here will no doubt speak to those issues. The Hindu pilgrim sets out for a well-defined purpose, he does not merge his personality or background temporarily with the other pilgrims even when he or she shares available amenities en route both ways, and pilgrimage is well established and touted within Hindu orthodox systems. Of course, all pilgrimage, whatever its initial decision or indecision, yields powerful experiences, but these are accidental in the sense of being part of the invasion of multiple, new, hence unaccustomed to sense impressions during the process.

It is necessary, therefore, to relinquish impressionistic reports altogether for the purpose of analysis, and to concentrate on some sort of underlying structure, of which the pilgrim is not conscious unless of course he or she is an anthropologist thinking in these terms

Back to Fritz Staal once more : "Our confusion in interpreting these (ritual) systems are largely caused by the disconcerting concatenation of two independent and unrelated facts" (1985 : 217). "Ritual systems are like language in that they are governed by rules, but unlike language in that they do not express meanings. For their study, we require syntactic theories that deal with rules, not semantic theories that deal with meanings. "Since I regard pilgrimage as a subvariety of ritual, the word "pilgrimage" can be substituted for "ritual systems." Very different people, alive and gone, would not agree with Staal or myself. When meaning, symbols, and all sorts of unconscious motives are seen as causal to ritualistic and to all other cultural behaviour, the suggestion of "chance concatenation" is odious. Yet I believe this is exactly what happens—the sequences and regularities in pilgrimage are mindboggling and boring to the frequent observer. To the actors, they are norm guided routine. When pilgrims and their guides act and interact with one another and with the paradigmatic objects as constituents of pilgrimage (shrines, bathing places, texts all included), their criteria for success are not what the pious or romantic outside observer imputes to them. Success for the pilgrim and the specialist means correct performance, which is norm guided, syntactic and paradigmatic performance. Pilgrims do not step out of line except in some minor accidental ways (slipping over a stone, breaking a vase or a bone, may be passing wind by mistake) just as speakers of a language do not step out of line by producing unintelligible syntactic sequences, even as they may mispronounce or misuse one phoneme or the other, or one sememe or the other.

## REFERENCES

1. Frits J. Staal, "The Sounds of Religion" in *Numen* xxxiii/1/2 1986; pp. 33-65, 185-244.
2. St. J. Tambiah, "A Performance Approach to Ritual", *Man*, Journal of the Royal Anthropological Institute, Vol. 65, 1979, 113-169.

3. I.M. Lewis, *Religion in Context* : *Cults and Charisma.* Cambridge University Press, 1987, 1-23, *et al.*
4. V. Turner, "Muchona the hornet : interpreting religion" in J.B. Casagrande (ed), *In the Company of Man,* New York : Harper, 1960.
5. M. Griaule, *Conversations with Ogotommeli.* London : Oxford University Press, 1965.
6. *Encyclopedia of Religion.* M. Eliade, (Ed. in chief), New York : Macmillan Co., 1987.

# 2

# History, Patronage and Social Organisation of a Sakta Pilgrimage Centre in India

## A Case Study of Kamakhya Temple of Assam

MAKHAN JHA

SOCIAL anthropologists have been studying the religion of both the primitive and complex societies since the inception of this discipline. In Indian anthropology, Hinduism has been studied by many anthropologists and among them special mention may be made of E. B. Harper's edited volume on *Religion in South India* (1964), Lawrence Babb's *The Divine Hierarchy* (1975), Vidyarthi's edited volume *Aspects of Religion in Indian Society* (1961), Milton Singer's *When a Great Tradition Modernizes* (1972), Srinivas' *Religion and Society among the Coorgs of South India* (1952) etc. The study of Hindu *Tirthas* (places of Pilgrimage), as a dimension of Indian civilization, are also many and among them special mention may be made of *The Sacred Complex of Hindu Gaya* (Vidyarthi : 1961), *The Sacred Complex of Janakpur* (in Nepal) (Jha : 1971), *The Sacred Complex of Kashi* (Vidyarthi, Saraswati and Jha : 1978), "*Dimension of Pilgrimage*" (ed. Jha : 1985) etc.

However, when we look at the anthropological study of Saktism, a very important cult in Hinduism we find that very few works have been done and among them I must mention the works of Agehanand Bharti—*The Tantrik Tradition* (1965),

Preston's volume on *Cult of the Goddess : Social and Religious Change in a Hindu Temple* (1980), Indological works on *Shakti and Shakta* (1929) by John Woodroofe etc.

## Shaktism in India

It is an important religious cult in India. There are many temples exclusively dedicated to the worship of Shakti[1] or the Mother Goddess, which is worshipped in ten major forms called as Das Mahavidya.

The followers of the Shaktism have always claimed a hoary antiquity for their faith and they trace its origin to the *Vedas* (Chakravarti : 1956, p. 408) and refer to a number of gods, kings and sages of the *pauranic* fame, like Shiva, Krishna, Vasistha, Parusrama and others, who are stated to have attained success in their spiritual endeavours through the practice of *tantrik* rites and propitiating the Mother Goddess. Parusrama, to whom is attributed the *Parusrama Kalpa-Sutra*, which deals with the details of the worship of *Srividya*, is incidentally referred to in the *Tripura-rahasya*, as a devotee of Tripura, another name of *Srividya*. According to the *Brahmananda Puran*, sage Agastya learnt the details of the worship of *Srividya* from *Hayagriva* (lord Vishnu). Sage Vasistha is stated to have been successful in his spiritual aspiration only after worshipping goddess Tara. Lopamudra, the wife of sage Agastya, became celebrated through her worship of *Srividya*, and the *mantra* with which she offered the worship, still goes by her name. An entire work, the *Radha-Tantra*, describes the life story of Krishna, an incarnation of Vishnu, who is represented in this work as an ardent worshipper of Shakti and as one who attained spiritual success through his union with Radha. Whatever be the value of these claims, as stated above, it cannot be doubted that Shaktism has a long history behind it.

Anthropological study of such a strong continuous cultural tradition has not been done on a large scale, although the rites and practices of Shaktism as well as its ideals are expounded in the extensive literature that has grown up from quite an early period. A critical appraisal of the vast *tantrik* literature, which is yet to be undertaken, will be very helpful, I believe, in distin-

guishing the "genuine" and the "spurious" (Sapir : 1924)
*tantrik* rites assimilated into the broader frame of Hinduism.

With this brief introduction, I now turn towards the
Kamakhya temple, the most celebrated Shakti *pitha* in the
*tantrik* world.

## The Kamakhya Temple of Assam

The present Kamakhya temple, located near Guwahati, Assam,
on the *Nilachal* (blue-hill) is full of ancient myths and legends,
which are still in vogue and are perpetuated by the people of
different parts of India, irrespective of their castes, faiths or
sectarian affiliations. The word "Kamakhya" or "Kamarupa"
is found in most of the sacred scriptures of the land. Among
the different important sacred scriptures, where Kamakhya is
referred to, special mention may be made of the great epic like
the Mahabharat, the Kalika Puran, the Yogni Tantra, the Devi
Bhagwat, the Tantra-Churamani, the Shiva Puran, the Vayu
Puran, the Brahma Puran, the Kamakhya-Tantra, the Raghu-
vansha of Kalidas etc. Besides these scriptures, the Jain lexico-
grapher, Hema Chandra (1200 A.D.) mentioned both Pragjyotishpur and Kamakhya simultaneously in his lexicon. The
Buddhist literature, specially the Majushri Mula Kalpa, though
mentions about Pragjyotishpur, it gives its location  somewhere
near Himalaya.

These sacred texts, as mentioned above, elaborately  contain
the various legends and myths about the origin of  Kamakhya.
However, it must be mentioned here that the word "Kamakhya"
finds no reference anywhere in the *Vedic* literatures like the
*Samhitas*, the *Brahmanas*, the *Upanishads* etc., and, therefore,
it may be argued that Kamakhya has a post-Vedic origin.

## Myths about the Origin of Kamakhya

Among all the sacred texts, however, the Kalika Puran  and the
Yogni-Tantra vividly describe the origin and the *mahatma*
(importance) of goddess Kamakhya. In the Kalika Puran we
get vivid description of Kamakhya, specially in chapters fifty-
one to fifty-eight and then in sixty-second. It narrates : "Formerly there were three mountains as high as one hundred *yojan*
i.e. corresponding to about 450 miles, which constituted the
*Nilachal* hill. In Indian mythology, the name of king Daksha[2]

is very familiar, whose daughter was Sati. She was married to Lord Shiva. King Daksha was not keeping good relation with his son-in-law. So when Daksha conducted a big *yagna*, he invited all the gods and goddesses, except Lord Shiva, to partake their offerings. Sati insisted to participate in her father's *yagna* even without getting a proper invitation. Thus, Sati, leaving behind her husband, Lord Shiva, at home, came to her father's place to participate in the *yagna*. She became very angry at the discourtesy shown to her husband, Lord Shiva, by her father, for no offerings had been kept by Daksha for Lord Shiva. We are further told that at this moment Sati jumped into the *havan-kund* (fire-place of the *yagna*) and died. After getting the news of Sati's death, the *Gans* (closed disciples) of Lord Shiva, specially Birbhadra etc. destroyed the *yagna* of Daksha. Lord Shiva finally came and killed Daksha and then with very heavy heart he took away the dead body of his consort, Sati. Shiva then wandered about the world carrying the dead body of his beloved consort on his shoulders. At this all the gods and goddesses got frightened and approached Lord Vishnu for the wellbeing of this universe. Then in order to put a stop to the sufferings of Lord Shiva, Lord Vishnu followed him and asked his *chakra* (sacred disk) to cut the dead body of Sati into pieces. The different pieces of Sati's body fell on the earth at fifty-one different places, spread from Kamakhya in the east to Hinglaj (Baluchistan) in the west and from Guheshwari in the north (Nepal) to Indrakshi (in Sri Lanka) in the south. And wherever it fell, it became a sacred centre for the Saktas, known as *Sakti-pitha*. Sati's organ of generation, called as *Yoni*, fell on Nilachal hill. Lord Shiva, seeing the genital part falling, held it over his breast on the top of that hill. It is said that previously the colour of the hill was red, but due to the immensity of the weight of the falling object and that of Shiva, the colour of the hill became blue. It began to go down towards the centre of the earth. Seeing this, Lord Brahma (the creator of this universe) held the eastern cliff and Lord Vishnu caught hold of the western cliff. Still the hill was going down. At last gooddess Mahamaya the (*Adi Shakti*) held all the cliffs together and, thus, prevented it from going down. The three cliffs, of the hill, i.e., Bhubneshwari, Kamakhya and the Barahi, therefore, represent the bodies of Lord Brahma, Lord Shiva and Lord

Vishnu respectively. This form of sectarian affiliation, thus, is unique.

The spot, where the *Yoni* (genital organ) of mother goddess fell, came to be regarded as Kamakhya. Why is it called Kamakhya ? There are many interpretations and arguments in the texts, some of which are discussed below.

In the Kalika Puran (Chapter 51) it is said that after the sad demise of goddess Sati, Lord Shiva sat for an endless meditation on Nilachal hill. Seeing the sufferings of Lord Shiva all the gods sent Kamadeva (the god of sex and passion) to put an end to Shiva's mourning and to awaken in him again the passion of creation. As soon as Kamadeva started his activities for creating passion before Lord Shiva, he was burnt to ashes by Lord Shiva. However, after great persuasion and prayer, offered by Rati, wife of Kamadeva, Lord Shiva bestowed upon him blessings to regain his original *rupam* (form) and Kamadeva, accordingly, got his old form. Therefore, this place was called Kamarupa, the sanskrit verse runs as. . . *"Kama rupam tato bhavet. . . . . ."* (Kalika Puran, ch. 51).

The *Yogni Tantra*, another important text on this subject, however, gives a little different account stressing upon the creative symbolism of the *Yoni* (the genital part). The Mahamaya, the *Adi Sakti*, was curious as to who was Kamakhya and wanted to know from Lord Shiva. In order to answer to her query, Shiva replied that Kamakhya was same as Kali, Bhubneshwari, Matangi, Bhairabi etc. In this way Lord Shiva also narrated the origin of *Das-Mahavidya* (ten forms of the goddess) which surround goddess Kamakhya at the blue hill. These ten forms are :

1. Kali,
2. Tara,
3. Khodshi,
4. Bhubneshwari,
5. Chhinmasta,
6. Dhumabati,
7. Baglamukhi,
8. Kamala,
9. Matangi,
10. Bhairabi.

Lord Shiva, after narrating the origin of these ten forms of Mahavidya which surround the goddess Kamakhya at Nilachal, further pointed out that Lord Brahma and Lord Vishnu had offered prayer to Mahamaya here for seeing a luminous divine light from the sky. In this way the Puran-writer laid emphasis on the importance of Vaishnav cult at the Sakti centre like Kamakhya, which is again unique from the point of view of sectarian integration which has rather strengthened the civilizational solidarity of India. Kakati (1948), a local historian, is of the opinion that the two sets of descriptions in the two Purans viz. the Kalika-Puran and the Yogni Tantra, as referred to above, are the views of two different sets of people who professed that cult in different periods of time.

The Devi-Bhagwat, another important text, gives the names of one hundred and eight places that were associated with the body of Sati one way or the other. These are, however, called *Up-pithas*.

Besides the great goddess Kamakhya and other ten Mahavidyas, as mentioned above, Lord Shiva himself lives at Kamakhya in five forms at five places. The first one is at Sidheshwar, which is located near the Gaya-kshetra and Amritkund. The Kalika-Puran says that it was dug by Lord Indra and other gods for the pleasure of Shiva. On its left is Kameshwar Shiva immersed in Kamakund. In between Sidheshwar and Kameshwar, there is *Kadar-ka-kshetra*, a place for Lord Vishnu. Lord Shiva stays in his *Aghor* form to the south of Kamakhya, where he is known as Bhairab. In the *Sri-Bhaba Gufa* (cave) Shiva stays in the form of Amriteshwar. It is believed that goddess Durga lives with Lord Shiva in this cave. Shiva, in form of *Kuti-linga*, lives to the north of Kamakhya. In this way the great goddess Kamakhya is surrounded by Lord Shiva in five different forms, besides the ten Mahavidyas, as already referred to above.

The Kalika-Puran further mentions that to the west of goddess Kamakhya is the abode of Lord Vishnu. The names of various other gods and goddesses are also mentioned in this text and among them special mention may be made of the Brama-sakti-sila, the Bhasmachal, the Kubjika-pitha, Kusmandi, Jogni, Chamunda, Puskar-kshetra, Bhubanand cave, Chandaghanta etc.

**What is Shakti ?**

In Hinduism there are many sects. Sakti is one of the most
dominating sects. Saundrya Lahiri (Barua & Murthy : 1965),
an important text on this subject, defines Sakti as "the concept
of divine energy in its dynamic aspect ; Sakti is inseparable
from Brahma ; She is the power of Existence, knowledge and
bliss of Brahma. She is the creative and preservative of energy
of Brahma. In this way we find that she is the *Adi-Sakti* and,
therefore, pervades all walks of life of human beings. At the
sectarian level, she influences followers of all the cults. Although
Lord Shiva is called the *Debadhideb* (god of all gods), but Shiva,
himself, is *shava* (corpse) without Sakti.

**Types of Saktas**

Those, who believe in the Sakti cult and worship Sakti, are
called Saktas. However, there are many types of Saktas according to the mode of worship they follow :

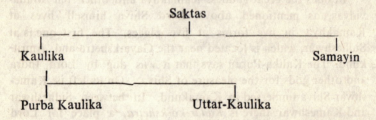

While the followers of *Purba-Kaulika*, who are now very few
in numbers, worship *Sri-Chakra* and the nine organs of a
female, the Uttar-Kaulikas believe in *Panch-Makar* practice.
The *Panch-Makars* are *Madya* (wine), *Mans* (meat), *Matsya*
(fish), *Mudra* (Tantrik calculation) and *Maithun* (sexual inter-
course). In the Sakti worship, the *Maithun* is also known as
*Bhramri-prayog*. Presently, the Purba-Kaulika worshippers
simply worship the *Sri-Chakra* which is drawn on golden-leaf,
silken cloth etc. I was told at Kamakhya that due to high cost
of gold, today *Sri-Chakra* is usually drawn on copper plates.
The worship of nine organs of an unmarried girl, as practiced
earlier, is no more in vogue. For, those who practiced it
earlier, had to pay a huge amount of wealth for the maintenance
of that unmarried girl, because once a girl has been selected for

*Purba-Kaulika* worship, she would not get herself married due to various reasons and, therefore, big zamindars, kings and wealthy persons used to practice it through their Tantrik *gurus*. That is why after the fall of the zamindari system and specially after India's independence the practice of *Purba-Kaulika* worship has become extinct.

The followers of the *Aghor* cult also claim themselves as the worshippers of Sakti. One of my Aghor informants at Kamakhya told me that in actual practice an Aghor is more related to the worship of *Panch-Mukhi* (five faced) Shiva.

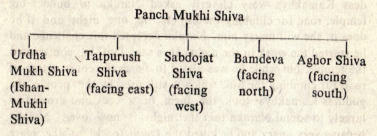

Panch Mukhi Shiva

| Urdha Mukh Shiva (Ishan-Mukhi Shiva) | Tatpurush Shiva (facing east) | Sabdojat Shiva (facing west) | Bamdeva (facing north) | Aghor Shiva (facing south) |

The *Aghors* actually worship the fifth one i.e. the Aghor-Shiva, which is called a stage of invisible whole in the universe. The *Aghors* call this stage as *Sunya-sirhi*, which is above the *Gyanmay-kosh* (stage of knowledge). Again, the *Aghors* worship the *Mahakal*—form of Panchmukhi Hanuman, which is nothing, but an enlarged form of lord Shiva. In this way the *Aghors*, whose famous centres are at Kashi, Vindhyachal, Kamakhya etc., combine in their worship both Sakti and Shiva, which are, as they believe, inseparable.

## History and Patronage

The first wave of Aryanisation of Assam and its neighbouring areas began with the establishment of Kamarupa kingdom by Prince Naraka, who was a Maithil Kshatriya by birth and was related to one of the Janaks of the Janakpur kingdom of ancient Mithila.[3] All the local historians like Kakati (1948), Barua (1965) Indologist like Mahamahopadhya Padmanava Bhattacharya (1931) and the British historian like Sir Edward Gait (1905) unanimously claim that Naraka was the Prince of the Janak dynasty of Mithila and he was the first patron of the goddess Kamakhya. Prior to the establishment of the Kamrup kingdom, this area was known as Pragjyotishpur. Gait writes (*ibid.*), "Prag means former or eastern and *Jyotish* means a star. Pragjyotishpur may be taken to mean the city of eastern astrology.

However, after the establishment of the Kamrup kingdom, king Naraka became the first patron of the goddess Kamakhya and built a small shrine for the deity at Nilachal hill. The goddess gave him *darshan* in her full form. But after seeing her, Naraka became so mad that he asked her to marry him. Goddess Kamakhya very cleverly asked Naraka to build a big temple, road for climbing the hill etc. in one night and if he does it, she will marry him. Naraka accepted this challenge and he started the work in the night. It is said that he constructed the temple, but while he was about to finish the construction of road for climbing the hill, which is still used by the people, the goddess Kamakhya took the form of a cock and crowed so largely to sound Naraka that the night is now over. Naraka became very angry and he killed the *kukut* (cock) at the place which is still called the *Kukut-katta* and it is located near the foothill. The people still offer worship at this place.

The famous Chinese traveller, Hiuen Tsiang, who visited and travelled throughout India from 629 A.D. to 645 A.D., as discussed by Cunningham in his *Ancient Geography of India* (London : 1871), visited Kamrup twice ; first in 638 A.D. and then in 641 A.D. He has used the word *Kia-mo-leu-po* for Kamrup. In his diary he writes that after Pubna near Champa (Bhagalpur) he proceeded for 990 *li* (about 150 miles) towards east and crossed over the *Lohitya* (ancient name of Brahmaputra) and entered *Kia-mo-leu-po* or Kamrup. The territory of this kingdom was estimated by Hiuen Tsiang at about 10,000 *li* or 1667 miles in circuit. The large extent shows that it must have comprised the whole valley of the Brahmaputra river, which then comprised of three tracts viz. Sadia, Assam proper and Kamrupa. The latter was the most powerful state and Kusa-Vihar near Bhutan, was the western division of Kamrupa kingdom. The old capital of Kamrupa, as said by Hiuen Tsiang, was near Kamatipura and the king, who ruled in the first-half of the 7th century A.D., was a Brahmin whose name was **Bhaskar Varman.**

The name of this king Bhaskar Varman, who ruled Kamrupa in early 7th century, coincides with the names of the kings of Kamrupa kingdom, known as *Kamarupa-sasanavali*. compiled by Mahamahopadhya Padmanava Bhattacharya in 1931 who was a great scholar of Sanskrit and taught this subject for a long time in Cotton College, Guwahati. His *Kamarupa-sasanavali* is based on the decipher of the copper plate inscriptions of the early Hindu kings of Assam.

There are ten inscriptions ranging from the seventh to twelfth century A.D., covering practically the entire Hindu period of Assam.

Some of the important kings, who ruled Kamrupa from 7th to 12th century, are given below :

| | | |
|---|---|---|
| 1. | Bhaskar Varman | 7th century |
| 2. | Harjan Varman | 9th century |
| 3. | Vanamala Deva | 9th century |
| 4. | Bala Varman | 10th century |
| 5 | Ratnapala | 11th century |
| 6. | Indrapala | 11th century |
| 7. | Dhramapala | 12th century |

After 12th century the kingdom of Kamrupa along with the whole of Assam passed into the hands of Ahoms, who came from Thailand and conquered the whole area and ruled for nearly 600 years till the British came towards the end of 18th century.

The Ahoms, who are also known as the *Shans*, have left a deep impression on the life and culture of Assam. The Bodo groups of tribes, who live to the west of the Kamarupa district are called *Mec*.

The Ahoms, who invaded Assam in 1228 A.D., built strong kingdoms with various fortunes and under various tribal names viz. the Chutiya, the Kachari, the Koch etc. The Koch kings like Durbala Narayana (13th century), Narayana (16th century), Chilakroy (16th century) etc., contributed much to the development of pilgrimage to Kamakhya. Other Shan tribes, who

followed the Ahoms were the Kamatis, the Phaliyats, the Naras,
the Aitoniyas etc., who now inhabit the eastern region.

The present temple of Kamakhya was constructed in Saka
1487 corresponding to 1565 A.D. by Prince Chilakroy, the
brother of king Narayana of the Koch kingdom. As mentioned
earlier, they were the Ahom kings, but had absorbed Hinduism.
The present mode of worship at the Kamakhya temple was
arranged by these Ahom kings. The existing pattern of the
sacred specialists and the sacred performances are also the gifts
of these great Koch kings (See Table 2.1).

## The Present Social Organisation of the Kamakhya Temple

Presently the temple of Kamakhya is controlled by the KTTB
(Kamakhya Temple Trust Board), which was established in
1972. The founder secretary of the KTTB was Pandit Hari
Prasad Sharma. The President and the Vice-President of the
KTTB were P. N. Sharma and Baroda Kant respectively. There
were eight members of the first KTTB which was dissolved in
1977. A new election of the KTTB was held in 1980 and Pandit
J. P. Sharma, a seasoned lawyer of Guwahati became its President and the Kaulikacharya Pandit Pran Ranjan Sharma became Vice-President. Pandit Tarni Sharma was elected to the
post of Secretary of the KTTB. There were nine members in
this Board and a committee of few members is actually looking
after the day to day affairs of the temple.

As mentioned earlier, the structural arrangements of the
priests and other temple functionaries along with the sacred
performances etc., are the gifts of the Koch kings which were
started by Chilakroy in 1565 A.D., which are still continuing.
However, there has been extinction of some of the posts of the
sacred specialists because their duties are no more required. It
will not be out of context here to put up a list of the sacred
specialists of Kamakhya, as done by prince Chilakroy in 1565
which is still in vogue at Kamakhya.

From the above mentioned types of *sevayats* (sacred specialists) at Kamakhya, one can easily imagine how elaborately the
Koch kings made arrangements for the various types of rites
and rituals for which different types of people were placed at
the disposal of the temple management. In course of time those
people got specialisations and in long run the posts became

TABLE 2.1 : **Types of Sevayats (Sacred Specialists) at Kamakhya (as in 1565)**

| Sr. No. | Name of the Sevayats | Caste | Duties |
|---|---|---|---|
| 1 | 2 | 3 | 4 |
| 1. | Deoriya/Vidhi Pathak | Brahmin | to supervise the rites and rituals from textual and tantrik point of view. |
| 2. | Pujari | Brahmin | to perform puja of the goddess inside sanctum sanctorum. |
| 3. | Jesthas (Supervisory posts) | Brahmin | to supervise all other works related to temple. |
| 4. | Pathak/Anusthanis | Brahmin | to recite tantras/mantras for pilgrims ; to conduct special rites for the fulfilment of the sacred vows etc. |
| 5. | Khowar | Brahmin | to cook for the goddess Kamakhya. |
| 6. | Mahasnani | Brahmin | to bath the goddess Kamakhya. |
| 7. | Ladoowala | Brahmin | to prepare sweets etc., for the goddess. |
| 8. | Dolai | Brahmin | to look after the managerial duties of the temple. |
| 9. | Bharal Khaith | Brahmin | Treasurer, but today he has been replaced. |
| 10. | Murar | Brahmin | Treasurer of the properties of goddess Kamakhya. |
| 11. | Jyotishi/Adhyapak | Brahmin | to calculate astronomical dates/time for religious functions. |

*(Contd.)*

TABLE 2.1—*Contd.*

| 1 | 2 | 3 | 4 |
|---|---|---|---|
| 12. | Cikdar | Kayastha | official goat sacrificer of goddess Kamakhya. |
| 13. | Mahari | Kayastha | Assistant of Murar. |
| 14. | Nitya-Asthpaharia | Kayastha | Assistant of Mahasnani. |
| 15. | Metarik | Kayastha | to supply *belpatra* leaf at the time of Puja in the Kamakhya temple. |
| 16. | Manghi | Kayastha | to distribute *Prasads* of the goddess. |
| 17. | Barah-Astha-paharia | Kayastha | to help in all other extra works. |
| 18. | Balidhara | Kayastha | to help the Balikatta (goat-sacrificer). |
| 19. | Balidhara-Gairia | Kayastha | to catch hold of goats at the time of sacrificing the goats. |
| 20. | Bara-Balli katta | Kayastha | Chief goat-sacrificer. |
| 21. | Astha-Paharia of Nanan-Devalia (priests) | Kayastha | to arrange all articles at the time of puja of goddess Kamakhya. |
| 22. | Nitya-dwaria | Kayastha | to watch and guard all gates of the Kamakhya temple. |
| 23. | Astha-Paharia of other temples like Bhubneshwari/Sidheshwar/Durga Kund etc. | Kayastha | Presently the posts of Astha-Paharia in all temples, except the Kamakhya temple, have been abolished. |
| 24. | Patnia | Kayastha | to help the priests at the time of Durga puja specially at the time of immersion of the idols in the river. |

TABLE 2.1—*Contd.*

| 1 | 2 | 3 | 4 |
|---|---|---|---|
| 25. Gayaks | Kayastha<br>Khatri<br>Das<br>in groups | | to perform bhajan/kirtan at the time of Arti in the Kamakhya temple. |
| 26. Rag-Gayak | Kayastha | | to recite the *slokas* (verses) of the Sam-Veda and other classical Ragas in honour of the goddess at the time of Mahasnan (great bath). |
| 27. Bara-Gayak | Kayastha | | Head singer, but in recent times, this post does not exist. |
| 28. Dhoba | Dhobi | | to wash the clothes of the goddess Kamakhya. |
| 29. Hindu Darjee (Tailors) | Kayastha/<br>Das | | to prepare and stitch the cloth of the deities. |
| 30. Khola sarahari | Das | | to clean the earthen pots and throw them into river Brahmaputra. |
| 31. Gwala | Gwala/Das (Milk-man) | | to supply milk to the goddess Kamakhya for sweets/offering etc. |
| 32. Sonari | Sonar (goldsmith) | | to prepare golden ornaments for the deities. |
| 33. Bhalli | Kayastha | | incharge of all utensils of the Kamakhya temple. |
| 34. Pathāsara | Kayastha | | to feed the goats kept/reserved for the official sacrifice in the Kamakhya temple. |
| 35. Chandan-piha | Kayastha | | to grind the sandle-wood meant for puja and offering in the Kamakhya temple. |

*(Contd.)*

TABLE 2.1—*Contd.*

| 1 | 2 | 3 | 4 |
|---|---|---|---|
| 36. | Bhog Panieri | Kayastha | to fetch water for supplying in the temple to clean the floor or to be used for preparing *bhog* of the deity etc. |
| 37. | Tāmoli | Tamoli | to arrange *nabeds* for the goddess as well as to supply betel nuts/leaves etc. to the deity. |
| 38. | Khitenia | Das | to grind spices to be used in cooking vegetables/goat meat etc. |
| 39. | Daud-dhara | Barber | to hold the flag of the deity at the times of Paridakshina (holi circumambulation) of the temple. |
| 40. | Darpan-dhara | Barber | to keep hold of big looking glass at the time of circumambulation of the temple. |
| 41. | Dau-dhara | Das | to clean the *dau* (scythe), which is used in sacrificing goats. |
| 42. | Dama-dhari | Das | to beat drums at the time of puja or on other occasions. |
| 43. | Homa-Parichalak | Das | to arrange things for *homa* and to help the *hota* (Brahmin priest) for conducting *homa*. |
| 44. | Chabal-kara | Das | to husk rice for cooking for the goddess. |
| 45. | Dar-Meria | Das | to drive boat in the river on the occasion of immersion of goddess |

TABLE 2.1—*Contd.*

| 1 | 2 | 3 | 4 |
|---|---|---|---|
| | | | Durga. But presently this post does not exist. |
| 46. | Jag-mukti kara | Das | to clean daily several times, whenever required, the place where goats are sacrificed for the goddess Kamakhya. |
| 47. | Kaha-Maria | Das | to play bells and other musical instruments at the time of puja/arti in the Kamakhya temple. |
| 48. | Siteniar | Das | to clean inside areas of temple, *bhog-ghar* etc. of Kamakhya temple. |
| 49. | Kharidia | Das | to supply wood (fuel) to the *Bhog-ghar* for preparing *bhog* (sacred food) for the goddess Kamakhya. |
| 50. | Kaur-Khenia | Das | to drive away the crows and other birds from temple precincts. |
| 51. | Bheru-sankh-badak | Kayastha | to blow conch-shells loudly specially at the time of *puja* daily or on some special occasions. |

specialised and hereditary. The temple got the royal patronage and the expenditures were used to be financed by the royal treasury. However, the first blow to this royal patronage came when the British took over the administration after 1765 when the right of *Diwani* was granted to the East India Company, but a major obstacle came after India's independence when the zamindari was abolished and the zamindars and the princes were deprived of their royal rights and privileges. Thus, many rites in the temple complex at Kamakhya became extinct and hence, the persons, associated with those rights, also became unemployed. Presently, therefore, there are altogether 21 major types of *sevayats*, out of 51, as mentioned above, in the Kamakhya temple complex, whose duties are very much defined and specified by the present KTTB. In this connection, it has also been found that a group of priests and other *sevayats* have been mixed up together, such as the *Nanan-Dewlia*. Under this category of *sevayats* many Brahmins and non-Brahmins have been incorporated ; like different types of *Astha-paharias*, *Snani-Brahmins* etc. who are now commonly addressed as *Nanan-Dewlia*. In this way, while a few *sevayats* have become extinct due to disuse of their services, few *sevayats* have already formed a new common group for their cultural identification and professional survival, which is a new phenomenon in the post-independence period of the socio-political organisation of the sacred specialists of the Hindu *tirthas*.

## REFERENCES

1. There are 51 *Shaktapithas*, spread from Hinglaj (Afghan-Pak border) in the west to Kamakhya in the east and from Guheshwari (in Nepal) in the north to Sri Lanka in the south.
2. King Daksha's kingdom was at Kankhal near Haridwar. The author conducted field-work at Kankhal and Haridwar in 1980 and visited all the sacred centres connected with Daksha, Sati, Shiva, Birbhadra etc.
3. For detail, see the author's book—The Sacred Complex of Janakpur ; the United Publishers, Allahabad, 1981, where the chronology of the kings of the Janak dynasty of ancient Mithila is given.

## NOTES

Barua, B.K. & H.V. Sreenivas Murthy, 1965, *Temples and Legends of Assam* ; Bhartiya Vidya Bhavan, Bombay.

Barua, K.L , 1933, *Early History of Kamakhya* ; Natesan & Co.

Babb, Lawrence, 1975, *The Divine Hierarchy* ; New York, Columbia University Press.

Bharti, Agehanand, 1965, *The Tantrik Tradition* ; Garden City, New York, Doubleday and Company.

Cunningham, 1871, *Ancient Geography of India* ; London.

Chakravarty, Chintamani, 1956, *Sakta Worship and the Sakta Saints, in Cultural Heritage of India*, Vol. IV, pp. 408-418.

Gait, Edward, 1905, *History of Assam* ; London.

Harper, E. B., 1964, *Religion in South Asia* (ed.) ; University of Washington Press, Seattle.

Kakati, Bani Kant, 1948, *The Mother Goddess Kamakhya* ; Lawyers Book Stall ; Guwahati.

Preston, James, 1980, *Cult of the Goddess* ; *Social and Religious Change in a Hindu Temple* ; Vikash Publishing Co., New Delhi.

Srinivas, M.N., 1952, *Religion and Society among the Coorgs of South India*, Oxford.

Singer, Milton, 1972. *When a Great Tradition Modernizes* ; New York ; Praeger Publishers.

Sapir, Edward, 1924, Culture : Genuine and Spurious ; *American Journal of Sociology*, Vol. 29, pp. 401-29.

Vidyarthi, L. P., 1961, *The Sacred Complex of Hindu* Gaya ; Asia Publishing House, Bombay.

Vidyarthi, L.P., B.N. Saraswati, & Makhan Jha, 1978 : *The Sacred Complex of Kashi* ; Concept Publishing Co., New Delhi.

   Sind, University [?]

# 3

# Aiyanar and Aiyappan in Tamil Nadu : Change and Continuity in South Indian Hinduism

## The Aiyappan Cult : The Meeting Ground of Hindu Militancy, Egalitarianism and Universalism

LARS KJAERHOLM

## Introduction

IN recent years the Aiyappan cult has attained enormous popularity. It has spread from Kerala and into Tamil Nadu, Andhra Pradesh and Karnataka and is now moving even further north. Obviously this fairly conventional *bhakti* cult is seen by many as the answer to their religious and social needs at the present time But what are these needs ? The answer to that question is rather complex.

There are conservative Hindu groups, who try to project the cult as the answer to all the forces, which seem to threaten Hinduism in the modern world, such as conversions to Islam and Christianity, as well as the rise of militant nationalism in conjunction with religious revivalism such as can be seen in all the states surrounding India, like Sri Lanka, Burma, Malaysia, Pakistan and Iran. No doubt this general trend in the area also affects people in India, who feel they must respond to this threat and rally round their endangered spiritual heritage. This aspect is stressed in much of the writings on the Aiyappan cult, which is often referred to as the proper religion of the Kaliyuga, the dark age in which we live where men and values are debased. Hence the need for austerity and self-control, so that one may withstand the prevailing negative tendencies of the modern world. There are numerous myths about Aiyappans prowess as a warrior and they are wellknown and popular. Since he is the eternal celibate, the link between sexual continence and spiritual and physical power is strongly brought out. This is also a prominent feature in the cult practice, since a period of sexual abstinence of at least forty days is mandatory for all who wish to go on pilgrimage to Aiyappan's temple at Sabari Malai.

However, there is also another tendency, which sustains the popularity of the cult, and that is the egalitarian element which is common to all *bhakti* cults. Most informants stressed this as the most attractive feature of the cult and said : "We are all equal in the eyes of Aiyappan". Obviously the pilgrimage and the preparation time preceding it are a welcome escape from the restrictions of traditional hierarchic norms.

A third aspect of the cult, closely linked to its egalitarian tendency, is its aspirations to become a universal religion. People of all castes, creeds and religions are welcomed without the slightest reservation. Anyone who wishes to participate can do so, provided he prepares himself in the prescribed manner. (On cult practice see Kjaerholm 1982).

The cult is truly open and willing to accept all. My participation in the pilgrimage on several occasions as participant observer was not seen by my fellow pilgrims as a conversion to Hinduism, but rather as evidence of the genuinely universal nature of this cult.

All these aspects of the cult cannot be treated within the limitations of this article, and some I have treated elsewhere. Here I present the results of a field study of the gradual spread of the Aiyappan cult in a region in Tamil Nadu, and how this new cult is integrated into the existing religious patterns in that area, and how newly formed Aiyappan groups in Tamil Nadu have allied themselves with an ancient royal lineage in Kerala, the traditional keepers of Aiyappan's jewels, and are forming a

new religious network, transcending the former impregnable
barrier between Kerala and the Tamil area.

In recent years there has been a spectacular growth in the
number of pilgrims, who gather at Sabari Malai in Kerala in
January every year in worship of Aiyappan, the peculiar South
Indian god. The rapidly growing interest in Aiyappan in
Tamil Nadu seems to be mainly responsible for this.

Aiyappan is a son of Shiva and Vishnu (in the female form
of Mohini), who is known only in South India, mainly in
Kerala and Tamil Nadu. There are now Aiyappan temples in
Bombay and New Delhi and a few other places in North India,
but these have all been built by Keralites residing in the North,
and are mainly attended by them. (concerning Aiyappan's
theogony see : Vaidynathan 1978, Kjaerholm 1982, and
appendix). Apart from these exceptions, Aiyappan worship is
not known further north than mid-Karnataka, where it was
probably introduced from Kerala (Srinivas 1965).

Although Aiyanar and Aiyappan are considered to be the
same god, (Gopinatha Rao 1916), there have emerged two
rather different modes of worship of Aiyappan in Kerala and
Karnataka, and of Aiyanar in the Tamil area. In Tamil Nadu
Aiyanar is worshipped as a village guardian god and his priests
are mainly from non-Brahman castes, like the Velar (potters).
In Kerala Aiyappan is worshipped in Shiva temples and has
Brahman priests. Another striking difference is, that Aiyappan
unlike Aiyanar has been made the object of *bhakti* devotion
(*i.e.* a popular emotional form of worship, which aims at
merging with the god in devotional love).

**The Return of the Native**

In this article I am not concerned with the historical development which led to the evolution of the Aiyanar Aiyappan forms
of worship (see : Clothey 1978, Adiceam 1967). What I am concerned with here is the unique and interesting historical situation, that a god—Aiyappan—is today being introduced in the
Tamil area with a mode of worship, which was unknown to
most people in that area before 1940. At the same time the
Tamils recognize Aiyappan as identical to Aiyanar or Sāstā,
the common village god of Tamil Nadu. Whether it is justified
or not the Tamils accept all references to "Sāstā" in classical

Tamil literature, which dates back—possibly—to 300 A.D. as clear evidence of the worship of Aiyanar/Aiyappan in the Tamil area in such ancient times.

## Aiyanar Worship in and around Madurai

Aiyanar is a village deity, and his temples are found—as a rule —only in villages. There are Aiyanar temples within the city limits of Madurai, but this is because the city has grown so much recently. Most Aiyanar priests in this area are of the Velar (potter) caste, who also make the terracotta figures of the gods in the temples, as well as the numerous votive offerings, cows, horses and other animals, which are so typical of the rural scene in Tamil Nadu. To seek better business opportunities many village potters have now moved to Madurai. There are important Velar settlements at Arappālaiyam and Tallā-kulam, but they retain their links to the surrounding villages.

The running of the temples is usually financed by temple lands, and the right to dispose of the income from these lands are inherited in individual potters families. Over the years these rights have been split between many heirs. For example, a group of eight male relatives may have inherited a priesthood and income from temple lands. This right is then shared in a rotation system, which means that each of them takes a turn to function as priest for one year. In spring there are many Aiyanar festivals, when villagers place votive offerings at their local Aiyanar temples. These offerings are usually terracotta figures, representing horse, cows, chickens, babies, scorpions, camels, elephants, and other things, given as thanks for boons bestowed on the worshipper. Such festivals take place at irregular intervals, every third year or so, depending on the wealth of the villagers. The terracotta figures are taken out in procession from the house of the potter, who is priest, and perhaps also made the figures, to the village temple. This is why so many processions can be seen going from the suburbs of Madurai to a great number of villages around Madurai.

## The Role of the Kodangi

The reason why people decide to donate votive offerings is usually that they have a problem. Then they consult a *kodangi*, a man who is able to get possessed by the village gods. He

beats an hour-glass shaped drum, sings, and when the god has
descended on him he can be consulted as oracle about what to
do to gain the help of the gods to solve the problem. The
*kodangi* then suggests which offering to make, and to which
god, and it is then ordered from the potter and offered at the
next festival. However, it is never Aiyanar himself, who is
consulted thus, because people who are possessed by him are
unable to speak; they stand stock-still while tears run from
their eyes. Aiyanar is thus too powerful for possession, so for
divine guidance lesser gods like Karuppaswami, a god always
found in Aiyanar temples, are invited to descend on the
possessed.

Aiyanar is the protector of the village against flood and evil
spirits, and Karuppaswami is the next-in-command in Aiyanar's
army in eternal combat against evil forces. The two gods are
often seen as statues of gigantic figures on horseback in front
of Aiyanar temples. There are also people who take vows to
go to an Aiyanar temple once a year and become possessed by
Karuppaswami. They are called *cāmi ādis* ("god dancers").
They have to prepare for this for weeks, abstaining from meat,
liquor and sex. On the appointed day they dress up in a
peculiar dress and hat supposedly worn by Karuppaswami and
start walking from their homes to the temple preceded by a
band with *nagaswaram* (oboe) and drums. Sometimes they also
carry the big chopping knife, which Karuppaswami holds in
his right hand. As they approach the temple they get more
and more possessed. People on the route come out and stop
the *cāmi ādi* and ask questions about their problems and how
to solve them. I once saw a mother place her child in a *cāmi
ādi's* arms and ask him about the child's future education.
When the *cāmi ādi* reaches the temple and faces the god, who
has possessed him, he is overpowered and passes out, and the
possession is over.

Someone in the family may also get possessed by
Karuppaswami or any other village deity and in oracle fashion
tell the family which offering to make to solve a particular
problem.

We may briefly sketch the Aiyanar worship as a closed
religious-economic village system largely devoted to solving
mental, health and economic problems of the villagers. This

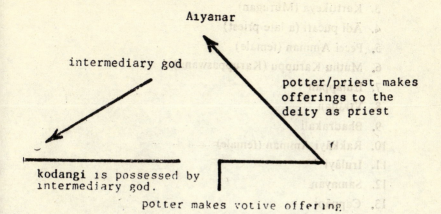

FIG. 3.1 : *Aiyanar Worship System*

system involves no higher deities and no Brahman priests. Only through Aiyanar is it formally connected with sanskritic Hinduism, since he is the son of Shiva and Vishnu (see Fig. 3.1).

**Aiyanar Temples and Village Hierarchy**

Aiyanar temples usually contain 21 gods. The other gods may vary from temple to temple. These gods may be the family deities—*kula deivam*—of particular lineages, which gather from all parts of the country once a year in order to worship and become possessed by the deity. In this way the lineage retains a geographical link to a place of origin, which all family members may have left long ago. There is also a certain hierarchy among the gods (Dumont 1970), which is based on the local principles of caste hierarchy. Some gods are vegetarian and hence purer than others, who will accept blood-offerings. As one particular example I list the gods in the Aiyanar temple at Kochidai near Arappalaiyam on the outskirts of Madurai in the order in which they receive offerings from the temple priest :

1. Ganesh (is always worshipped first as a matter of convention, not because of higher rank in this case)
2. Aiyanar

3. Karttikeya (Murugan)
4. Ādi pūcari (a late priest)
5. Pecci Amman (female)
6. Muthu Karuppu (Karuppaswami)
7. Irulappan
8. Vīranan
9. Bhadrakali
10. Rakkāyi Amman (female)
11. Irulāyi
12. Samayan
13. Cappāni
14. Mandi Karuppu
15. Conai
16. Muniyandi
17. Naga
18. Nagappa
19. Navangraha (nine planets)

and outside the temple wall :

20. Sangili Karuppu (Karuppuswami with the Chain)
21. Meiyandi

**iyanar, Karuppaswami and the Complex of the Village Religion**

In the minds of the Tamil villagers Aiyanar is the figure who links almost all the characteristics of Tamil village religion. He is the chief, so to speak, of almost all the village gods. This means that he is always implicitly present when one of the lesser gods is worshipped, even if he is not represented in the temple. This village religion also involves annual worship of the lineage deity during which lineage members are possessed by the deity.

Both the lineage deities and the lesser gods in the Aiyanar temples may be thought of as intermediaries in relation to Aiyanar, who is more powerful than they are. He is too powerful for people to be possessed by him, so Karuppaswami is often sought as intermediary. Karuppaswami is so closely linked to Aiyanar, that to mention one is to mention the other. This is why Karuppaswami plays such an important role as a linking figure—as we shall see later—in this religious complex. Karuppaswami is also important as a link between this village religious complex and the new version of Aiyanar worship, the Aiyappan pilgrimage cult, to which we shall now turn.

## Aiyappan Worship in Madurai

Through systematic interviews with a great number of Aiyappan devotees from various groups in Madurai, I have found that the cult was introduced in this area from Kerala beginning in 1945. I have found a few isolated instances of pilgrims going from Tamil Nadu to Sabari Malai as far back as the 1920s, but their activity seems to have left no trace in Tamil society. Prior to 1945 the cult seems to have been virtually unknown in the Tamil area. I reached this conclusion by asking the Aiyappan devotees who their gurus were, and when and how they came to know about Aiyappan. I then tried to find the gurus and ask them the same questions. Invariably I ended up with either a guru who had come to Madurai some time around or after 1945, or a Tamil guru who had gone to Kerala and became acquainted with the cult there around the same time.

There are now—to my knowledge—four Aiyappan temples in Madurai, and three of them have had Aiyappan statues installed between 1981-83. In January 1983, I witnessed the inauguration of an Aiyappan temple and the installation of a statue of Aiyappan in West Masi Street in the centre of Madurai. The ceremony started on 19th and lasted three days. I heard a long speech there by Kandaswami Pulavar, the well-known Tamil scholar. He explained that Aiyappan was not a foreign god, but really of Tamil origin, although the cult was being introduced from Kerala. As evidence of this he quoted the ancient Tamil epic, Silappadikaram. This information surprised the audience, but it is true, that there is mention of a god called Pātanda Sāstā in this epic, and Sāstā is another name for Aiyanar/Aiyappan. It seems that the Tamils accept all references in ancient literature to "Sāstā" as synonymous with Aiyanar/Aiyappan, although the texts give absolutely no information about these "Sāstās" apart from the name. Later Kandaswami Pulavar told me about the important role which

P.T. Rajan played in Madurai in spreading knowledge about
Aiyappan. P.T. Rajan was an industrialist who was active in
collection of money for a new Aiyappan statue for the temple
at Sabari Malai. An Aiyappan Sangam (society) started in
1955 is responsible for the collection for the new temple in
West Masi Street in Madurai. The sangam has about 200
members. From a brochure, printed by the sangam in order
to raise funds, I quote the following information about its
history :

> "From the early fifties quite a number of Aiyappan devotees
> would meet in West Masi Street, Madurai, in the months of
> Karthigai and Margali every year for singing bhajan in
> praise of Lord Aiyappan and offer worship to Him. That
> fraternity grew wider from year ro year and finally merged
> into Sri Sabari Malai Ayyappa Bakhtargal Sangam, and in
> course of time found an ideal president in the late Tamizhvel
> Sri P.T. Rajan.
> It was under the guiding and inspiring leadership of
> Tamizvel P.T. Rajan that the Ayyappa Bakktargal Sangam
> embarked upon the plan of erecting a pucca temple for
> Lord Ayyappa in Madurai city. It was on the first of March
> 1968 that the Sangam was registered . . . "

The text then mentions that :

> "Sri Ayyappa according to history was brought up by the
> then Pandian king who was reigning over the Pandala
> kingdom having his headquarters at Pandalam formerly of
> Tamil Nad but now forming part of Kerala."

In this way several things are brought to the attention of the
Tamil public, which is requested to donate money for this new
temple : that Aiyappan's place of origin was old Tamil territory,
that the king who adopted Aiyappan was of Pandyan decent
related to the old Pandyan rulers of ancient Madurai. Thus
not only literary sources, but also "history", are used to
demonstrate the links between Tamil culture and Aiyappan.
All this shows, that the Tamil audience needs to be told
about it.

Since many people mentioned P.T. Rajan's great importance, I went to see his son, Kamla Tyagarajan, who now manages the family's factory. One often hears P.T. Rajan described as a man who worked particularly to spread the worship of Aiyappan in Tamil Nadu, but during the talk I had with his son, I got a somewhat different picture of P.T. Rajan's involvement. He was an extremely pious man who supported many other religious causes. What prompted him to collect money for the new Aiyappan statue at Sabari Malai, was the fire accident there in 1949, in which both temple and idol were destroyed. Since it was rumoured that people from Tamil Nadu were behind the fire, P.T. Rajan felt that the Tamils should donate money to the temple. He was a prominent member of the group of people, who collected money all over Tamil Nadu for the Sabari temple. Thus, in his view, could the Tamils atone for the sin, which might have been committed by some of them. Fred Clothey (1982 : 47) also mentions P.T. Rajan's importance in spreading the Aiyappan cult. But although many of my informants have told me that they first came to know about the cult through his campaign, I think that the evaluation of P.T. Rajan's role presents a classical problem in history writing and evaluation of sources. The fact is, that most of my informants learned about Aiyappan through a variety of other sources, and that it was the example of close friends, and the boons they got by going to Sabari Malai, which actually prompted them to do likewise. The oldest members of the Sathagoparamanuja group, with which I went to Sabari Malai in January 1984, told me, that it was the example of Karuppa Pillai, a close friend of the guru, that really convinced them of Aiyappan's power. Karuppa Pillai had been unable to get children for a long time, and as a last attempt wanted to try to implore Aiyappan to grant him issue. Shortly after his return from Sabari, his wife conceived, and bore him a son, and this really made an impression on many people, and convinced them that they should worship Aiyappan. But as time goes by, and all these individual stories are forgotten, the importance of the personal contact is perhaps forgotten, and in retrospect the importance of famous men tend to grow larger than it actually was.

Simultaneous with the opening of the West Masi Street

temple, another Aiyappan temple was inaugurated at Tallāku-
lam near the tank of the Vishnu temple. This temple has been
built by a sangam centering around a guru from Kerala, now
settled in Madurai. A third temple is found near the Collector's
Office Bus Stand, but it is not functioning due to personal strife
in the sangam.

A fourth temple is located at Arappālaiyam near the by-
pass road south of Madurai. R. Sadasivasami, who was born
in Kerala in 1927 and came to Madurai in 1936, started building this temple in 1960. He spent most of his own money and
collected money from others. It got its final shape in 1973. In
1984 March, a stone statue of Aiyappan was installed at a
grand ceremony lasting three days and three nights. When
Sadasivasami came to Madurai, nobody there knew about
Aiyappan. He went himself to Sabari Malai in 1942 along
with 25 natives of Madurai. Their guru was from Kerala. Since
1945 he has functioned as guru and has every year taken about
60 people to Sabari Malai.

However, the most important part of Aiyappan worship is
the pilgrimage to Sabari Malai and the preparations for it. For
that reason, the following account of my observations of a
pilgrimage group in 1983-84 is important to explain what the
cult means in the present-day religious life of the Tamils.

## Report from a Pilgrimage : Preparation Time

On December 24th 1983 I went to an Aiyappan pūja in a
private house in Madurai. A number of Aiyappan devotees
had been invited to come and worship Aiyappan by a man,
who was just about to leave on a pilgrimage to Sabari Malai.
The one room in the house was transformed temporarily into
an Aiyappan temple, and only men were allowed to enter it.
As I have seen in many other houses, there were picture of
Aiyappan and other Hindu gods on the walls, and a special
Aiyappan altar with the indispensable model of the 18 steps
leading up to the temple at Sabari Malai. This temporary
transformation may last 40-50 days and starts, when the
pilgrims wear a necklace made of rudraksha beads given to him
by his guru.

After receiving the necklace the pilgrim lives a restricted
life. He stops shaving, walks bare-foot, and abstains from sex,

meat and alcohol. He wears the special dress of the Aiyappan pilgrim' a coarse cotton *vesti* (South Indian men's dress), which is either blue, green, saffron or black. Since the men gathered in that small house were all men, who had started preparing themselves for the pilgrimage about a month earlier, they all looked very much alike with their rudraksha necklaces (some wore several of them), coloured *vestis* and the grey smears of holy ash and red *kum-kum* on their foreheads. The devotees addressed each other as "swami", meaning Aiyappan, and they were in fact in the process of merging their identity with the god. Hence it was logical that they greeted each other by kneeling down and touching each others feet with their hands.

I had started growing a beard, but had not yet received my rudraksha necklace. My guru was present at the gathering, and after we had been served a meal on the roof terrace, I went with him to a small Murugan temple nearby. My guru was the son of the illustrious Aiyappan guru, Sathagoparamanuja, whose life-size portrait hung to the right in this Murugan temple. The guru and I made offerings of bananas, betel leaves and incense sticks. He garlanded me with a huge flower garland, which I took off immediately, as one is supposed to do. He then placed the rudraksha necklace round my neck. I had bought it earlier the same day in the Meenakshi temple in the centre of Madurai. Attached to it was a bronze medallion showing Aiyappan in yogic meditation posture. I was to wear this necklace day and night until the guru removed it after our return from Sabari. I knelt down to worship his feet, and the guru did the same to me. Then he applied holy ash and red *kum-kum* to my forehead. I was now a member of the Sathagoparamanuja group, which was to leave for Sabari Malai on January 10th in time for the very important annual festival, Makaravilakku. I had been told, that "our group is green", so I wore a green vesti.

During the two months before the pilgrimage, the pilgrims attend a great number of bhajans- religious song gatherings. I attended a number of bhajans arranged in the houses of members the Sathagoparamanuja group. The guru was invariably invited, but he was in such demand, that he could not always attend. The group had around 300 members, and no house could accommodate them all at the same time. It was inevitable, that our group members would occasionally arrange bhajans on the same dates.

When the Aiyappa swamis arrived at the bhajan dressed in their green or blue *vestis*, they would line up outside the house. The women of the house would then come out with water and wash their feet, apply sandel paste and *kum-kum* to them, and kneel down and touch their feet in worship. Then the swamis would enter the house and gather around the Aiyappan altar with the inevitable 18 steps in front, always profusely decorated with flowers. On some occasions the stress would be on ritual, and the Aiyappan service might last an hour or more depending on how many of Aiyappan's *saranams* (Aiyappan's holy epithets) were recited. In the ritual part of the bhajan was included worship of particular interest to the host and his family, and this might be performed by members of the family. Thus the Aiyappan devotion was woven into the religious life of the individual hosts and their families, and into the larger pattern of South Indian—and indeed pan-Indian—*bhakti* religion. Aiyappan devotion is rather novel in Tamil Nadu, but the worship of this god seems to be easily absorbed into the traditional patterns of religious life as yet another facet of Hinduism.

After the rituals would follow the true bhajan with songs, and sometimes dances. The songs would cover the whole range of well-known Hindu deities, and there were always songs on Murugan (Tamil name for Karttikeya), the god of war, so popular in Tamil Nadu, as well as Ganesh, Rama and Mariamman. The element of *bhakti* was very much stressed in these gatherings. Sometimes the devotees would sit in pairs with one swami resting his head on the other's lap while singing about the divine love between Radha and Krishna. Sometimes more energetic dances would be performed, for instance accompanying songs on Hanuman, the divine monkey warrior, with vigorous leaps, but more often the dance was a simple, slow circular dance with the swamis holding each other's hands. It was not easy to get the necessary room for dancing, because the house was invariably crowded with on-lookers, men who were not going on pilgrimage, and women who took great interest in the activities of the Aiyappa swāmis, although they could not participate themselves. (On the reasons for his see Kjaerholm 1982).

All through the evening swamis would arrive, greet the guru and the other swamis by kneeling down and touching their feet, and the greeting would be returned. Some swamis had been garlanded with huge flower garlands. To show proper humility one is supposed to very quickly present it to someone else. I received garlands quite often, and it was not easy to pass them on, because the other swamis protested in show of modesty.

After the bhajan a light meal would be served, and the host would be very particular that all the swamis ate his food and the fruit presented to Aiyappan. To feed swamis is an act which gives the host merit, like the feeding of Brahmans.

Once I tried to leave the bhajan discretely, but was told that I must ask the guru's permission to leave and greet him properly by kneeling and touching his feet. Apart from this recognition of the guru's superiority the stress in an Aiyappan bhajan group is on equality of all members, including the guru. The basic idea is to approach one's identity to the divine object of devotion, so that "we are all equal in the eyes of Aiyappan," as one swami put it.

I never received any formal teaching from the guru, since the cult's rituals and mythology are public knowledge. The Aiyappan guru is supposed to be just a good example for the devotees and to lead the way on the hazardous journey through the jungles and mountains around Sabari Malai. The pilgrims can learn about Aiyappan's mythology and rituals from a very large number of books and pamphlets on these matters, which are published or reprinted during the pilgrimage season. Also a large number of songs are available in books and cassettes. In fact, the pilgrim can learn everything necessary about the cult from the songs at bhajans and by watching the rituals on those occasions. Temple worship of Aiyappan is not necessary and not yet very common in Tamil Nadu, where there are not yet many Aiyappan temples.

The participants at the bhajan were not only members of our group but came also from other groups. Membership of a group is not a permanent or binding thing. One may join other groups at one's convenience. Since the groups leave at different

times, one may not be able to go with one's usual group, but
can then easily shift to another group.

During the preparation time there are also special *kanni
pūjas* (literally : virgin puja). These are special Aiyappan
services at which the swamis, who are going for the first time,
are worshipped. I was once invited to attend such a *puja* performed by another group. The *kanni swamis* were placed, one
after the other, on a low stool and people, mostly women, lined
up to worship the *kanni*. They bent down and touched the
swami's feet, which had been washed and anointed with sandel
paste and red *kum-kum*. When they got up and faced him with
their palm joined in greeting, he would apply sacred ash and
*kum-kum* on their foreheads, thus giving them the *kanni's*
blessing, which is considered especially powerful. Since I was
also a *kanni swami*, I was asked to receive homage like the
others.

At no time during this period of preparation did I meet any
obstacle in my quest for knowledge about the Aiyappan cult,
and nobody ever questioned my right to be present at any
gathering. On the contrary, I was greeted warmly by most and
it was never thought strange, that a *vellaikāran* ("white man")
should join them in worship of Aiyappan. This is because the
cult stands out from all others as a "universal" brand of
Hinduism. To worship Aiyappan is a seasonal thing which
during a short period can unite all men, be they Hindus of
different castes, or even Muslims or Christians, in universal
brotherhood. So the Hindu Aiyappa swamis did not consider
me as a Christian convert to Hinduism (which I never preten-
ded to be), but rather a Christian who temporarily wished to
share this universal brotherhood with them.

It was explained quite often to me, that the Aiyappan cult
is the religion of the Kaliyuga, this most difficult and conflict-
ridden and debased period, in which we are now considered to
live. It was to help man overcome conflict and base lust, that
Aiyappan came into being, and hence the stress on brotherhood,
love and friendship between men of different castes and
religions, as well as the stress on asceticism in the cult practice.

I often heard the claim, that Muslims and Christians participate in great numbers in the Aiyappan pilgrimage, but
although I was constantly on the look out for them, I never

came across any Muslim or Christian Aiyappa swamis. Those
I have met and interviewed were all Hindus from Tamil Nadu
or Kerala.

## The Pilgrimage

On January 10th all the members of the Sathagoparamanuja
group gathered in the evening in front of the guru's house in
the Raliway Colony in Madurai. A large leaf-thatched shelter
had been erected in front of the house—large enough to accommodate the 300 pilgrims with family and friends. Now the
*irumudi* ceremony was to take place, i.e. the pilgrim's cloth bag
with its two compartments was to be packed. The front part
contains a coconut filled with ghee and other offerings to
Aiyappan, the rear part contains the pilgrim's own food.
(Concerning the *irumudi* see Vaidyanathan 1978 and Kjaerholm
1982). Under the shelter were too Aiyappan altars with the 18
steps in front decorated with flowers and light bulbs. The
filling of the *irumudi* is an important ritual done by the guru,
and each swami comes forward and sits in front of the guru.
They both pour ghee in the coconut, and when it is filled it is
sealed and placed in the front part of the *irumudi*. Rice is taken
handful by handful and poured into the rear part of the *irumudi*,
and family members come forward to pour in rice. Although
not all were aware of it, the significance of this is that of the
Hindu death rite, where the relatives offer rice to the deceased.
Should the pilgrim die on the way, he would then not miss this
essential last rite.

When the *irumudi* was packed and tied securely by the guru,
the pilgrims placed blankets on their heads and knelt in front of
the guru, who then placed the bags on their heads. The pilgrims
then got up, were turned around thrice and respectfully backed
away from the guru, so as not to show him his back. The
pilgrims were now—so to speak—under the guru's command
and must stay with him, until they returned from pilgrimage.
They could not remove the *irumudi* from their heads without
the guru's permission. This ceremony lasted well into the night,
and once we had received the *irumudi* we were allowed to place
it in front of Aiyappan's altar and lie down to get some rest.
Once the pilgrim has received the *irumudi*, he is a member of

the sacred brotherhood and can under no circumstances go back to his home, until he has finished his pilgrimage.

In the morning on the 11th the *irumudis* were distributed (they were numbered) to their owners by the guru, and we proceeded one by one to the four buses to find the seat allotted to us, carrying the *irumudi* and blankets on our heads and other necessities for the journey in shoulder bags. On the way the pilgrims were greeted by relatives, many of whom knelt down and touched the pilgrim's feet and received his blessing. The pilgrims smashed coconuts on the ground and children fought eagerly to get the pieces. This ritual signifies the pilgrims departure and separation from his former social identity.

Our group consisted mostly of elderly and middle-aged men, but there were some small girls and older women as well. Women who are able to bear children are not allowed to participate in this pilgrimage. (On the reasons for this see Vaidyanathan 1978 and Kjaerholm 1982). I was given a seat in the guru's bus, in which the bhajan group was also travelling, so we had good music and singing on the way. The buses first went round the Meenakshi in the centre of Madurai and then proceeded south towards Sabari Malai. On the way we halted south of Madurai and had breakfast. This was prepared earlier in Madurai by our eight cooks and brought out to the spot in advance. The group had hired cooks, because cooking is of special importance—as we shall see below—to this particular group.

We proceeded south in our four buses with bhajan singing and the chorus call "*swamiye saranam Aiyappā*" which is repeated frequently all through the journey in order to urge the pilgrims on. We passed by Tenkasi, crossed the Kerala border and started climbing the Western Ghats. At 1 PM we reached one of the five important Aiyappan temples, the one at Ariyankavu. Here the group rested, worshipped Aiyappan, had lunch, bathed in the river, and the cooks and their volunteer helpers prepared lunch packs for the next day, when we were to start trekking, and cooking therefore would be difficult. Late in the afternoon we drove on to Erimeli, a village in the Western Ghats, which has another important Aiyappan temple, and with a brief stop for dinner on the way we reached Erimeli at 1 A.M. on the 12th. Since Erimeli is the starting point for the 48 miles trek to Sabari Malai, the crowd there was extremely dense. Our group, although fairly large, seemed to drown in this sea of people as we pushed our way to the place allotted to us in advance in front of the local school, where we lay down to sleep on the ground. We were awakened before dawn and prepared ourselves for an important ritual, which takes place at Erimeli, the Ottu Tullal dance. We adorned our heads with coloured balloons, (formerly feathers were used), decorated ourselves with powder in different colours and began a lively dance while singing *"swami tindakaṭōm-tōm"*. This meaningless phrase was explained to me as being a corrupted Malayalam phrase meaning "the swami (Aiyappan) is in your heart". We hired a local band consisting of nagaswaram (oboe) and drums, and with the musicians in front we joined the countless other dancing groups. It was quite a sight. I cannot even guess how many pilgrims were there, may be more than half a million, all gaily decorated with balloons and coloured powder, dancing and singing, while the bands competed with each other.

The dance started at the Ganesh temple, where make-up and balloons were put on, went around "Vāvar's Temple" (Vāvar is a Muslim warrior associated with Aiyappan; see Vaidyanathan 1978), and ended at the Aiyappan temple, where everybody had a bath in the river and washed the colours off. Some in the group carried the guru on their shoulders while dancing. This is a tradition started eight years earlier in the time of the present guru's father. I saw no other group carrying their guru in this fashion. The crowd was so thick, and the dancing so vigorous and the lanes so narrow in places, that people could have been easily trampled to death—as so frequently happens at film premiers in India—if people had not shown admirable regard for each other in spite of their abandon.

The whole idea of the Ottu Tullal was puzzling to me, and when I asked members of my group about it, I was told that the idea was, that we should humiliate by behaving like primitive forest people. Thus singing and dancing with child-like abandon we would get rid of our pride, forget our social position, and be able to merge more completely with the "Swami" (Aiyappan). (For further information on the Ottu Tullal see

Vaidaynathan 1978). The dance is in memory of Aiyappan's
visit to the jungle people during his sojourn in the jungle.

After this dance, on the morning of January 12th, our
group split in two, the elderly men and women went on by bus
to the river Pampa to take the short 8 miles route to Sabari,
but most of us started on the arduous 48 miles trek through
jungles and mountains. At the beginning of this route is a
Muslim "shrine" for Vāvar, where a fakir collects offerings of
money. After walking some hours we rested at Kālaikatti
Ashram, the place from where Shiva watched the fight between
Aiyappan and the buffalo demoness Mahisi. (For an account
of the relation between these mythological figures, see Vaidyanathan 1978, Kjaerholm 1982 and Appendix). We went on to
the Alutha river, where huge numbers of pilgrims were preparing lunch. Our cooks had gone there ahead of us and made the
food. However, it was not so easy to find the exact spot.
Fortunately, we could easily recognize members of our group
among the five million other pilgrims, because we all wore
yellow cloth tags with the name Sathagoparamanuja group
printed on it. Due to our number and the enormous mass of
people moving along the jungle path, we could not possibly
keep together while on the move.

On the banks of the Alutha river the battle between Mahishi
and Aiyappan took place. After killing her, Aiyappan was
informed by Brahma, that the demon's dead body would grow
until it darkened the sun and the moon, unless it was buried
under a heap of stones. This may be the origin of the custom
of taking a pebble from the river bed while crossing the Alutha
river and placing it on large heap of stones later on. However,
it seemed that not many pilgrims were aware of this mythological detail. The motive, I encountered most often, was
simply, that they wanted to have a wish fulfilled, and thought
this was a sure way of achieving it.

After a bath in the river we crossed the Alutha river, some
took up stones from the river bed, and we continued through
still rougher country to a night camp called Mukkuli. It was a
huge temporary camp, accommodating tens of thousands, with
huts covered with flimsy palm leaf thatch, that did not protect
us from the light rain throughout the night.

Along the route the Aiyappa Seva Sangham had laid electric

cables and in the big camps they had offices, which mainly
served as meeting places for lost pilgrims and their groups.
All through the night I heard the Aiyappa Seva Sangham's
loudspeakers blasting Aiyappan songs and religious discourses,
but mainly announcing the name of lost Aiyappan pilgrims and
where they hailed from, informing their groups where they
could be picked up. This was interesting to listen to, because I
could deduce—if we got a representative sample of the pilgrims
—that virtually all of the pilgrims were from Tamil Nadu, and
that all districts of Tamil Nadu were represented.

**Receiving Aiyappan's Jewels**

On the 13th morning we proceeded from Mukkuli before
dawn to reach another very large camp, Periya Yānai, at the
Pampa river and at the foot of Sabari Malai. Outside the pilgrimage season this is a watering place for elephants. Occasionally there are problems with elephants. Two pilgrims were
killed by elephants just after our departure. Most of our group
camped in the open on a ground reserved for us. Some of us
rented room in thatched huts. This camp was very densely
populated and there may have been anything between a half
and one million people. Day and night the pilgrims came
pouring in and out of the camp. Many individual styles of
religious worship could be seen here. Some groups of pilgrims
performed a peculiar ritual after they had eaten a meal on palm
leaves. The leaves were then placed in a row with the leftover
food on them, and one or several in the group would lie down
and role over the leaves, so they were smeared with rice and
various vegetable dishes all over. Then the group would proceed
to the river while singing and dancing, carrying the dirty leaves,
to take a bath in the Pampa river. Such groups could be seen
everywhere day and night. To my knowledge no explanation
for this ritual is found in Aiyappan's mythology, and some
groups frown on it. I was told by members of my group that,
"we don't do that", and that they found it irrelevant and in
bad taste. The reason I got, when I asked, was that through
this ritual "we wash away our sins". To touch other people's
food, especially left-over food, is normally highly polluting, so
this was certainly a "reversal rite". However, the idea might be
that since as we are all Aiyappans on this pilgrimage, none can

pollute the other. Later I was told, that this peculiar ritual is fairly common in Tamil Nadu, and that people do it in order to cure stomach ailments.

Another ritual performed on this spot is called "Pampa Vilakku" ("Pampa Lamp"). On structures made of sticks, candles are placed and lighted. Balloons are tied to the base of the structure, and the groups go singing and dancing to the river and place the floats on the water. The floats "carry our sins away", was the justification for this ritual, which also lacks any basis in the mythology, and it was not done by our group either. These two rituals are the only exceptions, I observed, to the general rule, that the whole pilgrimage is a detailed enactment of the very eventful Aiyappan mythology. This is in fact such a large subject, that I have only been able to give a few examples in this account.

In the evening our group performed *Ali puja*. (*Alis* are the huge demonic warriors, in this case the forest spirits, in the retinue of the gods). A big fire was built in the middle of the camp and offerings like camphor, coconut, ghee, apples and money were thrown into the fire. The pilgrims danced round the fire singing bhakti songs. After this, *puja* was performed for the *irumudis*, which were placed in a big heap while we camped. In the night, while everybody else in the group slept, 20 members of the Sathagoparamanuja group opened all the *irumudis*, took out the rice in them and closed them again. This rice was to be used for the great feast for the raja of Pandalam, when we were to serve lunch for him and his party the following day.

On the 14th, the first day in the Tamil month Tai, we had *Pongal* (rice boiled with brown sugar) for breakfast. This was the Tamil New Year, called *Pongal* (on this festival see Kjaerholm 1980). Because of this festival we took bath in the river, worshipped the guru and offered coins to him, which he gave back. The coins were kept in a special cloth bag with sacred ash as a sign of the spiritual bond between the guru and his disciple.

Now the Sathagoparamanuja group started hectic preparations to receive the Pandala raja and his party and serve them lunch. It is a special privilege of the group to do this. The custom was started in 1958, when Sathagoparamanuja insisted on the honour of serving a meal to the Pandala raja. No one and nothing may stop the raja and his party, when they carry Aiyappan's jewels to Sabari, so naturally they declined the offer. However, one of the men carrying the boxes was possessed and said that they must accept the invitation from Sathagoparamanuja. For five years after this, the raja was received by the Sathagoparamanuja group. The boxes were placed on a shelter, where a member of the group had the privilege of opening the boxes and worship the jewels. In the boxes were, according to this man, two elephants, two swords, and a large face mask made of gold. But after five years the police prohibited the opening of the boxes for security reasons.

After the camp was cleared, a shelter was built, and the entrance was roped in to keep the crowd away. The cooks and numerous helpers had been working since early morning to prepare a first class South Indian rice meal. Then the guru and four others went to invite the Pandala raja, who was resting in a camp two miles away. The guru invited the raja and his retinue, as well as five members of the Sathagoparamanuja group, who were travelling with the raja. They had left Madurai on the 10th and gone to Pandalam, where they received the *irumudi* from the raja. To have the coconut filled with ghee by him is very auspicious, since the raja is a relative of Aiyappan (see Vaidyanathan 1978 and Kjaerholm 1982). On the 12th day the raja's party and the five guests from our group started from Pandalam. They have two days to cover the long and arduous stretch to Sabari Malai, so they walk day and night. Two white-faced kites will precede the Pandala group all the way from Pandalam to Sabari, and we were waiting in the Periya Yānai camp for the kites to announce the imminent arrival of the raja. When we saw the two kites glide high in the air the entire crowd called out "Swamiye saranam Aiyappā", and worshipped the kites. There were also other signs that the raja was approaching. The police came with communication equipment to guard the three jewel boxes and their precious contents. The kingdom of Pandalam was abolished long ago, but still the descendants of the royal lineage claim the right to keep the jewels in their ancestral palace in Pandalam. Sabari is located in the former Pandalam territory, so the royal family are so to speak the hosts for all the pilgrims entering the area. The royal

Pandalam family must be present at the temple on this occasion still.

The members of the Sathagoparamanuja group received the raja with bhajan singing, as he and his party came rushing into our camp. The boxes containing the jewels were placed on the shelter and worshipped, and the raja and his relatives were welcomed by the guru. Under the shelter a very fine meal was served for them on palm leaves. The royal party ate the meal behind a curtain, so no one could see them eat. When they had finished the meal, members of our group went to kneel in front of the raja and receive his blessing. An enormous crowd had by now gathered, and our group had quite a job controlling them. They surged forward to see the boxes and receive the raja's blessing. After a brief rest the raja's party continued to Sabari and we all had lunch, and I must say that this meal— although prepared in the wilderness—was fit for a king. After the raja's departure our group packed quickly and started climbing Sabari Malai. We were to reach a place half way up in time to see the Makara Vilakku, the holy light, which appears on the hill tops above Sabari. We saw the light around 7 P.M.; it was rather tiny and shone very briefly but aroused huge enthusiasm among the hundreds of thousands of pilgrims around us. Our choice of this particular spot to watch the light was dictated by necessity. Along the entire width of the 6-8 yards wide path a flood of pilgrims was pouring down all evening, so it was impossible to go up. At 2 A.M. on the 15th it was possible for us to climb up to Sabari Malai, where we were let in groups of about 200. Then we rushed forward to climb the 18 steps while breaking a coconut. This was the culmination of the pilgrimage. At the temple a dense crowd was jostling to reach the temple door and get a glimpse of the deity. The Kerala police were out in strength and controlled the crowd efficiently. Those swamis who tried to ascend the stairs which were meant for descending were pulled down without the slightest regard for their sanctity.

After visiting the temple we went to rest in the Nambiar lodge, one of the permanent buildings in the otherwise uninhabited area, put at our disposal by Nambiar, the Tamil film actor and Aiyappan devotee. Later our group carried sandel paste in huge quantities as offerings to Aiyappan. In the evening a *puspanjali*—an offering of flowers—worth more than rupees 3000 was carried by our group to the temple. Our group decorated the 18 steps with lamps. The latter ceremony is a prerogative of the Sathagoparamanuja group and together with the lunch for the raja of Pandalam testifies to the special merit earned by the late Sathagoparamanuja. Flowers and sandel paste offerings are also made by many other groups, but the number of pilgrims at Sabari Malai is now so great it was estimated that year to be around 5 million people over three days—that they cannot all be allowed to bring their offerings to the sanctum sanctorum.

The ghee in the coconuts was poured out. Some was given to the temple and a small quantity was carried back by pilgrim in bottles. Many pilgrims regard this ghee as miracle-working medicine for all sorts of ailments, because it has been poured over Aiyappan's statue. In the early morning on the 1th we climbed down the 18th steps while breaking a coconut, thus taking leave of Aiyappan. Below the steps in a huge fire the coconuts which had contained the ghee were burning. This was explained to me as a symbolic funeral pyre. The ghee is the essence of life, the ever-living soul; the coconut is the body, which serves no purpose after the soul has passed on.

After a quick walk 8 miles downhill we came to the Pampa river, took a bath, boarded our buses and reached Madurai at 2 P.M. on the 18th. The guru then removed the necklace, received a symbolic offering of money from each, and the pilgrims dispersed in the night.

The journey had cost each of us about rupees 300, bus travel, meals, and *irumudi* included. On top of that some swamis had spent large sums on special pūja decorations and offerings on the way. Three hundred rupees is close to the average monthly income of a clerk or labourer in Tamil Nadu, and is a substantial sum of money for most people.

**Conclusion**

After two years of fieldwork in the Madurai area I can draw some conclusions about the relation between Aiyanar and Aiyappan worship, and what the introduction of a new version of an old god means in the cultural and religious system of the Tamils.

The rapid spread of the Aiyappan cult has the effect of
revitalizing Hinduism and certain of its traditions. This revitalization comes about because the Aiyappan devotees realize that
this new god is identical to the ubiquitous and familiar Tamil
village god, Aiyanar. At many Aiyanar temples can be seen
depictions of the Mohini myth. Ayappan/Aiyanar was the son
of Shiva and Vishnu in his female form, Mohini. (See Kjaerholm 1982). However, the two styles of worship and slightly
different identities of Aiyappan/Aiyanar are still kept separate.
This is because the Aiyanar worship is in the hands of the Velar
priests and closely connected with their artistic traditions, and
depends on hereditary rights. I found only one example,
where Aiyanar and Aiyappan had been merged into one
identity. This was an old Aiyanar temple at Panaiyūr about 10
miles South East of Madurai. This temple had been renamed
"Sri Sabari Aiyanar/Aiyappan temple", which was written
above the entrance to the sanctum sanctorum. Significantly the
hereditary priest of this temple was not a Velar but a Pillaimar.

When the identity between the two gods is realized, the
Aiyappan devotees tend to become more interested in worshipping Aiyanar and the god so closely associated with him,
Karuppaswami. Evidence of this is the fact that there is a
Karuppaswami temple at Sabari Malai to the right of the
Aiyappan temple, and the god's name is written in Tamil
letters, because this god obviously is the main concern of the
Tamil Aiyappa swamis, not those from Kerala. One member
of the Sathagoparamanuja group had "18-Steps-Karuppu" as his
*kula deyvam* and was frequently possessed by him. It so happens
that there are 18 steps leading up to some Karuppaswami
temples—hence the name 18-Steps—Karuppu. This is taken
as evidence of a link between Aiyappan and Karuppaswami.
This man took Karuppaswami's symbol, the chopping knife—
with him to Sabari and placed it on the 18 steps leading up to
Aiyappan's temple. Then he took the knife back and placed it on
his model of Aiyappan's 18 steps in his house when worshipping
Aiyappan there. To this man Karuppaswami's chopping knife
and 18 steps is tangible evidence of the link between his old village religion and the new *bhakti* cult. A closer look at the character of the Aiyappan worship shows a very conventional attitude, which is derived from the Aiyanar village cult. Having inter-

viewed a large number of devotees of Aiyappan and Aiyanar my conclusion is, that the goal, which is highest in the Aiyappan worship—according to the popular Aiyappan pilgrimage literature—namely merging with the god, is secondary. The most important motive for going on pilgrimage is the same, which makes people present votive offerings to Aiyanar : a certain material goal is desired. Most commonly the Aiyappa swamis desire offspring, success in business, farming or education, or relief of illness Although the Aiyappan cult introduces a new style of worship, the motive for worship has not changed significantly among the Tamils.

Another aspect of the revitalizing effect of the Aiyappan cult is the tendency, I observed in my sample of swamis, who had forgotten or ceased to worship their *kula deyvam*, and who took a renewed interest in the family deity, renovated the family deity temple, and gathered all the relatives at the annual *kula deyvam* festival. One swami told me how someone had said at an *irumudi* ceremony; he attended, "there is someone here who does not worship his *kula deyvam*". This had struck his bad conscience, because his family had not worshipped its *kula deyvam* for decades. So the family began to search for the *kula deyvam* temple, they did not even know where it was any more, and contacted other family members, and now worship the *kula deyvam* on a grand scale. The *kula deyvam* and its worship is of great importance in Tamil Nadu, but may easily be overlooked, because the deity is never represented in people's homes in any visible form, although numerous other god's may be represented either with prints or small bronze statues. Nevertheless, the *kula deyvam* is always thought of as present in the house, and whenever the family is afflicted with disease or financial problems, some coins are offered at the *kula deyvam* temple. The *kula deyvam* still looms large in the religious life of the family. Often family members—mainly the women—see the deity in their dreams and receive messages from it.

It is a plausible hypothesis that strong religious involvement in a cult like that of Aiyappan tends to remind people of other, more traditional aspects of their religious life, and to further their interest in religion in general. Aiyappan devotees tend to be very active in other religious spheres as well. They participate in bhajans for various other gods, they frequent a great

number of local temples, go on pilgrimages to temples all over
Tamil Nadu, and worship a great variety of gods. Only
to very few does Aiyappan worship become so important, that
all other gods are neglected. I have found only one devotee of
Aiyappan, a guru, who had taken Aiyappan as his *kula deyvam*
and ceased to worship his hereditary *kula deyvam*, because he
declared that now Aiyappan was his *kula deyvam*. But there was
no sign, that other Aiyappan devotees would do the same.
However, all this does not explain, why people in such great
numbers choose to worship Aiyappan, when there are so many
other gods and so many other *bhakti* cults in South India, and
so many other pilgrimage places, so naturally one must ask :

**Why Aiyappan ?**

There are several reasons, one might list, for Aiyappan's recent
popularity. In the first place, there is the very simple reason,
that Sabari Malai is geographically within reach. In my interviews I found very few, who had gone on pilgrimage outside
Tamil Nadu; many declared, that they wished to go to Benares
and other holy places in North India, but could not afford it.

Secondly, Aiyappan is a god, who is known only in South
India. Aiyappan's theogony is an exclusively South Indian
addition to the wellknown myth about the churning of the
ocean. Since Aiyappan is introduced to the Tamil public as a
product of Tamil culture, he is received as a lost son. When
references are made to ancient Tamil texts in order to demonstrate Aiyappan's Tamil birth right, the Tamil consciousness
about their cultural separateness is strengthened.

In the third place, the Aiyappan cult entails an adjustment
of the social forms of contact. Although Aiyappan and Aiyanar
may be identical, Aiyanar worship is socially very rigid and
connected with particular geographical spots, and local village
hierarchies. The Aiyanar cult expresses the social and political
exclusiveness of the village. This is seen in the fact that
Aiyanar is tied to a specific local pantheon and always has a
local name or epithet. Aiyappan, on the other hand, represents
the national level, that which is common to the Tamil
nation.

Aiyappan worship makes it possible to form groups of
people from different castes, who may have various motives to

be together. It is doubtful whether the Aiyappan cult activity as such creates new contacts but is obvious, that it gives people a plausible reason for gathering periodically.

The strongly publicized ideals of equality in this cult do not seem to have any socially revolutionary purpose. It is simply a new way of meeting, but what makes the meeting possible is that the lower castes must accept the purity ideals, (vegetarianism asceticism of the life style of the higher castes. So the meeting between high and low castes takes place on the terms of the high castes. This really means a universal acceptance of the hierarchic principles of ritual purity/impurity on which caste hierarchy largely rests in Tamil Nadu.

Now that an egalitarian cult like the Aiyappan cult is becoming popular, one might expect *kula deyvam* worship to die out, but the opposite seems to be the case. This is understandable once we consider, that the equality in the Aiyappan cult is only "in the eyes of Aiyappan". It is my hypothesis, that *kula deyvam* worship has an important role to play in the somewhat scizophrenic situation with two very different versions of the same god existing simultaneously. *Kula deyvam* worship seems to be the part of Tamil tradition, which is able to create a unity out of the village religious complex and the newly arrived Aiyappan cult. The lineage god was the link between the lineage and the common Aiyanar cult in many cases, perhaps the most important one, and now it seems to reconcile tradition and innovation in Tamil Hinduism as represented respectively by Aiyanar and Aiyappan.

## The Divine King—The Royal God

Two interesting aspects of the Aiyappan pilgrimage are the return of the royal god, Aiyappan, which is accompanied by the temporary resuscitation of the kingdom of Pandalam, on the one hand, and on the other, the evolving alliance between the descendants of the royal family of Pandalam and the Sathagoparamanuja group. The latter comes about because the Pandalam family is interested in retaining its mythical, hereditary rights as keepers of Aiyappan's jewels, and this is then just another example of the numerous battles in India between the traditional keepers of the god's possessions, lands and jewels, and the secular powers, the modern government, which

attempts to usurp these rights, as it has succeeded in many
cases in doing. In this particular instance of the ongoing
struggle between sacred and profane powerholders the Sathago-
paramanuju group enters as allies of the royal Pandalam lineage.
Together the two allies recreate symbolically—in the magnificent annual spectacle at Sabari—the political conditions as they
supposedly were during Aiyappan's avatar as prince of
Pandalam.

Politics and religion meet and merge to a certain extent in
the Aiyappan myth and in the pilgrimage. This expresses in
yet another way how the egalitarian mood of the Aiyappan
*bhakti* cult in the end will have to subject itself to the predominant hierarchic tendency in Hindu society. The Aiyappan
cult and the role played by the Pandalam raja is a good
demonstration of this, because even when the traditional Hindu
kingdoms have been abolished long ago and replaced by
secular political powers, the role of the king in this particular
cult is not only rejuvenated, its importance is growing. The
descendants of the royal lineage of Pandalam still claim the
right to keep Aiyappan's jewels in their ancestral palace in
Padalam. Sabari is located in the area which was formerly
Pandalam, so the royal family is so to speak the hosts for all
the pilgrims entering the area. The raja of Pandalam must be
present at the temple on this occasion to sanction the proceedings. So whereas the Aiyanar and Aiyappan cults formerly
served as legitimation for power, as writers like Fred Clothey
assume, we now have a curious reversal of this situation, in
which the phantom of an ancient is temporarily raised from the
dead in order to legitimize a religion.

## NOTES

Adiceam, Marguerite E. 1967, *Contribution a L'etude de Aiyanar Sasta.*
    Pondicherry.
Biardeau, Madeleine, 1971-72, *Brahmanes et potiers.* EPHE, Ve Section
    Sciences Reilgieuses, Annuaires. Tome lxxlx.
Chidambaram, V.N., 1977, *Aiyappan Tattuvankal and Sri Aiyappan
    Kavacam.* Tottira Padalkal. Madras.
Clothey, Fred. 1978, *Theogony and Power in South India : Clues from the
    Aiyappa Cult.* In : Bardwell L. Smith (Ed.) : *Religion and the Legiti-
    mation of Power in South Asia.* Leiden.

Clothey, Fred, 1982, *Sasta-Aiyanar-Aiyappan* : The God as Prism of
　Social History. In : Clothey (Ed.) : *Images of Man, Religion and
　Historical Process in South Asia.*
Diehl, C.G., 1976, *Who was Aiyappan* ? Actes du XXIXe Congress Inter-
　national des Orientalistes. Section organisee par Jean Filliozat.
　Vol. II. Paris.
Dumont, Louis 1970, *A Structural Definition of a Folk Deity of Tamil
　Nad* : Aiyanar the Lord. In : Dumont (Ed.) : *Religion, Politics and
　History in India.* Paris.
Inglis, Stephen, 1980, *A Village Art of South India. The Work of the
　Velar.* Madurai Kamraj University.
Kjaerholm, Lars, 1980, Vilakkidu Kalyanam. *Studia Orientalia.* Vol. 50.
　Helsinki.
*Kjaerholm, Lars,* 1982, Myth, Pilgrimage and Fascination in the Aiyappa
　Cult. *South Asia Research,* Vol. 2, No. 2, London.
Kalatu Aiyar, K.S., 1978, *Sri Dharma Sasta.* Madras.
Rao, T.A. Gopinatha, 1916, *Elements of Hindu Iconography,* 2.2.
　Madras.
Reiniche, Marie-Louise, 1979, *Les Dieux et les hommes. Etude des cultes
　d'un village du Tirunelveli Inde du Sud.* Paris.
Sarkar, H., 1978, Temples of Kerala, New Delhi.
Sathagoparamanuja Aiyappa Bhakta Sabha, 1982, *Sri Sathagoparamanuja
　Svamikalin ninaivalaya mandapa Ninaivu Malar.* Madurai.
Srinivas, M.N., 1952, *Religion and Society Among the Coorgs of South
　India.* Oxford.
Thapar, D.R., 1961, *Icons in Bronze.* Bombay.
Vaidyanathan, K.R., 1978, *Pilgrimage to Sabari,* Bombay.
*Viswa Hindu Parishad Calendar* 1984, Kottayam.

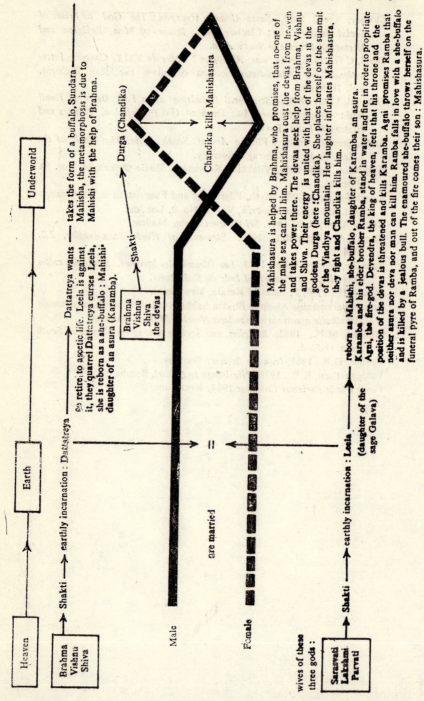

Heaven　Earth　Underworld

Brahma Vishnu Shiva → Shakti → earthly incarnation : Dattatreya → Dattatreya wants → takes the form of a buffalo, Sundara Mahisha, the metamorphosis is due to Mahishi with the help of Brahma.

to retire to ascetic life. Leela is against it, they quarrel Dattatreya curses Leela, she is reborn as a she-buffalo : Mahishi daughter of an asura (Karamba).

wives of these three gods :

Saraswati Lakshmi Parvati → Shakti → earthly incarnation : Leela (daughter of the sage Galava).

Male　Female　are married

Brahma Vishnu Shiva the devas → Shakti → Durga (Chandika)

Chandika kills Mahishasura

Mahishasura is helped by Brahma, who promises, that no-one of the male sex can kill him. Mahishasura oust the devas from heaven and takes power there. The devas seek help from Brahma, Vishnu and Shiva. Their energy is united with that of the devas in the goddess Durga (here : Chandika). She places herself on the summit of the Vindhya mountain. Her laughter infuriates Mahishasura, they fight and Chandika kills him.

reborn as Mahishi, she-buffalo, daughter of Karamba, an asura. Karamba and his elder brother Ramba, stand in water and fire in order to propitiate Agni, the fire-god. Devendra, the king of heaven, feels that his throne and the position of the devas is threatened and kills Karamba. Agni promises Ramba that neither asura nor deva nor man can kill him. Ramba falls in love with a she-buffalo and is killed by a jealous bull. The enamoured she-buffalo throws herself on the funeral pyre of Ramba, and out of the fire comes their son : Mahishasura.

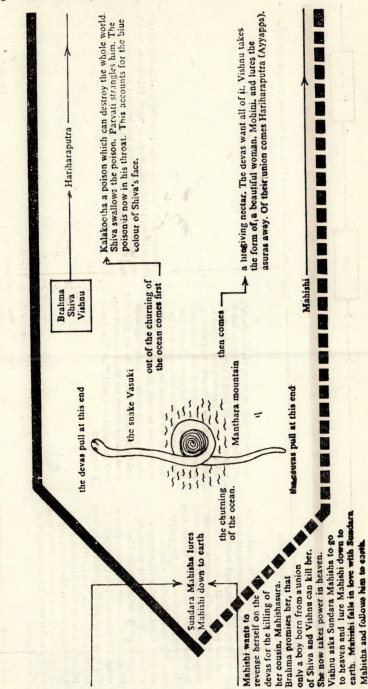

Underworld

Hariharaputra

Brahma
Shiva
Vishnu

Kalakoota a poison which can destroy the whole world. Shiva swallows the poison. Parvati strangles him. The poison is now in his throat. This accounts for the blue colour of Shiva's face.

the devas pull at this end

out of the churning of the ocean comes first

then comes

a lifegiving nectar. The devas want all of it. Vishnu takes the form of a beautiful woman. Mohini and lures the asuras away. Of their union comes Hariharaputra (Ayyappa).

the snake Vasuki

Manthara mountain

the churning of the ocean.

the asuras pull at this end

Mahishi

Sundara Mahisha lures Mahishi down to earth

Mahishi wants to revenge herself on the devas for the killing of her cousin, Mahishasura. Brahma promises her, that only a boy born from a union of Shiva and Vishnu can kill her. She now takes power in heaven. Vishnu asks Sundara Mahisha to go to heaven and lure Mahishi down to earth. Mahishi falls in love with Sundara Mahisha and follows him to earth.

Heaven

Earth

Manikanta leaves his human form and becomes the god Ayyappa

Manikanta, the divine boy.

Hariharaputra is left on the banks of the river Pampa. King Rajasekharan finds him, the childless king and queen adopt him and name him Manikanta. Later the queen has a son of her own. A courtier persuades the queen that Manikanta must be killed, so her own son can become king. The queen pretends to be ill, her doctor says, that only milk from a leopard can cure her. It is just before Manikanta's coronation, but he offers to go into the jungle to get the leopard milk. The 12-year old Manikanta departs carrying a coconut [represents Shiva (Trinetra)]. The devas now ask Manikanta to do, what fate has destined him to do and kill Mahishi. Near the river Alasa there is a fight between the two. Manikanta grips Mahishi's horns and kills her. While he is dancing on her body, Leela comes out of Mahishi's body.

Leela now wants to marry Manikanta, but he refuses because he is a celibate. She is allowed to sit on his left side as his shakti under the name Panchambika. Riding a tiger Manikanta returns to his foster-parents with the leopard milk. Manikanta informs them that his earthly avatar has ended, and he settles with them how he should be worshipped, and where his main temple must be built. He shoots an arrow into the air and where it lands, they must build a temple for him. To the left of it they must build a temple for Malikapurathamma (=Panchambika=Leela). Then Manikanta disappeared.

Manikanta kills Mahishi, who is thereby transformed into the human being, Leela. Leela wants to marry Manikanta, he refuses and becomes the god Ayyappa. She becomes his shakti, Malikapurathamma.

(human)
Leela

(divine)
Malikapurathamma

# 4

# Hindu Pilgrimage in America

Surinder M. Bhardwaj

Hindu Pilgrimage in America might seem a contradiction in terms, because most immigrants to the United States (and Canada) came in search of the legendary El Dorado, not for spiritual fulfilment. Some persecuted European religious communities to be sure found safe haven in America, and some, such as the Amish (Hostetler 1980 : 122-125), still continue to maintain their old lifestyle, even flourish in defiance of the high technology American culture. But these are exceptions to the rule. For most in India, America is the land of economic opportunity, professional advancement, and limitless freedom. Whereas most Hindus in India might perceive their expatriates as having adopted the Western culture to the fullest, Hindus in America have developed a heightened sense of religiosity. Hindus who return to India after many years, are frequently shocked to find that they, the American Hindus, are the ones trying hard to teach their children the Hindu epics, the Hindu philosophy, and high tech yoga. A heightened sense of religiosity among the expatriate communities, in general, has been observed (Abramson 1980 : 869-75). The developing practice of Pilgrimage among Hindu immigrants in America is only one of the religious phenomena which expresses such a renewed consciousness of Hindu spiritual heritage.

In order to appreciate the emerging nature of Hindu pilgrimage in America, it is necessary to realize the importance of religion in giving the immigrant communities a sense of security in the new adopted homeland. Most Hindu homes, whether in India or America, maintain a family altar where the images of the favourite deities, saints and even deceased elders are kept for daily religious worship (Bhardwaj and Rao, 1983). Frequently, calendars with pictures of a deity are kept in the home to remind of the dates of important religious events.

The family altar in the Hindu home of America, in fact, gives a sense of place in an otherwise alien world. It provides a sense of spatial and temporal anchor to ones own faith in ones own old homeland. Used for quiet meditation, occasional supplication, individual worship and even a focus of interfamily religious gatherings, the family altar is a source of security for the family, and manifestation of continuity of Hindu way of life.

Hindu religious landscape, which was confined to the outwardly invisible family altars, began to change as the number of Hindus rapidly increased due to sweeping changes in the U.S. immigration policy of 1965. It took about a decade for the first architecturally and ritually authentic Hindu temples to emerge, but since then, virtually every major concentration of Hindus in America has started, or already finished construction of a temple. News of such events are reported in the ethnic newspapers such as *India Abroad, India Tribune, India West, Lotus*, and others. *India Abroad* regularly publishes "Date Line" column as a community service, wherein religious organizations, especially temples give out information about the upcoming religious events. Consecration of Hindu temples in America, some still housed in adaptively reused buildings, halls, and even former churches, compellingly illustrate Eliade's idea that religious man cannot live except in an atmosphere impregnated with the sacred (Eliade, 1959 : 28).

### The Major Hindu Temples of America

Although Hindu temples are now found in virtually all significant clusters of Hindu population in America some have become prominent attractions for Hindus from more than just the surrounding communities. The bi-monthly *Hinduism Today* (January 1986 : 8) published a list of forty-six temples in the United States and Canada. Some of the temples have large and growing assets. For example, the Sri Venkateswara Swami

(Balaji) Temple of Greater Chicago, which was established as a non-profit organization only in 1983, has assets of well over two million dollars (S.V. Nivedika 1986 : 20). Similarly, The Hindu Temple of Greater Chicago, incorporated much earlier (1977), but inaugurated only on the 4th of July 1986, had total "receivables" of almost one million dollars in 1985 (HTGC 1986). The Sri Venkateswara Temple (Pittsburgh), inaugurated a decade earlier than the above two temples, posted its assets on December 31, 1986 at over $ 2.8 million (*Saptagiri Vani*, 1987 : 10). Other major temples of this type include the Ganesa Temple in Flushing (New York), the recently inaugurated Siva-Vishnu Temple at Livermore in Northern California, the Lord Venkateswara (Balaji) Temple in Malibu, Los Angeles, Paschima Kasi Sri Viswanatha Temple (Flint, Michigan), and the Minakshi Temple at Pearland near Houston Texas. Hindus in Canada are similarly in the process of building major (and local) temples in Toronto, Montreal, Edmonton, and Vancouver. Bengali Hindus of Toronto, for example, are in the process of building a Kali temple (*Toronto Star*, 1986 : L 12).

In addition to the major nonsectarian iconic temples where a variety of deities are installed (although one is normally considered a presiding deity), there is a growing number of sectarian temples and worship centres. The most influential of such places of worship are the almost exclusively Gujarati temples of Swaminarayan sect in Flushing (New York), Los Angeles, and Chicago. The preponderantly Punjabi congregation centres of the Nirankari Mission are located in several cities with substantial Punjabi speaking population such as Chicago (headquarters), Toronto, and New York. Although these organizations purport to spread a universal message, the following of each is primarily from language bound regional community.

International Society for Krishna Consciousness (ISKCON) has centres of worship in many American cities from Boston to Berkeley and from the Great Lakes to the Gulf Coast. Originally composed of American (predominantly white) followers of A.C. Bhaktivedanta Swami Prabhupada, the movement has gained Asian Indian devotees although the management remains in the hands of American leaders. Ridden by internal organizational and legal problems in the last few years (*Record*

*Courier*, August 23, 19 7 : A5), after the death of its founder, the image of this movement has been somewhat tarnished, but Asian Hindus seem to take these problems in stride. The movement has already built perhaps the most exquisite memorial to its founder Prabhupada, and has plans of building the Temple of Understanding—"The largest temple of its kind constructed in the last 500 years". Considering the large marble temple this movement has already built at Vrindaban in India, the Temple of Understanding at New Vrindaban (West Virginia) cannot be discounted if the movement does not die a legal death. The most interesting aspect of the movement currently is that "White Hindus" have been at least partly successful in forging links with the "Brown Hindus". This linkage is fortuitous because otherwise the movement might remain an American phenomenon, and could fade away as did the Transcendental Movement of Maharishi Mahesh Yogi. The Asian Indians admire, even envy the devotion to Krishna of the Hare Krishna sectarians but have not allowed their own children to follow the lifestyle of the White American Hindu devotees. New Vrindaban has become a place of great tourist attraction in the State of West Virginia for Americans, but a true place of pilgrimage for the devotees of Prabhupada and for immigrant Hindus from different parts of the world.

From among the many temples in America, a few have the potential to become great pilgrimage places at the national, even international level. Others will probably remain popular, but of relatively local or regional importance. It can be argued that places with some identifiable characteristics might develop into pilgrimage sites of great importance for the Hindus. We shall later identify some of these characteristics, and suggest that some places indeed already possess these attributes. The Sri Venkateswara Temple at Pittsburgh is the outstanding example.

The flurry of temple building activity in America is a visible expression of overt and heightened religiosity. The Hindus are in a hurry to make their adopted homeland a "sacred" place to be in.

## Emerging Hindu Pilgrimage Places

*The Sri Venkateswara Temple : an Established Pilgrimage Centre in America.*

The Sri Venkateswara Temple (henceforth referred to as the S.V. Temple), situated in a suburb of Pittsburgh (Penn Hills, Pennsylvania) has already become the most renowned Hindu pilgrimage site in North America. Consecrated in 1976, the Bicentennial year of American Independence, the temple attracts pilgrims from many areas of the United States and Canada. According to our survey of pilgrim origins, carried out in 1981-82, about a quarter of all the responding pilgrims from the United States (236), originated from within the State of Pennsylvania. A contiguous block of States, composed of Ohio, New York, New Jersey, Maryland (including D.C.), and Michigan, and the State of Illinois accounted for an additional 59.5 per cent of the American sample of responding pilgrims. Others came from farther off states, and those with a minuscule population of Hindus. An earlier map of pilgrim origins (Bhardwaj, 1985 : 244) however shows that even in the very first few years of this temple's inception pilgrims from virtually all over the United States had started to converge here. Pilgrims also come from various parts of Canada, especially Metropolitan Toronto., and other cities of Ontario.

Pilgrims to the S.V. Temple are generated from among the Hindu population clusters of the megalopolis communities which form the largest such concentration, and from the populous metropolitan areas of the Midwest. Note that few pilgrims originate from the Deep South, except from its growth centres such as Atlanta, New Orleans, and the "Research Triangle" communities of North Carolina (Durham, Chapel Hill and Raleigh). Although California has a large number of Hindus, both in the San Francisco Bay area and in Southern California (Mathur *ca.*, 1985), they are too far to effectively generate a large number of pilgrims. The S.V. Temple nevertheless has a vast distribution of donors in North America, and they form its basic pilgrim field.

*Donors of the S.V. Temple*

The *Saptagiri Vani*, the official journal of the S.V. Temple, publishes lists of donors, without mentioning the amount of donation. These lists are as complete as the temple can make them. There are also corporate donors. Some donors wish to remain anonymous. The April-December 1985 donor list contained 5057 donors from the United States and Canada.

Expectedly 4812 of them were from the United States and 245 from Canada (*Saptagiri Vani*, 1986 : 30-64). Hawaii was the only state not represented, but one donor was listed even from Guam. Likewise all Provinces of Canada were represented, although Ontario overshadowed the other provinces, by contributing more than 50 per cent of Canada's pilgrims to the S.V. Temple. Twelve states and the province of Ontario each had over 100 donors to the S.V. Temple. Even the distant California had 195 donors.

The July-December 1986 donor list had a total of 4696 from North America. This number is smaller than the 1985 list, partly because late spring and early summer are not included, and some people donate in person when they visit, but do not remit mail donation. But even then the two lists are in basic agreement regarding the pilgrim field of the S.V. Temple, which is clearly all of North America. The same twelve States and the same Canadian Province each had over one hundred donors.

The exact determinants of the number of donors in each state/province are not known because we do not know the exact number of Hindus in the United States and Canada. However, it is not unreasonable to assume that the number of Hindus might be closely related to the total Asian Indian population (composed of Asian Indians of various religions). With this assumption we might expect the S.V. Temple's donors to bear a reasonable positive relation to the Asian Indian Population, with the expectancy that distant States might suffer from distance decay effect. Hindus, however, are not a homogeneous group, because of sharp regional linguistic differences and the varying popularity of different deities (or manifestations of the same deity) in different regions. Thus, Hindus unfamiliar with the Dravidian temple ritual and perceiving a temple to be culturally different might not visit it, and more importantly not donate to it, even if they live in the proximity of the temple. Thus, donation rate may seem low as related to all the Asian Indian population, but may be quite high when the population of the specific cultural-linguistic group is taken into account with whom the temple is perceived to be associated. In our 1982-83 survey we found that vast majority of the S.V. Temple's pilgrims had Dravidian cultural linguistic roots. The last names of the donors give a general clue to their regional origin, although there is some room for error. Year after year the donor lists show a preponderance of southern Indian names appearing as donors from all over the United States and Canada.

## Other Temples as Probable Future Pilgrimage Centres

The Sri Venkateswara Swami (Balaji) Temple of Greater Chicago (henceforth called Balaji Temple) is also likely to become a major pilgrimage centre for the Hindus. Many of the reasons for the Balaji temple becoming an important place of pilgrimage are the same as with the S.V. Temple. For example, Chicago commands a superior location with respect to the population distribution of the United States Hindus East of the 100th meridian. The same locational attributes that have made Chicago the third largest city in the United States make it potentially a great location for the pilgrims to converge. Additionally, the Balaji Temple has the same deity, Sri Venkateswara, the most popular *vaisnavite* deity of the Dravidian cultural region of India. The management attributes are similarly of high quality. The drive of the Trustee Board and of the Executive committee of this temple is extremely strong. Within one year of the incorporation of this temple as a non-profit organization, the temple already had begun to take shape, and is now well on its way to completion, in competition with the Hindu Temple of Greater Chicago (henceforth called HTGC).

Although no formal survey comparable to the S.V. Temple has been conducted, it may be assumed that the donor distribution is a reasonable clue to the future of this place as a pilgrimage centre. The first major donor list was published by the Balaji Temple in mid-1986. A total of 1416 donors were listed, forty-one of which did not give their city origin. The donor list represents thirty-nine states and the District of Columbia. Surprisingly no names from Canada have been found in the list. Almost half (47.6%) of the donors are from the state of Illinois, followed by New Jersey (6.9%), New York (6.1%), California (3.9%), Michigan and Texas (each 3.6%).

A comparison between the Balaji temple's donation distribution and that of the S.V. Temple brings out the interesting fact that donors from the American state of each temple make a distinctly different percentage to total number of donors; Balaji temple is much more dependent upon in-state donors than is the S.V. Temple indicating the latter's more widespread appeal. However, this situation may change due to the greater geographic centrality of Chicago.

The Hindu Temple Society of Southern California is in the process of completing its Lord Venkateswara Temple (LV Temple). The list of donors to the L.V. Temple shows that 70 per cent of the 693 donors are from Los Angeles SMSA. Donors from the State of California alone make up 82 per cent of all contributors to this temple. But at the same time, twenty-six other States and the Province of British Columbia were also represented even though the location of this temple is far from central. Although the regional diversity of pilgrims from America at this temple may never match that of the S.V. or the Balaji Temple of Chicago, it will certainly increase because of the popularity of Southern California as a tourist area.

The S.V., the Balaji, and the L.V. Temple have a major common bond, and that is with the Hindu Temple Society of North America, and through it to the Tirupati temple in Andhra Pradesh in India (Alagappan, 1978 : 2'-29). All these temples have received encouragement and support from the Tirupati Temple, the wealthiest temple of India. These temples have been able to get trained *pujaris* (ritualist priests) temple architects, *shilpis* (artisans), and management advice from the Tirupati Temple. Stone images in these temples were made in India by the hereditary sculptors of temple images. In some instances the hereditary silversmiths and goldsmiths who make the decorative *kavachas* (precious metal ornaments) for the deities have been brought in the US to prepare these adorn-ments at the temple site in the traditional Indian manner. The S.V. Temple trustees even set up a small smithy shop for these artisans replicating the Indian style, complete with a wood charcoal using furnace to melt and forge silver.

The Sri Meenakshi Temple (Pearland) near Houston,

inaugurated in 1982 is one of the most interesting temples of the United States because a goddess is the presiding deity although she is flanked by Siva on her right and Sri Venkateswara on her left. Symbolically, this temple is located in the South of the United States, just as in the Indian homeland the Meenakshi Temple is located south of the Tirupati temple.

It is significant to note that major Hindu temples are now located in the cardinal directions, Ganesa and S.V. Temple in the East (New York, and Pittsburgh respectively), Paschima Kasi Sri Viswanath Temple in the North (Flint, Michigan), Lord Venkateswara Temple, and Shiva-Vishnu Hindu Temple in the West (California), and the Meenakshi Temple in the South (Pearland, Texas). The centre of the country is occupied by the two big temples in Chicago (Balaji and HTGC). Thus, from the Hindu perspective the land of their adoption has been sanctified and made fit for permanent residence. These major temples in the cardinal directions will one day be looked upon as the American *char dhams* of Hindu pilgrimage system that is currently evolving. Others will become part of the pilgrim circuit as the population of Hindus in the United States grows and ages, and finds more time to visit sacred spots, and as more elderly relatives of the permanently resident Hindus immigrate.

Temples that lack organizational affiliations in India, and are primarily the result of local efforts are a class by themselves. They are not really centres of pilgrimage, but rather places of worship and centres of Hindu festivals, and community activities. They do not have a local peculiarity, which makes them stand out. They are not sectarian, in the sense that people of that sect will make a special effort to visit these temples. Nevertheless they have needed a population threshold to emerge, and thus their draw area depends upon the peculiarity of the Hindu population distribution in a given area whose population has helped to build the temple. An example of such a temple is the Sri Lakshmi Narayan Temple of the Hindu Temple Society of North Eastern Ohio. The temple is conceived to be part of the local rather than the national scene. It does not significantly compete with the already established temples such as the S.V. Temple, but rather complements it by being a proximate religious centre. Most of its donors are from the neighbouring communities of Northeastern Ohio (personal information).

Hindu Temple of the Hindu Community Organization Inc., Dayton, Ohio, is a somewhat higher level centre. Although over 80 per cent of the donors are from Ohio (43 per cent from Dayton alone), twenty-three over states and even two provinces of Canada are represented. There is no "competition", as yet, from any other temple in the neighbouring states to the South because of relatively small Indian population in them. This temple is likely to become a regional level centre for the lower Midwest.

## Attributes of Emergent Hindu Pilgrimage Centres in America

The temples that may ultimately become major holy places of the evolving Hindu pilgrimage circulation system, are likely to have some or all of the following attributes :

1.  A specific deity whose temple in India is already a major pilgrimage centre. The most prominent example is Sri Venkateswara, whose temple at Tirupati is the most renowned place of pilgrimage for most of Southern India, and is gaining increasing popularity in the Western and even Northern India (Naidu : 1985). A deity such as generic Vishnu, or Shiva is less likely to attract adherents from far off places. A specific manifestation of Vishnu (e.g. Sri Venkateswara) whose symbolic regional identification is already well established in India, has a much better chance of attracting adherents from distant places in the adopted homeland of immigrant devotees. This is so; because the immigrants from any given of India are widely dispersed in the United States. Since manifestations of Vishnu have both a temporal and spatial specificity, legends about their actions have a regional basis. This regional strength, rooted in linguistic attachment, ensures regional following, and serves even as a regional sacred emblem. Similarly, Krishna *avatara* (incarnation), has a Hindi belt specificity, and although Krishna is worshipped in most parts of India, it is in Northern India that his popularity is maximum. Thus Krishna as a specific deity

is more likely to be generative of a new pilgrimage place, than his generic form as Vishnu. This explains the popularity of New Vrindaban among the Hindus of North America. Hindus of Northern Indian origin also identify themselves easily with Krishna because he had a temporal and spatial manifestation in human form, subject to earthly existence and corporeal attributes.

It is interesting to note that many people of Southern Indian origin visit the New Vrindaban as tourists, whereas Hindus from Northern India origin consider it a pilgrimage centre. When a deity is considered as a regional symbol, the fund raisers find it easier to raise money for the building of temples by appealing to a particular regional or linguistic group. Attachment to regional religious symbolism has a distinct potential for the emergence of pilgrimage sites, because appeal can be made to the devotees irrespective of where in America they live. Since the nature of immigration of Indians has ensured a nationwide distribution of people irrespective of their Indian regional origins, information about a deity symbolic of a region can spread among Hindu immigrants of that region rapidly. This process ensures widespread diffusion of the regionally symbolic deities of India. Temples with regionally symbolic deities are therefore more likely to emerge as pilgrimage places; the donors forming a nationwide distribution will sooner or later wish to visit the place.

2. A deity who is already famous for granting of wishes, at whose temples the concept of wish fulfilment, and healing, are already well developed. Temples of auto-nomous goddesses such as Kali, Meenakshi, and Durga, have also the potential to become pilgrimage places because of the special wish granting reputation of these goddesses. Non-autonomous female deities on the contrary (Lakshmi, Saraswati) are less likely to form the nuclei for potentially important pilgrimage sites. Autonomous deities alone, known for grace and wish fulfilment, are likely to generate significant pilgrimage sites.

Even in the affluent society of America, problems of

material well-being abound. More important, however, are the problems of adjustment to new culture and of raising children in a different culture. Such problems often produce stress but most Indians do not seek psychological counsel for stress related problems. Visitation to temples serves as a stress reducing, yet culturally acceptable, behaviour.

3. Favourable geographic location, for example, proximity to inter-state highways even though the actual site might be hilly. American Hindus, and their families may not wish to go too far away into the woods in search of the spiritual. Since spiritual and aspiritual journeys may be combined together, as they often are, pilgrimage places with a more convenient location are likely to supersede those that are excessively isolated in less populated states, unless the place has truly unique attributes, e.g. Prabhupada's Palace of Gold in West Virginia. Relatively convenient detours from the major circulation routes across the country are conducive to the development of pilgrimage sites. Places such as the Raja-rajeshwari Pitham (Pocono Mountains), and New Goloka (Hillsborough, North Carolina) on the Appalachian Piedmont in the vicinity of the Research Triangle, are in this category.

4. Topography symbolically replicating the Indian scene of the favourite pilgrimage site. Local site characteristics, especially topographic attributes of a holy place when found in a new holy place can act as a powerful impulse in evoking the sanctity of the "original" place. Recently while I was participating in the Sahastra Shiva-Linga Abhiseka at the Hindu-Jain Temple at Pittsburgh, one of the speakers on this occasion likened the confluence of Allegheny and Monongahela to form the Ohio River to the famous *tribeni* confluence of Ganga, Yamuna and the (mythical) Saraswati. Thus Pittsburgh was instantly made the holy Prayagraj of America; a remarkable transformation of the Steel City to a sacred centre. The deity Tirupati in India is also called the lord of "seven hills" because of the surrounding hills. Likewise, the S.V. Temple at Pittsburgh

surrounded by the hills of Pennsylvania evokes the
feeling of sanctity of the original temple in India. It is
not a mere coincidence that the News Letter of the
S.V. Temple is called *Saptagiri Vani* (The voice from
the seven hills). One of the songs in praise of the deity
Sri Venkateswara refers to him as the Lord whose
abode is Penn Hills. In an other instance, when the
Vivekananda Vedanta Society wanted to establish a
monastery and retreat for their Midwest mission at
Chicago, a site called "Ganges" was selected close to
Lake Michigan. According to the Golden Jubilee
Souvenir volume of the Vivekananda Vedanta Society
(Bhashyananda, 1981 : 15) the site Ganges was selected
partly because the word Ganges is synonymous with the
Society's faith and partly because a focal point of the
Society is in Chicago. Such attempts to see in either
topography or toponymy a reflection of the sacred in
India is consciously to make the newly consecrated place
an actualization of the original in India. The priest
(Mr. Ravi Chandra) of the Shiva Vishnu temple (Livermore CA, April 6, 1986) spoke to me of Springtown
localities of the temple as "Vasant Puri", and the state
of California to rhyme with Kapilaranya (the forest
home of sage Kapila). By the use of familiar evocative
names for the adopted alien landscape features the
land itself became immediately familiar, understandable,
and even holy. Uncertainty and the quality of alienness
immediately gave way to a sense of emotional bond
with the place. In short the unfamiliar became intimate,
and comprehensible. Tuan and others have examined
such ideas in detail (Tuan, 1974, 1977; Eyles, 1985).

5. Uniqueness about the place, that has some symbolic
value. Tanaka (1981) has admirably articulated the
spatial-symbolic dimension of pilgrimage. All individual
places are unique, but a striking uniqueness with a
clear symbolic value can enhance experiential feelings
about a pilgrimage place. The Meenakshi temple
(Pearland, Texas) is unique in that the presiding deity
there is a female. This could be a powerful symbol of
significance of the female in Hinduism for the second

generation Hindus both male and female. Similarly, the Shiva-Vishnu temple in Livermore, California is unique in bringing together two culturally different architectural symbols (Northern and Southern Indian) at one place. One wing of the sacred complex, beginning to be referred to as the Hari-Hara Kshetra, is composed of the temples and deities representing the Northern tradition, the other wing is architecturally Southern. Even the colours of the deities are reflective of the two different traditions. This temple is an emblem of two very different traditions of Indian Hinduism, willing and able to seek cultural accommodation, even if it has happened in a "foreign" land. Prabhupada's Palace of Gold in West Virginia is a unique example of a memorial to an Indian guru built by his incredibly hardworking and devoted American disciples. This sacred centre proclaims the beauty of love. The New Vrindaban community has become West Virginia's most popular *tourist attraction*, not so much for the Hindus but rather for the general American public, although its popularity is increasing among the Hindus as well.

6. Organizational ability. Temples that aspire to become well known, and thus become pilgrimage sites are extremely well managed. The components of this management include (but are not limited to) concept of the temple and its scope, fund raising, building, establishment of donor network, linking the temple with experienced and philanthropic organizations in India, and leadership in the community affairs. Some of the best organizational ability has been seen in the temples associated with the Hindu Temple Society of North America. Other organizational linkages include the Tirupati temple in India, Parmarth Niketan of Hardwar, the Birla Trust, the support from the State governments in India (especially Andhra), Endowments Department, and the Sankaracharya *Maths* (centres).

7. Authenticity. The potential pilgrimage place has to be authentic in its various dimensions. The temple architecture must be authentic to generate the feeling of at-homeness. It is sufficient to have a consecration cere-

mony. It must be followed by routine authentic ritual by *pujaris* who are traditional priests. The images must be made by the *shilpis*, they must be duly consecrated. installed and worshipped. Whereas modifications to suit the place are necessary, the temple must be an authentic Hindu place. The pilgrims cannot feel a sense of belonging unless the whole landscape, soundscape and even aroma evokes sacredness. The Siva-Linga at the Hindu-Jain Temple (Pittsburgh) was made authentic by bathing it with the holy water brought from numerous holy sources in different parts of India. Priests from the S.V. Temple were employed to perform absolutely authentic Shiva *puja*.

## Major Pilgrim Routes

The development of major temples in America has begun to generate certain popular pilgrimage routes and circuits. One of the most popular ones is from the Vighaneshwara (Ganesa) Temple of Flushing (New York) to the S.V. Temple, and then to New Vrindaban in West Virginia. A second major pilgrim route is from Montreal or Toronto to the S.V. Temple and from there to New Vrindaban. Both these routes may include sight seeing at Niagara Falls. Many pilgrims, most by automobiles and some by chartered buses, who visit the S.V. Temple, also visit the Hindu-Jain Temple, likewise those who visit the Hindu-Jain Temple try to visit the S.V. Temple. The pilgrims of the Dravidian language region of India primarily visit the S.V. Temple for very specific type of worship, and the fulfilment of vows and promises but also visit the Hindu-Jain Temple as a matter of courtesy and curiosity. Hindus of Northern Indian origin primarily visit the Hindu-Jain temple followed by a visit to the S.V. Temple.

It will not be long before a major new pilgrim circuit develops. That should be most likely from Toronto (or Montreal) to the Psychimakashi Temple at Flint, Balaji and HTGC at Chicago, New Vrindaban, S.V. Temple at Pittsburgh, and return via Niagara Falls. A variant of this circuit could be from New York to Pittsburgh, New Vrindaban, Paschimakashi, Ganges, Balaji and HTGC. Some chartered bus tours from New York have been operational since early 1980's.

Perhaps, in the not too distant a future will develop the *char dham* type yatra popular in India. The number of pilgrims in that type of circuit may never be very large, but it may become a respectable undertaking by the affluent or those that have the time. These latter type of people would include the elder relatives of the present residents, but also an increasing number of first generation retires toward the mid 1990s.

**Conclusion**

Hindu pilgrimage in America is a very recent phenomenon, based largely upon the temples. Although the visiting gurus and swamis attract "pilgrims", the real centres of pilgrimage in America at present are the temples developed primarily under the Southern Indian Hindu cultural motif. The leadership shown by the Southern Indian Hindus has its basis in the fact that temples have always played a crucial role in the life of people there (Appadurai, 1981) unlike the non-Dravidian people of India. We have discussed that aspect elsewhere (Bhardwaj and Rao, 1983). Other strong regional religious traditions will, undoubtedly, make their mark, for example the Kali tradition of Bengal, Jagganath of Orissa, Swaminarayan of Gujarat, and Ayappan of Kerala.

The development of temple based pilgrimages is tantamount to creating or recreating a religious landscape, a transference of holiness in which the Hindus can increasingly feel a sense of spiritual fulfilment as also temporal and spatial security. For the religious Hindus the various sacred nodes and the paths leading to them are beginning to create a sacred "circulation manifold" (a term I first heard used by Fred Lukermann) flowing through which they can experience no ill effects of the non-sacred realm to which they had originally migrated for entirely non-spiritual goals. Hindus have tried to reactualize their sacred landscape which they left behind. This sacred land-scape however is being continually nourished by strong spiritual links with Indian sacred centres and religious and philanthropic organizations. Emphasis on authenticity, and the ability to put this belief into practice has meant that Hindu holy places of America will be not only of value to the immigrants but a source of vitality to the original sacred hearth in India as well. The institution of pilgrimage in Hinduism is so deep rooted

(Jha, 1985 : 11-16; Morab, 1985 : 27-33) that it would be surprise if it did not transfer to America.

## Acknowledgement

I wish to thank the many dedicated individuals, members of the temple trustee boards, the *shilpis*, swamis, and the priests who were kind enough to talk to me, and in some cases even provided free lodging on my visits to the various Hindu temple sites in America.

## NOTES

Abramson, Harold J. 1980, Religion, In *Harvard Encyclopedia of American Ethnic Groups*, ed., Stephen Thernstrom, p. 869-875. Cambridge (Massachusettes) : Harvard University Press.

Alagappan, Alagappa, 1978, Links With Andhra Pradesh. In (Commemorative Souvenir), *The Hindu Temple Society of North America*, pp. 27-29.

Appadurai, Arjun, 1981, *Worship and Conflict Under Colonial Rule : A South Indian Case Study*. Cambridge : Cambridge University Press.

Bhardwaj, Surinder M. and Rao, Madhusudan N. 1983, Religious Reknitting of Ethnic Hindus in the 'New World' A paper presented at the 79th annual meeting of the Association of American Geographers, Denver, Colorado (April 24-27, 1983).

Bhardwaj, Surinder M. 1985, Religion and Circulation : Hindu Pilgrimage. In *Circulation in Third World Countries*, eds., R. Mansell Prothero and Murry Chapman, pp. 241-261. London : Routledge and Kegan Paul.

Eliade, Mircea, 1959, *The Sacred and the Profane : The Nature of Religion*, New York : Harper and Row.

Eyles, John, 1985, *Senses of Place*, Warrington (England) : Silverbrook Press.

Fisher, Maxine P., 1980, *The Indians of New York City*, Columbia (Missouri) : South Asia Books.

*Hinduism Today* (Originally bi-monthly, now monthly newspaper). January, 1986; August, 1987; September, 1987.

*The Hindu Temple Commemorative Issue 1985*, The Hindu Community Organization Inc., Dayton, Ohio.

Hostetler, John A., 1980, Amish. In *Harvard Encyclopedia of American Ethnic Groups*, ed., Stephen Thernstrom, pp. 123-125. Cambridge (Massachusetts) : Harvard University Press.

HTGC (see *Ramalaya Samachar*).

*India Abroad* (Weekly Newspaper). Various dates.

Jha, Makhan, 1985, The Origin, Type, Spread, and Nature of Hindu
    Pilgrimage. In *Dimensions of Pilgrimage*, ed., Makhan Jha, pp. 11-16,
    New Delhi : Inter-India Publications.

*Land of Krishna* (New Vrindaban) : New Vrindaban Community Monthly
    Newsletter.

Mathur, Raj, ed., 1985 (*ca.*), Asian Indians in Southern California (map.)
    Diamond Bar (California) : Cultural Map Service.

Morab, S.G. 1985, Concept of Pilgrimage in Folk Tradition : The Case
    of the Chamundesvari Ritual Complex. In Dimensions of Pilgrimage,
    ed., Makhan Jha, pp. 27-33. New Delhi : Inter-India publications.

Naidu, T.S. 1985, Pilgrims and Pilgrimage : A Case Study of Tirumala-
    Tirupati Devasthanam. In *Dimensions of Pilgrimage*, ed., Makhan
    Jha, pp. 17-25, New Delhi : Inter-India Publications.

*Ramalaya Samachar* (Official Newsletter of the Hindu Temple of Greater
    Chicago), 3(1), January-March, 1986.

*Record-Courier* (Newspaper). Sunday, August 23, 1987, "Thomas
    Drescher : Krishna Swami, convicted killer", p. A5.

*Saptagiri Vani* (inside cover *Sapthagiri Vani* : a publication of Sri
    Venkateswara Temple), 11(1), First Quarter, 1986; 12(2) Second
    Quarter, 1987.

*Sathya Vani* (Newsletter of the Hindu Temple Society of North Eastern
    Ohio).

Sopher, David, 1967, *Geography of Religions*, Englewood Cliffs (N.J.) :
    Prentice-Hall.

*Sri Lakshmi Narayan Temple Commemorative Issue* (October 10, 11,
    12, 1986). The Hindu Temple Society of North Eastern Ohio
    Liberty, Ohio.

Sri Minakshi Temple Society of Houston, 1982, *Main Temple Inaugura-
    tion*, June 27, 1982 (commemorative volume).

Sri Venkatesa Nivedika (a publication of Sri Venkateswara Swami,
    Balaji, Temple).

Tanaka, Hiroshi, 1981, Evolution of Pilgrimage as a Spatial Symbolic
    System. *Canadian Geographer*, 25, 240-251.

*The Toronto Star*, "Finally, Hindus have a place to call home", Saturday,
    June 28, 1986, p. L 12.

Tuan, Yi-Fu, 1977, *Space and Place : The Perspective of Experience*,
    Minneapolis : University of Minnesota Press.

# 5

# Panc Kosi Yatra: A Subregional Pilgrimage of Southern Chhattisgarh, India

EDWARD J. JAY

## Introduction

A PILGRIMAGE may be regarded as any visit to a sacred place undertaken as an act of religious devotion. Within this broad definition it is possible to conceptualize a whole range of types of pilgrimage, based on specific religious traditions. In every tradition the journey to the sacred place is always given several interpretations and enacted in a variety of ways. For example, pilgrims may undertake their journey voluntarily or as an obligation, alone or in association with others, may travel far or near, make a vow or fulfil one, go repeatedly or just in once a lifetime. Moreover, in some religions, such as Hinduism, there is a hierarchy into which the value of each type of pilgrimage is arranged, depending on the religious importance of the sacred place. In this chapter I discuss one type of Hindu pilgrimage carried out in southern Chhattīsgarh,[1] a cultural region of central India, and then assess its significance relative to its place in (*1*) the sacred complex of a religious town, and (*2*) Hinduism in general.

In 1967-68 and in the fall of 1970 I studied a peasant village (Devagaon) in the general vicinity of Rājim, a small but important temple town located 25 miles southeast of the city of Raipur, and in 1977-78 undertook field research in the town of

Social Anthropology of Pilgrimage

Rajim itself.[2] (see Fig. 5.1). My primary interest in the latter period was to understand the significance of Rajim temple worship within the wider context of Chhattisgarhi religion, a regional variant of Hinduism already summarized admirably by Babb (1975). It is apparent that there are at least three types of pilgrimage made by local Chhattisgarhi villagers and townspeople. These are "routine" visits to temples on an individual or family basis, attendance at major temple ceremonies and religious fairs, and undertaking a ritually structured journey on foot encompassing the town of Rajim plus five other sacred places within a 12-mile radius of the town. This last type of pilgrimage is known as *pañc kosī yātrā*, and is the major focus of this chapter. The other two types will be the subject of a future publication.[3]

**The Pilgrimage**

Rajim is an ancient town of about 5,000 inhabitants located on the east bank of the Mahānadī (literally "great river"), in Raipur District of Madhya Pradesh (see Fig 5.1). Immediately across from it, on the west bank, is the younger but much larger town of Navāpārā Rājim (locally referred to simply as Navāpārā), with a population of about 15,000. Although the two towns are in the same district, they are in different *tahsils* and have separate municipal administrations. Navapara is essentially a commercial centre with an important grain market, 15 rice mills, dozens of small retail shops and both daily and weekly markets where various local farm products and craft items are bought and sold. Rajim proper is distinguished by its religious significance. It is the site of two ancient temples protected by the Archaeological Survey of India as National Monuments, and one protected as a State Monument. In addition, there are numerous smaller temples and shrines, a Bairāgī Math, an *āśram* which serves as a traditional Sanskrit school for young boys, and two *dharmaśālās* (temple rest houses) for pilgrims. In 1973 a modern concrete bridge was completed, spanning the Mahanadi to connect Rajim and Navapara Rajim. Before that time the river could be crossed only by a risky boat trip during the rainy season, and by foot or vehicle over a makeshift earthen causeway at other times of the year.

The most important temple in Rajim is known as Rājīv

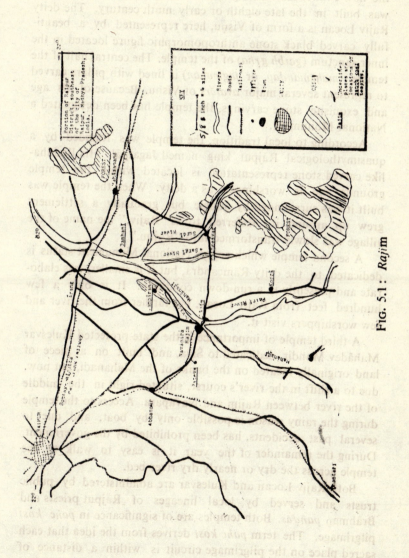

Fig. 5.1 : *Rajim*

Locan Mandīr, literally "temple of the lotus-eyed one" (*rājiv* : lotus; *locan* : eye; *mandīr* : temple). A *śilālekh* or inscription in the now extinct Kutila script inside the temple indicates that it was built in the late eighth or early ninth century. The deity Rajiv Locan is a form of Viṣṇu, here represented by a beautifully carved black stone anthropomorphic figure located in the inner sanctum (*garbh gṛha*) of the temple. The central hall of the temple (*mahāmaṇḍap* or *jagmohan*) is lined with pillars carved to represent several major *avatārs* of Visnu. Because of its age and exquisite stone carvings, the temple has been designated a National Monument.

According to local tradition, the temple was founded by a quasimythological Rājpūt king named Jagatpāl. His Buddha-like carved stone representation is located within the temple grounds and is worshipped as a deity. When the temple was built it was surrounded by jungle but gradually a settlement grew up around it. Referred to as "Rajiv," the name of the village was slowly transformed into "Rajim."

A second temple which enjoys National Monument status is dedicated to the deity Rāmcandra, but it is smaller, less elaborate and presently in a run-down condition. It is only a few hundred feet from Rajiv Locan, but farther from the river and few worshippers visit it.

A third temple of importance is the state-protected Kuleśvar Mahādev Mandir, dedicated to Śiva, and built on a piece of land originally located on the banks of the Mahanadi, but now, due to a shift in the river's course, situated right in the middle of the river between Rajim and Navapara. Access to the temple during the rainy season is possible only by boat, and due to several past accidents, has been prohibited by the government. During the remainder of the year it is easy to walk to the temple across the dry or nearly dry river bed.

Both Rajiv Locan and Kulesvar are administered by public trusts and served by local lineages of Rajput priests and Brāhmaṇ *paṇḍās*. Both temples are of significance in *pañc kosi* pilgrimage. The term *pañc kosi* derives from the idea that each sacred place on the pilgrimage circuit is within a distance of five *kosi* from Rajim. *Kosi* is the Chhattisgarhi form of *kos*, which in standard Hindi is a distance of about two miles.[4] But locally I received estimates of this measure varying from one and a half to three miles. Straight line distances on Fig 5.1 show that all of the sacred places are within twelve miles of Rajim. Estimates also vary as to the exact number of miles walked by the pilgrims on this journey, but most are within the 45 to 55 mile range. Direct distances on Fig. 5.1 total 52 miles, which would give a fairly accurate *minimum* estimate of the number of miles actually traversed. Since the routes are over winding roads and paths, the precise distance probably exceeds this minimum by at least 10-15 miles.

Although the pilgrims do not seem aware of it, the expression *pañc kosi* is also applied to a famous pilgrimage circuit around the sacred city of Vārāṇasī (Eck, 1982 : 41-42, 147, 238, 350-353; Havell, 1905: 186-187; Herbert, 1957; Saraswati, 1975; 11-12; Vidyarathi *et al.*, 1979 : 80-81) :

The names Kāshī, Vārānasī, and Avimukta may sometimes refer to progressively smaller circles of the sacred city. Each zone has its own pilgrimage of circumambulation (*pradakshinā*), that of Kāshī taking five days, and the others taking but a single day . . . . The area to which Kāshī refers includes all that is within the circular route around the city, called the Panchakroshī Road. A *krosha* is a unit of measurement equivalent to about two miles, and the term *pancha krosha*, "five *kroshas*," refers to the radius of the sacred circle of Kashi. Its geographical centre is said to be the Shiva temple of Madhyameshvara, the "Lord of the Centre . . . ." The Panchakroshī Yātrā, the "Pilgrimage of the Five Kroshas," makes the circuit around all of Kashi. The area, called the "Linga of the Five-Kroshas," is honoured by circumambulation, just as one would honour a deity by circumambulating the sanctum of its temple (Eck, 1982 : 350-352).

According to tradition there are 108 sacred places to be visited on the *pañc kosi* pilgrimage around Varanasi (Eck, 1982 : 352; Herbert, 1957 : 35), and five halting places called *chaṭṭis* (Vidyarthi *et al.*, 1979 : 83), where pilgrims stay over night. The area delimited by the pilgrimage is supposed to resemble a conch (Saraswati, 1975 : 11-12; Vidyarthi *et al.*, 1979 : 81). Rajim, too, has its sacred geography; the pilgrimage stations

here are visualized as five petals of a lotus flower. The specific
imagery is different, but the underlying conception of a sacred
centre encompassed by a sacred zone or field is an interesting
and significant parallel. Lotus imagery is characteristic of
Visnu and is prominent in the Rajim area, which was known at
one time as Kamalkṣetra Padmavatī Purī ("town of Visnu in
the place of the lotuses"), and even now sometimes is referred
to in Chhattisgarh as Kamalcetra, or "place of the lotuses").[5]

Two versions of the mythological basis of *pañc kosī yātrā*,
were encountered during the research. The first, which seems to be
more *ad hoc* and fanciful than the other, is that Rām, in his search
for Sita in the jungles of Daṇḍakāraṇya, made five stops in the
vicinity of Rajim. At each place he performed *darśan* at a local
Siva shrine. These five places correspond to the pilgrimage
stations of the *pañc kosī yātrā*. The second version establishing
the particular sanctity of these five stations is that the mythological founder of the Rajiv Locan temple, Mahārāja Jagatpāl,
stopped at the five places in search of the proper site for
construction of the temple. He is said to have completed the
entire circuit within twenty-four hours, a virtually impossible
task for a mere mortal. Divine inspiration finally guided him
to the place of the lotuses at the confluence of the Mahanadi,
Pairī and Sonṛhū rivers. The *pañc kosī yātrā*, therefore, can be
interpreted as a commemoration of one form or another of an
original sacred journey. However, many pilgrims have no idea
why the particular places on this journey originally were established, and simply cite "tradition" as the reason for their
inclusion. The allegation that three rivers converge at Rajim is
also a traditional or mythical statement. In fact, only two
rivers converge at this point, the Mahanadi and Pairi. But
people maintain that the waters of the Sonrhu can be distinguished by their own deep blue colour at the point where the
Mahanadi and Pairi join, immediately to the south of the
Kulesvar temple. The sacredness of rivers and particularly the
confluence (*sangam*) of rivers in Hinduism is well known.[6] The
contention that three rivers join at Rajim is consistent,
therefore, with the overarching Hindu world-view.[7]

*Pañc kosī yātrā* can be undertaken at any time, but the most
auspicious period is between Kārtik Pūrṇimā (full moon of the
month of Kārtik) and Māgh Pūrṇimā, roughly from mid-

November to late February. Magh Purnima is also the occasion of a large *melā*, or religious fair at Rajim, marking the "birthday" of Rajiv Locan, perhaps a metaphorical reference to the founding of the temple and the installation of its idol. Many *pañc kosi* pilgrims try to time the conclusion of their journey with this festival. According to temple priests and *paṇḍās* at Rajim, about 90 per cent of the pilgrims come from within a 50-mile radius of the town, which would constitute the "pilgrim field" in Bhardwaj's (1973 : 116-147) terminology, or the "pilgrim catchment area" in Turner's (1974 : 179). The vast majority of the pilgrims are women. They tend to travel in small groups of twenty to fifty each, and are often from the same village or from two or three adjacent villages. Most of the women are middle-aged or older, though some are young mothers who bring along their children. Each group usually includes one or more male relatives, who serve as guardians and chaperons, since it is not altogether proper for women to be travelling without male accompaniment. A typical example of such a group was one I observed in Rajim on December 29, 1977. It consisted of 47 persons, 5 of whom were men. Thirty-seven pilgrims were from the village of Ṭekaṛā, about 10 miles from Rajim. The others included 4 from the village of Bhainsā, 3 from Garaghāt, 1 from Sahasapur, 1 from Phingeśvar, and 1 from Rajim itself. Five different castes were represented : Rāvat, Sāhū, Goṇḍ Ṭhākur, Paṭel, and Daherīā Kṣatriyā. Ravats or cowherds are relatively high in the regional caste hierarchy. The Sahus are former oilpressers, most of whom now work as landless labourers. They and the Gond Thakurs (former tribals), who commonly work as labourers or servants, usually occupy middle to low ranks in the hierarchy. I am not familiar with the other two castes. Their names suggest "warriors" and "headmen," respectively, but these terms may represent only the assertion, rather than the attainment, of high rank. Interviews with villagers and temple personnel revealed that *pañc kosi* pilgrims are drawn from virtually all castes, including Brahmans, with the exception of untouchables.

Temple priests at Kulesvar, the starting point of the pilgrimage, estimated that about 5,000 people did *pañc kosi yātrā* during the winter of 1977-78, but since so many mingle with the crowds attending major festivals such as Cercera (Pūs Pūrṇimā) or Māgh Purṇimā, it is impossible to confirm this figure. This particular year was considered a "good" year in terms of numbers of visitors to the temples. The previous year had been one of relatively poor crops, so fewer people went on pilgrimage and fewer attended the big Magh Purnima *melā*. In 1978 temple priests and the local police independently estimated the number of persons attending the *mela* at 150,000. This is about one and a half times the number normally expected to attend.

Most of the pilgrim and former pilgrims interviewed mentioned various pragmatic concerns as the principal reasons for undergoing the journey, such as having more children, curing illness or achieving prosperity. Some declared that they felt "purified" by going on pilgrimage, and that it increased religious merit (*puñya*). One informant declared that it "cleansed the mind." However, many women also freely admitted that their main motive was just enjoyment. They like the hymn singing, conversation, sense of fellowship and freedom from everyday chores. One woman who has been a long-term informant, and who has never been on *pañc kosī yātrā*, expressed skepticism about the journeys benefits. She exclaimed that "all the women do is gossip; instead of *puñya* they get *pāp*" (sin).

To achieve optimum benefits from the pilgrimage it must be done on foot (*pad yātrā*). People are contemptuous of those who ride in bullock carts, cars or on bicycles. Although they admit that using vehicles rarely occurs in the case of *pañc kosī*, everyone "has heard" of people doing pilgrimage in this manner elsewhere. The journey begins in Rajim, where pilgrims arrive in the morning or sometimes the previous evening, depending on the distance they have to travel. Bathing in the river is mandatory as a ritually purifying act before entering a temple. This is done in a *sāṛī* by women or in a *dhotī* or undershorts by men, due to the lack of privacy in the river. Brightly-coloured *sāṛīs* are often seen later in the day, spread out to dry in the temple courtyard at Rajiv Locan or on the sand adjacent to Kulesvar.

After bathing, the pilgrims take *darśan* at Rajiv Locan temple. From here they typically proceed to the neighbouring Jagannāth Maṭh and several other temples in the town, includ-

ing those adjacent to Rajiv Locan and in the local *āśram* compound. *Darśan* literally means "viewing" the deity. It is an
essential element of Hindu religious observance everywhere in
India. The sight of the deity, the source of power in the
universe, is auspicious, bringing good fortune to the worshipper. The latter *pranāms* or gestures respectfully by joining his
or her hands, raising them to the forehead, and bowing the
head slightly. An even stronger expression of religious devotion
is total prostration before the deity. Depending on the occasion, and the nature of the particular deity, offerings are also
made in connection with *darśan*. These most frequently consist
of flowers, coconuts, coins or uncooked foodstuffs. Sometimes
pilgrims sing hymns as they enter the temple, or shout religious
slogans such as "Mahādev (Siva), we have come to see you,"
or "Śankar (Siva) Bhagvān *kī jay*" (long live Sankar the Lord) !
Other popular expressions, recited in unison, are : "We came
for shelter O God ! Preserve our modesty ! How can you sit
here alone O God, O God?"

In many temples a priest or *paṇḍā* (temple guide, often a
Brahman) provides the worshippers with *prasād* as they leave.
This is often in the form of three small dippers of water poured
into the open palm of the right hand, supported by the left,
along with a small piece of *tulsī* leaf. The water, which represents the bath water of the deity, is drunk and the leaf eaten.
In larger temples, or on special occasions more elaborate forms
of *prasad* are given, such as cooked rice and *dāl*, or sweets.
These foods represent the left over food of the deity. In accept-
ing *prasād*, the worshipper acknowledges his status as below
that of the deity, and at the same time expresses his connection
with and dependency on the deity. To accept *prasād* is an act
of respect and humility.

After visiting the various temples in the town, the pilgrims
arrive at Kulesvar, which is the official starting point of *pañc
kosī yātra*. Although some pilgrims argue that Rajiv Locan is
the first stop on the pilgrimage circuit, most agree with the
local priests that *pañc kosi* is devoted to Siva, and that Rajiv
Locan and the other Rajim temples are sometimes included
only because pilgrims feel compelled to visit them once present
in the sacred town. On the other hand, viewing Rajiv Locan as
an intrinsic part of the pilgrimage would be consistent with the

myth of its founding by Jagatpal after five earlier stops in the
surrounding villages. Following *darśan* at Kulesvar, the pilgrims prepare a midday meal, often eating on lengths of cloth
spread on the dry river sand adjacent to the temple. Each
pilgrims carries her own cooking utensils, fuel for cooking, a
quantity of rice, *dāl* and cooking oil, and one or two extra
*sāṛis*. In the afternoon the pilgrims may proceed to the next
stop on the circuit or remain overnight, spending their time
singing religious hymns and telling religious stories.

If they stay over, the pilgrims sleep on the sand or in a
nearby *dharmaśālā*, arising early the next morning, at daybreak
or before, then proceeding to the first of five pilgrimage locations outside of Rajim. They travel in a clockwise direction
around the town, beginning with the small village of Pateva,
some six miles west of Rajim. (see Fig. 5.1) The object of this
first stop is a very small Siva Ling temple on the bank of a
tank just outside the village. The deity is known as Patesvar.
*Iswar*, a general word for "god," in this region is applied
exclusively to Siva. When assimilated to a place such as Pateva,
it becomes the suffix *eśvar*, hence Patesvar, literally "Siva of
Pateva." Here the pilgrims bathe in the tank, perform *darśan*,
and again often remain overnight.

The second is Campāraṇ, a village approximately 10 or 12
miles to the north over unpaved bullock cart trails and back
road. Here the same routine is followed in relation to the
local version of Siva known as Campeśvar. Camparan is the
birthplace of the Gujarati saint Sri Vallabhai Mahāprabhu,
often identified with the god Kṛṣṇ. The annual celebration of
his birth draws Gujarati pilgrims throughout the area,
and many from Gujarat itself. *Pañc kosi* pilgrims sometimes
visit the temple built in honour of the saint, but their attention
is focused mainly on the small roofless temple housing the Siv
*liṅg* of Campeśvar. These temples, and one recently built to
house an image of Kṛṣṇ, are in a wooded area which is part of
a forest preserve adjacent to the village. The secluded nature
of the spot makes it one of the most pleasant on the pilgrimage
circuit.

The remaining pilgrimage stops are at Bamhanī, Phingeśvar
and Koprā (*see* Fig. 5.1). Bamhani is of particular interest
because of a *kuṇḍ* (pool or well) fed by an underground spring

which emerges from under the temple to Bamhanesvar. The spring is known as the Seth Ganga because it is believed that it is connected with the sacred Ganga (Ganges) river of northern India via an underground channel. The village barber of Devagaon (the village of research in 1967-68) tells a story about a Navapara merchant who once went on pilgrimage to Bamhani, where he fished an odd-looking stick out of the *kund*. On returning home he showed it to a *sādhu* who immediately recognized the stick and told the merchant to "open" it. When the latter did so, he discovered gold inside it. The *sādhu* claimed that he had deposited that stick in the Ganga years before, and gradually it found its way to Bamhani. From that time on the waterway known as the Seth Ganga (from *seth*, meaning merchant). Water is customarily taken from the Seth Ganga by pilgrims and carried back home where it is sometimes used in the establishment of ceremonial friendships.

Phingesvar is a large village and the residence of a *zamindar* (landlord) family in pre-Independence days. The old palace is in a state of decay, and the widow of the last *zamindar* lives in a small cottage nearby. In addition to the main temple of Phingesvar, which is the primary focus of *panc kosi* pilgrims, there is a temple devoted to several aspects of Krṣṇ, and a striking edifice known as *panc mindir* (five temples). This single structure consists of five adjacent sanctums, each with its own *śikhara* or tower. The sanctums contain images of (*1*) Satnārāyan with Rām and Sītā, (*2*) Lakṣmī-Nārayan, (*3*) Rāmchandra, (*4*) Rādhā-Krṣṇ and (*5*) Jagannāth.

The final place to be visited before returning to Rajim is Koprā to the south. Its rather undistinguished little temple to Kopeśvar is situated at the edge of a tank.

Upon their return to Rajim, the pilgrims terminate their journey with another visit to Kulesvar. Here participants often hire a Brahman *purohit* to perform a Satnārāyan *kī kathā* on their behalf. This is a popular ceremony in Chattisgarh, held on many different sorts of occasions. Some pilgrims have it performed at the onset of the journey instead of, or in addition to the end. I also witnessed one group of pilgrims at Kulesvar who had hired several musicians and a bard to perform for them when their journey was finished. They sat just outside the temple door and listened while the bard recited stories from the

Mahābhārata, interspersed with religious hymns sung and played by the musicians in *bhajan* style. When a group of pilgrims returns to the village, it is customary for their neighbours and relatives to welcome them with *pranāms* and gifts of coconuts and betel nut. If the reception is particularly elaborate, musicians may be hired and a Satnarayan *kī kathā* performed or a recitation of the Ramayana held. One pilgrim in the group mentioned above said that when they return to Tekara they expect to arrange for an elaborate Bhagavat Yagyān, held over a seven-day period. The *purohit* who does the recitation will be paid Rs. 1,200 (about $120) plus gifts of five types of utensils and other items valued at an additional Rs. 800 ($80). The pilgrims themselves and other villagers contribute to help pay the expenses. To a considerable extent all the villagers share in the merit gained by the pilgrims. Seth Ganga water and other *prasād* are brought back to the community for distribution and occasionally to establish ceremonial friendships (Jay, 1973).

## Summary and Conclusions

*Pañc Kosī yātrā* at Rajim is a popular form of religious activity in the southern Chhattisgarh area. The motivations of these pilgrims probably are quite similar to the motivations of those who go on more famous pilgrimages to pan-Indian sacred places, but the close proximity of Rajim and the relatively small expense involved make *pañc kosī yātrā* more accessible to villagers of the area. Considered within the broader context of religious activities of all kinds within this region, the significance of *pañc kosī yātrā* becomes especially apparent. Rajim serves as a focus of regional religious activity. Daily visits to its major temples by towns people and peasants from the surrounding villages, attendance at religious fairs by people from all over the district, and the beginning and termination of the *pañc kosī* pilgrimage circuit are all ways in which Rajim serves a wide geographical area. In addition, sermons (*pravācan*) are frequently arranged at Rajim temples, drawing people from surrounding areas to hear recitations and interpretations of religious scriptures, and group hymn-singing (*bhajan*) periodically occurs at the temples, involving men and women from nearby villages as well as from the town itself. In short, Rajim

is the centre of what Vidyarthi and his students have referred
to as a "sacred complex" (Vidyarthi, 1961, 1974; Vidyarthi *et
al.*, 1979). This sacred centre is surrounded by a field or zone
which appears to represent the limits of the power rādiated by
the centre. The symbolism is consistent with pan-Indian conceptions, in this context perhaps represented best by the sacred
city of Varanasi (Kashi) itself, as described by Eck (1982 :
146-147) :

> The city with its divine inhabitants may be likened to the
> symbolic structure of the *maṇḍala*. In a religious or ritual
> sense, a *maṇḍala* is a sacred circle that represents the entire
> universe, its powers, its interrelations, and its grounding
> centre. . . . The city of Kashi, with all its divine inhabitants,
> in such a *maṇḍala*. The radius of its sacred circle is a
> distance of five *kroshas*, about ten miles, and around its
> borders are a multitude of guardian deities. Within this
> outermost circle are increasingly smaller concentric circles,
> having Shiva as their common centre, especially Shiva as he
> abides in the city's inner sanctum, Vishvanātha Temple.

The circumabulation of pilgrims around the sacred centre
graphically delimits the sacred zone. Whether or not the
various representations of Siva on the route of *pañc kosī* pilgrims around Rajim may be conceptualized as "guardians," it
is hard to say. But the clockwise circumambulatory pettern in
which the periphery is traced, clearly is characteristics of the
common Hindu ritual practice of *pradaksiṇā* or *parikramā*. In
a given temple the worshipper may perform *parikramā* by walking around the inner sanctum (*garbh gṛh*), where the main deity
resides, in a special corridor built for the purpose, some seven
or twenty-one or one-hundred and eight times. This devotional
act is said to increase merit and cancel sin. Similar circumambulation of a sacred centre through a much larger space is also
considered a form of *parikramā*. But in this case various stops
are made at temples or shrines along the way. The route
followed may be quite restricted, such as the temple compound
itself with its four deities in the corners plus other shrines
within; or it may be still wider, encompassing a whole sacred

complex. Vidyarthi *et al.* describe the situation at Varanasi in this way (1979 : 77) :

> The custom of circumambulation, which is popularly refer-red to as *parikramā* in the various sacred scriptures, round certain sacred centres of Hindu pilgrimage, has been consi-dered as the best method of blotting out all sins committed during one's lifetime. In India there are a number of sacred centres ... where the devout Hindus go for *parikramā* and attach great religious importance to these sacred centres. In Kashi large number of *parikramās* of various types are made.

The authors go on to list sixteen types of *parikramās* which may be undertaken in Varanasi. According to their characteris-tics and the participation of pilgrims, *parikramās* may be classi-fied as local, regional, and all-India. The local *parikramās* consist of those undertaken within a small circle by residents of the city itself. Regional *parikramās* are slightly wider in scope and are undertaken by people from districts around Varanasi (1979 : 79). Finally, the widest circle is *pañc kosī*, and this is most popular with pilgrims who come from all over India (1979 : 80-89).

Conceptualized as a particular *genre* of pilgrimage, there-fore, *pañc kosī* pilgrimage around the sacred complex of Rajim may be considered a form of *parikramā* or ritual circumambu-lation. Of course in terms of its strictly local or regional significance, its simplicity of structure and execution, and the relatively small number of pilgrims who undertake it, the Rajim *pañc kosī* is far less important than that at Varanasi. But it is conceptually analogous to the Varanasi phenomenon and quite parallel in structure. Moreover, the persistent contacts of villages with this complex represent a continuous interaction of "great" and "little" traditions in the folk culture of the region. Although religious activities in Rajim temples do not attain the level of orthodoxy encountered in pan-Indian centres, they may actually represent more significant interaction of this type. Many villagers throughout the subcontinent attempt to make pilgrimages to the great pan-Indian religious centres, but rela-tively few are able to attain this goal, and many of those who do make such visits do so only once in a lifetime. A regional temple centre such as Rajim may be visited more frequently by anyone. Everybody in the area has been to many Magh Purnima *melās* during his life, and many people have been on *pañc kosi yātrā* at least once. It is likely that these frequently repeated, almost continuous interactions with a centre of higher, relatively more orthodox practices, have a greater effect on maintaining the traditional religious culture than the once-in-a-lifetime visits to the major pan-Indian centres. Although Hinduism has no official church organization or hierarchy analagous to Roman Catholicism, there is a network of religious places arranged in an implicit hierarchy from the most sacred pan-Indian centres, through regional centres, right down to the simplest village shrine. Rajim seems to occupy a low to intermediate position in this hierarchy, perhaps as a "sub-regional" sacred centre in the scheme devised by Bhardwaj (1973 : 116-162). It is hard to assess how "typical" of such places it is, but I suspect that similar functions are performed by thousands of other small religious towns throughout India.[8]

Bhardwaj (1973 : 173) maintains that "folk" elements are prominent in pilgrimage to lower-level (local, subregional and regional) sacred places, while Vedic or Sanskritic elements are more prominent in connection with high-level (supra-regional, pan-Hindu) places of pilgrimage. He also argues that the purposes of pilgrimage to high-level places is more "general" (perhaps one could say "transcendental," though the term is not his), while purposes are more "specific" at lower-level places (1973 : 148-162). The contrast is between vague or abstract goals, represented by statements of pilgrims that they have gone to a place simply for "pilgrimage," "*darśan*" or "holy bathing," and more specific ones, such as a child's first hair-cutting ceremony or making a vow to offer something of value if the deity fulfils a specific request (1973 : 153-154). Although his data, drawn from a particular sample of sacred places, do suggest that these generalizations are true, the pilgrims on Rajim's *pañc kosi yātrā* appear to have mixed motives, some of which correspond to Bhardwaj's "general", and some to his "specific" purposes. I observed *pañc kosi* pilgrims making their rounds at Rajim temples on many occasions; though intense in their devotion, they clearly were enjoy-

ing the recreational aspects of their experience as well. One
needs to understand the total configuration of that experience,
and not attempt narrow definitions of purpose or motive. It
appears that the configuration, for most pilgrims, is complex,
involving general conceptions of increased merit and ritual
"cleansing," as well as pragmatic goals of fertility and healing.
As for "folk" elements in particular pilgrimage traditions, their
identification is always problematical. There is no doubt,
however, that a subregional pilgrimage such as *pañc kosi* represents a level of orthodoxy somewhat above that of limited
experience within the village alone, but well below that of visits
to higher level places in the pan-Indian hierarchy. It provides
a small-scale model of Hindu values and world view, not identical with, but analogous to the configuration represented by
major sacred complexes such as Varanasi. Thus it intensifies
and reinforces commitment to pan-Hindu norms, but in a way
which is more accessible to more people.

Turner (1974 : 166; 175; 195-198) contends that pilgrimages
are liminal, or at least "liminoid" (1978 : 1-39) phenomena.
Any interpretation of the subregional pilgrimage described here
in terms of its liminal qualities, or in terms of Turner's other
incisive concept of "communitas," would take us beyond the
scope of this chapter and perhaps beyond the scope of the available data. But I do see this pilgrimage, and pilgrimage experience generally, as analogous to ascetic withdrawal from society.
In both monastic and non-monastic asceticism the initiates
remove themselves from profane space and time into the realm
of the sacred. Similarly, pilgrims are separated from the
mundane and work-a-day world, and ideally at least, are immersed in the sacred world of devotion and veneration. Neither the
depth nor the interval of their experience equals that of the
ascetic, since his commitment is total and his withdrawal
permanent, while the pilgrims' commitment is partial and their
withdrawal only temporary. But these two sorts of experiences
have something in common, both cognitively and affectively.
Both are characterized by transition and revelation, suggesting
the appropriateness of Turner's "liminoid" characterization.
These common features and their functional significance, both
for the participants and for the society, invite further
exploration.

Finally, some mention should be made of the predominance of women participants in *pañc kosī yātrā*. It is unlikely that the pilgrimage has any intrinsic characteristics which would make it more appropriate for female, rather than male, participation. *Pañc kosi* at Varanasi in fact shows just the opposite pattern : here about 70 per cent of the pilgrims are male and only 30 per cent female (Vidyarthi *et al.*, 1979 : 86). Unfortunately Bhardwaj (1973) provides no male-female breakdown for his figures in relation to the different levels of pilgrimage places. Local residents of the Rajim area mention going as families to the great pilgrimage places of India, or travelling late in life with just a spouse. Perhaps pilgrimage to more distant places involves more men, couples and families, while local pilgrimage is dominated by women.

People in the Rajim area, in response to questions about the large majority of female pilgrims on *pañc kosī*, usually give such explanations as : "Women are more religious than men," or "During the winter season men must spend more time in the fields and don't have the time to travel." These explanations are *ad hoc* and not very convincing, but they do indicate that most people have not given the matter much thought. All agree, too, that most pilgrims are women, but add that men are free to go if they wish. There is no custom of male exclusion. Possibly the motive of increasing fertility and the association of Siva with fertility are underlying factors. Yet the male guardian of one group of women pilgrims said that he hoped to be blessed with a son as a result of going on pilgrimage, which shows that men as well as women may be motivated by the desire for more children. I suspect that the popularity of this pilgrimage among women is the desire for female comradarie in a context outside the domestic sphere. Although the isolation or segregation of women is not as severe in Chhattisgarh as in some other areas of India, bound as they are to household chores and routines Chhattisgarhi women have few opportunities to enjoy freedom or the company of other women in the context of daily mundane activities. Religion provides a legitimate outlet in a variety of circumstances : attendance at local temple festivals, joining other devotees to sing *bhajans* in temples, attending sermons by religious teachers and of course going on *pañc kosi yātrā*. Since this pilgrimage is done close to home in just four or five days, neither expense nor time away from domestic duties is excessive, making the experience a feasible one for local peasant women. Perhaps the local people are right, that women *are* "more religious" in terms of participation at functions outside their homes and villages. But the underlying motives for this participation probably are more complex than devotion alone.

## REFERENCES

1. In this chapter standard Hindi orthography is employed, except for a few proper nouns such as "Chhattisgarh" (which otherwise would be rendered Chhattisgarh, reserving "c" alone for the unaspirated sound). Diacritics are used for place names, names of deities and other proper nouns on their first appearance only. Other Hindi and Chhattisgarhi words are italicized and written with diacritics throughout the chapter.

2. The 1967-68 research was conducted with the aid of a grant from the American Institute of Indian Studies. The 1970 work was made possible by a sabbatical leave of absence from California State University, Hayward, and a travel grant from AIIS. The 1977-78 field trip was undertaken on the basis of a sabbatical alone.

3. Obviously treating "routine" temple visits and attendence at religious fairs and temple festivals as forms of pilgrimage needs some justification. It is my contention that there are certain underlying common features of all these phenomena which allow them to be considered types of pilgrimage. However, a full discussion of this point is beyond the scope of the present chapter.

4. Eck (1982 : 147; 350) employs the Sanskrit term *krosa*, from which the Hindi is derived, and also gives its equivalent as about two miles.

5. Literally, in Sanskrit *ksetra* means "field or area of land." Eck (1982 : 373) refers to Kashi *kshetra*, the "sacred zone" of Kashi. In Chhattisgarhi *ksetra* becomes *cetra*.

6. See Bharati (1963 : 161-163) for a concise summary and discussion of this point.

7. The idea of a third or "hidden" river completing the triumvirate of a confluence (*sangam*) is not without parallels elsewhere. At Prayaga the Ganga and Yamuna rivers are said to be joined by the "mythical" Sarasvati (Eck, 1982 : 212). Bharati (1963 : 161) points out that "the Sarasvati is not entirely 'mythical'—there certainly was a small river flowing into the Ganges up to the early middle ages, but its merging with the two at Prayaga is almost definitely a myth."

8. Another example in Madhya Pradesh is Ratanpur, about 80 miles north of Rajim. The sacred complex there has been described by Jha

(1976), but he does not report a *pank kosi* type pilgrimage around the town.

## NOTES

Babb, Lawrence A. 1975, *The Divine Hierarchy : Popular Hinduism in Central India*, New York : Columbia University Press.

Bharati, Agehananda, 1963, *Pilgrimage in the Indian Tradition. History of Religions* 3(1) : 135-167.

Bhardwaj, Surinder Mohan 1973, *Hindu Places of Pilgrimage in India.* Berkeley : The University of California Press.

Eck, Diana L., 1982, *Banaras : City of Light.* New York : Alfred A. Knopf.

Havell, E.B., 1905 : *Benares, The Sacred City.* London : Thacker and Co.

Herbert, Jean, 1957, *Banaras : A Guide to Panch-Kroshi Yatra.* Calcutta : Saturday Mail Publications.

Jay, Edward J., 1973, Bridging the Gap between Castes : Ceremonial Friendship in Chhattisgarh. *Contributions to Indian Sociology*, New Series 7 : 144-158.

Jha, Makhan, 1976, The Sacred Complex of Ratanpur. Calcutta : *Bulletin of the Anthropological Survey of India* 25 (1 & 2): 46-116.

Saraswati, Baidyanath, 1975, *Kashi : Myth and Reality of a Classical Cultural Tradition.* Simla : Indian Institute of Advanced Study.

Turner, Victor, 1974, Pilgrimages as Social Processes. In *Dramas, Fields and Metaphors by Victor Turner*, pp. 167-230. Ithaca : Cornell University Press.

Turner, Victor and Edith Turner, 1978, *Image and Pilgrimage in Christian Culture : Anthropological Perspectives.* New York : Columbia University Press.

Vidyarthi, Lalit P., 1961, *The Sacred Complex in Hindu Gaya.* New York : Asia Publishing House.

Vidyarthi, Lalit P., 1974, Sacred Complex as a Dimension of Indian Civilization. *Journal of Social Research*, 17(1).

Vidyarthi, L.P., Makhan Jha and B.N. Saraswati, 1979, *The Sacred Complex of Kashi.* Delhi : Concept Publishing Co.

# 6

# Impact of Hindu Pilgrimage on Tribes of Chotanagpur

TRIBES in India have been much influenced by the Hindu mode
of life and that is why many theoretical concepts like 'tribe-
caste continuum' (Sinha, 1965) Rajputisation or Kshatrisati
(*ibid.*) Saskritisation (Srinivas, 1952) etc. were proposed to
establish cultural linkages and to demarcate the impact of
Hinduism on the different sections of the tribes of India. In this
context it must also be pointed out that since time immemorial
tribes have been in continuous interactions with the so-called
advanced form of Hinduism which are described in various
*Puranas and Epics* of the land. For example, we find references
of tribes in the *Vishnu Puran* where we are told that Khasa
(presently a tribe of Garhwal Himalaya) was a daughter of
Daksh, wife of Rishi Kashyap. The most famous reference to
the tribes in Indian antiquity is in the Valmikis' Ramayan
which describes how Ram and Lakshman, the two exiled sons
of King Dashrath of Ayodhya, came to the bank of a river
*Pampa* where an aged ascetic Savari, belonging to the famous
tribe of Central India, extended her hospitality to them.

In this way the tribes of India have been referred to in many
sacred texts of land. Some of the scholars have also pointed
out that in most of the cases the impact is so prominent that
one cannot easily make a demarcation between the two. Sir
Herbert Risely (1961) has pointed out, "No sharp line of

demarcation can be drawn between Hinduism and animism, the one shades away in sensibly into the other".

In the light of these impacts of Hinduism on the tribes of India, with special reference to Chotanagpur, when we look at the genesis of the tribal *yatras* (pilgrimage) we find that tribal *yatras* of Chotanagpur have been greatly influenced by Hindu pilgrimages, which may evidently be seen even today, although many changes have taken place in Chotanagpur due to industrialisation and urbanisation which have rapidly changed the cultural pattern of the people of Chotanagpur.

In this chapter I, thus, make an attempt to highlight the nature and trends of impact of Hindu pilgrimage on tribal *yatras* (pilgrimage) of Chotanagpur specially with the view to examine as to how different dominating Hindu sects centres are fairly represented in Chotanagpur. This chapter will also throw light, in brief, as to how the different tribes and castes of Chotanagpur participate in the tribal *yatras* (pilgrimage) without any discriminations, which ultimately helps them in strengthening the socio-cultural solidarity in the region.

While discussing the impact of Hindu pilgrimage on tribal *yatras* I have selected here for the present purpose only, three dominating Hindu sects and their sacred centres viz. the Vaishnavism, Shaivism, and Shaktism which are still in vogue in Chotanagpur. Here I must also point out that among the tribes of Chotanagpur, a demarcation may also be made firstly on the basis of Christian converted tribe and the non-converted who are called as 'Swainsar'. It in the latter section of the tribes of Chotanagpur who have been greatly influenced by Hindu pilgrimage, although they have also retained some of their very old customs and practices.

### VAISHNAVA PLACES OF PILGRIMAGE

### Jagannathpur and other Sacred Centres

The Jagannathpur temple is situated about 6 miles North-west of Ranchi town. The area is well known due to this temple and the Heavy Engineering Corporation, the famous Government establishment of its kind of India.

The temple was built in 1691 A.D. by Thakur Aini Sahi, a Khorposdar of the Nagvanshi family and the village was granted to Jagannath as a *Devottar*. The whole of the Ranchi District, before the abolition of the zamindari, comprised of one Tauzi and the Maharaja of Chotanagpur was the zamindar (landlord). The Maharaja of Chotanagpur belongs to the Nagvanshi Rajput family, the theory held by the Britishers that the family was of Munda origin, but became highly Hinduised, does not represent anonymous view. Even the Maharaja had the name of Phani Mukut Rai who was Hindu and not a Munda name. Phani Mukut Rai married a Rajput princess of Panchet Raj of Manbhum, but this also cannot be ruled out that his Raj was also ruled by Munda King named Madra Munda. Thus it put us into controversy. Researches are going on to make sure of it. There were about sixty to seventy successive Maharajas and taking the average duration of each at thirty years, it appears that the British ethnologists had put too much stress on the family name *"Nagvanshi"* and thought that since the family had taken it must be aboriginal in origin as the Munda are totemistic. The Nagvanshi Maharaja family was split into numerous branches.

The construction of Jagannath temple at Jagannathpur was not an isolated attempt at building a Hindu temple in land where predominantly the animistic tribes lived. At about the time the Jagannath temple at Jagannathpur was built, another Hindu temple was reared at Chutia, which is now a part of the town of Ranchi. There is an inscription in the northern wall of the temple, which shows that the temple was constructed in *Samvat* 1742 (1685 A.D.) by one Hari Brahamachari, the Guru of Raja during the reign of Raja Raghunath, the fifteen descent from Raja Phani Mukut Rai.

### Legends regarding the Origin of the Jagannath Temple at Jagannathpur

There are various legends about the origin of this temple. Firstly it is said that an Oraon servant of the Thakur of Barkagarh Estate within which Jagannath temple falls, had accompanied the Thakur to Puri. The Oraon servant became ardent devotee of Lord Jagannath at Puri and fasted continuously for seven days and nights. He felt hungry at about midnight and asked for food when everyone was asleep. He muttered a few words that he was hungry and suddenly he saw a man bringing him food and water in gold vessels. Next morning temple authorities at Puri in Orissa found that the gold vessels which were the property of the *Mandir* were missing from located room. The servant came to know of the commotion about the theft and produced the gold vessels which had been left by his side. Everyone understood that Lord Jagannath himself had brought food to him in the gold vessels. So pleased he was with the Oraon devotion. Next night Thakur had a dream that he must construct a temple of Jagannath and enshrine the images of Jagannath, Balbhadra and Subhadra at Jagannathpur in Chotanagpur and accordingly he did so after his return to Ranchi.

The second legend which is current among the non-tribal people is that the Thakur was a devotee of Lord Jagannath and used to go to Puri frequently and prayed to Lord Jagannath for help. The enemy were routed and after this the Thakur built the temple at Jagannathpur.

The third legend is that the Thakur had a dream in which Lord Jagannath himself directed the Thakur to build a temple at Jagannathpur which he did. The Jagannath temple is built according to the model of Jagannath temple at Puri.

## Rathayatra or Car Festival of Chotanagpur

Every year this annual Car Festival is held at Jagannathpur in Ranchi with great pomp and ceremony. This ceremony follows the customs and other practices as held at Puri. On the *Rathyatra* or car festival day thousands of people from different parts of Chotanagpur congregate and the idols are placed with due ceremonials in the *rathes* (chariots), just as the Raja of Puri ceremoniously sweeps the platforms of the chariots, the head of the family of the ex-Raja of Barka-Garh of Ranchi who was a close associate of the Raja of Chotanagpur, sprinkles scented water and sweeps. After this the chariot is drawn by the men, women and children accompanied with loud music of drums. The chariots with the deities of Lord Jagannath, Balbhadra and Subhadra are taken to *Mousi Bari* (Aunt's house), where they remain for a week. After a week on the *Ulta Ratha Yatra* day the chariot are pulled back. The *Rathyatra* at Jagannathpur is the biggest religious and social event connected with any religious creed in Ranchi district. At

the lowest estimate more than one lakh people visit the temple
on that day from different parts of Chotanagpur. The tribals
freely join the festival in pulling the ropes of the chariots and
worshipping the deities. As a matter of fact, the *Ratha Yatra*
festival is exercising a very strong influence in Hinduising the
tribals. The people of that area do not have any discrimination
regarding this Jagannath temple as both the tribals and non-
tribals show respect to the lord to a great extent.

The important tribes of Chotanagpur like the Kharias
worship the Sun god under the name of *Bero*. They address
him as *Parmeshwar*, a Hindu word for God. Similar is the case with the Oraon tribe who address the
Sun god as *Biri Deota*. The very adoption of the
*Parameswar* clearly shows the impact of Hinduism. The
Hinduised Kharias, the Oraons and the Mundas abstain from
taking meat which Hindus consider impure. The latter
aboriginal tribe, the Oraon, are distinguished from the Munda
so far as their symbols of worship are concerned. The Munda
normally have no symbol and make no representation to their
gods, where the Oraon, however, have some visible object of
worship though it may be a stone or a wooden post or a
lump of earth. The symbolisation on the part of the Oraon may
have been due to impact of Hinduism.

In this connection it has to be mentioned that the cult of
Vaishnavism has had a deep and significant impact on the tribal
people of Ranchi district from the day of Chaitanya Mahaprabhu in the 15th century, when the great Vaishnavite
apostle of Bengal had travelled through parts of Ranchi
district on his way to Puri to worship Lord Jagannath.
*Chaitanya Charitamrita* and host of other Vaishnava works
describe the travels of Chaitanya Mahaprabhu, through
Jharkhand area after crossing the Damodar river near Bankura.
Wending his way along portions of Bundu and Tamar Thana
and Ranchi he passed through Chaibasa and went to Puri via
Keonjhar and Jaipur. Even today in those areas vaishnavism
has such hold that there are many families who declare themselves vaishnava as by caste. Many of the tribes are *Khantidharis*
owing to direct impact of the cult of Vaishnavism. Thousands
of the tribals in Ranchi, district are strictly vegetarian. Some of
the tenets of the *Tana Bhagat* and *Vishnu Bhagat*, a class of

purists among the aboriginals that came into prominence in the 20th century, are based on Vaishnavism. They do not touch any intoxicant and do not eat meat. They have a high standard of values of love and truth and live in bonds of brotherhood with one another. *Tana Bhagat* also joined the non-co-operation movement launched by Father of Nation, Mahatma Gandhi. They did so with a religious fervour.

Another movement of the Puritans among the tribals known as *Safahor* movement in the later part of 19th century could also be directly traced to the influence of Vaishnavism. The Safahor movement wanted the people to live a clean life above intoxication and be strictly vegetarian. The Safahor adherents believe in *Gurus* respect and cherish fellowship and recognise love, peace and amity as the means to get nearer to God.

It is significant that *kirtans* accompanied by *khol* and *kartal* (musical instruments) are still prevalent in many of the villages in the interior of Ranchi District. *Kirtans* are gifts of the *Vaishnava* apostles. The cult of Vaishnavism had a deep impact on the Mundas, the Oraons and the Kharias just as the cult of Shaktism had influenced the Santhal tribes who live in Santhal Pargana district of Bihar State.

It is in this context that the temple of Lord Jagannath at Jagannathpur (Ranchi) occupies an extremely important position and could be described as a landmark in the history of religion in Bihar. The stone temple at Borya, five miles from Ranchi town, built during 1665-86 A.D. by Laxmi Narayan Tiwary may also be mentioned. It was dedicated to Lord Madan Mohan and has two inscriptions, probably the earliest in the local Hindu dialect and Devanagri script, which are eloquent of the temples origin. Other temples belonging to the Vaishnava group are the temple of Mahamaya at Hapamuni (Ghagra, P.S. of Gumla district). Old temples with images of Basudev, goddess Laxmi and Lord Shiva with inscriptions and engravings on stone slab at Nawagarh under Raidih P.S. of Gumla District are also very important. The famous Bansidhar temple of Nagar Untari (Palamau district) containing a life size *Astadhatu* (alloy of eight metals) image of Lord Krishna with flute in his hand is significant. In Deogen (Palamau district) there is an old Chero fort (Chero tribe's fort) where an old statue of Vishnu and Laxmi in black stone has been found which proves the tribal connection with the Hindu shrine.

In this wake of revivalistic movement in 19th century these sites became places of pilgrimage in the new religious order found by tribal leaders like Birsa. It was declared that these temples were made by the *Munda* in the *Satyuga* (golden age) for the worship of their God. It may be noted here that these temples were not merely centres of Hindu worship but they also played a positive role in the diffusion of Hindu culture in tribal areas.

### Shakti Places of Pilgrimages Divri Maa or Solabbuji Devi

The temple of *Divri* about two miles away from Tamar, Ranchi district of Bihar state, contains the image of the sixteen armed Mother-Goddess, popularly known as *Solabhuji Devi* with *Shiva* on the top and *Saraswati* and *Laxmi*, *Kartikeya* and *Ganesh* on the sides. It is believed that her image is of the elder sister of the Shakti group, the other being at Kera (Singhbhum) Palna (Tamar), Purna Nagar (Erki P.S.) and Dewli (Manbhoom). The local villagers believe that human sacrifice used to be offered at this temple till about the turn of the 20th century. Ruins of similar temples with a *Shivlinga* have also been found at Harin (Sonahatu) on the river Kanchi in Chotanagpur.

A significant feature about the religious services in the temple at Divri is that they are conducted by Munda Pahan (priest) on the all the day except Tuesday. A Brahmin priest worships the goddess after decorating her with golden *hasuli*, *nose-ring* and *ear ring* and dresssing her in a yellow and red *sari*. Thus we see both the tribal and non-tribal priests take part in performing the worship. The Pahan tribal priest of Divri is said to be the immediate in charge of the temple and conducts sacrifice of sheep, goats, and buffaloes, particularly during the Durga Puja in the month of October. Prevalence of these practices of Divri may be interpreted as cases of cultural synthesis between the Hindu and tribal elements.

### Maa Paudi

Worship of deity without a devotional *darshan* is rather rare in India and the deity of *Sri Sri Maa Paudi* enshrined at Porahat first and then at Saraikela, Singhbhum district in Bihar is the deity of same category. Nobody is permitted to see Maa Paudi except the ruler, the heir apparent, the heir presumptive and their consorts and the main *Dehuri* or *Pujari* (priest) of the temple. Formerly everyone could have *darshan* but since the beginning of 19th century a decision was taken in a convention of the people of Saraikela that none except those mentioned above would be allowed to have *darshan* of deity on ordinary days, but the ruler's family members also could have *darshan* only on the days of *Nua Khia* and *Jest Jental* days. The taboo still continues even after the termination of the rulership.

This unseen deity that has acquired a mysterious halo round her was the bone of contention between two ruling houses of the Maharaja of Singhbhum (Porahat) and the Raja of Saraikela. The deity first found her way to Porahat and the Raja of Saraikela. When the British wanted to draw up a treaty with Raja Ghanshyam Singh of Singhbhum the latter insisted among other terms on the possession of the Raja Saraikela. From the very beginning of the Parleys Capt. Ronghedge was insisting on the restoration of Sri Paudi Devi or Maa Paudi. British supremacy was acknowledged by the Maharaja of Singhbhum in 1820 while the ruler of Saraikela conceded it in 1823. Maa Paudi continued to remain with Saraikela because Raja Bikram Singh was adamantly refusing to part with the deity.

Maa Paudi is the presiding deity of the Singhbhum district in Chotanagpur which is called by the people of that area as *Ishta Devatas*. According io the *Vamsa Prava Lekhana* the Paudi Devi originally came from Ceylon (Sri Lanka).

*Vamsa Prava Lekhana* is a chronicle which has been faithfully recorded in palm leaves by a family of Dogras who have followed the Sinha Dynasty of Rathors from Rameshwaram to Singhbhum. The present palm leaf manuscript was copied by Maguni Rout Dogra, in 1643 A.D. during the reign of Kashiram Singh II, the 41st King of Sinha Dynasty. The script is Oriya.

Since Maa Paudi came to Singhbhum during the reign of Maharaja Kashiram Singh, she not only occupied a place in the hearts of every citizen of Singhbhum, but she has also been installed in the temple at Porahat and in the temple at Saraikela for the pilgrimage. Besides the two centres, whole of Singhbhum there are *Paudi Asthans*, scattered over the whole region. Maa Paudi has been the symbol of unity.

Maa Paudi, a female deity, is worshipped once in the month of *Jestha* (May-June) and again in the *Asadh* (June-July) or any two months fixed by the villagers, according to their convenience. At every worship a clay image of a horse and another of elephant, in miniature form are commonly purchased from potters and places at the place of worship. At Paudi Mela near the town of Saraikela, the goddess Paudi is worshipped. At Aharbandh near Saraikela there is a large circular stone known as Paudi, where once a year the tenants and lease holders assemble and sacrifice animals which are eaten on the spot.

Besides the festivals described above, there is another *Jantal* on the *Jestha Shukla Chaturthi*, the day Sri Paudi Devi was installed at Porahat during the reign of Achutya Singh in the 13th century A.D. and similarly installed at Saraikela much later, known as the birth day of Maa Paudi. Now this *Jantal* is performed in Saraikela, when tenants and lease holders bring their sacrifices to Sri Paudi Temple. This is followed by similar *Jantal* in other Paudi Sthan located in different parts of the region.

In addition to these worships, once in every ten years there is a national gathering at Paudi Mela just outside the Saraikela town in the Singhbhum Pir of Saraikela estate. People from all areas and from all castes and tribes participate without any discriminations. It is the greatest national festival of that area. However, after independence this festival literally remains a national unity in the name of Maa Paudi. It is significant that every ten years people must meet there and worship together the common goddess and feel that each and every one of them is of the same nationality and culture. Thre is no distinction of caste and creed there. Both tribals and non-tribals, a Ho, a Munda, a Santhal, a Bhumij, a Brahmin, a Khurmi, a Kshatriya, a Bhuinya, a Mahato, a Ghasi, a Dom, a Bhadri, a Teli and Oriya or one speaking tribal dialect, must all unite together in the name of God and feel that they are Saraikellian.

**Benu Sagar**

Benu sagar is a village in Singhbhum district of Bihar State.

Benusagar is now a hamlet with old age relic. It is situated seven miles south from Majhgaon road in the extreme south-west of the Kolhan area, on the border of Singhbhum district in Bihar and Mayurbhanj district in Orissa. There are a number of low mounds of bricks marking the ruins of several old temples and a number of beautifully sculptured images lying half buried in the ground. According to the local traditions there was a tank which was excavated and a fort was built round the township by Raja Benu, son of Raja Keshna of Keshnagarh.

Mr. Belgar, a researcher in the Archeological department, Government of India, after a close inspection ascribed the origin of the temples to the 7th century A.D.

Benusagar and its surrounding area had once evidently played a very great role in the history of Jainism, Buddhism and Brahmanism. The low mounds of bricks found at Benusagar belong to the Jain and Buddhistic shrines.

The medieval remains at Benusagar and as a matter of fact the remains throughout Singhbhum district have witnessed a chequerred history. The area is habited by aboriginal tribes like the *Hos* and the *Santhal*. There are eight phallic emblems of Shiva and the foundations of the four temples with their remains scattered around them.

### The Pilgrimage Centres of Tanginath

Tanginath is a hill shrine in village Majhgaon in Gumla District of Chotanagpur plateau. It is a famous place of pilgrimage for Shiva worship where almost all the tribes and castes of Chotanagpur and its neighbouring areas participate without any discrimination.

At Tanginath there are various sacred centres (Sahay, 1975) among which special mention may be made of different Shiva Lingas, sacred kinds, Devi Mandir, Surya Mandir etc., which attract the pilgrimage and devotees following the various sects and traditions.

The Tanginath temple is constructed of big walls with a thatched roof. Besides the temple there is a Shiva Linga with Argha of about five feet diameter. It is pointed out that in *Satyug* a sandal wood tree grew here but when *Kaliyug* approached Lord Shiva was pained to see every where sinful state of affairs and that is why he entered into that sandal wood tree and in course of time the whole tree turned into a Shiva Linga which is worshipped today. This ancient myth is still perpetuated by the priest and the pilgrims to Tanginath binds the people into the common fold of tradition.

Another significant sacred instrument which attracts the people of Tanginath is the *Iron Trisul* (trident) which is about seventeen feet in height as estimated by Roy (1915) several decades ago. In addition to the Shiva Linga, the sacred trident, the existence of *Devi Mandir*, *Surya Mandir* and various other kunds at Tanginath point out as to how the Hindu model of pilgrimage and the arrangement of the sacred counters belonging to the great traditions (Fedfield, 1955) or the Sahshric tradition (Saraswati, 1975) have influenced the tribal inhabitants of this region. We have also noted that besides the influence of Shiva worship on the people of Chotanagpur the inhabitants of this tribal region have also been influenced by the Vaishnava and Shakti centres of pilgrimage as discussed earlier.

**Observations**

Finally it may be suggested here that since time immemorial there has been a continuum of different traditions in Chotanagpur plateau. The give and take theory seems to be operative here which ultimately influenced the tribals. The Hindu modes of worship and the dominance of certain Hindu sects, have been absorbed by the local people in course of time which are now part and parcel of their own indigenous culture and civilization. However, some dominant trends of Hindu traditions, as reflected through the Jagannath Temple of Chotanagpur, the Shakti Centres (Maa Paudi, Benusagar) of Saraikela, the Saivite tradition of Tanginath still reveals the clear-cut influence of great Hindu tradition on the tribals of Chotanagpur. Here, it may also be pointed out that till today the indigenous religious institutions have survived, instead of growing trend of industrialisation and urbanisation, which are taking place so rapidly in this region and, I hope, the time alone will judge its future perspective.

## NOTES

Jha, M. 1979, *Dimensions of Indian Civilization*, Classical Publication, New Delhi.

Jha, M. 1983, *Hindu Pilgrimage and Patronage : As study in the History of Politicalisation of Hindu Tirth—Jagannathpur : A case study* : Presidential speech read at Vancouver, Canada.

Mishra Narayan, 1970, *Cultural Persistence and Change in Chotanagpur Village*, Classical Publications, New Delhi.

Roy, S.C., 1891, *The Oraon of Chotanagpur, Brambe*, Mission Press, Calcutta.

Roy, S.C., 1937, Caste, Race and Religion in India, *Man in India*, Vol. XVII, No. 4, Oct-Dec.

Roy, S.C., 1970, *Munda and their Country*, Asia Publishing House, Bombay, originally published in 1912.

Sahay, K.N., 1967, A study in the process of transformation from tribe to caste, *Parhaiyas of Social Research*, Vol. X, No. 1, 1967.

Sahay, K.N., 1975, *Hindu Shrines of Chotanagpur : Tanginath a case study*, Simla.

Saraswati, B.N., 1975, *Kashi : Myth and Reality of a Classical Cultural Tradition*, Indian Institute of Advance Study, Simla.

# 7

# Musicians of a Pilgrimage Centre in India

## Kashi : A Case Study

BALANAND SINHA

VARANASI or Kashi is perhaps the only city in the world which is known by three names—Varanasi, Kashi and Banaras.[1] It is mentioned in the Vedas, Puranas, Upanishads and the epics as the city of enlightenment.[2] Literally, Kashi means 'that which gives the light of knowledge'.[3] According to the Hindu belief one attains *moksha* (liberation) if he dies in Kashi.[4] Kashi, in fact is the most famous and ancient place of pilgrimage in India and can only be compared with Rome, Mecca and Jerusalem. Thus, Kashi as a *tirtha* (centre of pilgrimage) occupies an important place in the Hindu religious consciousness.

In the Vedic period and later during the time of Buddha Kashi established itself as a great seat of learning. People visited this sacred city to acquire true knowledge and divine wisdom. In the Jain texts too, Kashi is mentioned as an important centre of traditional learning.[5] Ramanand, Kabir, Tulsi and others enriched the religious and cultural heritage of this city through their preachings.[6] Some of these great men were also good musicians and their preachings were often in the form of bhajans and kirtans which they sang on *ektara* (a single-stringed instrument). In the seventeenth and eighteenth centuries various religious sects built temples of their own where religious festivals were frequently organized. For instance, Chaitanya Mahaprabhu and his disciples organized *kirtan mandalis*. Thus, in a way, because of the influence of men of such excellence the socio-cultural atmosphere of Kashi acquired a certain degree of sacredness in its appeal.

Kashi is one of the few Indian cities where music (traditional classical as well as folk) is "central" to the socio-cultural life of its people. The Kathaks, as a community of traditional musicians and dancers, have contributed significantly in this direction. As a sub-caste of the Brahmins the Kathaks have enriched the tradition of Indian classical music through their dedication to this field over many successive generations (Netl, 1978). Famous for its ornate Khayal, melodious thumri, lilting dadra and playful tappa Kashi is also well-known for kajri, chaiti and other lighter forms of (folk) music. Kashi, thus, represents a complete world of music.

In view of the above facts it was considered worth the effort to ascertain whether the musicians of Kashi are influenced by the fact that they reside in Kashi, a *tirtha*, and pursue music, a traditional Indian art-form. Consequently, a few researchable questions were raised for verification. These are :

1. Do the musicians of Kashi practise music as a *purusartha* ?
2. Do the musicians of Kashi uphold the traditional theory of music as a divine manifestation ?
3. Does Kashi, as *anandavana* (the Forest of Bliss), inspire its musicians to adopt the life-style of Banarasi which is characterized by *mauj*, *masti* and *phakkarpan*.

**Methodology**

*The Field : Its Importance*

Kashi, the most ancient and the most celebrated place of Hindu pilgrimage, was selected for the study of musicians for a number of reasons. Firstly, Kashi is the microcosm of Indian civilization. It is a place where diverse cultural traditions of India are presented and preserved in its best form (Saraswati, 1975; Eck, 1982). Secondly, it shapes the life and personality of the Kashivasi in a unique way. One of the several names of this city is *anandavana*, the "Forest of Bliss", that provides not only spiritual bliss but also the earthly joys of life. The *ananda* part of Kashi's character is amply reflected in the typical life-style of its people (be it musician, artisan, dancer, or any other) who call themselves "Banarasi". The personality of a "Banarasi" is characterized by *mauj* (delight), *masti* (joie de vivre) and *phakkarpan* (carefreeness). As Saraswati (1975) has observed :

> In their self-identification as a cultural group or as a community the people of Kashi address themselves by the term *banarasi*. The terms, such as *masti, phakkarpan* and even *akkharpan*, which gave cultural expressions to *banarsi* have no substitutes in any language, suffice it to say that these denote certain cultural characteristics whereby the people of this city are self-recognizable.

Kumar (1984) has also expressed a similar view :

> *mauj* or *masti*, these terms are untranslatable, even into other Hindi terms. In the Bhojpuri of Banaras another term used as synonym is *phakkarpan* : the special characteristics of Bhagwan Bholenath (Siva) of being "wild", eccentric, untraditional, unaccountable. Intellectuals describe *mauj* and *masti* as a "philosophy of pleasure" moulded to the truth of social life, or sometimes as *vigyan*, *vidya* (the science, the wisdom) of life. . . .These feelings are not only "mood" ensuing from and characterizing some actions; they are also "motivations", directing towards particular actions. .. . .Little wonder that the people of Banaras often refer to their motivations, and their activities, as *Banarasipan* or *Banarasness*. . . .

Thirdly, because of its sacred and gay atmosphere Kashi influences its people in a unique way. While on the one hand its people possess *mauj*, *masti* and *phakkarpan* in their personality, on the other hand there is a distinct tendency, conscious as well as unconscious, to behave according to the higher (transcendental) values of life. Religiosity constitutes the core of their personhood. Lastly, quite importantly, the musicians of Kashi are always aware of the fact that through

music they can attain *mukti* and at the same time help in the
growth of cultural awareness of its people.

## The Sample

Musician, as defined for the present study, was a person who
constantly contributed to his field of endeavour through music
performance and other activities related to music. The All India
Radio grading (such as B, B+, A, A— special) and affiliation
with authentic *gharana* (school) were the other markers of
musician. Sixteen typical cases were thus selected for indepth
life-historical study. Typicality was determined on the basis of
maximum suitability, comparability and appropriateness of the
subjects chosen for study.

## Method of Study

For the collection of life-histories the regular method of interview was utilized. The questions incorporated in the interview-
schedule were of the open-end variety so that the respondents
could freely report their feelings and attitudes relating to their
life in general and to their musical personality in particular.
Here are a few questions raised in the course of interviewing :
What do you think of the *Hindusthani Sangeet Parampara* ?
How old is it ? What have been its sources of origin ? Has Kashi
contributed significantly towards the growth of this *parampara* ?
If yes, how has it done so ?  Why have you chosen Varanasi as
your *sadhana-sthal* ? How much have you benefited by pursuing
music in Kashi ? What is the place and significance of music in
your life ? Is it just a means of livelihood, a medium of
recreation, or something more than that ? Do you perform
*pooja* ? Do you feel that music and *pooja* are related to each
other ? etc.

## Field Work

The field work in Kashi was undertaken in the summer of 1985.
The respondents were individually contacted either at their
place of residence or at pre-appointed places. They were made
to feel that the study had great relevance for the future of
Hindusthani music and musicians. Casual talking and exchange
of views on topics of general musical interest helped in establishing initial rapport with the respondents. They were also told

that the researcher himself came from a family devoted to the pursuit of music and that at the moment, too, was imbibing the subtleties and finer points of this art from one of the leading exponents of Hindusthani classical music (Pandit Jasraj of Bombay). This introduction worked well in establishing immediate and intense rapport with the respondents. Talking to me the respondents felt comfortable for two reasons : that I was one of them (i.e. a musician myself) and that I belonged to a family which has in the past done quite a lot for the musicians. Besides, they also enjoyed talking to me since I could appreciate what they were saying or demonstrating. In the course of interview, they often said, "Well, you are a musician yourself. You will understand and appreciate what I am saying." This type of identification between myself and the respondents was largely responsible for the successful and authentic collection of data.

Each of the respondents was interviewed for about two hours on the average. The interview-material was taperecorded and later transferred into written form for analysis. Some of the respondents showed reluctance in the recording of their interviews through a taperecorder. For such respondents the regular pen-and-paper method of recording was adopted. Material collected in such a manner naturally required more than one interview-session. The data gathered thus was carefully content-analyzed.

**Results and Discussion**

An analysis of the content of the material collected through intensive interviews revealed a few significant facts worthy of mention here.

*Music as Purusartha*

The theory of *purusartha* has an important place in the lifestyle and world-view of the Hindus. *Purusartha*, literally meaning "man's meaning", are four : *dharma, artha, kama* and *moksha*. These are, in fact, the psycho-moral bases of the Hindu personality.[7]

The word *dharma* originates from the Sanskrit *dhri* meaning 'to hold together', 'to preserve'.[8] *Dharma* roughly means moral duty or right action. It is the means through which man reaches the desired goal of his life. *Dharma* is that from which results happiness and final beatitude. *Artha*, on the other hand, is to be understood as referring to all the necessary means required for acquiring worldly prosperity, such as wealth or power. *Kama* refers to all the desires in man for enjoyment and satisfaction of the senses, including the sex drive to which the word *kama* more prominently refers. *Moksha* roughly means salvation, release from worldly involvement, from 'coming' and 'going'.[9] It is the direct experience of the unity of the self with the Infinite.

*Artha* and *kama* signify man's earthly belongings and dharma stands on a higher level. Nevertheless, it is widely accepted that an individual cannot conduct his life without *artha* (since it represents the material means of living) and *kama* (which is essential for the propagation of species). Therefore, it is required that the correct quantity and quality, the place and time of *artha* and *kama* be determined. This is done in terms of *dharma*, which defines, for man, the proper quantum, place and season, for the right functioning of *artha* and *kama*. However, Manu[10] declares that there ought to be a harmonious management of the *trivarga* : *dharma*, *artha* and *kama*. And that the good of humanity lies only in such an arrangement. But, it is also felt by many that this view is beneficial for only those who are after the immediate and worldly objectives of life. For those who go for the final purpose and meaning of life, *moksha* is the only aim of life. For them, *moksha* is achieved at the final stage of life. *Dharma, artha, kama* are the means for the attainment of that end.

The musicians of Kashi, by their behaviour and answers to queries, indicated that, by and large, music was their *dharma*. It was their moral duty, their right action and their means of achieving the supreme end of *moksha*. At the mundane level the repondents were seen to attach due importance to *artha* and *kama*, because while the former was helpful in attaining worldly prosperity (in the form of wealth and power) the latter assisted them in the propagation of species and thus ensured the continuity of their tradition. However, for the majority of the musicians of Kashi the final aim of life, the chief *purusartha*, was *moksha*. It way explicitly as well as implicitly acknowledged as the prime goal of their life. Music and *moksha* were not different but the same thing, they were synonymous to each other.

Thus, *dharma, artha, kama* and *moksha* constitute the core of the personality of the musicians of Kashi. It is a *purusartha* in the sense that it fulfils their needs of *dharma, artha, kama* and *moksha.*

## Music as a Divine Manifestation

Religiosity, as an expression of the Divine, is one of the "central" factors in the life and society of the Indians. Its importance has been highlighted by many Indian social scientists. Bose's analysis of the Hindu mode of tribal absorption (1941), Srinivas's study of religion and society among the Coorgs of South India (1952), Vidyarthi's work on the sacred complex in Gaya (1961), Sinha's treatment of Vaishnava influence of the Bhumij (1966) and Saraswati's work on the pottery-making cultures and Indian civilization (1967) are just a few examples. The role of religion in the cultivation of excellence has been described by Saraswati (1975). According to him :

Looking back at the history of Indian civilization, we find that religion has pervaded all aspects of India's creative life. From the very beginning Indian art and architecture, science and technology, language and literature have closely followed the course of Hinduism in their march of progress and decline. When Hinduism was in its prime they grew and flourished and when it was weakened they fell and became degenerated. . . .

The importance of the sacred element in the lives of Indian musicians has also been recognised by such writers as Coomaraswamy (1948), Ratanjankar (1959), Prajnananda (1973), Brihaspati (1982), Ranade (1984) and many others. It is felt that religion or sacredness drives a musician to a personal state of faith, a faith which invariably enhances his inner strength, skill and thought and thus enables him to perform the highest plane of excellence (both at the aesthetic and the transcendental level, sacred and secular sphere).

Musicians of Kashi, as expected, were found to be extremely religious in their approach towards life in general and music in particular. For them, music was not just a mundane activity, a means of livelihood, but, rather something very sacred and divine. A few statements of the respondents will serve as example.

"To tell you the truth, the sole purpose of singing is to attain *mukti*. *Sangeet*, as you must also be knowing, is a *naad-brahma upasana*. It is a divine art.

(MM : Brahmin : 74 Years)

"*Nadadhinan jagat*, that is, the universe is created by the divine sound *naad*. The modern scientists also believe this. But, for us this is nothing new. If we look at the sacred aspects of music it becomes evident that music is not only *mokshadayini* but also *sakshat parabrahmaswarupini*."

(RM ; Brahmin : 54 Years)

"The very origin of music, according to the *shastras* and our belief, is divine. I do not know about others but as far as I am concerned I always do *dhyan* of Maa Sharda before I start my performance irrespective of where and when I am singing."

(SM : Brahmin : 24 Years)

"For me music itself is a sort of *pooja*, a medium of merging with the *parabrahma parameswara*. I do not find the need for doing *pooja* separately."

(JV : Kayastha : 46 Years)

"Even the Muslim musicians do *dhyan* of Saraswati and Mahadeo. Allaudin Khan was a great devotee of Sharda Ma of Maihar. Bismillah Khan and others are also great devotees. Music is above religion."

(WK : Muslim : 52 Years)

Thus, evidently, the musicians of Kashi perceive and practice music as a divine art. Religiosity forms the nucleus of the personality of the musicians of Kashi. It is the driving force behind their urge to create.

### Kashi as Anandavana

Musicians of Kashi, with a few insignificant exceptions, expressed that being in Kashi and practising music was for them, to use an idiom, like having the cake and eating it too. The respondents felt that the sacred and gay atmosphere of Kashi, symbolizing *mouj, masti* and *mukti* (*moksha*) simultaneously, added much to their inherent motivation to become accomplished musicians. As expected, the respondents, most of them, were observed as being carefree people. Their behaviour (musical and otherwise) was consistent with their philosophy of *joie de vivre*. A few statements made by the respondents can be utilized here in support of the above observation :

"Well, I have been residing in Delhi for the last 12 or 13 years. I found that the life in those cities is artificial and materialistic. Hence, I have returned to Varanasi. What I have been missing all these years, the *mauj* and *masti*, I can enjoy it now."

(*RM : Brahmin* : 36 Years)

"I sincerely feel that Kashi is very different from other cities of India. Here you can enjoy life freely and simultaneously expected to be liberated by merely staying here. This you cannot expect to achieve in other cities."

(*BS : Vaishya* : 53 Years)

"It is quite natural for a musician to express desire for residing in Kashi. There is a lot of *ananda* here. You get both *ananda* and *moksha* at the same time. What else do you expect ?"

(*MS : Kshatriya* : 47 Years)

"Since, musicians are carefree people it is quite natural for them to opt for Kashi as their permanent place of residence. The atmosphere here is ideal for music-making."

(*JK : Muslim* : 61 Years)

## Conclusion

From the foregoing description of the musicians of Kashi the following conclusions can be drawn :

1. The musicians of Kashi pursue music as a *purusartha*. It fulfils their needs of *dharma, artha, kama* and *moksha*.

2. The musicians of Kashi carry the imprint of the traditional city, a *tirtha*, in so far as they uphold the traditional theory of music as a divine art.

3. The musicians of Kashi have tuned their life-style to the "Forest of Bliss" (*anandavana*), which this sacred city is. In their life-style they follow 'Banarasi' culture which is characterized by *mauj, masti* and *phakkarpan*—the earthly expressions of the spiritual bliss. However, in their performance of music they continue to strive for the realization of the "Ultimate Aesthetic Experience", that is *parmananda* or *moksha*.

## REFERENCES

1. Kedarnath Sharma, *Varanasi mein sangitagyon evam sangit rasikon ke parasparik sambandhon ke parivartanshil swarup.* Unpublished Ph.D. thesis, Sociology Department, Kashi Vidyapith, Varanasi, 1982, p. 48.
2. *Ibid.*, p. 48-49.
3. *Ibid* , p. 49.
4. *Ibid.*, p. 49.
5. *Ibid.*, p. 49-50.
6. *Ibid.*, p. 50.
7. Pandharinath H. Prabhu, Hindu Social Organization. Popular Prakashan, Bombay, 1963, p. 79.
8. Mahakarna, 69, 57.
9. Cited in Sudhir Kakar, *The Inner World,* Oxford University Press, New Delhi, 1978.
10. Man, II, 224.

## NOTES

Bose, N.K., The Hindu mode of tribal absorption, *Science and Culture,* Vol. VII, 188-194, 1941.

Brihaspati, A., *Musalman aur Bhartiya Sangit,* New Delhi, Rajkamal Prakashan, 1982.

Coomaraswamy, A.K., *The Dance of Shiva,* Calcutta, Asia Publishing House, 1948.

Eck, D., *Banaras : City of Light,* Princeton, University of Princeton, 1982.

Kumar, N., *Popular Culture in Urban India : The Artisans of Banaras, 1884-1984.* Unpublished Ph.D. thesis, The University of Chicago, Chicago, 1984.

Prajnananda, S., *Historical Development of Indian Music : A Critical Study*, K.L. Mukhopadhyaya, Calcutta, 1973.

Ranade, A.D., *On Music and Musicians of Hindustan*, New Delhi, Promilla and Company, 1984.

Ratanjankar, S.N., Individual notes and specific rasas. In *Aspects of Indian Music*, Delhi, Publication Division, Government of India, 1957.

Saraswati, B.N., *Kashi : Myth and Reality of a Classical Cultural Traditional*, Simla, Indian Institute of Advanced Studies, 1967.

Saraswati. B.N., Anthropological approach to the study of religions. In Surjit Sinha (Ed.), *Anthropology in India*, Vol. I, Cultural Anthropology, Calcutta, Anthropological Society of India, 1975.

Sinha, S., Vaishnava influence on a tribal culture. In Milton Singer (Ed.), *Krishna : Myths, Rites and Attitudes*, Honolulu, East-West Center Press, 1966.

Vidyarthi, L.P., *The Sacred Complex in Hindu Gaya*, Bombay, Asia Publishing House, 1961.

# 8

# History and Patronage of Tirumala-Tirupati Devasthanams

## An Anthropological Study of the Temples of Tirumala and Tirupati

V. NARAYANA REDDY & A. MUNIRATHNAM REDDY

## Introduction

THIS chapter examines the sources, kinds, scale, causes and results of the patronage that was provided to the temples of Tirumala and Tirupati (Tirumala-Tirupati Devasthanams or T.T.D.) in the Chittoor District of Andhra Pradesh over a period of about one thousand years between the tenth century and the present times. The findings illustrate the use of patronage in relation to the dynamics of the sacred complex of Tirumala and Tirupati.

The relevant data are collected from a number of sources namely the epigraphical reports (Subrahmanya Sastry : 1930) and history texts (Krishnaswami Ayyangar : 1952; Veeraraghavacharya, 1953, 1960, 1962; Ramesan : 1981; Subrahmanya Sastry : 1981) which embody almost a full account of when, how and for what reasons the temples of Tirumala and Tirupati were patronised by devotees with different socio-economic status and from different places of South India at different periods of history.

## Data and Results

Historical data going back over one thousand years reveals that the roots of patronage to the temples of Tirumala and Tirupati go back to the Pallava Dynasty (up to 900 A.D.) and that the extent of patronage steadily increase from the period of Chola Dynasty (900—1230 A.D.) to the period of Pandya Dynasty (1230—1360 A.D.) and it rises by leaps and bounds during the Vijayanagar Period (1360—1670 A.D.) but declines slowly from the Muslim Period (1670—1800 A.D.) to the British Period (1801—1947 A.D.) and steadily increasing during the post-Independence period (from 1947 A.D. on).

## Patronage during the Pallava Period

The historical data shows that during the Pallava Period there was only the temple of Tirumala and that Tirupati was non-existent. Only 6 people patronized the temple of Tirumala. Among the 6 patrons, one was a Pallava Queen, 3 were the vassals of the Pallavas, one was a royal officer, and 1 a private devotee. The following description gives the details of their patronage.

The first to patronize the temple of Tirumala was the Pallava Queen namely Samavai. In 614 A.D. she consecrated a processional image of silver, the first replica of Lord Venkateswara, under the appellation of Manavalapperumal, embellished it from head to foot with gold jewellery and inaugurated an elaborate expensive annual festival (brahmotsavam) to be celebrated twice a year. Through an endowment of land she made arrangements for the maintenance of a perpetually burning lamp before the silver image, and for providing fixed food-offerings for the silver image, and for the celebration of the newly inaugurated festival in honour of the silver image at the temple of Tirumala.[1]

The second and third to patronize the sacred complex of Tirumala were Ulagapperumanar, and Siyakan, the royal officers of some status during the regime of Ko-Vijaya-Danti-vikrama-Varman of the Pallava Dynasty. Ulagapperumanar (830 A.D.) gifted some quantity of gold (30 or 40 kalanjus) but Siyakan (833 A.D.) paid some money (*sem pon*) for the purpose of instituting the service of burning a lamp everyday before a processional image of silver, a second replica of Lord Venkateswara, newly installed in the temple at Tirumala.[2]

The vassals of the Pallava suzerains namely the Banas, the

Gangas and some local chiefs and princely families also evinced interest in the patronization of the temple at Tirumala. Among the Banas, Vijayaditiya (about 834 A.D.) deposited some quantity of gold (kalanju) and with it some lands were purchased and entrusted to cultivators to raise crops on the lands, and the temple officers were authorised to collect the rice from them and provide two food-offerings daily to the three different images of the Lord Venkateswara at Tirumala.[3]

Among the Gangas, Siyagangan (about 834 A.D.) made arrangements for the burning of a perpetual lamp in the temple of Tirumala. Another Ganga King by name Ranasingan (about 840 A.D.) made provision for an offering of food daily from the interest on the gold deposited by him.[4]

Apart from the Banas and the Gangas there were some local chiefs who were subordinate to the Pallava kings. One such subordinate was Tirungolakkon. Through a deposit of some weight of gold, he (about 896 A.D.) arranged for feeding two Brahmins daily for all time to come.[5]

One devotee whose name is not known made a provision for the utilization of the Tirumala temple of the income derived from the administration of a village.[6]

The data pertaining to the patronage of the sacred complex of Tirumala during the Pallava Period reveal several facts. First, there was only the temple of Tirumala during the Pallava Period and Tirupati did not exist at that time. Therefore, the Tirumala temple alone could have patronage from different devotees in those days. Secondly, through the patronage of affluent royal devotees, provision was made for fulfilling the prime requisites of the Tirumala temple, viz., two processional silver images representing the stationary idol of Lord Venkateswara, daily lamp-lighting and simple daily food-offerings; embellishment of the deity by means of gold jewellery and elaboration of the original annual festival. The prime requisites when a Deity is installed are lights in his presence to make Him visible to the worshippers and offerings of food, and flowers for His worship and celebration of festivals in His honour. All these basic requirements of the temple at Tirumala were fulfilled through patronage of royal families and royal office.[7]

The Pallavas were Brahmins. They supported both the

Vishnu and Siva temples. They also built several temples of
Siva and Vishnu in different parts of South India.

## Patronage during the Chola Period

Unlike the Pallavas, the Cholas were staunch supporters of
Siva temples. Nonetheless, they did not ignore patronization of
some of the Vishnu temples in their kingdom

In the Chola Period only 6 people patronized the temples of
Tirumala and Tirupati. Out of these, 2 were the queens of the
Chola emperors, one was an officer and 3 were private
individuals. The following account provides the details of the
patronage of all these 6 patrons.[8]

Among the Chola kings, none made any endowment to the
temple of Tirumala. But two of their queens made contributions to the temple of Tirumala. Parantakadevi-amman (1001
A.D.), the Chief Queen of Parantaka Chola II, presented to
Lord Venkateswara an ornament (*pattam*) of gold (52 *kalanjus*)
embedded with 6 rubies, 4 diamonds and 28 pearls. At about
the same time (1001 A.D.), Ulagamadevi, the queen consort of
Rajaraja Chola I, gifted 29 cows to the temple for supplying
ghee for a permanent lamp arranged in front of Lord Venkateswara at Tirumala.[9] While the first gift of jewellery to the
second silver image of the Lord was made by the Pallava Queen
Samanai in 966 A.D., the first gift of an ornament to the
stationary idol of the Lord was made by the Chola Queen of
Parantakadevi-amman in 1001 A.D. Likewise, the first gift of
cows to the temple of Tirumala was made by Ulagamadevi, the
queen consort of Rajaraja Chola I in about 1001 A.D.

One of the officers of the Cholas was Rayan Rajendra
Solan, the head of the village Kottur located at the foot of the
Tirumala Hills. This Kottur was formed towards the end of the
10th century A.D. In 1044, Rayan Rajendra Solan built the
Siva temple of Kapileswara, the same shrine as the present one
at Tirupati.[10]

Among the private devotees who patronized the temple of
Tirumala, Kodungoluran (936 A.D.) and Arulakki (1016 A.D.)
each deposited some quantity of gold (40 *kalanjus*) for arranging a perpetual lamp to Lord Venkateswara at Tirumala. Similarly another devotee (927 A.D.) whose name is not traceable
arranged a perpetual lamp in honour of Lord Venkateswara.[11]

During the Chola times another kind of patronage was offered to the temples of Tirumala and Tirupati. In a woody place like Tirumala wild flowers might have grown but they might not have been the proper ones useful for worship. Hence some devotees like Tirumala Nambi and Anantalvar chose to plant flower-garden (*nandanavanams*) at Tirumala and supply the flowers from them to the temple for daily worship of the deities and for special occasions and festivals.[12]

Almost 86 years later in 1130 A.D. Sri Ramanuja, the preceptor of Sri-Vaishnavas, obtained the patronage of several royal families and got the temple of Lord Govindaraja built at a place south to Kottur village. Following the instructions of Sri Ramanuja, the inhabitants of Kottur abandoned Kottur and moved to the sites available around the temple of Lord Govindaraja. As such a new settlement sprang up around the temple of Lord Govindaraja. This was designated as Tirupati.[13]

Further, Sri Ramanuja established several religious orders as the temples of Tirumala and Tirupati and also throughout South India for the propagation of Sri-Vaishnavism, for securing patronage in the form of permanent endowments for the temples, and for attracting numerous pilgrims to Tirumala and Tirupati. As a result, many affluent disciples of the religious orders made numerous permanent endowments of lands, villages, gold, gardens, and money to the temples and sacred specialists at Tirumala and Tirupati and thousands of pilgrims from different parts of South India converged at Tirumala and Tirupati and made gifts and offerings to the deities at Tirumala and Tirupati and the sacred specialists serving the temples of Tirumala and Tirupati also could earn more for their services.[14]

The data related to the patronage of the temples of Tirumala and Tirupati during the Chola Period brings to light several interesting points. First, the patronage of the sovereigns, the royal officers and the opulent devotees, the disciples of the religious orders and the thousands of pilgrims was far more substantial during the Chola Period than the patronage of the kings and their vassals besides some devotees during the Pallava period. Secondly, certain religious orders innovated during the Chola Period could become powerful agencies for securing permanent endowments for the temples and for attracting a large concourse of pilgrims everyday. Thirdly, the

primary necessities of lighting, flowers for worship and food-
offerings to the deities were still inadequate. As the means for
providing these primary requirements were insufficient, the
patrons made adequate provisions through endowments of
lands, villages, gold and money. For the first time in the history of the temples a new procedure was adopted in making
endowments. Instead of depositing gold, cows were gifted
because the ghee derived from them could be used for burning
a lamp in front of Lord Venkateswara. Again for the first time
in the history of temples, the service of supplying flowers to
the temples was made by raising flower gardens (*nandavanams*)
at Tirumala and Tirupati, Fourthly, jewellery and ornaments
were gifted to the deities to confer grace and beauty on them.
No new festivals were instituted in honour of the deities at
Tirumala and Tirupati. Fifthly, under the patronage of several
royal families the sacred complex along with the settlement of
Tirupati were formed. Finally, there was a rise in the pilgrim
influx and the sacred specialists earned more for rendering
their services to the temples of Tirumala and Tirupati.

### Patronage during the Pandya Period

After the fall of Cholas, the Pandyas came to power by the
beginning of the second quarter of the 13th century A.D. The
Kadava Rayas and the Yadava Rayas ruling the areas including
Tirumala and Tirupati, the Telugu-Cholas ruling the areas to
the south of Tirumala and Tirupati, and the Telugu-Pallavas
ruling the areas east and north-east to Tirumala and Tirupati
were the feudatories of the Pandyas. The Pandyas as well as
their psudatories save the Kadava Rayas patronized the
temples of Tirumala and Tirupati.

During the Pandya times, altogether 38 people patronized
the temples of Tirumala and Tirupati. Of these, one was a
Pandyan emperor, 7 were the vassals of the Pandyan kings, one
was a queen of one of the vassals of the Pandyan kings, 4 were
royal officers such as military commanders, palace official and
so on, 2 were officers of the non-Pandyan kings, one was a temple
functionary and 2 were private devotees of whom 20 were individuals, one was a political council and one was a group of
weavers. Among these at least 2 were Brahmins (priests), about
18 were Kshatriyas (warriors), 2 were Vaisyas or Komatis

(merchants), some were Salis (weavers) and the remaining 16 belonged to different castes. The following description gives the details of the actual patronage of all these 38 people to the temples of Tirumala and Tirupati.[15]

Of the many Pandyan emperors, only one by name Sundara Pandya Deva I (1216 A.D.) patronized the temple of Tirumala. He presented a gold vase (*kalasam*) to be placed over the sanctum tower or dome (*vimana*) of the temple of Tirumala, deposited some gold in the temple treasury for arranging a perpetual lamp in the temple of Tirumala and renewed and confirmed some old grants of villages made to the temple of Tirumala.[16]

The Yadava Rayas patronized the temple of Tirumala to a great extent. One of them was Tirukkalattideva Yadavaraya (1209 A.D.) who granted a village to the temple of Tirumala. The income from the village was meant for meeting the expenses towards the daily offerings and festivals.[17]

On the other hand, Virarakshasa Yadavaraya granted some land on the stipulation that the income derived from it should be used for making special food-offerings to the Lord at Tirumala. His successor was Vira Narasingadeva Yadavaraya. First (about 1240 A.D.), he got installed the image of Vira-Narasinga-Perumal, after his own name, somewhere in Tirupati. Secondly, (about 1225 A.D.) through one of his chiefs, he got the central shrine of Tirumala repaired. Thirdly (1263 A.D.), he weighed himself in scales against gold and presented that gold to the temple of Tirumala for gilding its sanctum tower (*vimanam*) and other structures. Fourthly, he instituted a new festival (*kodal tirunal* or *adi tirunal*) in honour of Lord Venkateswara. Fifthly, he made certain new grants and held enquiries pertaining to the progress of an old grant and passed decrees.[18]

Vira Narasingadeva Yadavaraya's queen Yadavaraya Nach-chiyar (1217 A.D.) presented 64 cows and one bull for supplying ghee for two lamps set up in the presence of Lord Venkates-wara at Tirumala and 32 big cows and one bull for supplying ghee for one lamp set up in the temple of Lord Govindaraja at Tirupati. She also instituted a new festival (*ani brahmotsavam*) for Lord Govindaraja, constructed a four-faced car and granted half of a village to meet the expenses of this festival, and for effecting repairs to the temple from the balance, if any.[19]

Tiruvenkatanatha Yadavaraya (about 1330 A.D.) granted half of a village to the temple of Tirumala to serve the expenses of celebrating a festival and conducting certain food-offerings. He (about 1333 A.D.) also converted Tirupati village besides another village as tax-free villages (*arvamanyam*) to the temple of Tirumala for propitiating the Lord daily with special food-offerings to the Lord at Tirumala. He also stipulated that the managers of the Tirumala temple should utilize any balance, left after meeting certain specific charges from the endowments concerned, for the institution of a water-shed (*tannir pandal*), a flower-garden (*nandavanam*), a free feeding house (*ramanuja-kootam*) and other acts of charity at Tirumala.[20]

The successor of Tiruvenkatanatha Yadavaraya was Sriran-ganadha Yadavaraya. He (1339 A.D) got the fields (which were donated certain to Ramanuja) situated at the north side of the big tank (*peri-eri*) in Tirupati repaired and rendered them worthy of irrigation. For allowing the transmission of water from the big tank to these lands, he paid a free (200 *panams*) to Lord Venkateswara because the village of Tirupati including the big tank belonged to Lord Venkateswara.[21]

On the whole, the Yadava Rayas endowed the temples of Tirumala with half a dozen villages including Tirupati, several acres of farm land, 96 cows and 2 bulls and not less than eighty kilogrammes of gold. They instituted a few new festivals, built a water-shed and free-feeding house for pilgrims, maintained a flower garden, repaired farm land, renovated some temple structures, and installed some idols of deities.

Among the Telugu-Cholas, only one by name Tikka or Gandagopala patronized the temple of Tirumala but none of the temples at Tirupati. He (1255 A.D.) gifted lands in one village to the temple of Tirumala.[22]

Among the Telugu-Cholas, the Telugu-Pallavas patronized temples of Tirumala and Tirupati to a lesser extent. Princess Devarasiyar, the queen of Vijaya Gandagopala, made (about 250 A.D.) a gift of 33 cows for setting up three lamps in the temple of Tirumala.[23]

Apart from the kings, queens and vassals some royal officers also patronized the temples of Tirumala and Tirupati. Ammaiappan (about 1250 A.D.), an officer serving the palace of Vijaya Gandagopala, gifted 33 cows and one bull and one lamp-stand for keeping a permanent light in the presence of Venkateswara from the ghee derived from the milk of the cows.[24]

Peria-Peruna-Nayakkar, the great commander under Sriranganatha Yadavaraya gifted (about 1360 A.D.) 32 cows and one bull on the condition that the ghee derived from the cow-milk should be used for burning a perpetual lamp in front of the Lord at Tirumala. His younger brother, also a military officer, made (1361 A.D.) a similar gift to Lord Venkateswara. Hobala Yadava, an officer under the Yadava Rayas, presented a gold covering for the hand (*varada hasta*) of Lord Venkateswara at Tirumala.[25]

There were some officers who were serving the rulers in the Karnataka country and the northern Andhra. They made contributions to the temple of Tirumala. One Brahmasetti, a minister of Kakatiya Ganapati ruling the northern parts of Andhra Pradesh, donated ( 285-1290 A.D.) a certain charity to the temple of Tirumala. Singaya-Dandanayaka entitled Sitakaragandan, a military commandant of Vira Kampana, the Hoyasaka king in Karnataka country, not only made available some endowments to but also contributed much to the services of the temple of Tirumala.[26]

Several private devotees also patronized the temples of Tirumala and Tirupati. The Peria-Nattuvar (1235 A.D.), members of the council of a particular group of villages, enshrined Tirumangaialvar in the compound of Govindaraja's temple at Tirupati and endowed a village stipulating that the income derived from the village should be used for worship and food-offering to Tirumangaialvar. One Amarakon, a merchant, gifted 33 cows, one bull and one lampstand for maintaining a perpetual light in front of Lord Venkateswara from the ghee derived from the milk of the cows.[27]

One devotee (about 1254 A.D.) deposited money (450 *panams*) for some food-offerings to Lord Venkateswara. A group of devotees who belonged to the weaver caste (sali) made several gifts to Venkateswara. First, they deposited a good sum of money (450 *panams*) for arranging a food-offering for Venkateswara. Secondly, they made a provision for arranging a light for Venkateswara for all time. Thirdly, they deposited some money (3 *madai*) as the capital for making a food-offring to the processional image of Lord Venkateswara. Different from these devotees, there was a devotee (about 1270 A.D.) who made some endowments for arranging a food-offering at the time of specific festivals in honour of Lord Venkateswara. Another devotee constructed a portico in a flower garden (*pu-mantapam*) at Tirumala and deposited some cash (3 *madai*) as capital for offering specific food when the processional image of Venkateswara visited that portico during some festival. Some devotee (1248 A.D.) made some provision for making food-offering at the shrine of Ramanuja at Tirumala. Vanaduttakaiyalagiyar alias Pallavarayan (1285-1290 A.D.) constructed the temple of Nammalvar near Kapilatirtham at Tirupati. A different devotee (1308 A.D.) made a provision for food-offerings and special worship for Lord Govindaraja at Tirupati on certain holy days of observance as per the Hindu calendar. One Tevapperumal (about 1330 A.D.) presented some cows and a bull for keeping a perpetual light in front of Lord Venkateswara. Taluvakkula alias Pallavarayan (1356 A.D.) deposited some cash (400 *panams*) as the capital on the interest of which the processional image of Venkateswara should be propitiated with offering at a particular porch (*chediyaraya mantapam*).[28]

There were several other private devotees who patronized the temples of Tirumala and Tirupati. One devotee gifted 6 lampstands to the temple of Tirumala. Another devotee gifted cows for offering milk to Lord Venkateswara each day at Tirumala. A third devotee presented some cows and a bull (about the value of 310 *panams*) for providing perpetual light for Lord Venkateswara. A different devotee made provision for keeping four lights burning before Venkateswara. Some other devotee also made some provision for similar purpose at the temple of Venkateswara. One devotee provided two lampstands and two lamps for the Lord of Tirumala. Another devotee gifted 32 cows and a bull and a lampstand for a light to the temple of Tirumala. Still another devotee made provision for food-offerings through a deposit of gold (400 *panams*) and through a gift of land (2000 *kulis*). Some donors paid some gold (40 *kalamju*) to the temple of the Lord for seeking the protection of the Sri-Vaishnavas. One devotee deposited gold and from the interest accrued on it he requested the temple to supply food-offerings everyday to the Lord of Tirumala. Another devotee provided for offerings of food for Lord Venkateswara 80 measures (10 *tumbu*) of rice and ingredients of ghee, vegetables, pulses, salt and curd and arecanuts, betel leaves, sandal paste, and oil for the lamp. A certain Kamavilli excavated a small tank near Alipiri at Tirupati.[29]

One temple functionary by name Anandavalan Venkata-thuraivar, who was an Acharya Purusha (religious teacher) at the temple of Tirumala excavated a fresh tank at Tirumala, made a charity of propitiation with food-offerings and decoration with flower-garlands and sandal-paste of Ramanuja's idol in the Lord's temple at Tirumala. He also maintained a flower-garden at Tirumala.[30]

In the 13th century A.D., the temples of Tirumala and Tirupati came to have qualified accountants (*tirunindrau-udaiyan*). They maintained an account of the temple properties and preserved the various documents related to the temple.[31]

The Sri-Vaishnava Brahmins connected with the temples of Tirumala and Tirupati established separate cadres meant for carrying on their evangelical activities amongst the people of South India. Their activities influenced the kings, chiefs, rich persons and common people to become the devotees of the deities at Tirumala and Tirupati. Simultaneously, they also benefited by procuring numerous gifts of villages, gold and money from their affluent devotees. The ruler and the ruled looked to the deity at Tirumala as a problem-solving supreme deity. The patronage was thus forthcoming from all classes of people from all over South India.[32]

The data related to the patronage of the temples of Tirumala and Tirupati during the Pandya Period shows how the patronage was almost adequate to meet the needs of the sacred complex of Tirumala and Tirupati. Firstly, apart from the royal benefactors, there were benefactors like the inhabitants of a village. Secondly, the patrons made ampler provision for lamp-lighting and food-offerings. The instances of provision of light at the Tirumala temple alone were about 40 in number. Thirdly, the patrons presented cows and bulls in large numbers in place of the then prevailing practice of paying a standard quantity of gold (40 *kalanju*) or money usually for lamp-

lighting. Fourthly, two new festivals were instituted in honour
of the Lord at Tirumala. Fifthly, provisions were made also
for offerings of food to the deities through gifts of several
villages. Several endowments were given to the sacred specialists. There was a rise in the pilgrim influx and to meet the
needs of the large concourse of pilgrims, free-feeding houses
and watersheds were provided by various classes of patrons.
Sixthly, as the primary necessities of lamp-lighting, food-
offering, and flowers for worship could be met adequately, the
patrons made every effort to embellish the deities and temple
structures. A golden vase was fixed on the sanctum dome at
Tirumala. Likewise the sanctum tower of Tirumala was
covered by gold gilded copper plates. The front right hand
(*varada hasta*) of Lord Venkateswara was covered by a gold
covering. Finally, till the thirteenth century, most of the
patrons of the temples of Tirumala and Tirupati were from the
extreme southern part of South India, save for a few from the
west coast. The first patron from the western area of South
India was a military officer serving the Hoyasala kings of
Karnataka country.

**Patronage during the Vijayanagar Period**

After the Pandayas, the Vijayanagar kings ruled South India
for more than 300 years almost between 1360 A.D. and 1670
A.D. During the Vijayanagar Period about 200 people patronized the temples of Tirumala and Tirupati. Of these 200
people, 16 were from royal families, 81 were military and
revenue officers, 31 were minor officers, 8 were religious
teachers, 33 were temple officers and the remaining 31 were
common citizens. Again, of these different classes of people 43
were Brahmins (priests), 138 were Kshatriyas (warriors), 3
were Vaisyas or Komatis (merchants), 3 were Reddis (agricul-
turists), 2 were Bhogams (temple dancers), and the remaining
18 belonged to different castes.

Among the 16 patrons from the royal families, 13 were
kings and 3 were queens. Out of the 16 kings, Bukka-I (about
1340 A.D.) endowed a village to the temple of Tirumala for
arranging food-offerings twice a day in his own name. Saluva
Mangideva (1359 A.D.) rendered his services to the temple of
Tirumala through old gilding of its dome (vimana) and through

the fixing of a gold vase (*kalasa*) over its dome. Harihara-II (1387 A.D.) instituted a new festival (*masi-tirunal*) for Venkateswara in his name by an endowment of annual income obtained from a village granted for this purpose. Devaraya-II (1429 A.D.) granted three villages and a gift of money (1200 *pan*) for certain daily offerings. Four years later (1433 A.D.) he granted half the share of farm produce obtained from a village to feed 24 Brahmins engaged for the recitation of holy texts (Vedas) at the temple of Tirumala. This endowment was made because it was felt that while Lord Venkateswara had all other attributes of greatness, the chanting of the holy texts was the one item wanting.[33]

Among the Vijayanagar kings, Saluva Narasimha, and his three sons besides his mother (1473 A.D.) granted a village to the temple of Venkateswara for the conduct of swinging festival (*dolamahotsavam*) started by him earlier together with certain food-offerings to be made to the Lord in the name of his mother. Several festivals came to be resuscitated in the temple of Tirumala during the region of Saluva Narasimha and his descendant Immadi Narasimha.[34]

King Vira-Narasimha (1510 A.D.) made nine kinds of extraordinary gifts (nava-vidhabahula mahadana) to several Vishnu temples including that of Tirumala.[35] During the reign of Krishnadevaraya and Achyutaraya, the temples of Tirumala and Tirupati received several endowments. Between 1513 A.D. and 1521 Krishnadevaraya made several gifts of gold, precious stones, diamonds, ornaments, silver plates, swords studded with many kinds of precious stones, gold strings, thirty thousand gold coins, a gold necklace embedded with red stones, emeralds, sapphires, cat's eyes, agates, topazes, old diamonds, pearls, corals, and others weighing about 31124 units, special silk clothes set with nine kinds of precious stones, head dress set with pearls, emeralds, and sapphires, fly whisks set with nine kinds of gems, several other jewels, hundreds and thousands of gold coins, and an endowment of three villages for the celebration of a festival (*brahmotsavam*) in the name of his mother at the temple of Tirumala.[36] He (1518 A.D.) gilded the sanctum tower of the temple of Tirumala with gold and granted some land to the Lord of Tirumala for the prosperity of his son. Again he (1524 A.D.) stipulated that the sacred specialist of Vyasatirtha be issued a part of his share of holy food from the temple of Tirumala which he was obtaining through an endowment of six and half villages to Lord Venkateswara.[37]

The successor of Krishnadevaraya was Achyutaraya. Over a period of eight years between 1533 A.D. and 1541 A.D. he made a number of gifts and had given many royal endowments to the temple of Tirumala and had given royal endowments. He presented several jewels and silk ornaments fully decked with pearls, rubies, emeralds and diamonds and many long strings of pearls of Lord Venkateswara, instituted two new festivals in honour of Lord Venkateswara at Tirumala and Lord Rama at Tirupati, constructed several pavilions (*manta-pams*), constructed tanks and buildings, laid gardens, established free feeding houses, and provided certain charities and services in the name of himself, his wife, son and parents at Tirumala and Tirupati. He endowed the temples at Tirumala and Tirupati with several villages. He granted ten villages to the descendant of a great musician-cum-poet and another two villages to the dancers at the temple of Govindaraja at Tirupati.[38]

Sadasivaraya (1553 A.D.) made magnificent charities for the free feeding houses at Tirupati, gifted some villages to some religious teachers to enable them to offer holy foods on certain occasions to Lord Venkateswara.[39]

Tirumalaraya was the successor of Sadasivaraya. He (1561 A.D.) constructed a pavilion after his name at the temple of Tirumala. Next, Venkatapatiraya (about 1640 A.D.) installed copper statues of his and his two queens besides some stone statues in the temple of Tirumala. Kumara Venkatapatiraya-II constructed a pavilion in a street opposite to the temple of Govindaraja.[40]

Some of the queens also were patrons of the temples of Tirumala and Tirupati. Queen Chinnajidevi and Queen Tirumaladevi, wives of Krishnadevaraya, presented (1513 A.D.) one gold cup each for offering milk at the night service to the Lord of Tirumala. Each one of them (1514 A.D.) also gifted an ornament to the Lord. Queen Chinnajidevi granted a village as an endowment for daily offering to the Lord. Varadajidevi, Queen of Achyutaraya, presented (1534 A.D.)

gold ornaments and endowed six villages to the Lord of Tirumala.[41-42]

As mentioned before, not merely the sovereigns and some of their queens but also their officers besides temple functionaries and private citizens, all numbering 184, patronized the temples of Tirumala and Tirupati. Among them 112 were officers under the kings. Of these, 2 were viceroys, 6 were ministers, 6 were commanders, 3 were military generals, 22 were royal officers and the remaining 73 were subordinate and tributary officers. of the 33 temple officers, 6 were temple managers (jiyyars), 8 were religious teachers (*acharyapurushas*), 7 were priests (*nambimars*), 3 were poet-musician (*sankirtanacharyas*), 3 were scholars, 2 were dancers (*tiruveedhisanis*), 2 were accountants, and 2 were musicians. Among the remaining 39 patrons 8 were spiritual teachers, and 31 were common citizens of whon 7 were merchants of Tirupati and the other 24 were private devotees.

Out of these 184 patrons of various categories, 33 instituted (1360-1551 A.D.) about 40 new festivals in honour of Venkateswara and Govindaraja, Rama and other deities. To meet the expenditure incurred on the celebration of these festivals they offered their gifts to the deities and made endowments to the temples at Tirumala and Tirupati.[43]

More than 33 of them gifted (1450-1543 A.D.) money in the form of gold coins (*panams*) to the deities to carry on certain services such as lamp-lighting and offerings to the deities at Tirumala and Tirupati. For offering certain special services at Tirumala and Tirupati 6 patrons donated one village each to the Lord, 2 gifted 3 villages each to the Lord, 1 gifted 4 villages to the Lord, 1 granted 5 villages to the Lord, 1 presented 50 villages to the Lord and many others donated either part or a hamlet to the deities of Tirumala and Tirupati. Four of them had even presented cows and bulls to the temples for providing ghee to the lamps arranged in their names.[44]

Almost 28 of the different classes of patrons constructed different shrines in Tirumala and Tirupati between 1407 A.D. and 1561 A.D. One of them instituted special holy bath to the deities at Tirumala and Tirupati by using perfumery such as civet oil, musk, refined camphor and so on. Two more donors deposited some capital of gold to continue this practice. Matla

Kumara Anantaraya presented two sets of golden elephant and horse vehicle to the temple of Venkateswara and Govindaraja. He also constructed the flight of stonesteps forming the pathway commencing from the foot of the hill and extending up to the summit of the front hill. Several officers, temple functionaries and private devotees arranged about 10 water-sheds (*tannir-pandals*), and 7 feeding houses (*ramanujakootams*) at Tirupati and Tirumala for the sake of pilgrims. Some devotees raised more than a dozen flower gardens at Tirumala and Tirupati for the supply of flowers to different divinities.[45]

The data shows that there were about 211 villages endowed to the temples of Tirumala and Tirupati of which 57 were given by kings and queens, 37 viceroys, ministers, generals, and other state officers, 64 by the sacred specialists such as temple managers, religious teachers, scholars, musician-poets, temple dancers, acolytes, accountants, and others and 53 were donated by citizens and merchants of Tirupati and other private devotees.[46]

Further, the money endowments made by all classes of patrons were also huge. The figures computed reveal that the the kings and queens gifted about 4,00,000 gold coins (*panams*), the viceroys, ministers, generals and other state officers contributed almost 3,37,000 gold coins (*panams*), the temple functionaries like the managers, religious teachers, poet-musicians, temple dancers and others donated about 2,05,070 gold coins (*panams*) and the private devotees granted 22,400 gold coins (*panams*) to the temples of Tirumala and Tirupati.[47-49]

The primary purpose of a land endowment or money endowment was to provide a perpetual income for a ritual service at the temples of Tirumala and Tirupati. All the villages granted by the kings, queens and state officers to the temples were crown villages. The villages granted by the temple functionaries were originally the donations made by the state officers and tributary chiefs. As such almost 90 per cent of the villages were crown villages and villages held on service tenure. And the remaining 10 per cent of the villages were peasant proprietary villages and they were from the private devotees. As per the custom, the income of the village under crown or service tenure was divided into major share and minor share. The major share was given to the state or the possessor, and the

minor share was retained by the cultivator. The same pattern
of division of village income was continued when the village
became a temple village. However, when the villages became
temple villages, they became the places for the investment of
monetary endowments by the temple trustees. The temple invested its capital endowments on the irrigation development of
its villages. In this context it improved the tanks and irrigation channels. This investment yielded a high monetary return
for doing a specific service intended by the donor to the Lord.
Thus the temple could mobilize adequate resources from its
villages and carry on its various ritual functions quite
successfully.[50]

The data shows that the temple functionaries also had
endowed good sums of money and a large number of villages
to the temples of Tirumala and Tirupati. It looks strange that
the temple functionaries who should really be receiving endowments would themselves endow as much as 64 of the 211 village
endowments to the Lord. There are economic and religious
reasons. The religious reason is to earn merit. But the economic reason is to earn profit. For the temple functionaries their
share of the holy food (*prasadam*) was their primary source of
livelihood. The greater the supply of holy food to the deities,
the greater was their income. As per custom a person who
made an endowment was entitled to one-fourth of the share of
the holy food and the other three-fourths of the total holy food
accrued to the temple as its share of income. When the temple
functionary had seen that the share of the holy food to the
person making an endowment was one-fourth of the total, he
too tried to make an endowment to the temple and received
one-fourth of the total holy food. Since sacred food was largely
in demand from devotees and pilgrims that thronged the temple,
the disposal of the one-fourth of total holy food he received as
his share on account of his endowment, was easy and it contributed a sizeable revenue income to him. This was a good
incentive to the temple functionary to invest his surplus income
as an endowment to the Lord, since the monetary conversion of
his one-fourth share of the holy food gave him enough monetary
return on the capital which he invested as an endowment. In
other words, an endowment to the Lord was a capital investment, and the holy food return was sold for cash, which was

enough of an annual return for the capital sunk by them, to motivate them to making greater and greater endowments. Thus, the endowments by the temple functionaries were in effect an investment which gave them a large return. This investment sunk in irrigation works by the temple increased the prosperity of the cultivators to the extent of their share, increased the income to the temple leading to greater celebration, which, by the expenditure involved gave rise to further economic prosperity and in addition acted as a large investment to the temple functionaries. This cycle was a self-sustaining and self-improving financial cycle since mere income meant more investment which gave more income and so in addition to improving the standard of living of the cultivators.[51]

For the above reasons processions, levies, and food offerings multiplied in numbers. New kinds of festivals were instituted. So much so at the close of the Vijayanagar Period there were 429 festivals for 365 days of the year. Obviously on some days two or three festivals were celebrated. Worship was free to every pilgrim. No fee was ever demanded. The aim was to provide food and shelter free to all pilgrims.[52]

An examination of the data related to the patronage of Tirumala and Tirupati temples during the Vijayanagar period reveals how it had provided embellishments and grandeur to the temples and made the temples carve a place of primary in South India during the Middle Ages. Firstly, the patronage regarding food-offerings took precedence over that concerning lamp-lighting. In certain cases of patronage, presentation of cows was preferred to payment of gold, since, besides yielding ghee for the lamps, they served the additional purpose of offering the dairy product to the deities.[53] Secondly, the patronage discloses the growth in the types of food-offerings from the simple cooked rice, green gram, ghee and curds of the Pallava, Chola and Pandya Periods to the much more gluttonous types of foods in the Vijayanagar Period. Thirdly, for the first time arrangements for the daily recitation of the Vedas in the temples were made. Fourthly, as the patronage in the earlier periods could fulfil almost all the prime necessities of lighting, flowers for worship and food-offerings, the patronage during the Vijayanagar period focussed its attention on embellishments and grandeur of the deities, temples and rituals. Through

patronage by different classes of people, the deities could be
decked with plenty of jewellery and hundreds of ornaments, the
shrines could be enlarged by means of several apartments,
corridors, and compound walls, numerous festivals could be
instituted and celebrated, the number of sacred specialists could
be multiplied, many seminaries could be established, free-feeding houses and water-sheds could be arranged for the pilgrims,
several flower gardens could be planted for adequate supply of
flowers to the temples, and the processions of the deities and
vehicles could amply be decorated and attended by bulls,
horses, camels and elephants nicely caparisoned, and accompanied by the music of pipe, chantings of sacred verses and
dances of damsels.[54] All this symbolized the pomp and splendour of the emperors in the Middle Ages [55] Fifthly, unlike in
the preceding periods, the patrons to the temples in Vijayanagara
Period were several categories including the temple functionaries. The patronage included only the private benefactions state
patronage was non-existent. Five kings, two queens, and several
others made their benefactions more than once. Sixthly, the
noticeable feature of the patronage was that while the smaller
benefactions were of the ordinary character, the larger benefactions took on the character of investment of money being made
for irrigation and other facilities for the lands already under
cultivation or bringing uncultivated lands into cultivation, and
making the income therefore served the purpose of the benefactions. This served double purpose : the acquisition of the religious merit of a benefaction in Tirumala and Tirupati, and
making this benefaction serve at the same time the secular
useful purpose of benefiting those who lived upon the land by
providing them facilities, and really bringing more land under
cultivation. This would be immediately for their benefit, so
that what was intended for the spiritual merit of the individual
donor proved benefit not only to the gods or to the temples,
or to the sacred specialists dependent thereon, but also served
equally to benefit the other communities concerned.[56]

## Patronage during the Muslim Period

After the fall of Vijayanagar empire, there came the struggle
for the supremacy of the Muslim kings and the fortunes of the
Tirumala and Tirupati temples underwent a notable change. In

1636 A.D. the Tirupati region became part of Golconda country. But it was declared part of Moghul empire in 1656 A.D. Thereafter, the Golconda ruler reconquered it and ruled it till 1688. In the year 1681, Akkanna and Madanna, the two ministers of Golconda visited Tirumala and made an endowment for food-offerings to Venkateswara and Varahaswami at Tirumala.[57]

In 1688 A.D. Aurangzeb extinguished Golconda rulers. By that time the Maratha empire of Sivaji arose in Western India. Sivaji proclaimed himself king in 1674 A.D. In 1684, through his envoy by name Dabisa, he sent an endowment of a gold ornament (*kanti*) to the Lord of Tirumala.[58]

In 1713, the Tirupati region became part of the Carnatic country. Sadatullah was the ruler of Carnatic country. Todar Mull was his general who wielded the greatest influence with him. He did some real good to the temple of Tirumala. Therefore, the bronze statues of Todar Mull, his mother and his wife were installed in the temple of Tirumala. These can be seen even today.[59]

When Daud Khan became the Nawab of Carnatic in 1724 A.D., the Tirumala and Tirupati temples came under his sway. He assured no molestation of the temples provided the Tirumala temple paid him every year Rs. 2,00,000. For realising this amount and for earning some more for their services, the temple administrators and the sacred specialists of the temple had to devise a scheme according to which a levy was made on pilgrims who resorted to the temple. Before bathing in the waters of holy-waterfalls and the sacred tank, every pilgrim had, according to custom, to recite certain sacred verses which a Brahmin priest would do. This right to dictate the sacred verses was leased out and the lessee levied a fee per head. So was the case when a pilgrim wanted to have his head tonsured. When camphor had to be lighted a fee of one rupee was levied. For attending worship a fee of seven rupees was levied for every item of worship. When an ornament or cloth was presented to the deity for perpetual wear, an amount equal to the value of the article had to be paid. When a food-offering was made by a pilgrim, an amount equal in value to the offering had to be deposited in addition to the cost of the food-offering. To attract to a large number of sacred spots and thereby realize large fees from them the sacred specialists made several water pools and waterfalls on the hills of Tirumala as sacred ones and innovated appropriate legends extolling their sanctity.[60] Such a scheme benefited the ruler and the temple functionaries.

When things were going on in this way at Tirumala and Tirupati, struggle for political power was brewing up in the Carnatic country. In 1740 A.D., Raghoji Bhonsle of the Maratha empire invaded the Carnatic country. At this time Raghoji visited the temple of Tirumala and endowed the Lord with several costly jewels worth Rs. 1,50,000 which are still preserved in a separate box.[61] Simultaneously another Maratha ruler Baji Rao gave Rs. 20,000 as charities to the temple of Tirumala.[62]

**Patronage during the British Period**

In the course of Carnatic wars which commenced in 1744, portions of Carnatic country were given to the British. The turmoil in the Carnatic country had one of its results the assignment of the revenues of Tirumala and Tirupati temples to the British in 1748 A.D. By 1801 A.D., the whole of Carnatic country, including the Tirupati region, passed into the hands of the British. As a result, the British became not only the owners but also managers of the temples of Tirumala and Tirupati from July 1801 A.D. They themselves instituted several special charities at the temple of Tirumala. To this class belongs the "Munro Taligai" which continues to this day.[63]

There was other side of the picture. With the acquisition of the Carnatic country, the British became its owners and all the temple lands and villages along with the other lands and villages in the Carnatic territory became the property of the British. The British got the right to enjoy the produce from those lands and villages. After some investigation, the British regranted the villages to the temple functionaries but kept only one village in the possession of the temple of Tirumala but no village in the possession of the other temples at Tirupati. Thus by 1801 A.D., the temples lost their landed property, while their servants benefited through the regrant of the villages.[64]

Due to loss of their lands and villages and consequent loss of their income, the temples at Tirumala and Tirupati had to stop the numerous festivals and food-offerings provided by the donors. Especially, the Tirumala temple had to stop celebrating all its 429 festivals except 24 in honour of its Lord and stop offering the hundreds of daily food-offerings of different varieties provided by different classes of patrons in the previous centuries.[65]

The annual income of the temples, particularly, that of Tirumala temple, had fallen so low that the British Government had to contribute not less than Rs. 25,000 every year towards the expenditure on temple worship. This contribution was only less than 50 per cent of the actual expenditure incurred on the temple worship.[66] The only material relief to the temples was the pilgrim contributions made substantially in the form of jewellery, money and other materials to the different deities. Even then the net income started declining from the year 1833 A.D. When the temple income was about Rs. 1,00,000 in 1823-24, it was only about Rs. 60,000 in the year 1983-84.[67]

The British passed on the administration of the temples of Tirumala and Tirupati to the heads of seminaries known as Mahants in the year 1843 A.D. From 1843 A.D. to 1933 A.D. six generations of Mahants by discipleship exercised authority as administrators (*vicharanakartas*) of the Tirumala and Tirupati temples. By using the temple funds they prepared several varieties of jewels to the deities, repaired and renovated several temple structures, offered many facilities to the pilgrims, resuscitated a few festivals, made certain vehicles and cars meant for the processional deities, opened some educational institutions and so on. Their services to the temples were satisfactory. None of them spent personal properties towards the development of the temples. Their administration involved lot of litigation and there was colossal waste of temple funds to meet the expenses towards law courts.[68]

The only activity that helped the development of the administration of the Mahants was the investment of Rs. 5,00,000 from the temple funds in the Bombay Development Loan and the resultant annual interest of Rs. 54,500. Further, for the temple of Tirumala the Mahants purchased about 600 villages from the Zamindars of Kalahasti and Karvetinagar.[69]

The only patron who contributed to the temple of Tirumala during the administration of the Mahants was Rani Adilakshmi

Devammagaru, the Princess of Gadwal. In 1931 she presented certain old jewels and gold and silver coins amounting in all to Rs. 20,000 in value to make a diamond crown to the processional image of Lord Venkateswara.[70]

To improve the administration of the temples, the Tirumala-Tirupati Devasthanams (T.T.D.) Act of 1933 was passed. Accordingly the temples of Tirumala and Tirupati were managed by a Commissioner. The patronage of the temples of Tirumala and Tirupati was almost non-existent from 1931 to 1947, the year of Independence to India.

The data related to the patronage of the temples of Tirumala and Tirupati during the British period reveals several significant points. The British treated the temple lands and villages as their own. Hence the temples lost their property, lost their source of perpetual income, and they had to stop almost 95 per cent of their ritual programmes. The income from the pilgrim contributions besides the grants made by the Government sustained the core ritual activities of the temple. The contribution of the Government towards the total expenditure was less than 50 per cent of the actual expenditure. When the Mahants became the administrators of the temples, they failed to claim the contribution from the Government or failed to get the Government contribution credited to the account of each temple. Thus a valuable source of income of the temples has been permanently lost. Except one affluent devotee none made any sort of endowment to the temples of Tirumala and Tirupati during the British Period.

**Patronage after Independence of India**

Two years after Independence, the temples of Tirumala and Tirupati had to face the problem of parting with some of their revenues. Under the Zamindari Abolition Act, in 1950, they had handed over their 600 villages with an income of Rs. 6,00,000 a year, to the Government and received a compensation of only Rs. 1,20,000 as against Rs. 7,00,000 already invested on those 600 villages. This was a huge loss to the temples of Tirumala and Tirupati.[71]

However, from 1950 on the income of the temple started steadily rising from year to year. It was Rs. 1,10,000 in 1933 but Rs. 2,10,000 in 1950, Rs. 2,00,00,000 in 1960 and

Rs. 70,00,00,000 in 1986. The number of pilgrims increased to about 6 thousands a day in 1950 and 40 thousands a day in 1986.

From 1951 on, several changes were effected in the administration of the temples of Tirumala and Tirupati by replacing the T.T.D. Act of 1933 with the new Acts of 1951, 1966, 1977 and 1983. Since 1951 a policy was laid down not only to have several schemes for obtaining the patronage of the people to the temples, but also to implement specific programmes for the maintenance of the temples, for providing facilities to the pilgrims, for the welfare of the public and for the propagation of Hindu religion and Dharma. In accordance with this policy half a dozen endowment schemes were innovated in the last 36 years to get patronage of the devotees to the temples and their various programmes.

One of the endowment schemes is the Cottage Donation Scheme inaugurated in 1959. Under this scheme 617 cottages and 704 suites were constructed collecting half and later two-thirds of the cost from the donor, ownership vesting with the temple of Tirumala and with the privilege of occupying the cottage or suite for a period of one month in a year free of rent by the donor and his successor. More than 1320 patrons made contributions to the tune of Rs. 5,81,40,000 towards this scheme in the last 36 years. These cottages aud suites accommodate more than 1320 families of the pilgrims everyday.

A different endowment scheme is the Guest House Building Scheme envisaged in the year 1980. Affluent devotees like industrialists and contractors had contributed to the tune of Rs, 1,00,00,000 to get seven guest houses constructed at Tirumala. For this kind of patronage, the donors are given the privilege of staying in one of the suites at any time in a year continuously for a week and of having free Darshan of the Lord on all those days at specified time periods.

There is the Sri Venkateswara Nitya Prasada Dana Endowment Scheme commenced in the year 1979. Under this scheme one can make an endowment of Rs. 500 for the distribution of 20 food packets or 15 sweets (*laddus*) or 15 black gram cakes (*vadas*) to pilgrims on a fixed day of one's choice *viz.*, birthday, wedding anniversary, specific date of ancestor worship and so on. The donor can make multiples of Rs. 500 as endowment. If the amount is Rs. 10,000, the T.T.D. with the interest accrued thereon, will arrange free males to pilgrims on a specified day. Further, the T.T.D. also arranges free Darshan for 5 persons of the donor. This contribution of the donors is exempted from income tax. By the end of 1986, about 10 thousand donors contributed to the tune of 1,00,00,000 towards this endowment scheme.

There is the Sri Venkateswara Nitya Laddu Dana Scheme opened in the year 1981. Under this scheme about 25 grams of *Laddu* (sweet) offered as holy food (*prasadam*) to the Lord will be distributed in the name of a donor on a fixed date of his choice. The minimum amount to be endowed is Rs. 1,00,000. There are now 9 donors, whose contribution is to the extent of Rs. 1,02,000.

Under another endowment scheme namely the Udayasthamana Serva Seva Scheme initiated in the year 1981 all rituals and services to the Lord will be performed on behalf of the donor on a fixed day of his choice. If the ritual services are to be performed on a Friday, the endowment to be deposited is Rs. 3,00,000. So far 68 members contributed to the extent of Rs. 90,00,000 towards this scheme.

There is the Balaji Archana Scheme commenced in the year 1982 under which the Lord will be worshipped in the donor's name on any day specified by the donor every year for a period of 10 years. The donor should make an endowment of Rs. 5,068. This amount with an accumulated interest will come to Rs. 15,000 in 10 years and the donor will have the satisfaction of donating Rs. 15,000 to the Lord. Till 1986, 300 donors deposited Rs. 15,50,000 towards this scheme.

There is also the Sri Venkateswara Nitya Anna Dana Scheme envisaged in the year 1985 which is aimed to provide free meals to the pilgrims at Tirumala. A donor can make an endowment of Rs. 10,00,000 or multiples thereof to the T.T.D. The T.T.D. will contribute an equal amount towards matching grant and deposit the entire amount in a nationalised bank to feed 500 pilgrims everyday on the interest earned on every Rs. 1,00,000 donated. Donations can be made by individuals, firms, companies and so on and they are eligible for exemption of income tax. Up to the end of 1986, 13 donors contributed Rs. 1,30,00,000 towards this endowment scheme.

Apart from the above, there is the Arjita Seva Scheme,

under which a devotee can get specified ritual services (*sevas*) performed in honour of the Lord at Tirumala after paying a stipulated fee to the temple. The income derived from such scheme runs to millions of rupees. In 1986 alone the income derived under this scheme was about Rs. 10 millions.

The T.T.D. is now investing its surplus income in fixed deposits in several nationalised banks. It is spending a part of its income of several temple activities, pilgrim facilities, educational institutions, welfare programmes and propagation of Hindu religion and dharma.

The data related to the patronage of the temples of Tirumala and Tirupati after Independence reveals many interesting points. First, among the patrons about 30 per cent are industrialists, contractors and businessmen, 60 per cent are employees and the remaining 10 per cent are prosperous landlords, merchants and others. Secondly, unlike in the pre-Independent times, in the period after Independence the patrons are from all parts of India. Thirdly, the number of patrons after Independence has gone to the extent of 20 thousands. Never in the history of the temples there were so many patrons. Fourthly, the quantum of patronage that the temples receive at present is several times more than provided at any time in the history of the temples. The various new endowment schemes have attracted thousands of patrons to contribute millions of rupees to the temples. In addition the rise in the pilgrim influx has resulted in the derivation of so much income every year that it is now to the tune of several millions of rupees. At no time in the history of the T.T.D. the ritual services had been so much commercialised as they are today. Further, the temple of Tirumala has become so famous that it has now its branches located in America and Australia. Now, it is called 'vatican of India'. Some of its patrons are foreigners. The annual income of the T.T.D. is more than 700 million rupees. The total assets of T.T.D. run into billions of rupees.

### DISCUSSION ON RESULTS

Historical data going back over one thousand years make it clear that the long involvement of kings, queens, royal officers, private devotees, and ecclesiastical orders in political, religious, economic and social matters and the successive policies of the colonial rulers and later of the various administrators of the temple have a great deal to do with the patronage of the Tirumala-Tirupati Devasthanams.

Here it may be suggested that the patronage of the Tirmala-Tirupati Devasthanams is intimately linked to the political power, religious popularity, spiritual benefits, economic advantage and social complexity over the course of several hundred years. The model assumes that the temples are progressively drawn into increasingly wider socio-economic systems and, as a result, larger and more complex modes of redistribution of resources. For the sake of convenience the process is divided into five phases : the formative phase (up to 1230 A.D.), the constructive phase (1230-1360 A.D.), the developmental phase (1360-1690 A.D.), the degradation phase (1670-1947 A.D.) and the expansion phase (1947 onwards).

The formative phase is characterized by the beginning of patronage in a definite mould to the temples. The existence of the Tirumala temple is known but it is not popular. Tirupati and its temples come into existence only towards the end of the formative phase. The Vaishnava saints (*alvars*) make the temples popular. They go about the country doing propaganda in the name of Vishnu temples. Rulers, royal officers and laity respect them. Royal families start making benefactions to the temple of Tirumala. As the royal patronage sets an example for laity, the private devotees also start making donations in small measure to the temples. The patronage by the royal families as well as the private devotees fulfils the prime requisites of lamplighting, food-offering, supply of flowers, inauguration of festivals and installation of portable images for daily worship and festival processions. What are the reasons for offering this kind of patronage to the temples ? For the sake of political advantage the royal families patronize both the Siva and Vishnu temples to please the Siva as well as Vishnu worshippers. To acquire spiritual benefit in consonance with the practice of perpetuating the memory of donors through designating the charities and services in temples after their names, the patrons endeavour to preserve their memory through their charities and endowments to the deity at the temples of Tirumala. Economically, the higher castes including the agricultural castes are affluent because the political conditions are such that they always favour the higher caste groups to have greater access to economic resources at all times. For this reason a vast majority of the patrons are from higher caste groups and opulent families. During the formative phase about two-thirds of the patrons are Brahmins and Kshatriyas and one-third of the patrons are from agricultural and other castes. Strong foundations laid by the Vaishnava saints for systematic propagation of Sri Vaishnava sect also influence the people to patronize the temples. Through propagation of Vishnu cult and proselytism, Sri-Vaishnava Brahmins hasten the popularity of the temples among all classes of people, encourage royal patronage and inspire all devotees to make pilgrimages to the temples of Tirumala and Tirupati.

The constructive phase of patronage is dominated by an upswing in the level of patronage and the adequacy of all prime requisites of the temples of Tirumala and Tirupati. The adequacy of bare necessities in the temples forms a starting point for making several charities, gifts and endowments for embellishment and grandeur of the divinities and temples in terms of presentation of special jewellery and ornaments, gold gilding of temple domes, augmentation of festivals and provision for pilgrim facilities. The process of patronizing the temples steadily gets accelerated towards the end of constructive phase as the demand for the divine grace to solve more and more problems and the temple requirements for more and more grandeur of divinities increases. In this context, the increased evangelical activities of the duly organised and extended religious orders, the increased monopoly of the higher caste groups over the economic resources, the dire political need for controlling the waves of Muslim hordes, and the desire for spiritual benefits help the flow of substantial donations from 38 people of whom about 60 per cent (22) are Brahmins, Kshatriyas and Vaisyas and the remaining 40 per cent are from other caste groups. Pilgrims from all parts of South India make holy pilgrimages to the temples of Tirumala and Tirupati.

The developmental phase of patronage is marked by an enormous increase in the scale of patronage for the embellishment and grandeur of divinities and temples by an addition of gorgeous jewellery and ornaments, imposing temple structures, elaborate festivals, pompous processions, gluttonous type of food-offerings, big flower-gardens, several seminaries, and numerous religious propagandists and temple functionaries. Of the 200 patrons, an overwhelming proportion (94%) includes Brahmins, Kshatriyas, Vaisyas and agricultural castes whereas a small proportion (6%) includes other castes. The monopoly of the higher castes over agricultural resources forms a basis for munificent grants of villages, gold and cash to the temples by rulers, sacred specialists, landlords, and merchants. Endowments become of increasing religious and economic significance to both the donors and the donees. The religious merit and the economic profit earned out of the endowments become so much attractive that the temple functionaries besides the religious teachers who are usually the donees become donors and come forward to endow the temples with villages, and cash and reap a rich harvest of economic profits and religious benefits. In this context, the temples invest money endowments on the irrigation facilities of their villages, thereby help the cultivators to get better produce from the land, help themselves to derive more income and celebrate the different festivals and functions on a grand scale and help their donors as well as their functionaries to earn more holy foods which can be easily converted into cash by selling them to the pilgrims. The returns obtained become sufficiently attractive to motivate people including the temple functionaries to invest their surplus cash as endowments to the Lord. This gives them the double advantage of religious merit and economic profit. Holy foods can be converted into cash because there is demand for them from thousands of pilgrims. Greater the number of pilgrims, greater is the demand for such foods. The best way to attract more pilgrims is to convert the people into Sri Vaishnava faith and make them devotees of the Lord of Tirumala. Such a conversion serves several purposes. It helps social integration of diversed castes and tribes in terms of common faith, and inspires devotees from all classes to make holy pilgrimages to the temples, to contribute something to the temples and their patrons and in return have holy foods and spiritual benefits. During the developmental phase of patronage a network of religious orders become firmly established all over South India to play a key role in guiding different classes of devotees in their pilgrimage and patronage to the temples of Tirumala and Tirupati.

The degradational phase of patronage is characterised by a negligible scale of patronage to the temples, annexation of the temple villages by the colonial rulers, a steep fall in the income of the temples and a fee levied on pilgrims for every ritual service they want to get performed at Tirumala and Tirupati. The only positive characteristic is that the temples become popular in Central and Western India as the Hindu rulers and their officers from these regions come to pay their homage and some donations to the temples during their compaigns against the Muslim and British rulers. Since then the temples of Tirumala and Tirupati become holy places of pilgrimage to the people in Central and Western India. Despite this rise in the pilgrim influx, the temple revenues are all time low. Neither the gifts of the pilgrims nor the fee imposed on the pilgrims make up the total loss of income on account of annexation of the 284 temples villages by the colonial rulers. The income of the temples become so low that it is hardly enough to celebrate 24 of the 429 festivals celebrated in the developmental phase. Towards the end of the degradational phase some 600 villages come into the possession of the temples after spending temple funds. The temples try to resume the role they have played during the developmental phase in terms of investments in the villages for derivation of good income from them. But they achieve success only to a limited extent. The degradational phase continues almost until India's Independence.

The expansion phase of patronage is marked by a rapid rise in the scale of patronage, an unprecedented increase in the monetary endowments, the using of a small fraction of monetary endowments merely as one time expenditure, the investing of a large number of money endowments as capital for deriving some income for carrying on the intended charities and ritual services in the name of the donors, and the investment of surplus income in fixed deposits in nationalised banks. Commercialization of different ritual services started in the degradational phase of patronage is now carried on on a large scale to obtain heavy monetary income from the pilgrims. At the same time as in the developmental phase of patronage, the temples are now investing a part of their income on pilgrim facilities to provide food, shelter and comfort to all classes of pilgrims. The monetary endowment schemes now in vogue also remind those made during the developmental phase of patronage. Notable monetary endowments come from kings, queens, royal officers and other opulent devotees in all the previous phases of patronage. Now, in the present expansion phase of patronage such endowments flow from several industrialists and businessmen. Monetary endowments made by the employees, merchants and others comprise bulk of the temple income in the present expansion phase of patronage. Unlike in the previous phases of patronage, all groups and classes of people all over India and several categories of people from outside India are drawn into the present phase of patronage of the temples of Tirumala and Tirupati. From the beginning of formative phase of patronage till the beginning of the present expansion phase of patronage different types of religious orders function as propaganda personnel and pilgrim guides on behalf of the temples. As middlemen between the people and the temples they try their best to make themselves prosperous. So, in their attempt to eliminate all these intermediaries between the people and themselves, the Tirumala-Tirupati Devasthanams replace the old religious orders by their own information centres, enquiry offices, and an array of personnel to do the kind of work that the religious orders were doing almost until the beginning of the present expansion phase of patronage. This effort proves beneficial to the pilgrims, donors, temple functionaries, and the whole sacred complex of the Tirumala-Tirupati Devasthanams.

### SUMMARY AND CONCLUSIONS

History provides the key to an understanding of the patronage of the temples under the management of Tirumala-Tirupati Devasthanams. The configuration of present day patronage is the result of specific political, religious, economic and social events that have occurred in the past several centuries.

The model presented in this context takes into consideration several historical processes : establishment of Vishnu cult by the saints (*alvars*), religious conversions of non-Vaishnavas into Vaishnavas, adequate motivation for flow of benefactions to the temples, commercialization of ritual services at the temples, fluctuations in political fortunes and modern innovations for attracting large scale patronage to the temples.

During the formative phase, the patronage is mostly in the form of charities and endowments which are inadequate to meet even the prime necessities of temples; but the later practice of patronizing the temples by means of abundant charities, gifts and endowments for embellishment and grandeur of divinities and temples which comes into vogue in the developmental phase is already visible in its nascent stage in the constructive phase. The degradational phase shows absence of patronage and loss of income and along with them the total disappearance of the type of grandeur that existed in the developmental phase. Even though the patronage in the present expansion phase is on a large scale unprecedented in the history of the temples, it is not able to restore the grandeur and splendour of the temples and their deities as existed in the developmental phase of patronage. The reason for this is that the present patronage is not meant for the institution and celebration of festivals as it was so in the developmental phase, rather it is largely concerned with the creation of several facilities for pilgrims.

In all the phases the sources of patronage are mostly from the higher castes. This is because the economic resources are a monopoly of the higher castes even to this day. In the degradational phase, colonial administrators become an additional class of patrons. Now in the expansion phase, all classes of people in India and different categories of people from numerous other countries are patrons of the temples of Tirumala and Tirupati.

The kinds of patronage include gifts of villages, gold, cash, cows, lamp-stands, lamps, silver images, jewellery, ornaments, special linen, precious stones, gold and silver cups, plates and spoons; flower-gardens, drinking water wells, water-sheds, feeding centres, pilgrim shelters, temple structures, chariots, fly whisks, gold vehicles, and so on in the formative, constructive, and developmental phases. But in the expansion phase, the patronage is mostly in the form of money and less in the form of gold, silver and several articles.

The scale of patronage gradually increases from the formative phase to the developmental phase and thereafter as the prime necessities of the temples are fulfilled first, embellishment and grandeur of the temples and deities come into play next, and finally more and more facilities for pilgrims are provided. Further, the rise in the cost of living from time to time in a single phase or across several phases is reflected in the increased amount of money which has to be paid by the donor for the same kind of food-offering, lamp-lighting and irrigation works.

The causes of patronage in all phases are political, religious, social and economic. Although political advantages, spiritual benefits and socio-religious harmony are sufficient motivations for patronizing the temples in all the five phases, economic profit becomes an additional motivation for patronizing the temples in the developmental phase. The patronage suddenly diminishes and disappears as the degradational phase sets in because the Muslim rulers treat the temples as their personal property and their successors namely the colonial rulers treat the temple villages as their own property. Obviously in the degradational phase, commercialization of ritual services becomes the only source of income to the temples. On the other hand, commercialization of ritual services to a degree that it was never before in the degradational phase, and creation of several monetary endowment schemes somewhat similar to those in the developmental phase comprise the main sources of income to the temples in the present expansion phase.

In every phase, the results of patronage of the temples of Tirumala and Tirupati are in terms of religious harmony, social integration and judicious redistribution of economic resources according to the ideals of the State. It is through patronage the whole temple complex of Tirumala and Tirupati have come into existence. Neither the patrons nor the sacred specialists make the temples as exclusive to them only. The temples are common to all Hindus and a special attraction to Sri Vaishnavas. But they allow people of all creeds, all religions, all classes, and all lands to enter them and worship their deities. The patronage is so meticulous in instituting the various ritual services on all the days of a year that these ritual services provide an opportunity to people to congregate at the temples and look to the central figures, *viz.*, the Lords. Further, in all the phases of patronage, the temples of Tirumala and Tirupati serve as redistribution centres in accordance with the ideals of the State. Even today, they collect resources contributed by patrons and pilgrims and give them out to people in a new pattern such as religious, educational, economic, welfare and other services to the citizens in consonance with the democratic ideals of India.

## REFERENCES

1. Subrahmanya Sastry 1981 : 99, 142, 162.
2. *Ibid.*, 1930 : 27, 20, 29.
3. Subrahmanya Sastry 1981 : 142.
4. *Ibid* , 1930 : 143.
5. *Ibid.*, 1981 : 143.
6. *Ibid.*
7. Ramesan 1981 : 347-350.
8. Subrahmanya Sastry 1981 : 143-5.
9. Subrahmanya Sastry 1981 : 143-4.
10. *Ibid.*, 143.
11. *Ibid.*, 143, 144.
12. *Ibid.*, 165.
13. Veeraraghavacharya 1953 : Vol-I 357-366.
14. Subrahmanya Sastry 1930 : 86-89.
15. Subrahmanya Sastry 1981 : 147-161.
16. Ramesan : 348, 351.
17. Subrahmanya Sastry 1981 : 152.
18. Subrahmanya Sastry 1981 : 152-53.
19. *Ibid.*, 152.
20. *Ibid.*, 1930 : 5, 46, 120-121.
21. *Ibid.*, 123-124.
22. Ramesan 1981 : 348.
23. *Ibid.*, 330-1.
24. *Ibid.*, 331.
25. Subrahmanya Sastry 1981 : 157-8.
26. *Ibid.*, 1930 : 93, 121, 128.
27. Ramesan 1981 : 331.
28. Subrahmanya Sastry 1981 : 150-7.
29. *Ibid.* 158-61.
30. Subrahmanya Sastry 1981 : 161
31. Ramesan 1981 : 340-342.
32. Veeraraghavacharya 1953 : Vol. I, 544-545.
33. Subrahmanya Sastry 1930 : 130-141.
34. Ramesan 1981 : 360, 362.
35. Subrahmanya Sastry 1930 : 150.
36. Ramesan 1981 : 364-368.
37. Subrahmanya Sastry 1930 : 166.
38. *Ibid* , 220-226.

39. *Ibid.*, 251-252.
40. *Ibid.*, 309, 314-315.
41. Ramesan 1981 : 365-366.
42. Subrahmanya Sastry 1930 : 226.
43. Subrahmanya Sastry 1981 : 170-286.
44. *Ibid.*, 1930 : 8-9.
45. *Ibid.*, 16-18, 30, 31-32, 42, 44-51.
46. *Ibid.*, 130-325.
47. Veeraraghavacharya 1960, Vol. 2 : 393-608.
48. *Ibid.*, 1962, Vol. 3 : 7-123.
49. Ramesan 1981 : 384-395.
50. *Ibid.*, 390-393.
51. *Ibid.*, 396-399.
52. Veeraraghavacharya 1953 : 101, 104.
53. Subrahmanya Sastry 1930 : 8-9.
54. *Ibid.*, 10-13.
55. Ramesan 1981 : 350-51.
56. *Ibid.*, 358.
57. *Ibid.*, 1981 : 432.
58. Veeraraghavacharya 1953 : 19, 25.
59. Ramesan 1981 : 256, 433.
60. Veeraraghavacharya 1953 : 25-6.
61. Subrahmanya Sastry 1981 : 300-1.
62. Ramesan 1981 : 434.
63. *Ibid.*, 443-4, 491.
64. *Ibid.*, 465.
65. Subrahmanya Sastry 1981 : 300-1.
66. Ramesan 1981 : 484.
67. *Ibid.*, 484-6, 502-3, 513-20, 543-4.
68. *Ibid.*, 551, 558-64.
69. *Ibid.*, 563.
70. *Ibid.*,
71. Anna Rao 1970 : Part II, 6.

## NOTES

Anna Rao, C., 1977, *Administration of Temples*, Tirupati : Tirumala-Tirupati Devasthanams Press.

Krishnaswami Aiyangar, S, 1952, *A History of the Holy Shrine of Sri Venkatesa in Tirupati*. Two Volumes, Sri Venkatesa Oriental Institute Series. Madras : Tirumala-Tirupati Devasthanams Committee.

Ramesan, N., 1981, *History of Tirumala-Tirupati*. Tirupati : Tirumala-Tirupati Devasthanams.

Subrahmanya Sastry, S., 1930, *Sri Tirumala Tirupati etc. Devasthanam Epigraphical Series*. Vol. I : Report on the Inscriptions of the

Devasthanam Collections with Illustrations. Madras : Tirupati
Sri Mahant's Press.

Subrahmanya Sastry, S., 1981, *Tirupati Sri Venkateswara*. Tirupati :
Tirumala-Tirupati Devasthanam.

Viraraghavacharya, T.K.T., 1953, *History of Tirupati*. (The Tiruven-
gadam Temple). Vol. I. Tirupati : Tirumala-Tirupati Devasthanam
Press.

Viraraghavacharya, T.K.T., 1960, *History of Tirupati*. (The Tiruvenga-
dam Temple). Vol. II. Tirupati : Tirumala-Tirupati Devasthanam
Press.

Viraraghavacharya, T.K.T., 1962, *History of Tirupati*. (The Tiruvenga-
dam Temple). Vol. III. Tirupati : Tirumala-Tirupati Devasthanam
Press.

# 9

# Srisailam : A Shivaite Pilgrimage Centre, Andhra Pradesh, India

S. VIJAYA KUMAR AND M. SURYANARAYANA

## Introduction

BEFORE going into the discussion about pilgrims and pilgrimage it is worthwhile to give a brief account of the sacred geography of Srisailam. Srisailam is a plateau situated about 1500 feet above the mean sea level. It is situated in the thick forest of Nallamalai hills (Eastern Ghats) in Atmakur taluk of Kurnool district, Andhra Pradesh, India. It is girdled round by the holy river Krishna on three sides i.e., North, West and East. The temple of Lord Mallikarjuna stand on a little hallow on the top of the hill at latitude 16° 12′ North and longitude 78° 85′ East. (See Fig. 9.1) The Lord Mallikarjuna is one of the twelve jyotherlingas in India and is self-born one. Once this holy place flourished as a great Shivaite centre and saints like Nagarjuna, Adi Sankaracharya penanced here. Since nineteenth century A.D. a number of choultries (rest houses) shops have come into existence. Besides, few new temples of little and great traditional ones came into existence. There are more than sixty sacred centres located all over Srisailam. It is served by both Brahmin and non-Brahmin sacred specialists to perform almost a nineteen-hour daily ritual worship and to carry on annual programmes and festivals. The temple has more than three hundred administrative personnel on its pay rolls to manage its

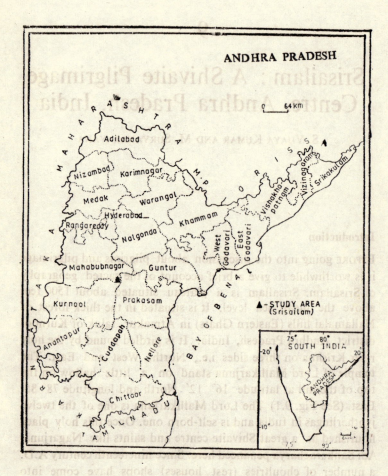

**FIG. 9.**1

dawn to dusk affairs, and to look after the thousands of pilgrims visiting it every day.

Pilgrimage is an institutionalised journey by an individual or a group to a holy place. Pilgrims hope to obtain material and spiritual benefits ranging from bodily cures, prosperity and progeny to peace of mind and salvation. They may go in a spirit of penance for more sin or of gratitude and devotion. According to *Aitareya Brahmana* (Vol. VII, p. 15) the origin of pilgrimage in India is the result of the animistic basis of the popular beliefs, reflected in the higher forms of Hinduism and even in the local developments of Islam. The *puranas* (ancient religious texts) are the main source of information on pilgrimage. *Kshetra Mahatyam* (importance of sacred centre), *Thirthasthalas* (sacred streams) are the important parts of the *puranas* which explain the efficacy of pilgrimage and the upright way of life a pilgrim is required to lead during *tirthayatra* (pilgrimage).

In India, pilgrimages at the time of seasonal festivals have long been important. Hindus visit holy places to attain blessings, atone for sins, and enjoy the carnival-like (merriment) atmosphere. There are some recommended performances to be done by a pilgrim at almost every important sacred centre, they are the *mundan* ceremony (tonsure ceremony), holy bath (holy dip in sacred rivers and sacred ponds), vow, prayer, worship, gifts, cremation as such.

### DISCUSSION

## Importance of Srisailam

As it has already been described earlier, Srisailam finds a prominent mention in various sacred scriptures. A special reference had been mentioned in '*Srisaila Kandha*' of *Skandapurana* about the most important shrine and *Phullas* (linga) which is popularly known as Lord *Srisaila Mallikarjunaswami*.

This holy place is mentioned in Mahabharata (*Vana* 85, VV 19-20). *Agni Purana* states that Srisailam is a Siddhakshitra where God Shiva and Parvathi always reside (*Agni.* Ch. 113 : VV 6, 7). The *Matsya-Purana* describes Srisailam as a seat of the mother Goddess Madhavi (*Matsya-Purana*, Ch 13; Verse 31).

Although the sectarian religion of Srisailam is essentially Saivism right from the ancient times, several sub-sects of that faith had their stronghold at his holy abode of Mallikarjuna (Shiva) claiming their individuality and control over the shrine. All the more interesting is the royal patronage enjoyed by these sects from time to time. The *Siddhas, Kapalikas, Kalamukhas, Pasupatas* and V*irasaivas* are the most prominent among these sects. Tantric schools of Saivism like *Yamila* and *Bhairava* also had their centres on this hill.

Tradition as well as epigraphical sources inform us that the shrine of Srisailam was approachable through four places on the plains, generally called the gateways of Srisailam on its four cardinal directions. They are Tripurantakam in the Prakasam district in the East; Siddhavatam in the Cuddapah district, in the South; Alampuram in the Mahabubnagar district in the West; and Umamaheswaram in Mahabubnagar district in the North. The concept of the gateways of Srisailam is traceable from 8th and 9th centuries A.D. All these four places developed as centres of pilgrimage. The pilgrims those who were making their journey towards Srisailam through these gateways were mainly helped and guided by the local tribal Chenchus. However, they are not being used now to reach Srisailam as bus route was made in the year 1961. Devotees now mainly make use of this facility.

### Pilgrims to Srisailam : Composition of Pilgrims

To analyse the pilgrimage to Srisailam a sample of 500 pilgrims representing the various cross-sections of Hindu society was drawn up. According to this sample analysis, pilgrims from all over India visit this sacred city.

From Table 9.1 we come to know that since Srisailam is located in Andhra Prdesh, a large number of pilgrims i.e. 33.6 per cent are from this State. The second position is occupied by the pilgrims of Karnataka, which is the neighbouring State, which formed 24.4 per cent of the total pilgrims interviewed. Next, subsequently third, fourth and fifth, places are occupied by the pilgrims of Maharashtra (18.4%), Tamil Nadu (12.4%), and Kerala (4.2%) respectively. From the Table it is evident that pilgrims from Orissa, West Bengal, Bihar and Madhya Pradesh have also visited, and thus, from the point of view of 'spreading

TABLE 9.1 : **Number of Pilgrims and their Percentages from Different States**

| Sl. No. | Name of State | No. of pilgrims | Percentage |
|---|---|---|---|
| 1. | Andhra Pradesh | 168 | 33.6 |
| 2. | Karnataka | 122 | 24.4 |
| 3. | Maharashtra | 92 | 18.4 |
| 4. | Tamil Nadu | 62 | 12.4 |
| 5. | Kerala | 21 | 4.2 |
| 6. | West Bengal | 9 | 1.8 |
| 7. | Uttar Pradesh | 8 | 1.6 |
| 8. | Bihar | 7 | 1.4 |
| 9. | Madhya Pradesh | 5 | 1.0 |
| 10. | Orissa | 6 | 1.2 |
| | Total | 500 | 100.0 |

importance', Srisailam may be called as important place of pilgrimage, which attracts pilgrims not only from local and regional but also from national levels.

The pilgrims to Srisailam have been categorised into five groups based on their number of visits to Srisailam. Table 9.2 will show their number and percentage.

TABLE 9.2 : **Number of Visits made by the Pilgrims**

| Sl. No. | Number of Visits | No. of pilgrims | Percentage |
|---|---|---|---|
| 1. | First | 167 | 33.4 |
| 2. | Second | 72 | 14.4 |
| 3. | Third | 68 | 13.6 |
| 4. | Fourth | 41 | 8.2 |
| 5. | Fifth and above | 152 | 30.4 |
| | Total | 500 | 100.0 |

Data showing the number of visits to sacred Srisailam by the pilgrims are very interesting. It reveals that while 33.4 per cent of the pilgrims had come to Srisailam for the first time, 30.4 per cent of the pilgrims had visited Srisailam for five times and even more. The pilgrims who had visited Srisailam second, third and fourth times are comparatively less i.e., 14.4 per cent, 13.6 per cent and 8.2 per cent.

People belonging to different castes visit this place. We find that Brahmins dominate others. Out of five hundred pilgrims interviewed at Srisailam, there were 187 (37.2%) Brahmins, 300 (60%) non-Brahmins. It is interesting to note that 11 (2.2%) pilgrims belong to Muslim community. Among non-Brahmins 98 (19.6%) members belong to Lingayat caste of Karnataka.

If the literacy rate among the pilgrims of Srisailam is considered, became to know that only 8.6 per cent were illiterate, who did not know even writing or reading, but they are well in touch with the 'myths' and 'kathas' (stories) of this sacred place. Table 9.3 shows the percentage figure of literacy among the pilgrims.

TABLE 9.3 : **Extent of Literacy of the Pilgrims**

| Sl. No. | Educational Qualification | No. of pilgrims | Percentage |
|---|---|---|---|
| 1. | Illiterate | 43 | 8.6 |
| 2. | Literate | 142 | 28.4 |
| 3. | Matriculate level | 93 | 18.6 |
| 4. | Graduate level | 119 | 23.8 |
| 5. | Post-graduate level | 66 | 13.2 |
| 6. | Professionals and Technicians | 37 | 7.4 |

According to Table 9.3, it appears that 28.4 per cent of pilgrims belong to literate group, who simply know reading and writing but are not having any educational qualification. The second largest group of total number of pilgrims were graduates (23.8%).

TABLE 9.4 : **The Analysis of Pilgrim's Professions**

| Sl. No. | Profession | No. of pilgrims | Percentage |
|---|---|---|---|
| 1. | Agriculture | 93 | 18.6 |
| 2. | Business | 126 | 25.2 |
| 3. | Higher Professionals (Doctors, Engineers, Lawyers, etc.) | 83 | 16.6 |
| 4. | Menial type of services | 76 | 15.2 |
| 5. | Other professions | 122 | 24.4 |

It appears from Table 9.4 that people from different professions come to Srisailam on pilgrimage. Among the pilgrims interviewed 18.6 per cent are peasants. Higher professionals like doctors, lawyers, etc., are 16.6 per cent. Business category people (25.3%) are also represented well. By this, we can conclude that all walks and ages of Hindus visit Srisailam.

**Preparation for Pilgrimage**

The Brahmanic scriptures have prescribed in great detail the rules regarding pilgrimage. The earliest reference of pilgrimage in Indian sacred scripture is reported to be found in the *Aitereya Brahmana*. The respectability attached to pilgrimage is not lost anywhere in India, for the pilgrims from different regions of the country have reported that the beliefs in the efficacy of *tirtha yatra* is well founded in their respective villages and towns. Attraction to pilgrimage towards Srisailam is evidenced from the fact that among the pilgrims interviewed 167 (33.4%) had visited sacred Srisailam for the first time, and 152 (30.4%) pilgrims visited Srisailam for more than five times so far, which is a remarkable one.

In most of the villages and even towns of South India, sometimes subscriptions are collected and those who wish to make a pilgrimage to Srisailam and other important *tirthas* enlist their names in advance to the organisers, thus, a collective pilgrimage is arranged. Special buses are arranged by the organisers.

This type of collective pilgrimage is reported from all parts of India.

In some of the South Indian villages, there is a custom that a person going on pilgrimage will announce his intention to the villagers who are invited to his house. On that occasion they worship the family deity and later on all the villagers will see off that person at the boundary of the village. After taking this type of sacred vow (*sankalpana*), one cannot return to his village unless he or she completes the intended pilgrimage. After returning from pilgrimage the pilgrim has to arrange a *katha* generally followed by a feast to the villagers. The *prasadam* and the *thirtha* (sacred river water) which he or she collects during the pilgrimage is also distributed to the invitees and to his kinsmen. Among the five hundred pilgrims interviewed at Srisailam, 273 (54.6%) had come with family members, 89 (17.8%) come with friends and 138 (27.6%) visited this sacred place alone. Most of the pilgrims visited Srisailam in groups.

It appears that today most of the pilgrims visiting Srisailam are not showing interest in the scriptural recommendations, which are the prescribed rules regarding the sacred performances in sacred texts. According to *puranic* recommendations, one has to spend in a place of pilgrimage at least three nights. This was violated by 59.8 per cent (299) pilgrims interviewed, because the most important point is time that it may not have permitted them to spend three days in a sacred place without attending to their regular duties. The detailed statistics regarding to duration of pilgrims stay at Srisailam are given in Table 9.5. Most of the recommended scriptual performances

#### TABLE 9.5 : **Pilgrims Stay at Srisailam**

| Sl. No. | Number of days | No. of pilgrims | Percentage |
|---------|----------------|-----------------|------------|
| 1. | One day | 299 | 59.8 |
| 2. | Two days | 128 | 25.6 |
| 3. | Three days | 54 | 10.8 |
| 4. | Six days | 10 | 2.0 |
| 5. | More than fifteen days | 9 | 1.8 |

are also not performed by the pilgrims now-a-days. When asked about the main purpose of their visit, the pilgrims response is shown in the Table 9.6. Regarding the movement

TABLE 9.6 : **The Main Purpose of Pilgrims Visit**

| Sl. No. | Main purpose of visit | Response in percentage |
|---|---|---|
| 1. | Tirthayatra (as a part of normal religious life) | 15.3% ( 76) |
| 2. | Special tirthayatra (on the occasion of festivals like Sivaratri) | 42.8% (214) |
| 3. | To observe special performances like (a) Rudrabhishekam (b) Koti Bilvarchana (c) Kalyanotchavam | 21.8% (109) |
| 4. | To perform tonsure ceremony (mundan) | 11.8% ( 59) |
| 5. | For recovering from sickness | 5.2% ( 26) |
| 6. | To perform funeral rites (like *pindadan*) | 3.2% ( 16) |

of pilgrims in the sacred geography of Srisailam, it appears that all the pilgrims do not visit all the sacred centres. Table 9.7 shows that 100 per cent of the pilgrims visited the temple of Sri Mallikarjuna and few other shrines within its cluster. The data further shows that Goddess Bramarambha temple is also visited by 100 per cent of the pilgrims this means, the pilgrims who visit Sri Mallikarjuna temple will also visit Goddess Bramarambha temple invariably.

It is interesting to note that 15.6 per cent (78) of the pilgrims visited not only the presiding deities of Srisailam but also few little traditional gods located within the sacred geography of Srisailam. They have performed rites in this little traditional sacred centres in accordance with the vows taken. Sometimes the pilgrims offer animal sacrifices to goddesses like Gangamma and Poleramma.

TABLE 9.7 : **Percentage of Pilgrims Visiting various Shrines**

| Sl. No. | Name of the temples visited by pilgrims | Percentage |
|---|---|---|
| 1. | Lord Mallikarjunaswami temple and other shrines within its cluster | 100 |
| 2. | Goddess Bramarambha temple | 100 |
| 3. | Shakshi Ganapathi temple | 69.8 (349) |
| 4. | Shikaraswara temple | 65.4 (327) |
| 5. | Hatakeswara temple | |
| 6. | Pathalaganga ghat | 79.6 (398) |
| 7. | Little traditional shrines (Poleramma, Gangamma etc.) | 15.6 (78) |

Many sacred bathing *ghats* and *gundams* are not equally used by all the pilgrims. In some of the *gundams* like *Mallikka-gundam, Manoharagundam, Rudhiragundam,* the sacred bathing is strictly prohibited by the temple administration, as the waters of these *gundams* are exclusively used for drinking and sacred purposes. 79.6 per cent (398) of the pilgrims had their sacred bath in holy river Krishna at a place known as *Pathalaganga.* Only 3.2 per cent (16) of the pilgrims visited *Veebhuti gundam* and 4.2 per cent (21) of the pilgrims visited *Sidhi Ramappa-kolanu* to take sacred bath.

Besides, there are nearly nineteen religious institutions like *mathams, ashrams,* located within the sacred geography of Srisailam. Pilgrims visit these places to get blessings of the *Sidha Sadhus* of that place. Only 9.2 per cent (46) pilgrims are reported to have visited these *mathams* and *ashrams.*

After making sacred performances in Lord Mallikarjuna-swami temple and other important temples, some pilgrims visit the project on the bank of river Krishna which is very near to Srisailam. 23.6 per cent (118) of pilgrims visited Sunnipenta where Srisailam Hydro-Electric Project is constructed on the river Krishna.

### TABLE 9.8 : The Household Deities of Pilgrims

| Sl. No. | Name of the household deity | No. of pilgrims | Percentage |
|---------|------------------------------|-----------------|------------|
| 1. | Lord Shiva | 163 | 32.6 |
| 2. | Lord Venkateswara | 116 | 23.2 |
| 3. | Lord Vigneswara | 65 | 13.0 |
| 4. | Lord Krishna | 76 | 15.2 |
| 5. | Lord Sri Rama | 30 | 6.0 |
| 6. | Goddess Lakshmi | 27 | 5.4 |
| 7. | Lord Hanuman | 16 | 3.2 |
| 8. | Goddess Kali | 7 | 1.4 |

Pilgrims whose family deities are Lord Shiva and His subordinate gods and pilgrims whose family deities are Lord Krishna and any of His 'Dasavatharams' visit Srisailam in almost equal number. Among the five hundred pilgrims interviewed 163 (32.6%) are staunch devotees of Lord Shiva, 65 (13%) worship of Lord Vigneswara, whereas 116 (23.2%) worship Lord Krishna. In addition to the above mentioned great tradition gods, goddess Kali a little tradition god is also worshipped by a few pilgrims as their family deity. From this it is clearly evident that both Shivites and Vaishnavites visit this holy place irrespective of their sectarian affiliations.

## Daily Routine of the Pilgrims

The daily routine of the pilgrims briefly recorded here is as such : A pilgrim who wants to worship Mallikarjunaswami takes a sacred bath in the holy river Krishna in the early hours of the day. After taking bath he performs some rituals at the ghats (*Pathalanganga*) and then proceeds to worship Mallikarjunaswami and other deities located in that cluster. During his stay over there he strictly commits himself to take vegetarian food and usually takes rest in the afternoon. He performs *abhishekam* to Lord Mallikarjunaswami in the early hours of the day. In the evening hours he goes to Mallikarjuna temple for having *darshan of the* Mallikarjunaswami at the time of *Susandhayam* and *Mahamangalaharathi*.

Afterwards he goes to Goddes Bramarambha temple for having *darshan* of the *Mangalaharathi* and *Rajapachara pujas* which are performed in the temple. On the second day he performs *rudrabhishekam* to Mallikarjunaswami and *kumkumarchana* to Goddess Bramarambha. On the second and third days, he goes for *puja* and *darshan* of the various shrines such as Vrudha Mallikarjuna temple, Sikharam, Hatakeswaram, Veerbhadra temple, Sakshi Ganapathi temple and few *gundams* and *mathams* like *Manohara gunndam, Mallika gundam, Panchamathams, Srisaila Jagadguru Panditaradhya Peetam*, Sri Sankaracharya Matham. Besides he may worship a *Trifala Vruksham* (peepul, fig and ficus trees grown together are called *thriphala* meaning three types of trees yielding fruits) by circumambulating it after having sacred bath at Krishna ghats in the morning hours. It is believed that by circumambulating this tree the persons get himself relieved from his sufferings immediately.

Apart from this, in Srisailam there is a peculiar custom known as '*dhuli darshan*'. This is mostly followed by the pilgrims who are from Karnataka. At the time of the *dasara* festival many pilgrims from Karnataka start pilgrimage towards Srisailam on foot. After climbing the footstairs of the hill the pilgrims straightaway walk into the sanctum sanctorum of the Mallikarjunaswami temple without taking bath at Krishna ghat for having *darshan*.

In the daily routine of a pilgrim, a holy bath in the Krishna *ghat* and *puja* performance to Lord Mallikarjunaswami are essential (the minimum sacred performances to be followed every day), and common to all, the performance of a ritual depends upon one's own interest. Hence, there are personal variations. Before going to the bed one remembers Lord Mallikarjuna, in the belief that it is the sacred place of Lord Mallikarjuna where he has come to spend a few days in peace. Generally in his stay, particularly in the morning he will be busy in making sacred performances, in the afternoons he participates in *Nithya Kalayanotsavam* which is performed to Lord Mallikarjuna and to Goddess Bramarambha. Since the merit of pilgrimage is proportioned to the time one devoted to sacred performances the daily routine of the devoted pilgrim is crowded with religious activities.

## Place of Pilgrims Stay at Srisailam

From the point of view of accommodation for pilgrims at Srisailam, 22.6 per cent (113) of the pilgrims stayed in *dharmashalas*, 35.8 per cent (179) stayed in choultries, 19.6 per cent (98) stayed in cottages and 4.8 per cent (24) stayed with their relatives, only 17.2 per cent (86) left Srisailam without staying anywhere.

## Pilgrim's Relations with the Sacred Specialists

The nature of relationship between a pilgrim and sacred specialist may reflect the attitude of pilgrim towards sacred specialist. Among the pilgrims interviewed maximum number i.e., 85.6 per cent (428) of pilgrims have temporary relationship with the sacred specialist, and only 9.8 per cent (49) pilgrims have hereditary relationship with the *tirthapurohitha*, 6.6 per cent (33) pilgrims did not utilise the services of the sacred specialists at all. They themselves performed the rituals of worship, *tarp.na* etc.

What has come out in the interviews, is that the motivating factors which inspires the pilgrims to visit Srisailam reveals that 38.8 per cent (194) of the pilgrims were motivated by their parents, kinsmen and friends, 24.4 per cent (122) come to perform necessary and obligatory rituals, 13.6 per cent (68) themselves decided to go on a pilgrimage, 7.4 per cent (37) followed the advice of the astrologers and family priests to overcome their misfortune and problems, and 15.8 per cent (79) of the pilgrims did not clarify the motivating factor of their pilgrimage to Srisailam.

By interviewing the pilgrims it is evident that most of the pilgrims do not have adequate knowledge of the sacred geography of Srisailam. Only 41.8 per cent (209) pilgrims had knowledge about the boundaries of Srisailam *Mahakshetram* as described in the scriptures. Roughly 95 per cent of the pilgrims had some knowledge of the *mahatyam* of Srisailam either through villagers and kinsmen or through sacred specialists and sacred texts, before coming to this sacred place on pilgrimage. This further testified the strength of the traditional media of communication through which the strength of the knowledge of the great tradition, pilgrimage etc. is continually transmitted.

Once the pilgrims arrive in this holy place the various sacred
specialists interact with them, and it is this interaction and
personal experiencing of the sacred phenomena which added to
the knowledge of the pilgrims and sustain their interest and
faith in the institution of pilgrimage.

## NOTES

Jha, Makhan, 1977, *The Cultural Contour of an Ancient Hindu
Kingdom of Mahakoshal*, Ranchi, M/s. Bengal Press.

Jha, Makhan, 1979, *Dimensions of Indian Civilization* New Delhi ;
Concept Publishing Company.

Jha, Makhan, 1978, *Rising India : An Urban Anthropological
Approach to Puri*, New Delhi : Classical Publications.

Jha, Makhan, 1982, *Cultural Regions of Mithila and Mahakoshal*,
Delhi : Capital Publishing House.

Jha, Makhan, 1981, *Civilization and Complex Societies in South Asia*,
Varanasi ; Jayanti Press and Prakashan.

Jha, Makhan, 1985, *Dimensions of Pilgrimage : An Anthropological
Appraisal*, New Delhi : Inter-India Publications.

Jha. Makhan and Vidyarthi, L.P., *The Symposium on Sacred
Complex in India*, Delhi : Capital Publishing House.

Parabrahma Sastry, P.V., 1982, *Srisailam : Its History and Cult*
Hyderabad : Srinivasa Printers.

Saraswati, B.N., 1974, "Studying Sacred Complex in Kashi", *Journal
of Social Research*, Ranchi, Vol. XVII, 1.

Singer, Milton, 1961, Text and Context in the Study of Contemporary Hinduism, Madras : *The Adyar Library Bulletin*,
No. XXV.

Vidyarthi, L.P., 1961, *Sacred Complex of Hindu Gaya* Bombay :
Asian Publishing House.

Vidyarthi. L.P., Jha, Makhan and Saraswathi, B.N., 1979, *The
Sacred Complex of Kashi*, New Delhi : Concept Publishing Company.

# 10

# Studying The Sacred Complex of Kathmandu[1]

## A Case Study of Pashupatinath Temple : Some Preliminary Observations

### MAKHAN JHA[2]

I have been studying the centre of pilgrimage of both India and Nepal in terms of "Sacred Complexes" since over two decades, which are referred to or reviewed elsewhere. During last two decades the social anthropologists, sociologists, cultural geographers, linguists etc. have been attracted towards the study of pilgrim centres of different religions, which are verified by the facts that different international symposis (Jha : 1985) are being organised on this theme in different parts of the world. Thus, keeping in view the growing importance of the subject, in general, and very rich field of studying the "sacred complex" of the Himalayan Kingdom of Nepal, in particular, which is like the crest jewel of the great Himalayas, the abode of gods and goddesses, particularly owing allegiance to Lord Shiva of Mount Kailash. I undertook a major research project, *"The Sacred Complex of Kathmandu"*, sponsored by the Indian Council of Social Science Research, New Delhi, in December, 1986, which is still in progress. In this research project, I have attempted to understand in brief, the impact of ecology on the nature and social organisation of these Himalayan sacred centres of Kathmandu, on one hand, and to unfold the channels of continuum existing between Hinduism and Buddhism in Nepal, on the other.

In the present chapter, however, I confine my discussion only on Pashupatinath Shiva temple, which is the guardian deity of the King of Nepal and worshipped by both the Hindus and Buddhists of Nepal, besides other Hindu pilgrims coming from India and elsewhere.

## Pashupati Mahakshetra

In Kathmandu, Pashupati,[3] situated on the western bank of river Bagmati, where a large galaxy of gods and goddesses reside, is not only considered as a sacred *kshetra* (sacred zone), but a *mahakshetra* (very big zone). In the *Nepal Mahatmya* (a sacred text on the sacred centres of Nepal) Pashupati is referred to as *Mahatirtha* (a great pilgrimage centre).

In the seventy-first chapter of the *Skandapurana* we get a detailed description of the Pashupati *kshetra*, *Rishi* (saint) Skanda, while talking to *Rishi* Agastya, says that Pashupati *kshetra* is the place where one can get a daily dose of *dharma* (religion), *artha* (wealth), *kama* (pleasure) and *moksha* (salvation), four most desired wishes of every pious Hindu. The *Puranas* dealing with the Pashupati *Mahakshetra* make a clear cut demarcation of the four sub-*kshetras* within the Pashupati *Mahakshetra*, for bestowing the four cherished desires and blessings, as mentioned above. This *pauranic* (textual) classification of the Pashupati *Mahakshetra* is an excellent geographical location of the various ancient sacred centres, which are still in vogue in spite of so many changes taking place in the Pashupati area.

The ancient *Rishis* (saints), among whom special mention is made of Rishi *Ne*, who did severe penance and meditation for several years on the bank of river Bagmati, and who was made *"pal"* (protector) of this Himalayan kingdom, as the Nepal, country is presently known, made the four sub-*kshetras* within the Pashupati *Mahakshetra* as follows :

The place from Koteshwar to Tileshwar is the place called *Mrigendra*[4] *kshetra*, which provides *Kama* (pleasure). The area between Vikateshwar to Chandra Bharteshwar is a sacred sub-*kshetra*, which provides devotees with fortunes and *artha* (wealth). The place between the Yogdhara river beyond the Vishnu *tirtha* provides *moksha* (salvation). The area between these places is the holiest and best Pashupati *kshetra* which provides both *bhakti* (devotion) and *mukti* (salvation). This is the area where lord Shiva lives in form of Pashupatinath and it is one of the twelve Jyotirlinga.[5] These four sub-*kshetra*, as referred to above, make a big Pashupati *Mahashetra*, which is famous for bestowing *sidhis* (supernatural power), chiranjivis longevity) etc. and that is why the ascetics and other pilgrims consider this *kshetra* (zone) as very sacred and the holiest among the holy centres of pilgrimage.

The most important sacred segment of the Pashupati *Mahakshetra* is the *Shleshmantak* forest where Lord Shiva lives in the company of Gopal *Sidhi Gans*, Vinayak (lord Ganesh), Chhetrapals, and various other goddesses like Guheshwari[6], Bageshwari, Brahmi, Maheshwari, Kaumari, Varahi, Narsinghi, Shivadhatri, Batshala, Mangala, Raj Rajeshwari etc. Thus, this *Mahakshetra* of Pashupati is Shiva-Sakti dominant region, which further testifies that Shiva is *shava* (corpse) without *Shakti*.

In the four directions of this Pashupati *Mahakshetra*, there are eight *Bhairavas*, who guard this *Mahakshetra*. The names of these eight *Bhairavas* are Unmatta Bhairava, Asintas Bhairava, Ruru Bhairava, Kal Bhairava, Sangharak Bhairava, Krodha Bhairava, Ananda Bhairava, and Chanda Bhairava. In the midst of all is Basuki, a dear friend of Lord Pashupati.

**Pashupati Nath Temple of Deopatan**

The name of the ancient village, where the present temple of Pashupatinath exists, was Deopatan, which is presently only 6 km. from central Kathmandu. According to a traditional belief the village Deopatan existed as early as 3rd century B.C., when this temple was also in existence. Historians (Parcival, London : 1928) have described Deopatan as a shrine-packed town with various public resting places and welfare centres around the Pashupatinath temple[7].

The definite historical evidences of Pashupati are found from 533 A.D. onwards (Gopal & Verma : 1977) when the Lichchvis (Slusser : 1982) were ruling Kathmandu. Before that period even the *vanshavalis* (genealogies of the kings of the Kiranta or the Lichvis dynasties) are silent over the Pashupati temple. Thus, the earliest epigraphic reference to the Pashupati *Kshetra* is found in the Bhasmeshwar Pashupati inscription of 533 A.D. However, some local historians also point out that even during 4th century A.D. the temple of Pashupatinath existed when a king of Kathmandu named Pushpush Deo dedicated some land and other gifts to Pashupati Mahadeva. Thus, whatever may be the exact date of its origin, one thing is very clear that the Pashupati temple of Deopatan is of very ancient origin over which no historical records in chronological order are still available.

### Royal Patronage of the Pashupatinath Temple

The present temple of Pashupatinath was constructed in 1692 A.D. after it was badly damaged by the white ants. However, most of the structural complex around the present Pashupatinath temple had been erected around 1640 A.D. during the regime of king Partap Malla, who resided at Pashupati for some years by way of atoning for his sins. Before king Partap Malla, the temple of Pashupati had been restored and repaired several times and among them special mention may be made of queen Ganga Rani, wife of King Shiva Simha Malla (1584-1614) who not only repaired the temple, but also donated gold and other ornaments to the treasure of Lord Pashupati.

The kings and queens of Nepal have patronised Lord Pashupati and have donated much to its treasure. However, among them special mention may be made of king Anantamalla (1274-1307) who donated all his wealth and treasure to Lord Pashupati and went to retire at Banepa and died thereafter some time.

While most of the kings of Nepal, irrespective of their ruling dynasties, have donated wealth and other gifts to the treasure of Pashupati, a few kings of very exceptional nature have also taken away from the treasure of Pashupati. King Jaya Prakash Malla (1768), the last king of the Kirtipur (Kathmandu), who was defeated by Pirthivi Narayan Shah, the founder of the present Shah (or Gorkha as some people say) dynasty, was one of them, People in Nepal generally believe that Jaya Prakash Malla was cursed by Lord Pashupati because he had taken away some money from the sacred treasure of Pashupatinath, and that is why he was dethroned by the Gorkha king Pirthivi Narayan Shah in the night of Indrapuja (September) of 1768. After the fall of Kirtipur (Kathmandu) kingdom of the Malla dynasty, the other two seats of Malla[8] Kingdom at Patan and Bhaktapur were also taken away by Pirthvi Narayan Shah, the first Gorkha king in 1769 and Vishal (unified) Nepal Kingdom was established.

During the Shah (Gorkha) dynasty the entire decorative surface of Pashupatinath temple have been constructed and the kings and queens have provided, from time to time, various structural and attractive look to the temple and other shrines, located in the Pashupatinath sacred cluster.

## Pashupati Shiva Linga

The temple of Pashupatinath is a large two-storeyed edifice covered with gilt copper. The architectural plan is similar to that of other pagoda style temples of this Himalayan valley. The main pavilion is panelled with silver and gold plates with beautiful patterns carved in relief on them. Therefore, it looks more gorgeous and elegant than any other temple of Nepal. The two roofs of the balconies are screened. The screened balconies are enclosed and are used as the treasure for storing in the costly offerings made to Lord Pashupati. There is *kinkin malla* (metal-border) hanging along the edges of the roof. Small bells with pendant leaves below the roofs are kept hanging. The wooden strufs have beautifully carved images of gods and goddesses.

Towards the main entrances, facing west, there are beautifully and majestically carved images of Hanuman, Ram, Sita, Lakshman etc.; while towards south, Yudhistira, Draupati, Bhim, Arjun etc. (the Pandava characters of the Mahabharata) are seen. Towards east, we find the images of Balrama, Guheswari, Saraswati, Ganga, Jamuna, Vishwakarma etc. are found and towards north the images of Ganesh, Brahma, Vishnu, Kumar etc. are seen. There are four struts on the upper roofs one each side, besides one in the corner. Sixteen goddesses are beautifully carved on them. These are called sixteen *matrikas* (divine mothers).

The pinnacle of the shrine, which consisted of a long central spire with a rod to support a towering umbrella is fairly big. Four small spires surround the base. Each pinnacle consists of an inverted bell along with a lotus, a *kalash* and a *chintamani* (magic jewel). Besides the pinnacle there are a trident (trishul), a *damru* (mini-drum) and a *pharsa* (axe), which are the emblems of Lord Shiva. There is, however, no *dhwaja* (banner) hanging on the pinnacle. On the sides of the pinnacle some-times there are some weeds found growing and the pilgrims believe that those are the shoots of Shiva's favourite plant *dhatura* (Dhatura stromonium) which has a narcotic effect.

The floor on the corridor around the main shrine and in the interior part of the sanctum has some silver coins embedded in it by the Rana Prime Minister Chandra Shamsher (1901-1928). On each of the four sides of the temple there is a door. Each door has silver-polished *torana* (tympanum) All the four doors of the temple were renovated by king Mahendra (1955-1971). The temple has a plinth of about one metre in height and is surrounded by a double railing which has on it several open oil lamps made of brass. Besides, there are four big lamp stands, one each of the four sides while there is an additional one on the south side. The lamps fed with mustard of sesame oil are lighted at the time of various festive occasions (like Shivaratri etc.).

In the courtyard there are several porches where one can sit down for saying prayers. The gigantic image on a pedestal near the main entrance i.e. on the west, is that of a gilded bull or Nandi the vehicle of Lord Shiva. It is about 3 metres long and 1.5 metres high. It is a massive figure and is the biggest metal sculpture in Nepal. The Nandi is kneeling down in a gentle reverential posture. Although there are three images of Nandi in this temple, but one that is in the western side, as referred to above, is the biggest one.

On the right side of the temple there is a large bronze trident (about 6 metres long) supported on a pole. On the south side of the temple, there are various statues of former kings, queens and other distinguished persons. The metallic statue of the late King Mahendra (father of the present king) cast in a devotional mood, is an excellent master-piece in the metal work in Nepal. In one small enclosure all the kings of the Shah dynasty are also dipicted.

On the left side of the temple one old tree of *belpatra*[9] (Aegle marmelos) is seen, while at the right side near the main entrance (western side) recently a plant of *rudraksha*[10] (Elaeo-carpus), brought from Dingla, has been planted.

With these descriptions of the Pashupati temple of Kathmandu, I now discuss, in brief, the Pashupati form of Shiva linga, which is unique from many angles.

## Pashupati form of Shiva Linga

The Pashupatinath, which literally means "lord of animals" is considered to be half Jyotirlinga, for it is half of Kedarnath.[11] 'The linga' (male sex organ) stands fixed in a *yoni* (female sex organ) and it has five faces, four of which are on the four sides while the fifth (presumably on the top) is shapeless. It is believed that this Shivalinga has a cosmic effect. Pashupati is also known as *Parasnath* and accordingly to a popular belief, it has the power of alchemy which turns all kinds of metals into gold. Nobody except the authorised priest is allowed to enter into the precinct or to touch the linga.

The height of the Shivalinga of Pashupati is between 0.9 and 1.20 metres. The face towards the east is called *Tatpurush,* This word means *Parambrahma* or *Parampurush.* Indra is *Tatpurush* of the eastern direction. He is king of all deities and, therefore, the face towards the east is called *Bhava* in the Vedas. Therefore, *Tatpurush* is worshipped in the eastern direction. The face of Pashupati towards the south is called *Aghor.* This is the symbolic representation of *Yamraj,* the god of death. He has three eyes and brows are dreadful. Pashupati, therefore, in the form of *Aghor* is worshipped, who is considered to be terror-striking for the enemies and benignant for the devotees.

The north side of the Pashupati form of Shivalinga is called *Vamadeva.* The north face is very peculiar. On the left ear there is *Nagkundla* (an ear-ring of snake). On the right side there is a lock of hair. The hair lock on the right side is smaller to that of a lady and is just like a crown. *Vamadeva* is benign and boon-giving and is worshipped as such.

The face of Pashupati towards the west is called *Sadyojat* which is the ruling deity of the western direction. *Sadyojat* means just born and, therefore, it depicts a face of a child. It has also three eyes and on the head there is a crown. Ear-ring on both the ears are similar.

On all the faces of Pashupati two hands are shown. Each right hand has a sixteen-beaded rosary of 12-forrowed *rudraksha* (Elaeocarpus). In each left hand a *kumandulu* or *kalash* (sacred pitcher) which is full of *amrit* or ambrosia.

The upper face of Pashupati is shapeless which is called *Ishan*. This face is symbolic representation of sex and there- fore, it is called *Linga-Sharita*. The upper form is considered to be full of energy and happiness. It is nucleus of all forms, therefore, it is the greatest form of Shakti or energy, which is worshipped for knowledge, fulfilment of desires etc. Pilgrims are also told that all four directions of Pashupati represent the four *dhams* of the Hindus.

The idol of Pashupatinath is, thus, considered to be not only Shivalinga alone, but also a Hindu *tirtha* in totality.

## The Sacred Specialists of Pashupati

Besides a large number of temple servants, *bhandaris* (store- keepers) and other ritual associates, the Pashupati temple has four main priests, who are selected specially from the Brahmins, south of Vindhyachal in India. Presently, they come from Karnataka (India). The priest cannot become the Nepalese citizen. The post of the priest is not hereditary.

The following are the priests of Pashupatinath of Kathmandu :

1. Shri Padmanabham Shastri,[12] called a *Mul-Bhatta* or Rawal (Chief-priest).
2. Shri Rama Krishna Shastri—Assistant Priest.
3. Shri Ananta Krishna Shastri-Assistant Priest.
4. Shri Subramanya Joshi—Assistant Priest.

Shri Padmanabham Shastri became the chief-priest in 1965. He worships the south side of Pashupati temple. He is an expert in Rig-Veda and, therefore, he is called *Rigveda-Kovid*. He is also addressed as *Mul-Bhatta* of Pashupati. He is one of the three[13] important religious personalities who is entitled to apply *tilak* to the king on his forehead.

Besides, the four main priests, there is another important priest, Shri Rama Chandra Bhatta, who worships the Vasuki- narayan and he also comes from Karnataka (India).

The selection of the priest is made by the chief-priest and *Bara-Guruji*. A candidate for priestship should be well-versed in the vedic rites and rituals. He is interviewed by the *Bara-Guruji* and if he is recommended then he is to have *darashan* (audience) of the king after presenting a coconut. The selection is final when the king approves the appointment. The priest starts doing worship in the temple of Lord Pashupati after he is initiated in the *Pashumantra*. The dress, a priest has to wear during worship, is *dusala, labeda, kamarpeti* and *srimala* (rosary of *rudraksha*). Without putting it on, a priest cannot enter into the Pashupati temple.

A priest of Pashupati must be *sansari* (house-holder); he must come from the south of Vindhyachal (in India); must not be a Nepalese citizen and should be well-versed in Sanskrit and the Vedic rituals.[14]

## Remuneration of the Priests

The four main priests, who are appointed on the basis of their selection, as discussed above, and the *Bhandaris*, whose posts are hereditary, do not get any salary. They however, get paddy instead of cash money and the quantity of paddy is fixed according to their seniority.

The offerings, made to Lord Pashupati are distributed in three main parts. One part is shared by the *Bhandaris*, while the remaining two parts are divided among the four main priests. However, the share of the *Mul-Bhatta*, (chief-priest) is double of what the assistant priests get. The gold, silver and other precious items, offered to Lord Pashupati, are deposited in the treasury of the temple.

## The Sacred Performances at the Pashupati Temple

The sacred performances at the Pashupati temple may be broadly divided into two main types viz., the daily performances and the special performances.

The daily performances start at 4 A.M. in the morning when the doors of the temple are opened. However, at that time only one door facing west remains open. At half-past nine all doors are opened. From 4 o'clock to half-past nine in the morning the *Bhandari* (store-keeper) looks after the temple and he offers garlands and other items to the devotees.

At 9-30 A.M. the elegant adornment or the attire of Lord Pasupati is taken off. At 9.45 the lingam bathed with water brought from the holy places i.e. the *tirthas* of India and Nepal. From 9.45 to 12.30 the lingam is further bathed with holy water of Bagmati which is brought in *kalash* (holy pots) from the eastern gate. Pasaupati is bathed with hot water from *Balchaturdashi* (i.e. the 14th day of dark moon fortnight) in Margsir (November-December) up to *Ghoda-yatra* in *Chaitra* (March-April). Thus, during severe cold at the higher altitude, specially from November to March, as people feel much cold take bath with hot water, similarly the Lord Pashupati is also bathed during that period with hot water. During bathing time the priests recite *slokas* (verses) from Vedas and other texts, which is called *rudri*. It is of three types : (i) Akrudri, which Brahmins, numbering from one to eleven, recite rudri for one hour; (ii) Maharudri, in which Brahmins, numbering from 11 to 21, recite rudri for two and half hours, and (iii) Lahurudri, in which Brahmins, numbering about 121, recite rudri and other *slokas* for several hours. After rudri the lingam is bathed with *Panchamrit* (milk, ghee, curd, honey etc.) After that from 1 to 1.30 P.M. the lingam is elegantly adorned and is attired in gorgeous dresses of golden cloth. On the head of the lingam *Shri-Yantra* is made. *Arti* (waving of light) is performed thereafter and *chamuru* (fly-whisk), made of yak's tail, is also swayed before the Lord. Mirror is also shown to Lord Pashupati and *shahanai* (musical instrument) is played. And at 1.30 P.M. *balbhog* (light meal) is offered to Pashupati. In the *balbhog* generally *halua* (pudding of semolina), fruits etc. are offered. *Balbhog* is cooked by the *bhandaris* (store-keepers) or some time by a Brahmin. After *balbhog*, the Lord Pashupati is offered *bhog* (meal), which includes rice, pulse, khir (rice-pudding), vegetable, *achar* (pickles) etc. This *bhog* is prepared by the assistant priest in rotation, except the chief priest. The *bhog* is afterward carried away by the *Bhandari* (store-keeper) to his home and it is not distributed. All the doors are closed during *bhog* and *balbhog*. After *bhog* doors of the temple are closed.

The temple doors are again opened at 6 P.M. in the evening. Between 7 to 8 P.M. *arti* is performed. Thereafter, the *bhog* is offered to Lord Pashupati. This *bhog*, which is offered in the night, consists of 9 *mooris* and 9 *manas* (163 kg) rice and 84 types of delicious items, vegetables etc. which are placed before the deity on the cooper platform at the south side. Inside the heap of the cooked rice, one *tola* (13 gram) of gold is kept hidden. At that time a string is used to connect the food offerings with the south face of Pashupatinath. This offered food is eaten by the people of Kushale caste. They just search for the gold in the food. One who gets it has to return to the treasury of Lord Pashupati and he is paid only one *mohar* (i.e. 50 paisa). After this night *bhog* the Lord Pashupati goes to retire for the night.

So far the special types[15] of sacred performances are concerned, special mention may be made of the Shiva-ratri, Purnamashi, Ekadashi, Janmastami, Diwali, Holi, Sankranti etc. when thousands of pilgrims and other devotees of both India and Nepal, belonging to different castes and sects, assemble and worship Lord Pashupati. Recently, the pilgrims of the Tarai region of Nepal have started undertaking the *Kamaur* pilgrimage to Kathmandu, carrying the holy water from river Narayani or Bagmati and offer them to Lord Pashupati on the occasion of Shivaratri.

To sum up, Lord Pasupati, as discussed above, is the guardian deity of the King of Nepal. The Hindu kings, since the days of Lichchivis (4th century A.D.) till the Shah (present) dynasty have patronised it. But the significant point is that even at the textual level, there is an excellent harmony between Hinduism and Buddhism in Nepal. It can be aptly said that in Nepal. Buddhism and Hinduism criss-cross each other in perfect co-existence. Nepalese Brahmins not only tolerate, but accept Buddhism. According to the *Nepal Mahatmya* "to worship Buddha is to worship Shiva" (Maujpuria 1981, p. 94). The *Swembhu puran*, an important Buddhist text on the Swembhunath (Buddhist centre of Kathmandu) in reciprocation, recommends to the Buddhists to worship Pashupati. Sometimes the followers of both the religion worship the same image under different names. Several Hindu gods have been absorbed into Buddhism. There are several idols of Buddha near the Pashupati temple. There are also several idols of *Nagas* (serpant god), which are worshipped by the tribal groups, Buddhists and the Hindus without any discrimination. Thus, the Nepalese religious pantheon has three main elements viz. the aboriginal deities like the *Nagas*, the Buddhist deities and the Hindu gods and goddesses, which have been combined together to form the Nepalese religion of this Himalayan Kingdom.

As discussed above, the Pashupati form of Shivalinga combined in himself the entire Hindu *tirthas,* spread in different parts of India. Since last three hundred years the priests of the Pashupati temple come from South India and serve this Himalayan shrine. Thus, this Pashupatinath temple of Kathmandu has caused to promote the cooperation and socio-religious solidarity of the two neighbouring nations, India and Nepal.

## REFERENCES

1. The Sacred Complex of Kathmandu is a major research project, sponsored by ICSSR, New Delhi and Professor Jha is the Director of the project, which is still in progress.
2. Paper presented at Zagreb on the occasion of XII ICAES held at Zagreb, Yugoslavia from 24th to 31st July, 1988.
3. There are three temples of Pashupati in Kathmandu valley : (i) Pashupatinath (Deopatan), (ii) Pashupatinath (Bhaktapur) and (iii) Pashupatinath near Hanuman Dhoka (in Basantpur). However, the Pashupati of Deopatan is the ancient one, which is visited by most of the pilgrims.
4. In ancient time, it is said, Lord Shiva lived here along with his consort Parvati in form of *Mriga* (deer) and spent the days and nights in pleasure. Later on when Lord Shiva was located by the *devatas* (gods) and *rishis* (saints), Lord Shiva announced that whosoever will visit this area, will live in pleasure. Since Lord Shiva was in the form of *Mriga* (dear), this *Kshetra* is known as Mrigendra Kshetra.
5. Many people say that Pashupatinath is not a Jyotirlinga, as it is not mentioned in the list of Jyotirlingas. But the sacred specialists of Pashupati argue that it is half-jyotirlinga, because it is half of Kedarnath, which is an important Jyotirlinga. There is an important myth associated with Kedarnath-Pashupatinath about the half Jyotirlinga, which will be discussed elsewhere.
6. In Kathmandu Guheshwari is one of the fifty-one Shakti *Pithas* is very important sacred centre for the Shakta worshippers.
7. Presently there are many welfare centres like-Bridha-Shram (old-men house), Samaj Kalyan Kendra (Social Public Welfare centre) etc. adjacent to the Pashupatinath temple at Kathmandu.
8. When Pirthvi Narayan Shah, the founder of the present Shah dynasty, attacked on Kirtipur (Kathmandu) in September, 1768 where king Jaya Prakash Malla was ruling, at that time king Tejnara

Simha and king Ranjit Simha were ruling at Patan and Bhaktapur respectively. While Ranjit was exiled to Kashi (India), king Tejnara Simha was imprisoned and jailed by the Gorkha king. Thereafter all 24 smaller kingdoms spread all over Nepal, were incorporated in United Nepal under Pirthvi Narayan Shah in 1769. From Pirthvi Narayan Shah the first Gorkha king, the descendants of Gorkha kings have been ruling Nepal and the present king is tenth in that order.

9. It is a very old tree, but due to higher altitude which is not favourable for the growth of a *bel* tree, leaves remain absent in the tree or leaves are not fully grown.

10. Dingla is in Koshi Anchal of Nepal, which is very famous for *rudraksha* cultivation. Now *rudraksha* trade is very much growing in Nepal in which hundred of people of Nepal and India are engaged in.

11. It is said while half portion of Shiva, in form of a buffalo, is in Kedarnath, the half portion is enshrined in Pashupati. Hence both Kedarnath and Pashupatinath should be visited by the devotees to obtain the full *punya* (religious merit).

12. He was interviewed by the author in depth and his full life-history will be described in detail in the main report.

13. The three persons are the Bara Guruji, the Mul-Bhatta and the Mahantha of Gorakhnath temple, who apply *tilak* on the forehead of king of Nepal specially on the occasion of coronation and other festive and auspicious occasions.

14. The detail discussion on their percentage of share and other descriptions concerning their remunerations, honorarium etc., will be made in the main report on "The Sacred Complex of Kathmandu", which is likely to be submitted to the ICSSR soon by the author.

15. The details of special types of sacred performances will be discussed in the main report.

## NOTES

Allen, Michael R., 1975 : *The Cult of Kumari : Virjin Worship in Nepal*; CNAS, Tribhuvan University, Kathmandu.

Chitrkar, Ratan Lal, 1970 : *Shri Pashupati Mahatmya* (in Nepali and Hindi) : Kathmandu.

Jha, Makhan, 1971 : *The Sacred Complex of Janakpur* (Nepal); United Publishers, Allahabad, India.

Jha, Makhan, 1978 : *Aspects of Great Traditional City in Nepal*; Kishor Vidyaniketan, Varanasi, India.

Jha, Makhan, 1980 : The Sacred Centres of Kathmandu : History and Typology; *Journal of Social Research*, Vol. XXIII, No. 1.

Jha, Makhan, 1985 : *Dimensions of Pilgrimage* (ed); Inter-India Publication, New Delhi.

Majupuria, T.C. and I. Majupuria, 1979 : *Glimpses of Nepal*; Gwalior, India.

Majupuria, T.C. and I. Majupuria, 1981 : *Pashupatinath : The Divine Glory of the Guardian Deity of Nepal*; Lashkar, Gwalior, India.

Slusser, Marry Shepherd, 1982 : *Nepal Mandal : A Cultural History of Nepal Valley*; Princeton University Press, Princeton, U.S.A.

# 11

# The Sacred Complex of Badrinath
## A Study in Himalayan Pilgrimage

DINESH KUMAR

## Introduction

ANTHROPOLOGICAL approach to study the places of pilgrimage, as a dimension of civilization, has now become an important and independent subject of research not only in Indian anthropology, but also in World Anthropology. In India there are a numbers of Hindu sacred centres, belonging to various sects and traditions, of which some have been studied by anthropologists and it will not be out of context to review some of these works with a view to throw light on the nature of the study of "the sacred complex" of Hindu sacred centres.

Vidyarthi (1961), a student of Redfield, studied a great traditional city of Hindu Gaya (India), located in the ancient cultural zone of Magadh which actually initiated the rise of "sacred complex" studies in Indian anthropology". Following the foot-steps of Vidyarthi's concept of "sacred complex", Jha (1971) studied the "sacred complex of Janakpur (Nepal)" and brought out the main theses that the civilizational boundary oversides the political and administrative boundaries. However, it was found that the concept of "sacred complex" has a wider acceptability and universality in the study of Hindu places of pilgrimage.

After these two major works, a number of Hindu places of pilgrimage have been studied, which have been described and reviewed elsewhere.[1]

However, when we look at the Himalayan sacred centres, we find that no significant work has been done and, therefore, I undertook the study of Badrinath, located in the Garhwal Himalaya, which is the super-most *tirtha* (place of pilgrimage) of the Hindus.

## Badrinath

Among the four *dhams* of the Hindus Badrinath is the most important *dham* located in the Garhwal Himalaya region which is mentioned in the sacred texts of the land as *Uttarakhand*.

The cultural boundary of Uttarakhand more or less coincides with the political boundary of the eight hill districts of Uttar Pradesh i.e. Dehradun, Tehri Garhwal, Uttar-Kashi, Pauri Garhwal, Nainital, Almora, Pithoragarh and Chamoli. The sacred centres of Badrinath, however, fall in the district of Chamoli.

As discussed earlier a number of Hindu-tirthas have been studied by the anthropologists but all these centres of pilgrimage are located in plain lands of the country. But all of us know that ecological set-up plays a very important role in moulding the mode of worship, organisation of sacred specialist, their life patterns, dresses etc. which have not been studied in detail in Indian anthropology.

In Himalaya the sacred centre of Badrinath is located at an altitude of more than 10,000 ft. in the Garhwal area, where the Yatra season (pilgrimage) continues only for six months from May to late October every year, and thereafter the doors of Badrinath temple are closed for six months. This is mainly done due to ecological obstacle, because no pilgrim or any devotee can stay at Badrinath during the severe cold season when the heaviest snowfall is recorded in Badrinath.

## The Sacred Geography of Badrinath

The presiding deity of Uttarakhand is Lord Badrinath. There are various sacred centres, located and distributed in the Uttarakhand and therefore the word "Uttarakhand" is found in many "Purans" and other sacred texts of the land. The sacred centres, found in and around Badrinath, are also very important for understanding the complexities of the sacred geography of the area.

## Textual Dimension of the Himalayan Shrines

The largest number of the sacred centres are located in Central Himalayas. The central boundary of the Central Himalayas coincides more or less with Uttarakhand, which has been vividly mentioned in the Purans. In various sacred texts Uttarakhand is also known as Brahampur, Bhu-Swarg, Swapna-Brahampur etc. In the Rigveda as well as in the Sat-path Brahman the word Gangotri occurs for the first time. In the Buddhist literature especially in different *Jatkas* we find the word Uttarakhand as a place of pilgrimage. In the various Purans like Skanda Purans (especially Shristy Khand) and Shiv Puran etc. we get a vivid description of Uttarakhand and its various sacred centres. In the Aswamedha-parva of Mahabharat, Uttarakhand is described in detail when Arjun defeats the inhabitants of the Uttarakhand. Again in the works of Kalidas (4th century A.D.) we find a detailed description of the places of Uttarakhand especially in the *Raghuvansham*, the *Kumarsambhavam* and the *Meghdootam* etc. which reveal as to how Himalayas attracted the attention of writers, poets, saints and sages even during those days when there was lack of developed means of communication.

Adi Shankaracharya (788-820 A.D.) visited the Himalayan shrines around 814 A.D. and lived there for 6 years till he died in 820 A.D. in Kedarnath. We are further told that each year during summer he used to stay for six months in the Vyas Gupha near Mana village in Badridham and six months during winter at Kartikepur (now modern Joshimath). It was he who established the idols of Badrivishal at Badrinath after taking them out from the Narad Kund near Garur-Gupha.

Through historical documents we also come to know that during the ancient period of Indian History there were many sites for pilgrimage in Uttarakhand which were patronised by various ancient kingdoms of the central Himalayas like Rinida, Yodhem, etc. whose cultural patronage is still there. Shiv Prasad Dabral (1970), a local historian, has deciphered and described the various coins, written in the Karothi and Brahmini scripts of these Himalayan scripts of ancient India. Again, during the medieval period there were many kingdoms and among them special mention may be made of Kulinda

Nagar, Kartikepur, Chandragarhi, Deoalgarh, and Champabat etc.

## Myth and Legends of Badrinath

About the origin of present Badrinath there is a myth according to which Lord Vishnu along with his spouse Laxmi left Thuling (very interior place in the Himalayas) as the place got corrupted by the meat-eating monks and other licentious people. He set up his *ashram* 4 km south of the village Mana on the bank of river Alakhnanda. He sat for a long severe meditation. Laxmi, finding her husband exposed to weather, assumed the form of a big Badri tree (jujubi) protecting him with her foliage. Having been pleased with her devotion, Lord Vishnu named the place after the Badri tree and therefore it was called Badrika Ashram. Atkinson (1973) holds that there used to be jujubi forest (Badri-van) here which are presently not found at Badrinath.

There is another tradition which is also mentioned in the Vishnu-Puran about the origin of Badrinath. Here the *pauranic* version is slightly different and also mentions for the first time about five types of Badrinath. According to the tradition Dharam had two sons—Nar and Narayan Parvat, where they selected their sites and since they desired to spread their religious activities on a large scale, they wedded spacious valley in this part of the higher Himalayas. In their search for an ideal place, they set up *ashram* at different places of natural beauty viz Bridha-Badri, Yog-Badri, Dhyan-Badri and Bhavish-Badri, conclusively they found the present Badrinath more suitable for having hot and cold spring besides the river Alakhnanda and it was called Badri-Vishal.

## Contextual Dimensions of Badrinath

The Badrinath Dham, as all of us know, is situated on the western bank of the river Alaknanda which flows from north to south and makes a natural division between the sacred and secular zones at Badrinath. Towards west of Alaknanda river the famous Badrinath temple is situated besides various other sacred centres like the temple of Shankaracharya. Different *tapta* (hot) Kund and different *shilas* (stones) represent various sacred centres.

While the western sites of the Alaknanda river represent the sacred zones, the eastern sites of the river represent the secular zones which are represented by a large numbers of Dharamshala's (pilgrims inn), tourist lodge, P.W.D. Office, police station, hotels, restaurants, shopping centres etc.

Besides these two zones there may be another cluster of sacred centres located in and around the Mana village (about 3 km. extreme north of the Badrinath temple). Among them special mention may be made of the Vyas Gupha (the cave), Ganesh Gupha (cave) Bhim-Pula, Mata-Mandir and Basudhara etc.

## Sacred Performances at Badrinath

In the study of sacred complexes of the different Hindu-tirtha (Vidyarthi, 1961; Jha 1971; Vidyarthi and Jha, 1974; Vidyarthi, Saraswati and Jha 1978 etc.) every act of worship, performed at a sacred centre has been called as sacred performance. This may vary from simple *jap* (uttering of God's name) to Darshan (glimpses of the idols) or from different types of Arti and Bhog to the complex form of *rituals* like yagana and *havan* or Maha *Abhisekham*

The Pujas performed in the morning are Mahabhisekham, Abhisekh, Geeta Path, Veda-Path, Bhagwat Path, Kapoor Arti, Swarna Arti, Astotari Vishnu Sahasranam Path, Vishnu Sahasranamabali, Atka, Geet Govind Path, Shyam Arti and Khir Bhog.

## The Sacred Specialists of Badrinath

In the anthropological studies of the Hindu-tirtha, the sacred specialists play very important role in perpetuation of rites and rituals as well as to establish a continuity between the centres of civilization and the people of India. The sacred specialists are of different types, because they are specialised in a variety of sacred activities, and therefore in most of the studies on the sacred complexes carried out earlier (Vidyarthi : 1961, Makhan Jha : 1971, Vidyarthi, Saraswati and Jha : 1978) different types of sacred specialists have been discussed.

At Badrinath, when we look at the sacred specialists from this point of view we get a large number of the sacred specialists engaged in perpituating the different types of sacred performances. The sacred specialists of Badrinath work in different

210 Social Anthropology of Pilgrimage

ecological set-up and, therefore they have a distinct style of life, dresses and food habits.

The Chief Priest of Badrinath temple is known as Rawal, who comes from Namboodri Brahmin family from Kerala. According to the present rule the Government of Uttar Pradesh has to write to Government of Kerala for the selection of a suitable Namboodri bachelor Brahmin for the post of Chief Priest at Badrinath. Among the essential qualifications for the post of Rawal, it is obligatory that the candidate should possess the degree of Acharya in Sanskrit, he should be bachelor, he should be well-versed in reciting the *mantras* and *vaishnav* mode of worship. Considering these qualifications and in consultation with the present Rawal of Badrinath, a candidate is recommended by the Kerala Government to Uttar Pradesh to forward his name to the king of Tehri-Garhwal, who is the tutelary head of the Badrinath, for he is called as ,'Balond-Badri" (Movable Badri or Chalanti Badri), for his Tilak ceremony. As soon as the Tilak ceremony is held in Tehri, he becomes the chief priest of Badrinath and is addressed as Rawal. He resides at Badrinath permanently for six months from Baisakh to Kartik till the temple of Badrinath remains open and, thereafter, he either goes on pilgrimage or resides at his native village in Kerala state. The topology of other sacred specialists, who assist him in conducting daily retuals at Badrinath temple like Nayab Rawal, Dharma-Dhikari, Ved-Pathi, a group of priests and Pandas Samadhini, Bhandari, Rasoiyas (cooks), Devotional Singer, Clerk of Dev-ashram, Water-keeper, Jal Bhariya, Guards etc., is very interesting.

The duties distributed to the staff of the Badrinath temple is shown in the Table 11.1. It appears from Table 11.1 that besides the chief priest there are varieties of sacred specialists who earn their livelihood by "religious services" (Vidyarthi : 1961) by performing different types of duties in honour of Lord Badrinath.

Among the different types of sacred specialist the word 'Panda' is rather a generic term which includes a number of Brahmins of Dev-Prayag and other Brahmins of the Garhwal region, who are associated with the sacred services of Badrinath since time immemorial.

All sacred specialists are engaged in Badrinath temple only

TABLE 11.1 : **Duties of Staff of Badrinath Temple**

| Sl. No. | Name of the Sacred specialist | Caste | Duties |
|---|---|---|---|
| 1. | Rawal | Namboodri Brahmins of Kerala | Chief Priest of Badrinath Temple. |
| 2. | Nayab-Rawal | Namboodri Brahmins of Kerala | To assist Rawal. |
| 3. | Dharmadhikari | Brahmin | Astrological works. |
| 4. | Ved-Pathi | Brahmins | To recite Veda. |
| 5. | Panda | Brahmins | To assist pilgrims |
| 6. | Samadhini (tailor) | Dimri Brahmins | Stitching cloth work of Badrinath-jee. |
| 7. | Bhandari | Dimri Brahmin | To maintain the store. |
| 8. | Rasoiya (cook) | Dimri Brahmins | To prepare Bhog etc. for Lord Badrinath. |
| 9. | Devotional singer | Sikh or any caste | To sing in honour of Lord Badrinath. |
| 10. | Clerk of Devasthan | Dimri Brahmin and Nautiyal. | To maintain register of the temple. |
| 11. | Water-keeper | Dimri Brahmin. | To sprinkle water in the courtyard of the temple. |
| 12. | Jal Bhariya | Brahmin | To fetch sacred water from Alaknanda river for bathing of Lord Badrinath. |
| 13. | Guard | Rajput and Brahmins. | To guard temple and door of the temple. |

for six months because in the winter season the door of the
Badrinath temple is closed. Then the movable idol of Badrinath
is brought to Joshimath for sojourn during next six months.

So far the dresses of the sacred specialists in general are
concerned they wear the woollen garments of different types
because of the higher altitude. In the plain land we have
observed that the sacred specialist of the Hindu Tirtha especially
those who perform the ritual inside the temple, remain naked
and usually and do not wear *banian* or any other cloth on their
body. But as the situation at Badrinath is quite different because
of ecological set up sacred specialists have to wear heavy
garments. Ecological conditions mould not only the mode of
worship, but also their dresses, diets etc.

## The Pilgrims : Their Typology

The concept of pilgrimage exists in all major religions, although,
not unexpectedly, its meaning varies to a great extent within
the conical structures of each religion. In Hinduism, the
pilgrimage to holy places is an ancient and continuing religious
tradition. Numerous sacred centres distributed in various parts
of India, attract millions of pilgrims. Some sacred centres draw
pilgrims from all over the country while others attract largely
from the local and regional area.

In Hinduism the institution of pilgrimage has been mainly
described as a religious tradition, but in addition to it, the
pilgrimage has many significant dimensions. The innumerable
sacred centres can be conceived as a system of nodes having
varying degree of socio-religious traits. It is found that while
some places are focal points for pilgrims from the entire vast
Indian Sub-continent with the variegated cultural mosaic, other
from modest places may serve as centres of congregation of
devotees from the immediate vicinity and between these two
extremes there are sacred centres of several intermediate levels.
The sacred centres of several levels, thus, have their corresponding pilgrim "field" and those pilgrims interact freely at several
stages. In this way the sacred centres in India generate a
gigantic network of socio-religious circulation in compassing
the entire Hindu population.

## Development of Hindu Pilgrimage

Several scholars have expressed their view on the origin and the development of the practice of *Tirtha-Yatra* (pilgrimage) and in many sacred texts we find reference about different types of pilgrimage. Its antiquity is evidenced by both the Brahminical and Buddhist literature.

The Purana and Uppurans also elaborately describe various types of pilgrimages. In addition to epics and the Purans, the writers of the Nibandhas (digest and commentaries) also emphasized on the types, nature and importance of *Tirtha-Yatra.* Among the various Nibandhas which deals with Hindu Pilgrimage of Medieval India, special mention may be made of Laxidhar's *Tirtha-Kalpataru*, Narayanbhatt's *Tirthalisetu*, Hemadri's *Chaturbarna-Chintamani*, Mitra-Mishra's *Tirtha Prakash* etc.

## Democratic Nature of Pilgrimage

The pilgrimage is a sacred act, and hence those who go for pilgrimage are all sacred "(Saraswati, 1965, pp. 30-43) besides that pilgrims are also guided by certain rules and traditions which may be said of liberal and democratic nature. For example, there is no caste and sex restriction on going to the pilgrimage as have been found in the study of Janakpur (Jha : 1971), Kashi (Vidyarthi, Saraswati and Jha : 1978) etc. It has been found in Janakpur that pilgrims belonging to different castes participate in *Parikarmas* (holy circumambulation) and nobody makes any objection from any section of the societies.

## Changing taking place in the Himalayan Pilgrimage

The socio-cultural milieu in Uttarakhand is deeply shaped by the Himalayan ecology. The mountainous terrain and the cold climate not only regulate dietary habits but also enforce certain clothing requirement.

Thus, unlike the pilgrimage undertaken at the. *tirthas* of the plain land, the pilgrimage of the Himalayan shrines requires extraordinary preparation from the very beginning till it is concluded either at Haridwar or at Rishikesh.

Previously when Pilgrims used to go on foot, they took about 45 days to cover the distance from Haridwar to the

Badrinath Dham. But after India's independence motorable road was constructed from Rishikesh to Joshimath and after Joshimath pilgrims used to go on foot to Badrinath, till 1962. When Indo-China war broke out in 1962 and Chinese soldiers entered in Mana village and killed many Indian soldiers, the Government of India made a pucca all-weather road not only from Joshimath to Badrinath but also repaired the road going up to different valleys in the Himalayas. I consider this development as the landmark in the changing pattern of Himalayan pilgrimage. When the on-foot pilgrimage turned into wheel-born pilgrimage, it gave birth to many subsidiary and satellite business, like hotels and restaurants, taxi hiring etc. and therefore, Himalayan pilgrimage has become an "industry" through which the people of the Himalayan region earn their livelihood.

## Conclusion

Badrinath is considered a Hindu Tirtha of supreme importance among the Hindus of the world. Badrinath has been called as a Tirtha of *Satyug*. Its importance lies not only in its beautiful location in the high Himalayas but also in its existence and location in the midst of several Himalayan sacred centres which have deep mythological, textual and historical importance. Badrinath is nicely described in various texts. It is deeply associated with various myths and is surrounded by various legends of the epic period of the great Bharat-war etc. Thus, from all respects the Badrinath is the greatest Hindu-Tirtha.

In Badrinath, various facets of "sacred complex" have moulded due to the ecological factors of the higher altitude. The dresses of the pilgrims and priests have changed because of severe cold. Lord Badrivishal, the God of Universe, is bathed with hot water whereas in the plains there are a large numbers of sacred centres and nowhere the deity is bathed with hot water even in the winter season. It can be concluded that ecological factors do play an important role in moulding the mode of worship.

The chief sacred specialist of this Himalayan shrines who comes from south India, is called Rawal. He is a Namboodri Brahman, a bachelor, a well versed scholar of Sanskrit and is appointed as chief priest on the recommendation of the Government of Uttar Pradesh. He becomes "Rawal" after *Tilak* ceremony, performed by the King of Tehri Garhwal, who is the tutelary head of Badrinath. Garhwal *Naresh* is also called as "Balond Badri", for he is Badri-incarnate. The chief sacred specialist of Badrinath dominates over all other priests of this high Himalayan shrine and he distinguishes himself not only in conducting the sacred performance inside the Badrinath temple, but also in matters of several socio-religious context of the Badrinath temple management.

The people in general have strong feeling that Lord Badri-Vishal will save us in case of any insurgency by the neighbouring country. Badri-Vishal, therefore, is considered to be a symbol of national unity.

### REFERENCES

1. "For detail, see Professor Jha's book—*Aspects of a Great Traditional City of Nepal*, (Introduction), 1978.

### NOTES

Chakraborti, P., 1974, Some observations on the pilgrims and their Pilgrimage. A case study at Tarkeshwar, *Journal of Social Research*, Ranchi XVIII—1, pp. 104-115.

Dubey, S.C., 1958, Approach to study of complex culture, *Journal of Social Research*, (Vol. 1, No. L).

Dashmana, M.M., 1982, Himalayan Pilgrimage, *Journal of Social Research*, Vol. XXI, No. II, Ranchi.

Jha, M., 1971, *The Sacred Complex of Janakpur*, The United Publishers, Allahabad.

Jha, M., 1974, *Symposium on Sacred Complexes in India*, Ranchi (Ed. Jointly).

Jha, M., 1978, *Aspects of a Great Traditional City in Nepal*, The Kishore Vidya Niketan, Varanasi.

Jha, M., 1978, *The Sacred Complex of Kashi*, Concept Publishing Co., New Delhi, (Jointly).

Jha, M, 1982, *Transactions of the Centre of Himalayan Study*; (Ed. Jointly), Ranchi.

Jha, M., 1985, *Dimensions of Pilgrimage* (Ed.), Inter-India Publications, New Delhi.

Jha, M., 1986, *Ecology, Economy and Religion of the Himalaya*, (Ed. Jointly); Orient Publication, New Delhi.

Jha, M., 1989, *The Sacred Complex of Kathmandu (Nepal)*, ICSSR Project Report, (in Manuscript).

Kumar, Dinesh, 1988, *The Sacred Complex of Badrinath*, Unpublished Ph.D. Thesis (R.U.).

Madan, B.S., 1980, *An Introduction to Uttarakhand*, Karan Singh Amar Singh Publishing House, Haridwar.

Rawat, S.S.R. Singh, 1983, *Badrinath Dham Darpan*, Narayan Jayanti Publishing House, Chamoli Garhwal (U.P.).

Raha, M.K., 1987, *The Himalayan Heritage*, Gian Publishing House, New Delhi.

Singh, M.M., 1985, *Call of Uttarakhand, Mainly Badrinath-Kedarnath*, Randhir Book Publishing Haridwar.

Vidyarthi, L.P., 1961, *The Sacred Complex of Gaya*, Asia Publishing House, Bombay.

# 12

# Puri : A Centre of Pilgrimage of an Eclectic Shrine

## Sabita Acharya

PURI is one of the most important centres of pilgrimage in India. This sacred place owes its size and importance entirely to its connection with the famous temple of Jagannath. Puri is the centre of a great cultural tradition consisting of sacred and secular institutions with their religious and social functions, cultural values and symbolic configurations. It is widely known as a great religious and sacred centre (*kshetra*) and a place of pilgrimage (*tirtha*) since the days history could reckon.

Puri, the site of Lord Jagannath, is situated right on the coast of Bay of Bengal in Orissa. It lies between 19° 28'N and 20° 35'N latitude and between 84°29'E and 86°25'E longitude. Puri has a population of 2,911.720 persons (1981 census).

Puri forms one of the four *dhams* of the Hindu, renovated according to the traditions, at the instance of Adi Shankar (788 A.D. to 820 A.D.), the great teacher and a revivalist of philosophic Hinduism, at the four corners of India. In North, *Badrinath* is situated which is dedicated to Lord Vishnu, in South *Kanchipuram*, associated with the worship of Lord Siva, established by Sri Rama, the reincarnation of Lord Vishnu. In west, *Dwarika* which is dedicated to Lork Krishna—Vishnu incarnate. For every pious Hindu, a visit to all the *dhams* is almost obligatory.

The temple of Lord Jagannath is 214 feet high. It is crowned with Vishnu's sacred wheel and flag which catch the eyes of the tourists and pilgrims, from a long distance. The architecture of the temple is more impressive. The sculptural and architectural heritage of Puri coupled with its sanctity as Vishnu or Purushottam *kshetra* since early mediaeval days, attracts thousands of visitors from all corners of the world throughout the year. The importance of the town as a seat of vaishnavism increased when Chodaganga Deva constructed the temple of Purushottam Jagannath and installed the image of the deities.

The data have been collected at Puri through field work following different anthropological methods and techniques such as preparation of schedules, observations, interviews, case-study etc. The method of observation was of non-participant type but observations have invariably been carried out on natural situations. Both individual and group interviews were taken. This is a structural-functional type of study. Interviews were taken from 200 pilgrims of India who were from Orissa M.P., U.P., West Bengal, Bihar, Rajasthan, Gujarat, Maharashtra, Karnatak and Andhra Pradesh. Different types of pilgrims belonging to different caste-groups, income-groups and educational status groups were interviewed.

The image of Lord Jagannath, be a synonym of either a Buddhist or Brahminical deity, in origin, is not found anywhere else in ancient India except at Puri. The structure of the present temple was put up during the rule of king of Orissa, namely Ananga Bhima Dev, who ruled Kalinga Kingdom in 1174 A.D.

Jagannath is an unsectarian name which is an eclectic one. The crude figures of the Jagannath triad do not approximate to any anthropomorphic concept of the known gods and goddesses of Hindu pantheon. In daily ritual practices and festivals of temple, Jaina, Buddhist, Saiva, Tantric and Vaishnavite influence are clearly discernible on the Jagannath cult. Hinduism has an extraordinary capacity to incorporate and amalgamate other religious and alien cults. Thus, the Jagannath temple at Puri attracts pilgrims from all over India, and therefore Puri may be called as a religious certre of all-India importance, and further it is bound up with the culture and history of Orissa—Jagannath cult and Oriya culture.

The concept of pilgrimage to reputed holy places has always

been very popular in India. But no pilgrimage was ever so extensively practised and so generally famed as that of pilgrimage to Jagannath. Hindu religion and Hindu superstitions have stood at Puri for 18 centuries against the ever-changing world. This is a national Hindu temple where the devotees flock to worship Lord Jagannath from every corner of India.

The institution of pilgrimage at Puri has knitted the linguistically diverse Hindu pilgrims of different certres who are living even beyond the national boundary of India and came from different political and geographical regions as well as from various social and economic strata. In Hinduism, the institution of pilgrimage to holy places is an ancient and continuing religious tradition. It assumes an important role in generating a circulation mechanism in which all the social strata of Hinduism participate.

The Puri temple of Lord Jagannath occupies a unique position not only in the State of Orissa, but also in relation to the whole of the country, because pilgrims from different parts of the country constantly throng into Puri. Lord Jagannath, primarily a Hindu deity, had been made to symbolize the Orissan culture, a collection of heterogeneous elements. The history of Jagannath is the religious history of Orissa. Lord Jagannath is the oldest deity in the world; who is still being worshipped. The worship of Jagannath cult has its mutual relationships with the political power in Orissa. The relation between the Jagannath cult and kingship in Orissa found their lasting manifestation in the construction of the present monumental Jagannath temple in the middle of the 12th centry.

The *sebaks* or servants of Lord Jagannath are classified into 36 types, whose number is more than 2000. There are nearly 500 members in the association of the cooks who are working in the temple kitchen. The cooks again employ about 500 servants to help them in cooking. The total number of people being directly dependent on the temple for their livelihood is about 4000. The total number of people directly employed within the secular organisation is approximately 300 who work under temple administration from different angles.

Pilgrims visit Puri—a Brahminical shrine i.e a Brahmanic deity worshipped by the Brahman priests in accordance with the Brahmanical mode of worship. Gajapati (King) of Puri is treated as the superintendent of the temple of Lord Jagannath, who has got some important *sevas* (service) in the temple, for which he enjoys unique privileges for himself and his family.

Every Hindu has to meet the requirement of his religion and must be taught the sacred books by a Brahman and his religious sacrifices are also administered by a Brahman. The functional abilities of Brahman are fixed and transmitted from generation to generation that the exchange of services must be on and asymmetrical level and that ethical and ideal elements in the thinking of individuals remain constant (Wiser : 1936).

From the very beginning of Hindu society, in Hindu pilgrimage, there lies service relationships between the pilgrim and priest. However a pilgrims gets the required services from the priest of the temple when he comes on pilgrimage to the sacred centres.

The traditional Vedic Brahmans of Orissa could adapt their position to recent political and socio-economic changes and within the framework of new media of influence, they could retain their status. According to tradition, the priests of Puri temple were powerful in the past both in the regional political power structure and religious leadership. Today, the pilgrims get the services from the traditional priests or *sevaks* of Lord Jagannath and observe all the opportunities during their pilgrimage at Puri. Priests are always appointed for the ritual service of pilgrims, in the temple of Lord Jagannath at Puri. The power prestige and influence of the priests of Lord Jagannath were considerable in the past; but these have declined since the State government took over the management of the temple.

A time-honoured relationship exists between the pilgrims and the priests of Jagannath. The priests employ pilgrim agents to keep contact with the pilgrims who come from different parts of the country. They maintain a list of the pilgrims who are under their supervision and whom they escort to Puri on pilgrimage. The pilgrims agents or *"Jatri Pandas"* are not necessarily all Brahmans. In the past, they visited remote corners of India with a view to recruiting pilgrims before important festivals and accompanied them all the way to Puri for which they are known as *batua* (Journeyman) or *sathua* (fellow travellers). Now-a-days, as the pilgrims travel by trains and buses, the agents are no more required to accompany them from their home but usually await them to receive at important railway junctions and other pilgrim centres and then conduct them to Puri.

It is calculated that about 40 regions are there all over India from where pilgrims come to Puri and handled by priests. For each region, separate priests are allotted to guide the pilgrims on their pilgrimage. Each priest has to maintain his own official records of pilgrims to handle them properly which is a large and complex organisational network of different personnel. The priests have a reputation for hospitality and they take all possible care to the pilgrims during their stay at Puri. *Pandas* or priests give company to the pilgrims round the important shrines and other holy places where certain ceremonies are performed within the Puri town.

The pilgrims coming to Puri temple are directly concerned with the economy of the Jagannath temple which appears to be very complex in nature. The religious importance of Puri attracts hundreds of thousands of pilgrims throughout the year. Within the temple compound there are many small shops or sheds where a variety of articles are sold to the pilgrims and the selling of these articles is the source of income of the temple whose total value cannot be figured out. The pilgrims also give offerings and make donations to the priests and temple. Now-a-days, there is a *hundi* (a container for money-collection) which has been set up inside the temple for the receipt of pilgrims' donations. It is introduced recently by the Government of Orissa.

Through a study of 200 pilgrims the nature of social interaction between the priests and pilgrims has been found out. Out of the total, 56 per cent of pilgrims appointed priests (guides) for their pilgrimage to guide them at Puri who belong to higher income group. 44 per cent of pilgrims did not appoint any guide who were mostly the regional pilgrims. It is also found that maximum number (63%) of pilgrims communicated with their priests/guides in Hindi language whereas minimum number (18%) of pilgrims communicated in Oriya language who were the regional pilgrims. 82 per cent of pilgrims opined that guides were professionally good. 64 per cent of the pilgrims got their guides easily whereas 4 per cent only got their guides with difficulties.

There are different types of Pilgrims who come to Puri—the sacred seat of Lord Jagannath—from different strata of Indian society. Puri is the meeting place for different kinds of people and traditions where exchange of ideas, way of life and traditions take place. The tradition of Puri is a network of different social and cultural relations within and between communities of different levels of socio-cultural integration. Hindu pilgrim keep more or less their traditions and social customs intact from generation to generation. In the present study, there are four types of pilgrims namely local pilgrims, regional pilgrims, national pilgrims and also the non-Hindu and international pilgrims.

Out of the total sample taken, 11.11 per cent were local pilgrims who were residents of Puri town. 24.24 per cent were regional pilgrims, who were residents of different districts of Orissa. National pilgrims who were residents of other States of India, constituted 62.77 per cent of the total population. The non-Hindu and international (foreigners) pilgrims constitute 1.66 per cent of the sample taken. They generally come to Puri occasionally and seasonally. Amongst the non-Hindu pilgrims, Muslims, Sikhs, Jains and Christians are included.

The sample included 33.33 per cent female pilgrims and 66.66 per cent male pilgrims. Out of it, 87.77 per cent pilgrims were married and 7.22 per cent were unmarried, 1.66 per cent were widows and 3.33 per cent were widowers. Between the age-group from 30 years to 39 years, maximum number (23.33%) of pilgrims came to Puri. Service-holders came to Puri in maximum number (42.22%). The income-group whose monthly income was between Rs. 750 to Rs. 1000 came to Puri in majority (16.66%), pilgrims came to Puri in maximum number (22.22%) who are passed matric standard only. The sample included majority pilgrims of Brahman caste (40%) and maximum (35%) Oriya speaking pilgrims.

There are a number of hotels, *dharmasalas, maths* (monasteries), lodging houses, *ashrams* available for pilgrims' accommodation during their pilgrimage at Puri. It has been found that maximum number (80.24%) of pilgrims prefer to stay at different *dharmasalas* which are free of cost.

At Puri, 92 licenced lodging houses are located whose total strength of accommodation is about 10,000 persons at a time. Besides these, there are six licenced dharmasalas which have the capacity to accommodate 2,000 pilgrims at a time. The total number of hotels is around 300, including luxurious, moderate, and medium. All of them are not licenced. There are also five licenced ashrams situated at Puri to accommodate people of different sects. These ashrams can accommodate about 500 to 600 persons. Besides, there are government accommodations namely circuit house, P.W.D. Inspection Bangalow, Forest Rest House, Youth Hostel, Pantha Nivas etc. for pilgrims. It is observed that during Rath Yatra, the most important and famous festival of Lord Jagannath, all the hostels, lodging houses, dharmasalas, ashrams, maths are over-crowded by pilgrims. Not only the corners and centres in each apartment are occupied but also the entire space including the verandahs, and steps of these houses overflow with pilgrims. Even the private houses of pandas are filled up by the pilgrims for accommodation.

In the past there were no roads to come to Puri; pilgrims had to come across deep forests walking. Roads were not well-connected or safe and few people could return home safely from a long trip; there was fear of an attack by wild animals from all sides while passing through the dense forest. Pilgrims of distant places could hardly reach Puri for a *darshan* or audience of Lord Jagannath.

The first road connection to Puri was built between 1811 to 1826 and the first railway connection to Puri was made in 1896. Now Puri is easily accessible by train and also by roads with all kinds of comforts from distant places of India.

It is estimated that about 13 lakhs pilgrims visited Puri in 1986. Around 10 lakh people came by trains and around 3 lakh pilgrims by road. The average floating population of Puri per day is about 6,000 in ordinary days, but it rises up to 10,000 per day during festive occasions. *Rath Yatra* (car festival) is the most important and famous festival of Lord Jagannath which has worldwide reputation. Last year, around 3 lakh pilgrims assembled at Puri to attend the car-festival. The total income of Indian Railways during *Rath Yatra* of last year was more than 12 lakh rupees. Maximum number (72.83%) of pilgrims come to Puri on pilgrimage by trains. During their journey to Puri, 91.97 per cent of pilgrims faced no difficulties.

Partaking of *mahaprasad* (food offered to Lord Jagannath daily) is a distinctive feature of pilgrimage at Puri. People of all status groups, castes, creeds may join together in eating the *mahaprasad*. Which proclaims the equality of all men before God. *Mahaprasad*, the cooked food, is the main offering made to Lord Jagannath. During their pilgrimage, maximum pilgrims (97.22%) preferred *mahaprasad* as their principal food at Puri which is easily available in the temple. For 58.33% pilgrims, the cost of *mahaprasad* was not expensive. The hygienic condition of *mahaprasad* was satisfactory for 80 per cent pilgrims. 20 per cent pilgrims who belonged to higher income group and higher educational group, were not satisfied with it.

The concept of purity and pollution attain their form within the bounded structure of particular societies and cultures. Each and every Hindu pilgrim has this concept in his/her mind, but the belief pattern of pilgrims may differ from society to society. Ceremonies refer to the religious and ritualistic orientation manifested in the observance of the festivals, worships, pilgrimages, sacred baths etc. They are generally observed with certain stereotypic formalities in the names of gods obeying the social customs and traditional beliefs. In the sacred centres, ceremonial performances are motivated by socio-religious consideration.

The very concept of pilgrimage is treated as a socio-cultural dimension of Indian civilization. It acts as an important socio-cultural phenomenon in Indian society by which socio-cultural interaction of people is taking place. As a Hindu pilgrim centre, Puri has similarities in many respects with other sacred centres of India like Tirupati, Banaras, Allahabad, Haridwar, Mathura, Brindaban, Dwarika etc. the number of pilgrims coming to Puri is very conspicuous.

It is observed that at present, the functioning of pilgrimage at Puri is much more wider than in the past mainly due to modern facilities provided for the pilgrims. The present-day moderate transport and accommodation systems attract hundreds of thousand of pilgrims to Puri throughout the year. Being an attractive tourist centre of the country, Puri with its sea beach and other scenic beauties attracts people of all walks to visit at least once during their life-time. Now-a-days pilgrims of even distant places come to Puri due to availability of modern transport systems. It is observed that modern amenities provided by the tourist department of Government of Orissa encourage the visitors and tourists to come to Puri in large numbers to perform their pilgrimages.

## NOTES

Dash, G.M., 1978, The Evaluation of Priestly Power : The Gangavamsa period—*Cult of Jagannath and Regional Traditions of Orissa* (eds.) A. Eschmann *et al.*, New Delhi : Manohar Publications.

Hein, E.. 1978, Temple, Town, and Hinterland : The Present Network of Religious Economy in Puri. *Cult of Jagannath and Regional Traditions of Orissa*. (eds. A. Eschmann *et al.*, New Delhi, Manohar Publications.

Jha, Makhan, 1971, *The Sacred Complex in Janakpur*, Allahabad, United publishers.

Jha, Makhan, 1978. *Rising India*—An Urban Anthropological Approach to Puri, New Delhi, Classical Publications.

Mohapatra, Kedarnath, 1954, Antiquity of Jagannath Puri as a place of pilgrimage; *Orissa Historical Research Journal*, Vol. 3(1) p. (6-21).

Mohapatra, L.K. and Behura, N.K., 1981, *Man in Society* : Bulletin of the Department of Anthropology; Utkal University, Bhubaneswar, Vol. II.

Pattnaik. N., 1977, *Cultural Tradition in Puri*, India Institute of Advanced Study, Simla.

Vidyarthi, L P., 1961, *The Sacred Complex in Hindu Gaya*, Asia Publishing House, Bombay.

# 13

# Studying a Vaishnava Sacred Centre of Chotanagpur

## An Anthropological Appraisal

CHANDRA MOULI JHA

ONE of the recent trends in the world anthropology has been to study the anthropology of civilisations, and now it has occupied an important place in the anthropological researches. The methodological approach to the study of Indian Civilisation not only added a new dimension to Indian Anthropology, but also created an academic atmosphere in India, for taking up different studies on various dimensions of this indigenous civilisation.

**Works so far done**

The anthropological investigations in the field of Indian civilisation were accelerated after the researches of Robert Redfield (1955, 1956, 1957) McKim Marriott (1955, 1959, 1960, 1961), Milton Singer (1955, 1958, 1972) and L.P. Vidyarthi (1953, 1960, 1961) and thereafter, a band of young Indian anthropologists were attracted towards this new fascinating field of research in contemporary Indian anthropology. While a few Hindu places of pilgrimage were studied in detail, many small articles were published on different sacred centres of India. B.N. Saraswati—'Kashi : Myth Reality of a Cultural Tradition' (1975) throws light on the dimension of Indian civilisation. In the mean time, the study of the Sacred Complex of Janakpur (1971) was taken up by M. Jha and it was the first intensive work following the pattern of the work done on Gaya (1961). After studying Janakpur, M. Jha took up the study of the Sacred Complex of Ratanpur (1970) which was the ancient Hindu capital in Central India. Several scientific papers of Indian Civilisation as far as reflected through the study of this ancient Hindu kingdom have been published by him (1970-74).

His most pioneering research work of two civilisational regions *viz.* Mithila and Mahakoshal (1980) reveals that a civilisational region, irrespective of its location and extension, is an aggregate of local cultures and histories.

## Location

The famous historic temple of Lord Krishna named as Bansidharjee is situated in Nagar Utanri under Palamau district in Chotanagpur. Chotanagpur was known to the Aryans as Jharkhand or the 'Forest tract'. Throughout the Muslim rule the word 'Jharkhand' appears to have survived although the word Kokrah became a common epithet for this region. In the *Ain-i-Akbari*, Kokrah formed a part of Suba Bihar and was the realm of the Raja of Kokrah. It was also known to the Mugals as Nagpur. The name Nagpur probably dates back to the 15th or 16th century A.D. It was ceded in 1765 under the grant of Diwani to the East India Company. In the covenants granted to the Nagbansi Raja the settlement was given of the Nagpur Pargana. James Rennel in his map of Hindoostan (1792) prefixed the word 'Chutia' to Nagpur; but it was not till 1812 that Nagpur was officially recognised as Chota Nagpur by the British Parliament.

Palamau is a district of this Chota-Nagpur division. The origin of the name Palamau is doubtful. According to one account it is derived from the Hindi word Palana, to flee and means a 'place of refuge'. Another suggestion is that the name is combination of Pala meaning 'forest' and 'mu' the patois root for 'dead' the whole word meaning 'dead from forest'. Another suggestion is that Palamau is a Dravidian name, that it may be a corruption of Pall-ammu-pall meaning 'tooth' and amm meaning 'water' while U is a kind of genitive or possessive case meaning 'village, country, forests' etc. In support of this theory it may be mentioned that the name is spelt Palamau in the vernacular and was originally applied to the village which was the seat of the Chero chief.

## History

The early history of this area is not authentic but we have legends about it. It is, however, certain that Kharwars, Oraons and Cheros, the three aboriginal races, practically ruled over the tract. The Kharwars claim to be Suryavansi Kshatriyas. They trace their descent from Ajanagara or Ayodhya. Karsua was the sixth son of Manu vaivashta and he was assigned the eastern territory. The descendants of Kharwars were called Karsas who subsequently came to be known as Kharwars or Khawrars. According to tradition they were the rulers of Rohtasgarh. The Kharwars point to the days of Pratapdhaval, one of the line chiefs who ruled there in the twelfth century A.D. during the time of their greatest prosperity.

The Cheros have been spoken in very high terms in the Aitareya Aranyaka alongwith the Vougas and Magadhas. They did not observe the Vedic sacrifices and still they are termed as revered Cheros 'Cheropadas'.

The family of Bhaiya Sahab of Untari is a branch of Sonepura family of Surajbansi Rajput, being descendant of an elder wife of the 44th Raja of Sonepura. Her son lost his right to succeed the Sonepura estate through being absent on a pilgrimage when his father died. On his return he was given an estate via Belanrija with the title of Bhaiya or brother. The 3rd Bhaiya subdued Untari under the order of Mugal Emperor at the end of the 17th century and received it from the Emperor as a rent free Jagir. This grant was confirmed by the British Government a hundred years later. The Khorposhdars of Bhaiya Saheb live in village Silidag. Adhaura, Kochea, Ramna, Marwaria and Kathar all situated in Nagar Block.

## Bansidhar Temple

Nagar Untari is situated on the north-west of the district and is connected by a 35 km. long road with Garhwa. It is situated on the bank of river Banki. This place is a border of Bihar, M.P. and Uttar Pradesh. M.P. is about 15 km. distance across the river Kanhar in south. Uttar Pradesh is 9 km. west across the Malia river. The area of village Untari is 260 acres. There is a temple behind the Garh of Bhaiya Saheb containing the idol of Shri Bansidhar. The idol is made of 'Ashta Dhatu' (eight metals) and is one of the beautiful idols of its kind in northern India. The idol weighs about 30 maunds. Rani Saheba Srimati Sheomani Kaur of Nagar Estate is said to have brought this idol about 150 years ago. Rani Saheba was a widow of Raja Bhawani Singh. She was a kind lady and had a firm faith on Lord Krishna. Once on Janmastami (Birth day of Lord Krishna) she was observing the festival and was on fasting. At night she saw Lord Krishna in dream calling her that he is on the crest of Shivhari Pahari across the river Kanhar. Rani Saheba alongwith priest and her men went and brought this big idol of Bansidhar (Lord Krishna) on an elephant. She wanted to establish this idol inside her fort but the elephant sat behind the fort and ultimately the idol was put there and a temple was made. Lord Krishna is always worshipped with Radha so a beautiful idol of Radhajee was built and brought there and placed beside the Bansidhar.

In a Hindu place of pilgrimage the structure of the sacred centre may be single or multiple. The multiple sacred centre is that where more than one sacred structures are built up within the precinct of a shrine dedicated to a specific deity. Most important in this category of shrines is the famous Bansidhar temple where in addition to Radha Krishna, there are a number of deities and godlings, such as Sita and Ram, Hanuman, Shivalinga of Vishwanath, Ridhi Sidhi and Ganesh. There is a Surya Mandir (Sun temple) beside the temple of Bansidhar. Here, there an idol of sun seated on his rath with seven horses.

**Sacred Performances**

The sacred centres of Chotanagpur, prospectively of its location either in the hilly area or in the plains of Chotanagpur may be broadly classified under three main sects of the Hinduism *viz.* the sacred centres belonging to the (i) Shiva sect, (ii) belonging to the Shakti sect and (iii) those which have allegiance to the Vaishnav sect of Hinduism. This sacred centre of Palamau, besides various others belonging to the Vaishnava sect is mentioned in various sacred scriptures like the Puranas, epics etc. and are deeply associated with several myths and mythology. The mythological stories of the sacred centres are perpetuated in such a way that ultimately these sacred centres are linked with the other sacred centres of Hindu universe.

The Hindu sacred centres belonging to various sects are found all over Chotanagpur and at Palamau itself many shrines of these sects are still existing where people come from different corners of the area. Although Untari is considered as the biggest and the most famous place. The various sacred performances observed by the people of this area from brief floral offerings and *jap* (mutterings of the God's name) to the complicated performances of Ramnavmi, Janmastami Jhulan, Shivratri etc. Besides these, there is a number of daily sacred performances which is performed in this temple.

The mode of performing worship of the deities is not certain. One can also worship after washing hands and legs but to take bath is the religious necessity for making a sacred performance. The sacred bath at any place is considered meritorious but to bath on the Bansidhar well is considered to be endowed with special virtue. After taking bath, one generally makes a brief personal worship and recites *mantras* while making oblation to gods and ancestors, then one moves to the temple. The time of Darsan is fixed from 6.30 a.m. to 7 p.m. Darshan can only be had from the gate. No. one is allowed to touch Bansidhar.

Parikrama, the custom of circumambulation in the sacred centre, has been considered as the best method of blotting out all sins committed during one's life time. According to the nature of Parikrama and the pilgrim's participation therein, it can be mentioned that Parikrama is Laghu and Dirgh. Laghu Parikrama means to move once around the temple and Dirgh represent five times movement around the temple. Both men and women are allowed to undertake the Parikrama. There is no castes and age restriction, persons of any caste or of any age can perform this Parikrama. However, there are certain rules which are strictly followed. For instance Parikrama is started from the right side of the temple. The pilgrims are neither allowed to put on shoes in the course of Parikrama nor are they supposed to carry any cooked meal with them. Menstruating women do not undertake this Parikrama.

Another sacred performance related to the fulfilment of a vow is called Dudhadharia (pouring milk) over the Shivlinga, and other deities. Milk is poured on the Shivalinga by those persons whose desires have been fulfilled. For this one has to contact the priest.

Since Bansidhar has the power to fulfil human desires, men and women in crisis approach them and pray for quick remedies. A couple generally keeps a vow in connection with the desire to have a son, and when this is fulfilled the Mundan ceremony (shaving off the head for the first time) of the baby takes place before Bansidhar. In Mundan ceremony the role of the barber is important in so far as he shaves off the hair of the child, while the priest of the temple utters certain verses on this occasion. The client may offer a piece of *dhoti* to the priest and also the barber, besides paying them in cash and making them available some eatables.

Visiting the deity is an important act of sacred performance which the orthodox devotees regularly do. In formal worship one is involved in an act of Darshana and the devotee is required to be present when the Bansidhar is being worshipped by the priest. A crowd of the devotees is seen during the Arati which is organised in Bansidhar temple. At the end of the Arati, the devotees offer some flowers if they have brought there with them or may have a look at the Bansidhar which is enough for acquiring the Darshana.

## Fairs and Festivals

A large number of fairs and festivals are periodically organised in Nagar Untari. But the festivals of Shivaratri and Chhath are attended by pilgrims from Bihar, M.P. and U.P. other festivals are celebrated locally.

## Shivaratri

An annual fair for one month is observed on the eve of Shivaratri. According to Hindu calendar, Shivaratri falls on Krishna Paksha Chaturdashi (fourteenth day of the dark lunar fortnight) in the month of Phalgun (falling in February-March). As the tradition has it, Shiva was married on this auspicious day. In this connection it may be pointed out that Shiva's first marriage with Sati, the daughter of Raja Daksha is not celebrated by the devotees. It is only the anniversary of his second marriage with Parvati, the daughter of King Hemant of the Himalayas, which is celebrated as Shivaratri by the devotees all over India.

Shivaratri is celebrated here with pomp and show attracting a large number of pilgrims from all over the region. People also visit from Madhya Pradesh and Uttar Pradesh.

As regards its ritual observance, the festival of Shivaratri may be divided into two parts. First part is known as Shiva Upas (fast in the name of Shiva) and the second part is called the Shiva Darshan. The first part usually precedes the later, when the devotees keep fast for the whole day and night. Shiva's marriage is celebrated at midnight, and the devotees break their fast next morning. The second part of the ritual i.e. Shiva Darshan starts after the culmination of the marriage of the divine couple. While the day marked for Shiva Upas is spent on observing wedding rites, the Shiva Darshan is meant for rejoicing and giving and Dana Dakshina to Brahmins and beggars.

On the occasion of Shivaratri, the pilgrims as well as the local devotees organise Kirtan and Bhajan. In many families, the ladies remain engaged in Kirtan and Bhajan for the whole night of Shivaratri. Throwing of Abir on one another; singing songs and taking of Bhang are the order of the day.

On the occasion of Chhath (sixth day of Kartik Shukla) a fair is organised and people from every corner of the area come to perform Ardhya to sun and worship in Surya Mandir. The fair continues for two days.

It is clear that Untari is situated in the midst of the tribal belt of Chotanagpur and the region is designated as the tribalised one. This characteristic of the region is clearly reflected in the composition of the pilgrims who attend this Mela at Untari. Most of them belong to the various lower and so-called untouchable castes and tribes of the neighbouring areas and among them mention may be made of Teli, Sonar, Chamar, Ghasi, Oraon and Manjhis etc.

Thus, the analysis of the sacred performance of the fair at Untari brings into light the complex interaction pattern of people from various castes and tribes and belonging to different sects and traditions. Further, this fair brings together ideas and rituals from diverse sources of the Hindu tradition.

Besides this sacred centres each and every village of Chotanagpur has a sacred centre for its village deity called

Gram Devata. These village devatas belong to the varied gods and goddesses of the Hindu pantheon. However, most of them belong to the folk and *laukik* traditions of the land. The performances and the priests of these shrines usually vary from village to village as well as from caste to caste who inhabit the village. In addition to this there is a common belief among the people that the village spirits protect the village from evil spirits which may come from any direction. Different folktales are attached to prove the existence of this deity who is believed to guard the villagers. This deity goes with the bride, bridegroom, individuals going for any difficult job outside the village and protects him or her in all possible ways.

**Sacred Specialist**

The priest of the temple is called Pujari; presently the Pujari is Pandit Ridheshwar Tiwari, about 90 years old. He is performing the duty of a Pujari since more than 50 years. Pujari is not a paid servant but he takes the amount which is offered in the temple.

The Pujari remains very clean, wears simple dress, gets up in the morning and maintains more or less a routine life. The traditional dress of the sacred specialist is not much different from one another. The dress consists of Dhoti, Kurta and silken Chaddar, Baniyan etc. He also puts a red Gamchha or Angocha (a thin long towel) hung on the shoulder. From the point of view of food habits the Pujari is vegetarian and he takes meal at his home only and takes a simple diet of rice, pulse, vegetables, curd, ghee etc. He resides in his own house at Untari. The daily routine of the sacred specialist is according to his profession. He leaves his bed early in the morning and after attending the call of nature, he takes bath before sunrise. He pointed out that by the sunrise he usually completed half of the Puja and Path (recitation of the sacred book).

An important feature of the priest of the sacred centre is his regular habit of reciting the sacred books like the epics, the Puranas, the Geeta, the Hanuman Chalisa, as well as muttering of the sacred names and Mantras on the Mala. He is a well travelled person and has visited most of the places of pilgrimage in India. Thus, the religious experiences gained by him during the visits of pilgrimages, which are located in far off areas of different linguistic zones, different geographical regions and ecological settings, helped him in communicating the 'essence of great tradition' and thus establish continuity with the masses.

## Conclusion

In conclusion it can be said that the structure of the sacred complex viz. the sacred geography, the sacred performances, and the sacred specialists, is so built that it subsists heterogeneous population and varieties of traditions. The change in the sacred geography has also been noticed, the reason assigned for this is largely historical. There has been a natural rise that some new constructions have taken place. The sacred performances are made according to Vedic or Shastric and Laukik. The performances are made according to oral tradition or what is called Laukik parampara, distinguishable both in content and manner from the Vedic performances. The structure of the sacred performances is operative at all Hindu shrines, and hence all the places of Hindu pilgrimage have the unity of biliefs and practices. But the places of pilgrimage may be differentiated from one another also on the basis of the sacred performances peculiar to them. For instance, in Gaya the main sacred performance is ancestor-worship but in Untari it is difficult to say what is the main sacred performance.

The sacred specialist who have the requisite knowledge of the Shastric rituals sometimes also perform the Laukik rituals free from Shastric injunctions, though they may sometimes be appended to Shastric rituals.

The human desires of Artha, Kama and Moksha is being fulfilled by the Bansidhar. Though there are various gods for various functions but Bansidhar is common and people come here with various desires for fulfilment. Certain types of sacred performances are consciously conducted with earthly consideration. Man's final desire of enjoying beauty and his sense of aesthetics are amply fulfilled in his sacred performances. This is truly reflected in the selection of sacred objects or motifs, in the style of performances, in the choice of place, the choice of time and season, and such other considerations which make a ritual pleasant or pleasing and absorbing. All ritual performance are made with a perfect sense of aesthetics held with deep devotion.

One of the important function of the sacred complex is the pattern of cultures. As has been discussed in foregoing pages, on the basis of their physical features, organisation of functionaries, the sacred centre of Untari is characterized as local and regional.

In the sacred geography of Untari people from all corners of Bihar, M.P. and U.P. are settled in linguistic clusters, each preserving its identity in respect of food, dress, language, rituals, ceremonies and at the same time they also commonly interact at these centres.

The institution of pilgrimage, has undoubtedly been a levelling influence on diverse social life. Sex, colour, civil condition, economic inequality, traditions of servitude which have made some people untouchables, become unreal distinctions in course of pilgrimage. It is only during the pilgrimage that unity of faith in Hindu society and religion can be seen at its best.

Summing up, it may be said that the sacred centre is not an abstruse together against the geographical diversities, and social and linguistic heterogeneities. Whether the modern secular mechanism and institutions are equally viable and lasting means of cultural integration is a question that awaits time. But there is no doubt that the mechanism of sacred complex and the institution of pilgrimage are dependable and effective means of integration, for they have already stood the test of time, and hence their relevance.

## NOTES

Bose, N.K., *Organisation of Services in Bhubaneswar Tample* Culture and Society in India, Asia Publishing House, Calcutta, 1967.

Chakrabarti, P., *Some Observations on the Pilgrims and their Pilgrimage. A case study of Tarkeshwar*, Journal of Social Research, Ranchi, 1974 XVII—I.

Jha, Makhan, '*The Sacred Complex in Janakpur*, The United Publishers, Allahabad, 1971.

Jha, Makhan, *Pilgrims and Centre of Pilgrimage in Chhatisgarh*, Journal of Social Research, Ranchi, 1974, XVII-I.

Jha, Makhan, *The Sacred Complex of Kashi*, Concept Publishing Company, Delhi, 1979.

Saraswati, B.N., *Kasi : Myths and Reality of a Classical Cultural Tradition*, Indian Institute of Advanced Study. Simla, 1975.

Vidyarthi, L.P., *Thinking about a Sacred City*, Eastern Anthropologists, 1960, XIII, No. 4.

Vidyarthi, L.P., *Sacred Complex in Hindu Gaya*, Asia Publishing House, Bombay, 1961.

Vidyarthi, L.P. and Jha, M., *Symposium on the Sacred Complex in India*, published by the Council of Social Research Bihar and Department of Anthropology, Ranchi University, 1974.

# 14

# The Tradition of Kumbh

## A Study in Continuity and Change

JAGADISH CHANDRA DAS AND JITENDRA SINGH

UNLIKE other religions, the Hinduism is not to be viewed as a mere religious doctrine alone, but more than that it represents a way of life. In fact, the canvas of the Hindu idiom *dharm* is far more pervasive and encompassing upon traditional Hindu life-ways than its inappropriately translated English equivalent 'religion'. Derived from the Sanskrit root *dhri* which means 'to sustain, to uphold, to hold together', *dharm* stands for diverse aspects such as religious observance, righteousness, justice, conformity to social traditions and customary laws etc. and thus has religious, moral, ethical and socio-legal significances to Hindu socio-cultural life. *Dharm* is, therefore, an all-comprehensive guideline which regulates other important mundane omponents of Hindu life *viz.* *arth* (*i.e.* pursuits of acquirings wealth) and *kam* (*i.e.* propagation of family through procreation) and thereby qualifies one for *moksh i.e.*, final liberation from all worldly ties.

Traditional Hindu outlook about cosmos concerning the life of mortals comprises the existence of *ih-lok* (*i.e.* this world) and *par-lok* (*i.e.* the other world). The Hindus deeply believe that the status, position and treatment of an individual's soul at *par-lok* is directly determined by quality of his all life-time activities (including the apparently negligible ones too) at *ih-lok*. This belief-system is intimately linked with the concept of *pap-punya* (sin-virtue) which is quality-accountability syndrome of

all human actions, weighed/assessed with reference to framework of *dharm* or righteous conduct. Obviously, the actions of
an individual which conformed with *dharm* were deemed as
meritorious ones and thus earned *punya* (virtue/merit) for the
doer while the actions which infringed *dharm*-guideline, earned
*pap* (sin) for him. Existence of such an ideological system therefore, has crucial bearing on almost all socio-cultural and socio-
religious actions, aspirations or even thinking pattern in Hindu
society. Although Hinduism does not make pilgrimage obligatory, yet the ordinary Hindu attribute great importance to
*tirth-yatra* where they resort to a host of merit-earning activities like taking a holy dip, *darshan* (respectful sight with sense of
devotion and surrender) of deities, temples and ascetics, performing worship, listening to religious discourses, hymns and
devotional songs in praise of deity, doing charity to Brahman,
beggar and ascetics—all these believed to earn *punya* for an
individual thereby advancing him towards the ultimate goal of
*moksh*. The mass Hindu participation in *Kumbh* may be understood in this frame of Hindu psyche though other dimensions
like its being a powerful medium of communication, cohesion
and integration etc. are equally important.

This chapter proposes to examine the *Kumbh* tradition
in the framework of continuity and change. First, a general
background of *Kumbh* tradition has been given in historical
perspective in order to bring out its multi-dimensional implications. Secondly, the *Kumbh*, held at Hardwar during 1986, is
discussed as a case study to examine the elements of continuity
of *Kumbh* tradition alongwith its changing dimensions.

## General Background of Kumbh Tradition : Origin and Historical Sketch

The tradition of *Kumbh* is very ancient. There exist several
opinions regarding its origin. However, the most popular
*pauranic* legend relates to the churning of ocean (*Samudra
manthan*) by the gods and the demons jointly, which resulted in
the extraction of various precious objects amongst which *amrit
kumbh* (pitcher filled with nectar) was an important one: In
order to deprive the demons from drinking *amrit* which bestowed immortality, the divine-king Indra's son Jayant fled with
*amrit kumbh* who was chased by demons. It is said that Jayant

rested at twelve spots where he kept the *amrit kumbh* while resting; and of these spots, eight are located in heaven and four on earth. The spots on earth are Hardwar, Prayag, Ujjain and Nasik where, it is believed, drops of *amrit* also fell which enhanced the holiness of these places. This battle for *amrit kumbha* lasted for twelve days : One day of gods being equivalent to one year of man. And by this simple reckoning, twelve days of gods amount to twelve years on earth hence the tradition of holding *kumbh* at the interval of twelve years on each of the four spots in clock-wise cyclic order. In other words, the Kumbh at Hardwar is followed by Prayag, Nasik and Ujjain. That is why the time-gap between the two *kumbh* is three years.

A slightly different version of the above legend is that Lord Vishnu entrusted Garuda with the task of carrying *amrit kumbh* to the heavenly abode of gods. On his way, Garuda halted at these four spots and kept the *kumbh* for some time while resting which acquired sanctity thus and hence the tradition of holding *kumbh* at those spots.

Apart from the above legends, there exists another opinion regarding the origin of *kumbh* congregation. According to this, the learned Hindu ascetics of high order used to congregate at these four places at regular intervals to discuss religious scriptures as means of exchanging views and knowledge that they attained individually out of constant meditation and self-cultivation. It is believed that ordinary householders took this opportunity to listen to the discourses of these great souls whose sight (*darshan*) was also deemed as an act of earning *punya* (virtue) and hence they assembled in large numbers. And in course of time, such pan-India level assemblages gradually transformed into traditions like *Kumbh Mela*.

In determining exact date and time of *kumbh*, the position of constellation *viz.*, Sun, Moon, Jupiter and Saturn and their conjunctions are considered according to Hindu astrology. The position and conjunction of these are important since these constellation-gods had played important roles with regard to protection, supervision and preservation of *amrit kumbh* during the god-demon struggle as narrated in mythology. Besides, the positions of these planets during *kumbh yog* (precise timing of *kumbh*) also astrologically signify the struggle phase of god-demon battle,

The required planetary conjunctions occur at different dates at the different four places of *kumbh* fair. At Hardwar, the *kumbh* is held as the sun enters the zodiac sign of Aries (*Mesha*) while Jupiter enters Aquaris (*kumbh*). Such planetary positions occur at the interval of twelve years and hence *kumbh* is held at every twelve years. The tradition of *ardh-kumbh* (that is, six-yearly *kumbh*), in addition, is observed at Hardwar and Prayag (Allahabad), to have religious assembly in between.

A close view of the *kumbh* during historical past is important, because of its key-role in social and religious resurgence in Hindu society. Two sets of diverse forces during those days, which were causing stress and strain on the Hindu social polity, contributed to this. The first one was endemic. Briefly speaking, the then Hindu society was under convulsions due to rigid Brahmanical orthodoxy. Secondly, the discriminatory policy followed by a few non-Hindu rulers of medieval times was also causing lot of pressure on the socio-religious institutions of Hindu society. As consequence of simultaneous affect of these two forces, a state of flux was noticeable in Hindu society. To withstand the decay that had set in, and also to effect greater cohesiveness, solidarity and integration, some measures were to be initiated, and *kumbh* mela was perhaps one of the best occasions for such purpose as it attracted huge attendance of both *grihasthi* (householder) and *sadhu* (ascetic) from all corners of the country.

The earliest recorded description of *kumbh* occurs in the travelogue by Hiuen Tsang who visited India during the reign of king Harsh Vardhan. Hiuen Tsang estimated about two-and-a-half lakhs of people taking holy bath in Ganga at Prayag (Allahabad) and called it *"Dharm Mahasabha"* i.e. "great assembly for religious discourses". As a sect of Hinduism, they enjoyed political patronage at that time and hence the presence of Buddhist monks at the Kumbh was also noticed by him, which is still to be found in each Kumbh. It may also be noted that a few centuries later when Addya Sankaracharyya organized the *Samnyasi* (Shaivite ascetics) under different *math, marhi, akhara* etc. he allotted one *marhi* to the 'Lama' i.e. Buddhist monk, which was, perhaps, an effort to bring all the Hindu ascetics of different sects under a common banner.

In order to organize the *Samnyasis* (Shaiva-ascetic), Addya

Shankaracharyya established four principal *math, viz.* Sringeri, Sarada, Gobardhan and Jyotirmath in four cardinal directions (South, West, East and North respectively) of the country and delineated the jurisdiction of each *math.* Thus, Sringeri *math* of Kerala covered the entire Southern India, up to Maharashtra; Gobardhan *math* of Puri covered the entire eastern India, Jyotirmath (Joshimath) of Garhwal Himalaya covered the whole of Northern India while Sarada *math* at Dwaraka covered Western India. Then he appointed four *acharya* each to head one *math* who was well versed in one *Ved.* Thus, the *acharya* of Sringeri *math* was a scholar of *Yajurved,* the *acharya* of Jyotirmath (Joshimath) in *Atharv Ved,* the acharya of Gobardhan math in *Rig Ved* while the acharya of Sarada *math* in *Sam Ved* These four *Acharyas* then recruited ten disciples in accordance with ten directions or *'disha'* who were decorated with titles like Giri, Puri, Bharati, Saraswati, Tirth, Sagar etc. who are often collectively referred to as *"Das nami Samnyasi".* In order to recruit desirous persons and offering them identity and absorbing such people into the *Samnyasi* fold, 52 *marhi* were created. The *marhi* is like an initiation centre (*Diksha Kendra*) of the persons seeking admission into Samnyasi fold and thus *marhi* becomes "identity-reference" of the new *Samnyasi* after initiation thereby giving him some clear social identity within the vast *Samnyasi* community. Of these 52 *marhi,* the Giri *Das nami Samnyasi* controlled 27 *marhi,* the Duri had 16 *marhi,* Bharati had 4 *marhi,* Lama has one *marhi,* and so on. In a way, the *marhi* institution acted as 'operational field stations' of *Samnyasi* community.

The challenges faced by Hindu religion and society during fourteenth century from some of the political rulers necessitated further organizational evolution among the *Samnyasis.* It was felt that the protection and perpetuation of religion and cultural heritage could not be accomplished by only resorting to theological exercises (*Shastra Charcha*) rather militarisation was also necessary in this regard. This contributed towards the militarisation of *Naga Samnyasis* who constituted defence wing to safeguard Hindu religious institutions, temples, and the organizations and the entire gamut of Hindu ethics and values. Thus, the *Samnyasis* were broadly divided into two categories :

    (*a*)  *Shastradhari, i.e.* those practised religious were engaged
             in purely religious activities.

    (*b*)  *Astradhari, i.e.* those devoted to learning the art of
             handling weapons (Shastra) in order to defend religion
             by means of physical fighting. The *Nagas* fell into this
             category.

As a token of their sacrifice for the cause of religion and
society, the *Naga Samnyasis* renounced cloth and fully devoted
themselves in military trainings. Initially they formed one
*akhara*, known as *Avahan akhara* with *Bhairav* as their presiding deity (*Ista dev*). Subsequently other *akhara* like Bairagi,
Nirmohi, Narvani, Digambar etc., belonging to Vaisnavite sect
while still other *akhara* like Nirmal, Udasi etc., belonging to
Sikh sect came into existence.

    The history of Naga *Samnyasi* is full of heroic sacrifices who
not only fought to protect religion but also stood against
British power during sepoy mutiny of 1857.

    *Kumbh* has special significance in relation to the Sanyasi
organization as this occasion offered opportunity of mass con-
tract and exhibited structural effectiveness, solidarity and
strength of various Hindu ascetic organizations. The tradition
of holding long colourful procession by different *akhara* with
enough pomp and show on the auspicious bathing-dates during
kumbh, commonly referred to as *Shahi Snan,* which is enthusiastically witnessed by millions of ordinary devotees, act as
powerful stimulus to generate socio-religious consciousness
among common mass and thus boost society's morale. Millions
of common devotees feel inspired and confident and this sense
of psychological reassurance regarding the protection of their
religion and culture are important relevances of kumbh. Saptashrot, Maya Devi, Neeldhara, Mansha Devi, Chandi Devi etc.
Of the various sacred bathing-*ghat* (spot), the Har-ki-Pauri is
considered to be of particular significance. During *kumbh* its
sanctity is believed to enhance many-fold since according to
mythology, a few drops of *amrit* dripped from the *Amrit kumbh*
at this spot. Due to this, taking a holy dip at Hari-ki-Pauri
Ghat remains the foremost objective of all the pilgrims irrespective of their being ascetic of common householder.

## Kumbh Mela of Hardwar

In the preceding pages, the mythical origin of the *kumbh* tradition and its role in ushering some transformation and rejuvenation in the Hindu socio-religious polity in response to a set of then-existing circumstances have been highlighted. We may now turn our attention to the latest *Maha Kumbh* (the 12-yearly *kumbh*), held at Hardwar in 1986 in order to bring out the still-persisting traditional attributes of *kumbh* alongwith the aspects of change. At the outset, however, it is necessary to delineate the "sacred geography" (of Vidyarthi : 1961) of Hardwar since the numerous sacred-spots which together comprise it, are the principal locales of the pilgrims' varied interests and ritual performances.

The holy city of Hardwar, a premier Hindu *tirth*, is situated on the bank of Ganga, the most sacred river of the Hindus. An exceedingly large number of shrines of various Hindu gods and goddesses, several *ashram* (hermitage), *math*, *akhara* etc. are thronged in this city which have greatly enhanced the spiritual sanctity of this place. Some of the most prominent sacred spots which compose the sacred geography of Hardwar are : Har-ki-Pauri, Kushavart, Vishnughat, Ramghat, Gaughat, Saptashrot, Mayadevi, Manshadevi, Chandidevi, Bilwa, Neeldhara, Kankhal etc. each of which has its own religio-historical or *Pauranik* significance thereby reflecting tremendous sacred/religious relevances for the pilgrims. The most popular bathing-*ghat* (spot) at Hardwar is Har-ki-Pauri or Hari-ki-Pauri, meaning the stepping stone to Vishnu or the holy feet of Shiva. Apart from the sacred spots, Hardwar is also a unique place for the propagation of traditional Hindu socio-cultural and religious idioms through institutions established for and functioning towards these ends. The Gurukul Kangri University, Rishikul Medical School and many such institutions, located in and around Hardwar, offer excellent examples in this regard. Mention of these institutions are made here due to the paramount role these play in reassertion of traditional Indian education system, medicine etc. After this brief introduction of Hardwar we may now focus attention on the *Mahakumbh*, held here during the early part of 1986.

The *Mahakumbh* being the most sacred occasion has always

attracted huge number of pilgrims from every corner of the
country and even beyond. This is evidenced from some early
accounts also as mentioned earlier. Owing to this tremendous
pilgrim traffic inflow and assemblage of *kumbh* venue, suitable
administrative management and civic arrangements in order to
avoid untoward happenings, protect law and order as well as
cater to the pilgrims' health and other needs are necessary. In
view of these, the Uttar Pradesh Government constituted a
special *kumbh* mela district comprising Roorkee, Hardwar,
Rishikesh, Laxman Jhula and Muni-ki-Reti. For convenience
of administration, the entire *mela* area was divided into 20
sectors. Each sector was looked after by a sector magistrate, a
Deputy Superintendent of police, a medical officer and engi-
neers of electricity and water supply. Besides these, certain
procedures are followed by all sects of ascetics with respect to
bathing, that is, which sect of ascetic would get precedence in
taking holy bath over others. The question of precedence in
bathing on these occasions had led to bloody fights but the
British Government after enquiry into the time-honoured practices, laid down the following rules which are strictly imposed by
the Mela Incharge. Thus, the Shaiva Naga lead the Vaishnava
Naga during *Kumbh Snan* (holy bath), in the *kumbh* bathing
procession the following order of precedence is observed :
(1) *Shaiva Naga*, (2) *Vaishnava Bairagi*, (3) *Udasi-Naya Akhara*
(4) *Udasi Purana or Bara Akhara*, (5) *Nanak Panthi*, (6) *Nirmala*.
Among the various *Shaiva akharas*, the following order is
observed at Hardwar. The *Niranjani akhara* is followed by
*Juna, Awahan* and *Anand akharas*. The *Nirwani akhara* is followed by *Atal akhara* and then come other *akharas*. The *Vaishnava
Nagas'* procession at the *kumbh* assemblage is conducted in the
following manner. "In the formal procession for the bath on
the occasion of *kumbh* assemblage, the *Digambar Ani* with its
standard banner as well as the sectarian flag marches in the
centre. The *Nirmohi Ani* with its two banners marches on its
right and the *Nirwani* keeps to the left. A big kettle-drum is
beaten in front of the banner of the *Digambar Ani* and a
number of smaller ones satisfy the martial spirit of the *Nirwani*.
The drum of the *Digambar Ani* is called *Garbha Ganj* (loud and
fearful enough to cause abortion or miscarriage)". (Tripathi :
1978 : 39).

The lavish display of human and material resources at the command of various *akharas* of different sects on the days of *Shahi Snan* (main bathing dates) of *kumbh mela* is explicitly observable in terms of rightly caprisioned elephants, elaborately equipped camels and horses and the religious/patriotic slogan-shouting hordes of Naga *Samnyasis* and *Sadhus* who march in procession. This practice was very much in the past and is still continuing which, in a way, may be viewed as the vibrant throbbing of *kumbh* assemblages that almost hypnotizes and enchants the mammoth crowd of pilgrims from different parts of India. The visual observation of the holy grandeur in the religiously charged environment of *kumbh mela* reinforces latent traditionalism and rekindles a sense of pride about the rich heritages of the Hindu culture.

Let us now turn our attention to other eternal attributes of *kumbh* assemblage which have sustained the tradition and contributed to its perpetuation. The basic one among these is the attitude and world view of pilgrims who participate in *Kumbh*. In fact, our discussion with scores of *kumbh*-pilgrims in course of fieldwork at Hardwar revealed that the pilgrim's fundamental approach and motivations towards this great assemblage are still entrenched in their traditional Hindu socio-religious value-system despite apparently observable modernization of Hindu society. In other words, the traditional Hindu socio-religious outlook characterized by continual craving for earning *punya* (merit) and thereby advancing towards the *moksh* (salvation), remains the most primary and most compelling factor behind abnormally large-scale pilgrim attendance in *kumbh*. Irrespective of their age, sex, caste status or economic, educational and regional-linguistic background, all the pilgrim-respondents were unanimous in their opinion that their primary objective for attending *kumbh* was to take a holy dip at Ganga which was an act of earning rare merit which they think, would advance their cause of attaining *moksh*. In addition, other activities such as sacred performances, *darshan* of so many ascetics as well as listening to their socio-religious preachings and singing devotional songs in chorus *i.e. kirtan*, are generally undertaken by pilgrims which are deemed to accumulate *punya* for them. In fact, *kumbh* presents the greatest Hindu religious event where large-scale participation of ascetics belonging to various path (sect) take place and hence it offers a rare opportunity to the common householders to interact with them. According to the traditional Hindu value, all these acts are unique ways of accumulating merit by ordinary householders. Perpetuation of such a value-system is primarily responsible for continuance of the traditional elements of *kumbh* assemblage as well as sustaining its relevances to the pilgrims participating in it.

The non-traditional dimensions of *kumbh mela* are equally important in view of its being an extraordinary occasion of mass-scale gathering of pilgrims from every linguistic regional or cultural areas of the greater Hindu universe. The *kumbh* celebration, though retained most of its traditional characteristics intact, has also attracted some new attributes because of its being a powerful forum affording mass communication. Social reformist organizations as well as renowned ascetics utilize the occasion to act towards removal of misconceptions, social discriminations etc. that exist in society and create barrier among men. Similarly, *kumbh* offered golden opportunity for various propaganda—both at Government and non-Government levels, and festoons conveying "messages" abound the city. Child health care messages were disseminated through festoons, boards, hydrogen balloons sponsored by UNICEF. Government publicity departments raised giant pandals and arranged puppet shows, movies etc., for millions of pilgrims in order to convey messages ranging from family planning to adult education. Businessmen of different breeds and hues earned manifold through brisk business thereby underlining the great commercial potential of *kumbh*

## NOTES

Tripathi, B.D., 1978, *Sadhus of India*, Popular Prakashan, Bombay.
Vidyarthi, L.P., 1961, *The Sacred Complex in Hindu Gaya*, Asia Publishing House.

# 15

# Concept of Teerth and Tradition of Teerth-Yatra in the Himalaya

JITENDRA SINGH AND JAGDISH CHANDRA DAS

TRANSCENDENTAL as well as mundane merits of *Teerth* are superfluous in the Hindu horizons of mind. The *Teerth* is held as a point between the two entirely different entities—the *Ihlaukik* (mundane) and *Parlaukik* (spiritual) and served as stepping stone from former to latter. Sacred dips and associated observances at a *Teerth* are deemed to wash away mundane sins and earn added virtues to one's credit. These in subsequent *Teerth* visits accumulate in considerable extent and help one for leading righteous life essentially required for *Moksh* (salvation) after death. The Hindu culture attaches highest value to *Moksh* to end rebirth or transmigration of life. The Hindu philosophy mentions *karm*—controlled (deed based) birth-rebirth cycle and attribute present like merely as a phase between several past and future births. This cycle would not stop unless one gets *Moksh* and unites with the Brahm. It is envisaged that obtaining *Moksh* in present life is easier, as in subsequent rebirths there are more chances of accumulating more sins, which may result even into a non-human life, leaving no chance of earning virtues required for *Moksh*. Thus for earning merits for *Moksh*, the *teerth* are of paramount importance, where a Hindu adhering to *Varnashram* system performs some of the *Panch-Mahayazya*, gets redemption from the *tri-rin* and enjoys *Navdha Bhakti*, obtains knowledge and invokes meditation.

Derived from the word *Teer*[1] (bank of any water resource),
the term *Teerth*[2] and its concept has frequently occurred in the
Sanskrit textual works to elucidate crossing of *Bhavodadhi*
(cycle of birth and death) for unifications with the Brahm.
There are various typologies of *Teerth* given in our Sanskrit
literature. A brief review will suffice our present purpose.
Kashikhand of Skand Puran[3] illustrates three types of *Teerth*—
the *Jangam* (movable), the *Sthavar* (immovable) and the *Manas*
(mental). The *Jangam* teerth is equated with the Brahmin varn,
as it symbolizes the virtues of supreme piety attributed to
Brahmin. The people having such Brahminical virtues are
worthy to get worship. The *teerth* of *Stavar* category are
explicitly the places or locations in the country having been
famous for learning, devotion and meditation etc. The third
category of *Manas-teerth* is mentioned to be composed to
people's positive personal mental dispositions and motivations
required essentially for a coherent and peaceful social life such
as—*Satya* (truth), *Ksahma* (pardon), *Indiriya-nigrah* (sensual
control); *Daya* (kindness), *Rijuta* (simplicity), *Dan* (charity),
*Dam* (austerity), *Santosh* (satisfaction) *Brahmacharya* (cele-
bacy), *Gyan* (knowledge), *Dhairya* (patience), *Priyavadita* (soft
speech) and sublime to all these is spoken as *Adhyatmik
Shuddhi* (spiritual refinement of soul).

For an ideal, prosperous, systematic and symbiotic social
living in *Ihlok* (the world) and after life for the achievement of
*M ksh*, Bhumikhand of Padam-Puran[4] has recognised the
following social relationships to be of crucial importance and
provided the status of *Teerth*. These are *Guru* (teacher), *Mata-
Pita* (Parents) and *Pati-Patni* (spouse) who respectively discharge
the duties of imparting time-tested knowledge and experience
to their pupil, have unfathomable sense of love, welfare and
progress for their offspring, and share unique mutual love,
trust, honour and cooperation at all walks of life. These indi-
spensible qualities of the three fundamental social relationships
ensure a life, which is full of peace, success and prosperity.

However with the passage of time, the general conception
of the concept on *Teerth* has shrunk to the limits of *Sthawar
Teerth*. The locate of such a Teerth is invariably conceived to be
a *teer* (bank) of any water resource, where people may assemble
on ritual occasions, take sacred dips, enjoy *Satsang* (congrega-

tion) and acquire knowledge from the preachings of various learned saints and other great men. Through such congregations they invoke the inert germs of knowledge, devotion and meditation, which ultimately help patterning the mode of model life-style conducive to the achievement of *Moksh*.

Ambition of attaining *Moksh* has encouraged Hindu since the dawn of civilization to undertake on foot hazardous journeys involving life-risks to reach every Teerth in Hindu universe. Spreading over the whole of the continent, the Hindu *Teerth* are situated amidst seas, deserts plateaus, plains, hillocks and mountains. Among mountains, the Himalaya has been conceived to be the embodiment of divinity, hence doing meditation and other religious activities in the near-divine serene atmosphere has added merits to meet the desired goal of *Moksh*. The great virtuous ascetics and philosophers of their times, have been meditating and building up sacred shrines in the Hamalaya, which in course of time converted to famous *Teerth*. Garhwal is one such part of the holy Himalaya which has attracted the foremost attention in the context of religiosity.

This article aims to delineate the characteristic features of the *Teerth* (pilgrim centres) and the aspects of mental and bodily purity brought forth by the *Teerth-Yatra* (Pilgrimage) to Badrinath, Kedarnath, Gangotri and Yamunotri, called locally as *Char-Dham** (four divine abodes) of Garhwal Himalaya.

The territory of 'Garhwal', presently divided in Dehradun, Chamoli, Uttarkashi, Tehri and Paudi-Garhwal district, was formerly a princedom by the same name from the time immemorial. In Mahabharat mention has been made of Garhwal as 'Kulind'[5] while in Skand Puran as 'Kedar Khand'.[6] The geographical particulars of Garhwal, described centuries ago, can still be recognised by identical names, cultural zone etc.

As stated in 'Skand Puran', the territory of 'Kedar Khand' extended from 'Gangadwar' (Haridwar) in South to 'Shwetant' (Himalayan peaks with perpetual snow) in north and from 'Tamsa' (Tons river) in west to 'Baudhachal' (Nanda Devi Mountain) in east as an apparent *Swarg-bhavan* (heavenly abode) and remained tempting attraction even for the gods. The territory of Garhwal has been associated at different times,

---

* The Char-Dham of universal Hindu usuage contain the sacred shrine of Badrinath, Jagannathpuri, Rameshwaram and Dwarika.

to Hari (Lord Vishnu) and 'Har' (Lord Shiva) and their consorts. The famous shrine of Badrinath as a presiding deity of
the Garhwal kings of later times alongwith 'Panch Badri' and
numerous other temples, is dedicated to Lord Vishnu, while
the shrine of Kedarnath remained the presiding deity of
the former Garhwal kings, alongwith Panch-Kedar and other
temples, dedicated to Lord Shiva.

As remnants of a systematic fortification of the so-called
'Swarg-bhavan' of Garhwal, we still find two *Dwar* (gates)—
'Hardwar' called due to the prominence of Lord Shiva or
'Haridwar' (due to prominence of Lord Vishnu) and 'Kotdwar'
(gate of the fort) for getting into it and several 'Paudi' (stepp-
ing stones) for stepping up into the Bhavan, starting from the
'Har' or 'Hari-ki-Paudi' (threshold step at Haridwar). The
so-called 'Swarg-bhavan' contains innumerable places of
pilgrimage and temples in the name of different deities but the
most famous among these are the *Char Dham* of Garhwal
(Badrinath, Kedarnath, Gangotri and Yamunotri), 'Panch
Prayag' (Vishnu, Nand, Karn, Rudra, and Deo-Prayag) and
'Kashi' (Gupt and Uttar-Kashi). Besides, the 'Swarg Bhavan'
of Garhwal contains world's famous and biggest flower valleys
like Hari-ki-Doon and Bhyundar Ghati, with countless varieties
of flower species alongwith several attractive natural ponds,
mountain peaks, rivers, fauna and flora contributing to emana-
tion of mystique realm of sacredness. Most sacred rivers of the
Hindu, the Ganga and the Jamuna, originate from here. Among
the innumerable sacred centres of the Garhwal Himalaya the
main objective as already mentioned, is based on the description of the so-called Garhwal-ke-*Char-Dham*, associated sacred
centres and sacred offerings conducted in those.

## Badrinath

The divine shrine of Badrinath (10,284 ft.) is situated at 25
miles down to Mana pass, between Nar-Narayan mountains
along the left bank of Vishnu Ganga flowing amidst a forest
called Badrivan in the district of Chamoli. It is one of the
Char-Dham of pan-Hindu concept. It is also called, Bishalapuri
after Bishal Vaksh.

Within the sacred 'Kshetra' (geography) of the Badrivan,
other than Badrinath, there are the temples of Panch Badri

(Vishal, Yog, Bhavishya, Dhyan and Vriddh) at different places.

According to Skand Puran, Badrivan extended over an area from Kanva Ashram to Nandadevi mountain nearly 12 miles in breadth and 48 miles in length encircling several *Teerth* such as Gandhmadan, Nar-Narayan, Kuvershila and *Vanhi-teerth* (springs of hot and cold water). The Kshetra is stated to be very favourite to the gods and bestower of popularity, prosperity and *Moksh* to the devotees but remains beyond the approach of sinners.

Regarding the *Mahatmya* (sacred importance) of the sacred centre of Badrinath, it is held that the peak of Mount Badri, which lie adjacent to the peak of Mount Kedar once belonged to Lord Shiva but later on taken and occupied by Lord Vishnu. Afterwards as a mark of respect, a Brahmin called Subrat or Shalyabrat by name, installed the shrine of Badrinath at the confluence of Vishnu Ganga, Rashiganga and Saraswati rivers. The shrine was connected by an underground tunnel to the shrine of Kedarnath and the distance was covered within two hours only.

It is also believed that Mahabharat fame Arjun in the form of Nar and Srikrishna in the form of Narayan penanced for a long time respectively on the peaks of Nar and Narayan mounts and hence the area belongs to Lord Vishnu.

According to another current belief there Nar and the Narayan were the sons of Dharamraj and Matamurti. Disgusted by the sensual pleasures of Indralok they approached saint Narad for peace who advised them to penance in Badrivan. As per promise to meet their parents regularly they did not went back, so when their parents came to meet them, they disguised themselves in the mountain called Nar-Narayan. However, today as per their promise and unfulfilled wish, Nar-Narayan in the form of 'Utsav Murti' visit to the sacred centre dedicated to their parents as 'Matamurti' on Baman Dwadashi day for seeking *Ashirbad* (blessings).

## The Badrinath Complex

The temple of Badrinath bear the symbol of *Sudarshan Chakra* and has three apartments, the outer most *Sabha Mandap* or *Singh Dwar* the middle one *Darshan Mandap* and the inner one

*Garbh Grih Mandap* (sanctum sanctorum). The sanctum sanctorum has the idol of Akhil Brahm Badrinath, accompanied with the idols of Nar-Narayan at right hand, Narad and Kuver at left hand and Udhav and Garud in front. The other sacred centres of the complex are as follows.

Right to Badri Temple in Parikrama, there is a headless idol of Ghantakarn, who is worshipped prior to Badrinath. Ghantakarn has special importance in the temple of Badrinath and who is also symbolically represented by bell.

Behind the temple of Badrinath, there is a separate temple for Goddess Laxmi, and Shankracharya Gaddi also situate.

A huge stone slab known as 'Brahm Kapal' is famous for *Pitra Shradh* (oblations to manes) and lies in the vicinity of the temple. It is believed that at this sacred centre Lord Shiva got rid of *Brahm hatya*—the sin for chopping off the fifth head of Brahma.

Besides these, there are two *Taptkund* (hot water springs) called by the names Narad and Surya Kund where people take sacred dips to get rid of skin diseases. The water in these springs is so hot that it can boil rice, pulse and potatoes.

Embedded within Vishnu Ganga are *Panch Shila* (Narad, Barah, Narsingh, Markandeya, and Garud) where once these saints sat and meditated to appease Lord Vishnu.

At the left bank of Rishi Ganga, there is a temple dedicated to Urbashi, who was produced by Narayan to counter and ashame the 'Apsara' sent by Indra for distracting him from his meditation.

During winters, the doors of Badrinath temple are closed and for that time the idol of Lord Badri is worshipped at Joshimath. At Joshimath, Rawal—the chief priest of the shrine and temple committee office is also situate.

**Kedarnath**

The shrine of Kedarnath (11,753 ft.) is one of the *Dwadash Jyotirling* (Twelve illuminating phalluses) of Lord Shiva and situates amidst Kedar, Bharkhand and Kharcha peaks at the root of mountain Mahapatti in Mandakini river valley.

It is believed that the present shrine of Kedarnath was built by the Pandavas and will be extinct with the blockade of the passage leading ro Badrinath. The Pandavas having committed the sin of *Gotra-ghat* (clan destruction) in the battle of Mahabharat intended expiation from the grave sin, through the sacred 'darshan' of Lord Shiva. They visited for Darshan to Uttarakhand, but Lord Shiva disappeared at Guptkashi and appeared in disguised form as a bullock amidst a hoard of cattle. Bhim with the help of his brothers Nakul and Sahdeo came to know this trick and in order to recognise Lord Shiva, stood spreading his legs over the path. All the cattle passed through the space between his legs but Lord Shiva did not do so and tried to enter into the earth. While entering into the earth, Bhim recognised him and caught hold of his hind portion so firmly that Lord Shiva could not enter into the earth. By this incidence Lord Shiva became very happy with the Pandavas, resumed his real form and gave *Darshan*.

To immortalise the incident, the back of the bull form of Lord Shiva touched by Bhim is being worshipped at Kedarnath, while the other parts which entered into the earth appeared at different places in human form are being worshipped there. The *Nabhi* (navel) at Madhya, Mahesh, the face at Rudranath, the hands at Tungnath and the hairs at Kalpeshwar and all these places became famous by the name Panch-Kedar. The mouth appeared in Nepal and is worshipped as Pashupatinath.

Within the sanctum sanctorum of Kedar temple a place is dedicated to Annpurna Devi and outside the gate, Sringi-Bhringi gatekeepers find their place. On the left of Kedar temple at about 4000 ft. above, a sacred centre of Bhirav is situated at Bhairav Shila.

Around Kedar temple within its sacred geography there are three water reservoirs—Hemkund at left, Udakkund in front and Retkund in south. Hemkund is famous for sacred dips and for the immersion of horoscopes of the dead ancestors for enhancing their salvation. Udakkund is famous for taking dips for ones own salvation and the Retkund for the *Darshan* of Lord Shiva. It is held that as soon as one pronunciates the sacred dictum of *Om Namh Shivaye* a lot of bubbles would appear over the water of Retkund, to show the pleasure of Lord Shiva but if Lord Shiva remained unpleased these would not appear.

Besides these there are other sacred centres like Bhrigu Panth, Madhu Ganga, Ksheer Ganga, Basuki Tal, Gugal Kund,

Hanskund, Amrit Kund etc. Bhrigu Panth is famous for *Pranotsarg* (jumping to death for *Moksh*). Basuki Tal is sacred place where worship is conducted during Krisnashtmi and Rakshabandhan.

The doors of Kedar temple are opened 3-4 days before the opening of Badrinath shrine in late April or early May. The decision to this effect is taken by the temple authorities during Mahashivratri worship at Ukhimath temple, which is the winter abode of Kedar for six months. The temple of Kedarnath is closed down for the winter on the second day after Diwali. Lord Kedar migrates to Ukhimath with His divine *Gaddi* (seat) and office. There are several temples at Ukhimath dedicated to Siva, Parvati, Mandhata, Usha, Andiruddh, Brahi and Navdurga.

Before the opening and closing of the Kedar temple Lord Bhairav is worshipped and given the offerings of '*Bhandara*' (feast) during *Asarh* month.

## The Kedar Complex

The Kedar Complex includes several shrines which mainly remain dependent on the income of Kedar temple and are governed by the rules and regulations of the Shaiv philosophy, the centre of which is considered to be Kedarnath. Thus the Kedar-complex extends to the temples of Agastmuni, Gupt Kashi. Triyuginarayan, Laxminarayan, Gaura Devi, Madmaheshwar, Tungnath Kalimath, Rudranath, Gopeshwar and Ukhimath.

## Gangotri

The famous shrine of Gangotri (10,020 ft.) commemorates the descendence of Goddess Ganga on the earth in the form of a holy river to provide salvation to the sixty thousand fore-fathers of Bhagirath, the king of Ayodhya. And hence the river, before joining to Alaknanda at Dev Prayag is still called Bhagirathi, while afterwards as Ganga. The sacred centre of Goddess Ganga confines to a temple constructed by the Raja of Jaipur, over a huge black Shila (stone rock) at the right hand side of Gauri Kund (Bhagirathi and Kedar Gad confluence) behind Kedarnath peak.

The sanctum sanctorum of the Ganga temple is furnished

with the idols in which the prominent are Goddess Ganga, Raja
Bhagirath, Yamuna and Saraswati. A number of other deities
occupy their positions in the courtyard, in the smaller temples.
Within the sacred geography, there are Brahmkund and Vishnu-
kund. The rest of the part of the huge Bhagirath Shila (rock)
constitutes the famous sacred centre for offering oblations to
ancestors. At the confluence of Rudra Ganga and Bhagirathi,
the place called 'Patangan' is a famous centre for offering Pind
to ancestors.

Six miles down at the confluence of Bhagirathi and Janhavi,
a temple of Bhairon situates who is the protector of Gangotri
shrine. And further down at Jangla, the sage Janhu is said to
have his meditation.

Downwards from Jangla at the right hand side of Bhagirathi,
there is a place near Mukhwa and Dharali called Markandeya,
a sacred centre with few temples which serves as the winter
abode of Goddess Ganga. Gangotri priests and Panda of
Semuwal caste live at Mukhwa. The temple of Gangotri opens
on the occasion of Akshaya Tratiya day and closed down for
winters on the occasion of Gobardhan Puja day after Diwali.

Goddess Ganga, the consort of Lord Vishnu, due to
animosity between the co-consort was sent on earth. Co-
incidentally Raja Bhagirath was also granted a vow after his long
and rigorous meditations for bringing Ganga from heaven to
guarantee salvation to his sixty thousand great grand parents
who were reduced to ashes by the anger of Sage Kapil. Later
on, Kapil advised that the curse would be automatically removed
if any one from their dynasty succeeds in bringing Ganga to
earth and the curse-stricken princes would thus achieve salvation
by the touch of holy water of Ganga.

**Yamunotri**

The sacred shrine of Yamunotri (10,844 ft.) is situated at the
bank of Yamuna river flowing in north and as so thus named.
The river originates from Bandarpunchh of Kalindi mountain
in the Geethpatti of Rawain Pargana of Uttarkashi district.

Some nine kilometres downwards, at the confluence of river
Yamuna and Hanuman Ganga, a place called Kharsali situates
within the sacred geography of Yamunotri Teerth. Kharsali is a
famous *'chatti'* (halt for pilgrim) with Someshwar temple and

the winter abode of the Goddess Yamuna. The panda of Yamunotri belonging to Uniyal caste live here.

The Goddess Yamuna or Kalindi—the consort of Lord Krishna—is mentioned to be the daughter of Surya and Sangya and the sister of Yam or Dharmraja and the half-sister of Shani and Tapti who were born of her step-mother Chhaya.

Goddess Yamuna, before descending on earth in the form of a river, meditated hard and received a boon from Lord Brahma, by which she was blessed to be the reliever of all sufferings of mankind. Before her departure, she received another boon from her brother to the effect that a mortal sinner would always attain salvation, if he takes a sacred dip in the river Yamuna.

The sacred temple of Yamunotri contains the black marble icon of goddess Yamuna and that of white marble of goddess Ganga, the icons of Lord Krishna and Yamraj.

In the sacred geography of Yamunotri there exist sacred centres of Suryakund and Gaurikund. The water in Surya-kund comes from a hot spring and is so hot that it boils rice and pulse. The sacred prasad of Yamunotri is cooked in Surya-kund. Sacred dips for pilgrims are prescribed in Gaurikund. There is big rock constituting a sacred centre near Surya-kund called 'Divya Shila'.

The doors of the shrine are closed on Yam-Dwitiya day of Kartik Diwali and opened on the tritiya of Shukla-Paksh of Baisakh.

## The Sacred Performances

At all the prominent sacred centres of the Himalayan shrines of Garhwal, a large variety of ritual and devotional activities are performed to pacify the deities associated with the centres along with those responsible for shaping and controlling different aspects of destiny of a Hindu. Provision for the appeasement of manes also exists within the framework. They include ritual bath, floral ritual, individual worships, *Darshan* and *Aarati* ritual, *Havan-yagya*, artistic devotional performances, *Dan-Dakshina* offerings, exorcistic performances, fairs-festivals, *Tarpan pind* offerings etc., covering almost all the elements of *Navadha Bhakti* (nine types of devotion i.e. Shravan, Kirtan, Smaran, Padsevan, Archan, Vandan, Dasya, Sakhya, and

Atmnivedan), *Yog* (meditation) and *Gyan* (knowledge) prescribed for *Moksh*. Besides these performances by the pilgrims, there are shrine linked daily performances conducted by the Pujari regularly such as *Snan* (bathing of the idol), *Sringar* (decoration by clothings, ornaments, sandal, vermillion etc.) *Arti* (waving of burning incense around the idol), *Deep* (lighting earthen lamp), *stuti* (appeal), *Vandan* (salutation); *Bhog Lagana* (offering of food and Vishram (offering rest). Among these temple-linked sacred performances, the pilgrims are invited for having the blessings of *Aarti*, through salutation and offering of coins, taking part in *Stuti* and *Vandan* and are distributed with the *Prasad* after offering *Bhog*. The sacred performances commonly held at each of the four shrines of Garhwal and performed by the pilgrims are detailed below.

## Holy Snan

The ritual of taking dips in the sacred water of a Teerth is a primary sacred performance, essentially needed for bodily purity. The bodily cleanliness is a symbol of ones liberation from the worldly impurities of birth-death cycle. Though this performance is of daily occurrence but extra-ordinary virtues are attributed to taking dips on Purnima, Amavas, eclipse and other festive days of the Hindu calendar. Any water source of a *Teerth* is conceived to divine and taking bath in it, is in a way, establishing contact with the supernatural entity. This observance is of simplest type in which all of those, who are ignorant of other observances can take part but total devotion to it is required.

## Floral Ritual

The term 'floral ritual' is applied to a number of observances such as offering of water, flowers, leaves, fruits, milk, 'akshat' (rice), incense, sandal and vermillion together by the worshipper normally called *Puja* (worship). Usually, the Pujari of each of the shrines supervises the performances of *Puja* or *Archan*. This type is not abundantly practised in all the shrines.

## Individual Puja

The term individual *Puja* extends to all observances followed such as *Arghya* (offering of water mixed sometimes with milk, flowers fruits) *Prarthana* (prayer), *Stuti* (appeal), *Path* (reading and recitation of sacred texts), *Jaap* (repeatedly pronouncing of sacred words or Mantra and *Dhyan* (meditation). Through these performances, the individual worshipper tries to establish direct personal communication with the supreme power. Individual worship may be mental with utter silence or through verbalized utterances but the aspects of *Jaap* and *Dhyan* are done in utter silence and concentration. These are very rare in practice in the actual shrines. These are performed in the lonely places within the sacred geography of a Teerth.

## Havan and Yagya

Fire sacrifice of *Sankalaya*—a material consisting of barley, rice, sesamum, dry fruits, sandalwood, sugar, jaiphal, ghee etc. under the supervision of a priest is called *Havan*. This is performed in *Vedi* (fire pit) prepared by *Samidha* (dry woods of mango or palas) under the verbal utterance of sacred *Havan* hymns by the priest. This is arranged on request at each shrine.

The *yagya* is an elaborate form of *Havan*, which runs from hours to days and sometimes even lingers for a week or a fortnight. Different types of *yagya* performances, at all the Himalayan shrines of Garhwal, are arranged on the request of the pilgrims through advance payment of the expenses.

## Artistic Devotional Performances

The constituents of this category are invariably *Katha of Satyanarayan* (story recitation of Satyanarayan), *Keertan* or *Sankeertan* (group recitation of sacred poems). The pilgrims willing of earning *Punya* (merits) through these performance usually contact shrine's organising committee, pay the amount and observe on the given dates.

## Philanthropic Performances

The category is contained by *Dan* (alms) to beggars, saints and other needy persons, *Dakshina* (gift) to priests, *Nag* (customary payments) to other sacred specialists, *Brahm Bhog* (offering food to Brahmin), *Bhandara* (offering food to saints) and donations to shrines in terms of cash for meeting daily Puja expenditure, repair or construction of temple or Dharmashala, and purchase of idol etc. The Dan is also made in terms of gold for making 'Chhatra' or other ornaments for the presiding deity of the shrine.

**Exorcistic Performances**

The regional deities of Garhwal, mostly presiding village deities inclusive of the Bhotia Valleys also make their visit to the local *Char-Dham* of Garhwal, to offer their homage and sacred dips. It is customary to the regional culture to have *Deo-Doli* (palanquin for the deity) in each village for carrying them for rituals and for making visits within the region. The Doli is carried by the persons, who feel the effect of the spirit of the deity coming to them. Under the influence of the deity the *Deo-Doli* carrier do exorcistic performance called as *'Devta Jhulana'* locally. By offering some coins and a piece of red cloth, any pilgrim can request the deity to tell remedies for the sufferings. The deity speak through the spirit-possessors, who express their answer through hints, which are uncoded by the trained interpreters to the questioner. Likewise *Dhol-Deity* (Drum deity) exorcism is also seen in these shrines.

**Fairs and Festivals**

On the festive occasions of Hindu calendar a lot of people gather from the nearby villages and also from the distant parts of the country providing a special attraction to the shrines, which normally does not find place in ordinary routine. This kind of special gathering may occur sometimes in particular, on 'Yam Dwatiya' (at Yamunotri), 'Ganga Dashahra' (at Gangotri), 'Ram Navmi', 'Krishna Janmashtmi' (at Badrinath) and 'Rakshabandhan' (Annkoot) and other occasions related to Lord Shiva and Goddess Parvati (at Kedarnath) and ordinarily Sankranti, Amavas etc. at all the Teerth.

**Man-Dan Performances**

These are the vows of different kinds, which people promise to perform in particular *Teerth*, after the fulfilment of desires of property, job, mate, offspring and such others. These are done in accordance with promises from simple worship to offering of gold.

## Obsequal Observances

At each of the four Himalayan *Teerth* of Garhwal, there is provision for obsequal offerings and that is associated with some famous incidence of *Pauranic* or Vedic times. Usually the people of neighbouring Himalayan states, inclusive of Nepal visit the *Teerth* for the immersion of the bones or idol of their dead and for observing associated rituals. The pilgrims from other parts very rarely take part in such performances. The main observances of this category are as follows.

### Sacred Tonsure

The pilgrims eager for obsequal offerings are required to get shaved their hair, moustaches and beard from the barber sacred specialist, before taking the ritual bath in the *Teerth*. Those people who have come to the Teerth for immersion of ashes, bones or idol of their parents are required to '*Marjan*' (sprinkling of sacred water) before the ceremonial immersion and subsequently shaving and taking of sacred bath. It is believed that unshaved person remains polluted and hence any offering made to ancestors would not reach to them unless they observe purificatory tonsure.

### Tarpan and Pind-Dan

'*Tarpan*' (libation) and offerings of '*Pind*' (rice balls) are integral to obsequal sacrifices. The *Tarpan* is an elaborate form of offering of water starting with deities (Deo-Tarpan) to saints (Rishi-Tarpan) to God of death (Yam-Tarpan) and coming to manes (Pitra-Tarpan). The Deo and Rishi Tarpan are done by facing north while the Yam and Pitra-Tarpan are done by facing south. The act of Tarpan is conducted by the sacred specialist, who chants sacred hymns and names the ancestors.

The *Pind-Dan* offerings is very elaborate performance but the '*Sanklap*' (dedication), '*Gayatri mantra*' (Vedic recitation) '*Sthapana*' (symbolization of gods and manes), '*Sapindikaran*' (joining of Pind of manes and gods) and '*Pind-Puja*' (worship of Pind) are main elements. The sacred specialist invites the gods and manes by chanting Vedic hymns, represents them with different symbols, offers Pind to them and then cuts these Pind of the gods and manes and joins them to symbolise the deceased's unification with the Brahm.

## The Sacred Specialist

In the category of sacred specialists, all those persons belonging to Brahmin and other castes of the Hindu are to be placed who earn their livelihood, wholly or partially, depending upon the sacred services performed in the Teerth of Garhwal Himalaya and associated temples. They are panda, pujari, purohit or acharya, pachak, saints, astrologers, palmists drummers and singers, barbers, florists, and shopkeepers who sell sacred objects.

### Panda

The sacred specialists of Panda category belong to Garhwali Brahmin castes and serve as important mediators between the Teerth and the pilgrims, the Panda of Yamunotri live in Kharsali, those of Gangotri in Mukhwa, those of Badrinath in Joshimath and those of Kedarnath in Deoprayag. The Panda of each shrine have traditional hereditary rights over the clientele and as per their right, they serve the pilgrims of the different regions of the Hindu universe. They extend facilities of stay and worship to their clients and receive handsome rewards. The Panda and the Pujari belong to same caste and work as Panda, when they do not have Pujari duties. The *Jajman* (pilgrim) donate money to temples and other philanthropic activities through their Panda. The Panda are not to be viewed in isolation as sacred specialists. In true sense they form an institution in which other than Pujari, a number of functionaries such as Acharya, barber, florist, drummers and singers contribute their important roles. Therefore, they become entitled to share the remuneration, the pilgrims offer to Panda. The Panda serve as agent of the shrines, who travel in the different corners of the Hindu universe and invite the people to visit the Teerth.

### Pujari

The Pujaris sacred specialists are regular priests of the shrines, who perform daily temple-linked worships such as 'Snan' 'Sringar', 'Aarti', 'Deep-Dan', 'Stuti-Vandan' and 'Bhog' etc.

In the temples of Kedarnath and Badrinath, customarily the Pujari are appointed from the celebate Nambudari Brahmin of south and are called as *Rawal*. The *Rawal* are allowed to keep disciples and one of these disciples is entrusted with the duties of daily temple-linked worships. In Gangotri and Yamunotri the Pujari hails from Garhwali Brahmin caste and is entitled to lead married life. They have hereditary rights over the worship in respective temples which they perform as per their share in turns. They have claim over the '*Dan-Dakshina*' offered to them personally by the pilgrims and over the money offered to '*Aarti* ritual' held twice daily.

### Purohit or Acharya

The sacred specialists of the category are required to have versatile and detailed knowledge of the procedures of Hindu '*Karm-Kand*' (rituals and ceremonies). They are supposed to conduct different types of '*Jaap*', *Path*', '*Yagya*', '*Havan*', and even mortuary ceremonies as per textual guidance. They belong to Brahmin caste. They earn a lot from the remuneration received for conducting these performances.

### Pachak

The '*Pachak*' sacred specialists in the shrines of Garhwal Teerth act as cook for the divinity. They cook twice a day for the divine *Bhog*. The amount of *Bhog* differs in each of the four shrines. After the offering of *Bhog* to the presiding and secondary deities of the shrines, the cooked items are distributed as '*Prasad*' to pilgrims and the functionaries of the temple. The Pachak belong to Brahmin caste of Garhwal and are paid by the temple management. They also cook *Bhog* in different quantities on requests of the pilgrims as per their promises of Bhog offerings to the deities. They get extra remunerations for such cookings.

### Drummers and Singers

This category of sacred specialists come from the caste of their profession and have versatile knowledge of the ceremonial and deity-linked songs. They, as per the vows of the pilgrims, perform the sacred services and receive payments. They eulogize the respective deities and request for the welfare of their clients.

## Barber

The sacred specialist, barber performs *Mundan* ceremony and also ritual shaving for conducting obsequal ceremonies. They hail from the barber caste and earn their livelihood from the handsome payments of the pilgrims.

## Florist

The florist category of sacred specialists in the Himalayan *Teerth* of Garhwal do not belong to florist caste found elsewhere in the country. In these shrines local Rajput supply flowers traditionally and receive remuneration from the temple management. When they supply flowers or garlands to pilgrims they are paid for it separately.

## Astrologers and Palmists

This category of sacred specialists, contribute their sacred services to future telling of the pilgrims. They point out the harmful stars and prescribe pacificatory measures to appease the bad stars through performances like, *Yogya, Havan, Jaap* etc. besides wearing precious stone (*ratan*). They are paid for their consultations by the pilgrims. Some of them also keep ready-stocks of gems of various types and sell to pilgrims.

## Sacred Object Sellers

People engaged in the selling of sacred objects such as, *Ganga Jal*, containers, religious books, conch-shells, utensils used in worship, prasad, vermillion, rings, tulsi, bead necklace, Rudraksh etc. also constitute a category of sacred specialists. They provide the pilgrims with sacred objects and thus help in the sacred activities of the shrines. They can be considered as positive agents for the diffusion of material objects of a region, to the far off areas of the Hindu universe spreading beyond the political limits of the country.

## The Saints

The division of sacred specialist constituted by the saints in each of the Teerth contribute to the sacredness as Guru and motivators for observing various performances. They infuse religiosity in the pilgrims through their preachings and narrating importance of the various Teerth and the deities. '*Banprasth*' and '*Sanya*s' being important stages in Hindu life, from the view point of renunciation and Moksh, their recruitment is voluntary, honorific and easy. They are the pivotal figures of Hindu culture and civilization, as they have successfully passed through the stages of '*Brahmacharya*' and '*Grihast*' and gained varied experiences of life.

## Concluding Remarks

The preceding account reflects that Hindu view of life is far penetrating one and provides emphasis to enjoy all the worldly things through different *Sanskar* of the *Ashram* system. With the passage of age it is recommended that one should distract his mind gradually from the worldly pleasures through intermittent visits to Teerth required for mental and bodily purification. These contributed increasingly to righteous way of life and help in the accumulation of merits required for one's liberation from the cycle of birth and death and unification with the Brahm.

As is evident in the introductory paragraphs that the Hindu concept of *Teerth* is not only limited to '*Sthavar Teerth*' (places of pilgrimage but it extends to cultivation of positive mental virtues and amicable social relationships also, which are needed for peaceful and prosperous living. Thus, there has been a lot of emphasis over the mental and social achievements besides ritual attainments in Hindu Dharm.

Spread of the Hindu *Teerth* in different types of terrains, climates and in every corner of the Hindu universe regardless of isolation, direction and inaccessibility, reflects the basic sentiment of functional integration. It was deliberately designed so that inter-regional visits may occur frequently and people may learn things from each other despite sharing distant habitats.

In every *Teerth* and associated temples of the Garhwal Himalaya we find representation of almost all major deities from local, regional and pan-Hindu levels indicating mythical and conceptual solidarity of all Hindu sects like Shaivism, Shaktism, Vaishnavism, Buddhism etc. The various sacred specialists found in the above Teerth, belonging to different castes and regions have assembled at a place, to contribute to the sacred functioning through their specialized jobs. Despite vast apparent regional-cultural variation in the different castes and regions of Hindu universe, spreading even across national boundaries, we find them in each of the *Teerth*, sharing similar inherent under-currents of ideas, faiths and sacred performances. Observing and concluding from all the points we can attribute that the Hindu *Teerth* spreading in all directions, regions and climates of the country and beyond, are not only the cradles of Hindu culture and civilization but also those of ritual, rather *Dharmik* (relating to way of life) integration. The *Dharmik* unity of the Teerth have surpassed regional, linguistic, nationalistic narrowness in each of the historical eras of Hindu civilization.

## REFERENCES

1. *Teeryte bharodadhiruen, asmat, asminniti va teertham. cf.* Hindi Vishwa Kosh, 1965, Khand 5, p. 339, Nagri Pracharini Sabha, Varanashi.

2. *Tasmatu teertheshu gantavyam nareih Sansarbhirubhin, Punyodakeshu satatam sadhu shreni Virajishu,* cf. *ibid,* p. 389.

3. Cf. *Ibid,* p. 387-388.

4. Cf. *Hindu Vishwa Kosh,* p. 387.

5. Singh, J. 1987, Nritatvik Darpan Me Uttarkashi Ke Garhwali Samaj Aur Sanskrit Ka Pratibimb, p. 8-9.

6. *Ibid.,* p. 8-9.

## NOTES

Bhardwaj, S.M., 1973, Hindu places of Pilgrimage in India, Thompson Press (India Limited) Delhi.

Ratudi, H.K., 1928, Garhwal ka Ithas, Garhwali Press, Dehradun.

Sharma, M.M., 1977, Through the Valley of Gods, Vision Books, Delhi.

Singh J., 1986, Ecological Bearing in the Religious Milieu of Garhwal, Himalaya in Ecology, Economy and Religion of the Himalaya (ed.) Vidyarthi and Jha, Orient Publication, New Delhi.

Singh J., 1987, Nritatvik Darpan Me Uttarkashi Ke Garhwali Samaj Aur Sanskrit Ka Pratibimb, An. S.I., Calcutta.

Vidyarthi, L.P., 1961, Sacred Complex in Hindu Gaya, Asia Publishing House, Delhi.

# 16

# Parasuram Kund

## A Hindu Centre of Pilgrimage in North East India

ASIM MAITRA

## Introduction

HUMAN society, culture or civilization, in Redfieldian sense of the term, is fundamentally amorphous in nature which is further characterised by its complexity and diversity. To study it in different contexts, space and time dimension, different approaches and techniques are needed and evolved accordingly by social and cultural anthropologists. In India, in the recent past, inspired and influenced by the concepts and theoretical propositions of Chicago School of anthropologists such as Redfield, Singer, Marriot and so on, Prof. L.P. Vidyarthi, studying the sacred city of Hindu Gaya, located in ancient cultural zone of Magadh, developed 'Sacred Complex', a new social anthropological approach to study the Hindu places of pilgrimage as a dimension of Indian civilization. This is really a new trend, a new area of study in Indian anthropology, more precisely in social anthropology, as it marks the beginning of a new era of an anthropological tradition of studying the sacred complex in India and in other countries of the world. The trichotomic components—the sacred geography, the sacred performances and the sacred specialists are accreted to 'Sacred Complex'. Following the lead given by Prof. Vidyarthi, a band of Indian scholars have successfully studied the institution of pilgrimage in different ecological set-ups. Foremost among the Indians who devoted their genius to this new dimension of study are Prof. M. Jha (1971, 1973, 1974, 1978, 1979, 1982 and 1985), a specialist in conducting scientific studies in sacred complex, and Prof. Saraswati (1963, 1965, 1974, 1975, 1984 and 1985). Prof. Jha, along with other scholars, has amply demonstrated that the concept of 'Sacred Complex' has wider applicability and pan-Indian pattern. He (19 5) has given the concept a firm footing by studying the origin, classifying the types, and delineating the spread and nature of Hindu pilgrimages in India. Prof. Saraswati (1984) has refined the concept of 'Sacred Complex' further and brought sophistication in its analysis defining the term 'sacred' from Indian point of view, and propounding a theory of 'Sacred-Secular continuum'.

The institution of pilgrimage is intimately related with religion, and the historians of religion have recorded that almost every religion or recognised faith of the world has the concept of pilgrimage or the sacred places to which men and women of faith periodically converge, though its attributes differ from one religion to another. In general sense, pilgrimage means the journey undertaken by a devotee or believer to visit a sacred or holy place. It is generally equated with the Hindu term *tirtha-yatra* which does not fully connote the English term pilgrimage. Literally, *tirtha* means holy or sacred place, and *yatra* denotes journey or visit. The Hindu term *tirtha* implies many other meanings as well. Prof. Saraswati (1984 : 36) has etymologically explained the various meanings, forms and significance attached to the term *tirtha* using materials from *Brahma Purana*. According to *Skandapurana*, a religious scripture, control of senses, truth, forgiveness, and kindness to all living beings, and simplicity are also *tirtha*. Thus the *tirtha yatra* not only means the physical act of visiting the holy places but it also implies mental and moral discipline (Bhardwaj, 1973). In fact, without the latter pilgrimage in physical sense has little value or significance in the Hindu religious tradition. Again, according to Hindu religious thought (Radhakrishnan, 1968) four predominant ideas have been persisting in Hindu society concerning attitude to life. They are *dharma*, *astha*, *kama* and *moksha*. *Dharma* characterized by the considerations of righteousness, dutifulness and virtue. *Artha* entails materials gain, worldly advantage and success. *Kama* denotes love and pleasure; and the fourth, *moksa*, connotes spiritual realisation and self-emancipation which has been equated with salvation or freedom from transmigration. The first three aspects of life converge towards the final goal, i.e. spiritual bliss. Within this philosophical concept of life those activities, observances, rituals and ceremonies become meaningful in the attainment of liberation of the self from the bondage of re-birth. Hinduism provides a variety of courses that individuals may take towards religious fulfilment, for example, there is a path of knowledge, *jnana-yoga*, and the path of unmixed devotion *bhakti-yoga*. Pilgrimage, though not one of the major recognised paths of achieving *moksa*, is nevertheless accepted as a desirable practice to earn religious merit, within a life lived according to *dharma*, pilgrimage is one of the many ways for self-realisation and bliss. Moreover, journey to sacred places provides opportunity for the householder to detach himself for some time from the cares and worries of daily life and to devote that time to prayer, contemplation, and listening to the spiritual discourses of holy men. With these introductory sentences, let us turn to the discussion of the sacred centre referred as Parasuram Kund. For empirical data, field-work was conducted during January 1986. Besides, religious scriptures available historical records, archeological evidences, the myths related with the Kund, guide books and pamphlets have been utilised to study this sacred centre.

## Geographical Setting

Parasuram Kund is located in the district of Lohit in the present state of Arunachal Pradesh, the fascinating land of rising sun. It lies between the latitudes 27°33'N and 29°22'N, and the longitudes 95°15'E and 97°24'E. Kund is situated on the bank of river Lohit at a distance of 35 km. from Tezu, the district headquarters. The district of Lohit lies in the north eastern corner of India, and adjoins Tibet now China on the north and Burma on the east. Situated at the tri-junction of three countries, the place has assumed paramount importance. Besides, the district occupies a unique position in the history of India as a meeting place of various cultures, both indigenous and exotic. The place is also fascinating for its natural grandeur and scenic beauties. The lofty snow-cloud mountains cascading down into the profusely wooded lower hills, and the innumerable streams flowing through deep gorges and glens, and through the verdant valleys till they merge with the great tributaries of Brahmaputra, namely Lohit and Dibang rumbling on the plain, constitute a topography which is at once formidable, sublime and magnificent.

## The Kund

The Kund is actually a big and deep water hole or well of approximately 30 metres in diameter in a rocky bed protruding into the river from the left bank hill. There was a separate Kund named Brahmakund adjacent to Parasuram Kund which, at present, cannot be distinguished from the main course of the turbulent river because of topographical change came about due to earthquake in 1950. That is why the present Parasuram Kund is also known as Brahmakund. The river Brahmaputra is said to be originated from Brahmakund. Kund can be reached by boat or by bus.

The surrounding area of the Parasuram Kund is inhabited by a Mongoloid tribe or community known as Mishmi. They are divided into three sub-groups—the Idu or Chulikata, the Taraon or Digaru, and the Kamaon or Miju. They are migrants from Burma, and arrived in different batches in the Lohit valley. The last group i.e. the Kamaon or Miju came about 500 years ago. But they claim themselves as the autochthons of the area. They practise agriculture by the method of shifting cultivation. The Mishmi are animist, but have the concept of Supreme Being. It is the Mishmi people who generally carry the pilgrims by boat to Parasuram Kund.

## The Legend

Almost every centre of pilgrimage in India has a legend. The Kund is associated with the legend of Parasuram, the great mythological hero who, it is mentioned in *Kalikapurana*, religious scripture, composed in ninth century A.D., had massacred Kshatriyas and killed his own mother. The story goes like this. In ancient times, there lived a Brahman *rishi* (sage) named Jamadagni, an eccentric person, hot tempered, with his wife and five sons. One day he sent his wife Renuka to fetch water from the Ganges for bath. She was delayed in bringing water, and this made Jamadagni very angry. He became furious and ordered his eldest son to kill his mother. He refused to obey his father and so did the other three sons. Then Jamadagni ordered his youngest son Parasuram who severed the head of his mother with an axe, i.e. *kuthar*; but as a result of the killing the handle of the axe got stuck to his hand. However, his father was very pleased with him for carrying out the order and he asked his son to pray for a boon. Parasuram first prayed for bringing his mother back to life and then enquired as to how to expiate the crime of killing his mother. Jamadagni told his son to visit the sacred places throughout the country. Parasuram did so, and ultimately came to the Brahmakund in the present Lohit district. He faced difficulty to reach the *Kund* and made a passage for the water to come out by digging the bank of the Brahmakund. Then he took bath there and expiated the sin. While taking bath, the axe dropped on from his hand, and the spot where the axe fell down came to be known as Parasuram Kund. In allusion to this legend, the place is also known as Prabhu Kuthar.

There is a rational or speculative account of how the place derived its name. It is said that the roaming sages of ancient times named the mount-Kailash and made or imagined it the abode of god Siva. They visited the area and called the ever growing lake Brahmaputra having seen its source waters emerging from the depth of silvery, glazing glaciers resembling Brahmaloka (abode of god Brahma). May be it was some of those roaming sages who found the Kund during their sojourns, then named and consecrated in Brahmakund or Parasuram Kund. According to some scholars the (Toseswar Sarma, and others), incident might have happened during pre-historic or epic times when a civilisation called 'Bhisneak Nagar' during Shri Krishna's time, nearly 5000 years ago, flourished in the area.

**Sacred Performance**

It is mentioned in the Yogini Tantra, a Hindu scripture, that a mere bath in the Brahma or Parasuram Kund washes away all the bodily and mental sins of a person. That belief still guides thousands of Hindus who come as pilgrims from far and near to visit the Kund for a holy dip during the 'Magh Sankranti

Mela' (a festive occasion on the first day of Hindu month-Magh) held in the mid-January every year. To facilitate the sacred performances of the pilgrim, a *dharamsala* (resting place for pilgrims or visitors) has been established at the foothills on the way to the Kund. A Siva temple has also come into existence recently on the slope of the hill near the *dharamsala*. A sacred specialist has little role to play in this centre. Pilgrims come, change dresses, take holy bath then go away. They rarely engage priest for the purpose. This place may be designated as a 'natural sacred centre', and the tradition of the performance of the complex network of rituals is yet to be construed. Here, sacred performance, means a holy dip in the Kund which continues for 15 days. Ascetics of different denominations visit this centre regularly. Besides, a good number of pilgrims also come from Assam, Bihar, Bengal, Orissa and Uttar Pradesh. In addition, the government servants who are posted in North East India come with their families to take a sacred bath in the Kund. Some pilgrims prefer to stay in the *dharamsala* a few days more to enjoy natural beauty of the area. Across section of the ethnic composition of the pilgrims at the Parasuram Kund reveals that they hail mainly from the upper strata of the Hindu society.

## Concluding Remarks

Pilgrimage is a world-wide phenomenon. At least in India and other South-Asian countries, sacred centres still exert a powerful influence on the believers, though its impact on the people of industrially and technologically advanced countries is on the wane. Pilgrimage is a religious institution continuing in the Hindu society since time immemorial. The form of this religious tradition or institution is mostly non-rational and extra-necessities from technological point of view. This may be a reason or a factor for its persistence and perpetuation. Again, the earnest and supreme desire for *moksa* (salvation) in life of the Hindu is another reason for the continuity of this religious tradition.

The Parasuram Kund is a *nadi-tirtha* (river shrine). This sacred centre is unique in that it is located in the heart of a Mongoloid tribe i.e. the Mishmi in the sub-Himalayan region. Parasuram Kund provides a vivid or glaring example of interactions or linkages between the peoples of great tradition and little or local tradition. Here, 'great tradition' means the traditions of the Hindu and little tradition denotes the traditions of the Mishmi and other local people. This linkage can be viewed at three levels—historical, mythical and empirical. At the historical level, the students of ancient cultures provide us relevant information or evidences of direct link of this place with other areas. At the foot of the present Mishmi hills in the district of Lohit hidden in a dense forest, lies the fortress of King Bhismaka. Protected by an earthen rampart from three sides, and by the mountainous wall in the north, the fortress extends over an area of four square kilometres. At the centre of the fort lie the ruins of a large brick-built palace which, according to experts of this line, reveals that the builders of Bhismaknagar were inspired and guided by the canons formulated by Kautilya and Manu. The recently excavated wheel turned pottery and the terracotta industry are the evidences of direct contact this region had with the Gangetic basin since ancient times. At Bhisnaknagar, remains of tanks, broad and high roads, have been found. It is very interesting, and surprising too, to know that the Mishmi still identify one of these roads as 'Rukmini Ali', ali means road. Heroes of Mahabharata, such as Bhismaka, Rukmini, Sishupal and Krishna had found local habitation in this area.

At the mythical level, a faith very fundamental to the Idu, a sub-group of the Mishmi, who inhabit this region, is that Rukmini, the consort of Krishna, belonged to their community, and Bhismaknagar, was the home of her father—king Bhismaka. The story goes like this. Bhismaka declared the betrothal of his daughter Rukmini with Sishupal. But Rukmini who was in love with Lord Krishna, eloped with him. Rukmo, Bhismaka's son was sent to bring them back. In the encounter that followed Krishna overpowered Rukmo. But, at Rukmini's intervention, Krishna spared Rukmo's life chopping off his (Rukmo's) head hair. Since then, all the Idu Mishmi, the men-folk, cut their hair in the same fashion which is still continuing, and the community still prefers marriage by elopement.

Some scholars believe that the Mishmi, the present inhabitants of the district of Lohit, are the progenies or the descendants of one of the seven Brahman families who had come along with Parasuram, but it has no historical evidence.

At the empirical level, a significant secular aspect of this sacred centre is the colourful fair (*mela*) held every year on the Kund site, where various departments of the government of Arunachal Pradesh, and the local people i.e. the Mishmi put up stalls displaying varieties of handicrafts and other artistic products which easily attract the attention of the pilgrims. This fair and the Kund itself expose the Mishmi and other local people to pan-Indian communities, who come over here as pilgrims as well as tourists—where diffusion of cultural traits, exchange of views and ideas takes place automatically. Incident of marriage between the Mishmi girls and Hindu boys, though not very common, crystallises the linkages between great and local traditions. Besides, the manner, the behaviour, the performance of little bit rituals, and the act of holy-dip of the pilgrims of this centre reflect the integration of their beliefs, practices and thought thereby confirming the oneness of Hindu society which is basically religious in form. Moreover, this centre is playing an integrative role to the Hindu. The fair, the construction of *dharamsala*, and the arrangements made by the local government for the transport, accommodation and medical facilities for the pilgrims are definitely the secular aspects of this sacred centre which go to prove the theory of 'Sacred-Secular Continuum' developed by Saraswati (1984).

In addition to the four types of *tirtha's daiva* (created by god), *asura* (associated with asuras), *arsa* (established by sages) and *meanus* (made by man) mentioned in our sacred texts, as an anthropologist looking from the explicit point of view, I propose, rather venture to classify, roughly the Hindu places of pilgrimage or the pilgrimage centres of all religions into two types—natural and artificial. Natural sacred centre means made by nature, where the beliefs of man have not yet taken the concrete shape in reality. All the river shrines or water shrines, mountain or hill shrines, stone or tree shrines may be designated as natural sacred centres or shrines. Artificial sacred centres or shrines are those that are created by the art or skill of man, in fact it is artistic product of man. Here the term 'artificial' has been used to mean real or reality. All the temples, churches, mosques and so on are artificial shrines. Here the supernatural beliefs of man and woman have been concretised into reality in the shape of temple, church and so on. In both the types of sacred centres or shrines religious merits are attributed by gods. Parasuram Kund is still functioning as a natural sacred centre, and it will grow into an artificial sacred centre in the long run, and the process has already started, the recently constructed Siva temple is an indicator. Generally, in the natural sacred centres, rituals or ceremonies are not elaborately performed by the pilgrims whereas in the artificial sacred centres, the ritual or ceremonies are observed in a complex and complicated manner. though the actual performance of rituals or ceremonies depends on multiple factors.

## NOTES

Bharadwaj, S.M., 1973, *Hindu Places of Pilgrimage in India* : *A Study in Cultural Geography*. University of California Press.

Bhowmick, P.K., 1960, Four temples in Midnapur. *Man in India*. 40(2), pp. 81.

Bowman, G., 1985, Anthropology of Pilgrimage. In Dimensions of Pilgrimage, (ed.) M. Jha.

Chakrabarti, P., and K.C. Malhotra, 1979, Social Structure of a Pilgrim Town Tarakeswar (West Bengal). An Exploratory study—*Journal of Social Research*. Vol. XXII, No. 11.

Chaudhuri, B., 1985, A Rural Temple and the Devotees : A study on continuity and change. *In Dimensions of Pilgrimage*, (ed.) M. Jha.

Datta Choudhury S., 1978, *Lohit District*, Arunachal Pradesh District Gazetteers. Director of Public Relations and Information, Shillong.

Goswami, B.B. and S.G. Morab, 1975, *Chamundeswari Temple in Mysore*. Anthropological Survey of India, Calcutta.

Jha, M., 1971, *The Sacred Complex in Janakpur*, Allahabad. United Publishers.

Jha, M., 1978, Studies on Sacred Complex : A Methodological Approach to Study Indian Civilisation, *Journal of Social Research*. Vol. XXI, No. 11, pp. 23-46.

Jha, M., 1981, The Sacred Complex in Himalaya : Some Notes and Observations. *Journal of Social Research*. Vol. XXIV, No. 11, pp. 61-71.

Jha, M. (ed.), 1985, *Dimensions of Pilgrimage : An Anthropological Appraisal*, New Delhi : Inter-India Publications.

Jha, M., 1985, The Origin, Type, Spread and Nature of Hindu Pilgrimage. *In Dimensions of Pilgrimage*, (ed.) M. Jha.

Jha, M. 1985, Hindu Pilgrimage and Patronage : A Study in the History of Politicalisation of Hindu Tirtha-Jagannath Puri : A case study. In *Dimensions of Pilgrimage*, (ed.) M. Jha.

Morab, S.G., 1985, Concept of Pilgrimage in Folk-Tradition : The case of the Chamundeshwari Ritual Complex. In *Dimensions of Pilgrimage*, (ed) M. Jha.

Negi, R.S. and J. Singh 1931, Makar Sankranti in the Garhwal Himalaya : A Study in Sacred Performance. *Journal of Social Research*. Vol. XXIV, No. 11, pp. 113-123.

Sahay, K., 1974, The Sacred Geography of Rameshwaram and Tirupati : In *Symposium on the Sacred Complex in India*, (eds.) L.P. Vidyarthi and M. Jha.

Samanta, D.K., 1985, Ujjain : A Centre of Pilgrimage in Central India. In *Dimensions of Pilgrimage*, (ed.) M. Jha.

Saraswati, B.N., 1961, Holi Circuit of Nimsar. *Journal of Social Research*. Vol. 8, No. 2, pp. 35-43.

Saraswati, B.N., 1962, The Temple Organization in Goa. *Man in India*. Vol. 42, No. 4.

Saraswati, B.N., 1975, *Kashi Myth and Reality of a Classical Cultural Tradition*. Indian Institute of Advanced Study, Simla.

Saraswati, B.N., 1984, *The Spectrum of the Sacred*. Concept Publishing Company, New Delhi.

Saraswati, B.N., 1985, Kashi Pilgrimage—The End of an Endless Journey. In *Dimensions of Pilgrimage*, (ed.) M. Jha.

Sinha, S., 1972, Kali Temple of Kalighat and the city of Calcutta. In *Cultural Profile of Calcutta*, (ed.) S. Sinha.

Upadhyay, V.S., 1974, The Sacred Geography of Dwaraka. *In Symposium on Sacred Complex in India*. (eds.) L.P. Vidyarthi and M. Jha.

Vidyarthi, L.P., 1961, *The Sacred Complex in Hindu Gaya*. Bombay, Asia Publishing House.

Vidyarthi, L.P. and M. Jha, 1974, *Symposium on Sacred Complex in India*, Ranchi Council of Social and Cultural Research, Ranchi University.

Vidyarthi, L.P., B.N. Saraswati and M. Jha, 1978, *The Sacred Complex of Kashi* : New Delhi : Concept Publishing Company.

# 17

# Formal Replication in Costa Rican Pilgrimages

LESLIE ELLEN STRAUB, O.P.

PILGRIMAGES in Costa Rica occur on local, regional, and national levels of society; differ in structure, ritual behaviour and meaning for participants; and very both in the Spanish terms, namely, *'romeria'* and *'peregrinacion'*, by which are they identified, and the degree to which they reflect Spanish models of pilgrimage (Straub 1985 : 105-113). Given such diversity, the question arises as to what components of these pilgrimages provide consistency and unity either among the various pilgrimages in the Republic, or among the expressions of a single pilgrimage tradition which differ according to locale.

This chapter addresses that question using data drawn from an ethnographic and ethnohistorical study of the Costa Rican pilgrimage tradition of Our Lady of the Angels (Nuestra Señora delos Angeles) carried out in the Republic in 1984, 1985, and 1987;[1] and focuses on four expressions of that tradition, namely, pilgrimages to the city of Cartago, to Barrio Los Angeles in San Ramön de Alajuela, to Juanilama de Puntarenas, and within Llano Grand de Cartago. A description of the pilgrimages with attention to similarities and differences among them, is followed by an examination of a unifying element, namely, the replication of iconographic form, with a view to contibuting material to what is to date a very small pool of ethnographic data on Central American pilgrimages and to offering some conceptual analysis of interest to students of Latin American pilgrimage and of pilgrimage in general.

## The Pilgrimage Tradition of our Lady of the Angels : Four Expressions

The national pilgrimage in honour of Our Lady of the Angels is the most well-known pilgrimage in Costa Rica and the one highest in rank. It is a striking manifestation of the intense devotion of Costa Rican Catholics to Mary, Virgin of the Angels, who, as of September 23, 1824, by decree of the Congress Constituyente of the State of Costa Rica, is and will be in the time to come, the Patroness of the nation (Sanabria 1945 : 213-214). Although it is the virgin of the Angels herself who is Patroness, and not the Image of her under this advocation, the Image is the tangible focus of devotion and the magnet which attracts thousands of pilgrims to her official sanctuary, the Basilica de Nuestra Señora de los Angeles in the city of Cart ago, Province of Cartago.

The Image is a dark-stone figure of the Virgin with the Child Jesus on her arm. According to tradition, it was found in 1635, on a boulder in a place called "La Gotera" in the outskirts of Cartago, by a *mulata* named Juana Pereira. The narrative recounts five instances in which the women and then the parish priest secured the Image only to find it on the boulder again. After each new encounter with the Image—the Little Black One, the Negrita—it was guarded more closely, until, finally, having placed it in the Tabernacle where the Blessed Sacrament was reserved and discovering that the Image had fled once more to the boulder, the priest concluded that the site was the Virgin's choice for her church. Because the Image was first found by the *mulata* on 2 August, the day on which the Roman Catholic Church was accustomed to celebrate the feast of Our Lady of the Angels, the stone figure was given that name.[2]

The exact date of the origin of the annual national pilgrimage to Cartago is on 1 and 2 August in honour of the Negrita is unknown, but Don Francisco del Valle Guzmán, former goldsmith for the Image, estimates that the pilgrimage, called traditionally a *romería*, is at least fifty years old. Thousands of people make this *romería*, mostly on foot, from all parts of the Republic, and from Nicaragua and Panama. Streams of people converge on the highways, including the one going through the town of San Pedro de Montes de Oca where, in 1984, I joined a group to walk across the rest of the Valle Occidental, over the mountain, Ochomogo, and into the Valle Oriental to Cartago.

Though some participants make the *romería* solely for the enjoyment of the trip, most pilgrims go to Cartago the fulfil a promise—a *promesa*—and to thank the Virgin for favours received or to make other requests. At the Basilica built on the site where the Image of Our Lady of the Angels was found in 1635, pilgrims travel the length of the central aisle on their knees to venerate the Image of the Negrita, which is housed high above the main altar except on her feast day, when it remains for the day in the sanctuary. While it is there, ordinarily no one but a priest may touch it. After visiting the Negrita, pilgrims proceed to a crypt where the boulder on which the stone Image was found is preserved, and then visit the well where water which springs from beneath the boulder is channelled into shallow basins to be used for drinking, bathing, or collection into bottles to care for future needs.

The *romería* is over when the destination has been reached. However, many pilgrims who arrive on 1 August assist at Mass and, after eating and resting, return to their homes, usually by bus. Those who remain overnight to assist at the Solemn Mass and procession on the feast day, enjoy music and folk dancers, and find somewhere to stay. Because there are no adequate hotels and the grounds which once surrounded the church of the Negrita are now largely given over to houses, pilgrims sleep at friends' homes, in the Basilica, or in the park in front of it. After the solemnities on 2 August, they take the bus home.

Not all Costa Ricans who wish to fulfil their promises or honour the Patroness through a pilgrimage make the *romería* to Cartago. Although the national *romería* remains the preferred pilgrimage, some people are participating in local level or regional *romerías* which take place on 2 August. One of these *romerías* is undertaken to a small sanctuary where there is an image of the Virgin of the Angels, located in a *barrio* named Angeles Sur or Los Angeles, in the canton and parish of San Ramon, Province of Alajuela. This *romería* is younger than that to Cartago, having been inaugurated in 1978 by the Pastor of the parish at that time, Fray Alvaro Montes de Oca, O.P. However, like its national counterpart, it has grown larger in the past few years.

In 1987, I joined the group of pilgrims from the parish church of San Ramon, in the town of that name which is the centre of the canton. They were setting out for the sanctuary in Barrio Los Angeles six kilometres away, carrying with them the parish church's image of the Virgin of the Angels. Following the announcement of a communal intention for the pilgrimage of prayer for peace, the group walked along a customary route through outlying settlements and past fields of cardomom, sugarcane, coffee, bananas, and corn. People prayed and sang hymns the entire way except when climbing the final—and steepest—hill, at which time they were asked to meditate in silence. Some participants paused en route to buy refreshments, but the group as a whole did not stop until it reached its destination where pilgrims who had come, unaccompanied by any image, from approximately twenty-three other settlements in the canton, were waiting.

The *romeria* officially consists only in going to the sanctuary of the Negrita, but once there, pilgrims assisted at Mass, followed by dinner. Ordinarily, pilgrims would have enjoyed the meal, which most brought with them, outdoors in the environs of the sanctuary; but because of torrential rain, they were permitted to eat inside of the chapel. Afterwards, pilgrims started home, generally on foot or by bus.

Though most pilgrims join the *romeria* from San Ramōn Centro or travel to Barrio Los Angeles from elsewhere in time for Mass on 2 August, others go there to pay promises or simply to visit the Negrita later that afternoon or the day before. The former enjoy the sociability and conviviality of the *romeria* which unites the main town with villages within the parish of San Ramon, some of which are quite isolated. People in this rural area depend on religious and social events, including this *romeria* to bring them together—a facet of pilgrimage activity which is not prominent, if at all present, in the national *romeria* to Cartago.

There is another pilgrimage on 2 August to the village of Juanilama, situated about two kilometres from the town of Esparza, Province of Puntarenas, where there is a chapel housing an image of Our Lady of the Angels. The pilgrimage, referred to as *romerio* or *turno* by the local inhabitants, is much older than the *romería* in San Ramon. It is rooted in devotion to the Virgin of the Angels which predates the first chapel built in Juanilama about sixty years ago; and apparently developed out of two sources : (*1*) taking the image of the Virgin house-to-house on 2 August, concluding the visits with a six-hour trek on foot to a house near the community of Jesús-María, where the image was left until the next day, (*2*) the fidelity of the owner of the present image, and then his son, to killing a steer for a feast and praying all day once a year. When the son, who like his father had kept the image in his house, could no longer sustain the cost of the celebration, he gave the image to the chapel in Juanilama: and the custom of honouring the Virgin of the Angels in the established way continued.

Because I was participating in *romerías* elsewhere on 2 August, I have not yet made this one. However, I did visit the chapel, study the image of the Virgin of the Angels there, and talk with informants in Juanilama and Esparza. From them I learned that on 2 August; people travel to Juanilama from at least ten of the *pueblos* in the area, from the town of Esparza where the church for the parish to which Juanilama belongs is located, and, in 1987, from the port city of Puntarenas. People make the *romería* mostly in small family groups. They ordinarily travel on foot, though in 1987, for the first time, many pilgrims reached Juanilama via bus service provided for the day. A formal group walks from Esparza together with the Pastor of the parish and, if possible, musicians. In various years including 1987, the group has taken with them an image of the Negrita. In this regard, this *romería* is similar to that to Barrio Los Angeles. However, in contrast to the latter, the image does not belong to the parish church : People in Juanilama take their image of Our Lady of the Angels to Esparza prior to the departure of the *romería* in order for the Virgin to accompany the pilgrims.

When the group arrives in Juanilama, Mass is celebrated followed by a procession. Afterwards, pilgrims enjoy their meal in the meadows which surround the chapel : They carry their own food or purchase local fare. Some of the pilgrims arrive in the village on 1 August and remain overnight. Others confine their visit to the feast day itself. Still others arrive on 2 August and remain until the following day in order to attend the dance on the night of the Virgin's feast. Yet, however much pilgrims vary in the length of time they spend in Juanilama and the events in which they participate, they all share the primary motive for their visit, implicit in a sign which greeted pilgrims from Esparza in 1987 and read (in translation), "Welcome to Juanilama, the Second House of Our Lady of the Angels." The greeting indicates that while villagers agree that the Basilica in Cartago is the first house of the Patroness of the Republic, that is to say, her official sanctuary, they consider their chapel a *bona fide* sanctuary of the Negrita—the second in rank—to which one can go to pay promises. Even when in reference to this event, local people use the term, '*turno*', which suggests a fair, rather than the word, '*romeria*', the intention is the same : "*Vamos al turno a pagar promesa*".

In the district of Llano Grande, Province of Cartago, located high on a mountain near Volcano Irazū, the church, which presently belongs to the parish of San Nicolās de Taras, houses an image of Our Lady of the Angels in whose honour there are annual *romerias*. Payment of individually-made promises is one motive for participation in them; but as will be seen below, such payment is not the primary reason for the maintenance of these pilgrimages year after year. This is one respect in which pilgrimages in the district differ from the three described above. There are other differences. First, in Llano Grande, there is a complex of daily *romerias* carried out over a period of fifteen-to-twenty days rather than a single *romeria*. Second, these *romerias* take place in May. Third, they originate in an event of local importance rather than in one deemed fundamental for the Republic of Costa Rica as a whole. Fourth, in Llano Grande, the custom of undertaking these local *romarias* is honoured in addition to that of going in pilgrimage to Cartago on 2 August. Fifth, going to visit the Virgin in her church in Llano Grande Centro is not the objective of the pilgrims : Their destinations are houses, fields, sheds, barns, greenhouses and work areas where flowers are grown and prepared for sale, repair shops, places where cheese is made or firecrackers are manufactured, schools, children's nutritional centre, quarries, graves, a chapel in Barrio Los Angeles (a population nucleus within the district farther down the mountain), springs the place where chunks of the mountain side threaten to break off to choke the Río Reventado flowing down through a gorge to the valley below; and the shrine built where a miracle which is the *raison d'entre* of the *romerías* is believed to have occurred. Sixth, it is the Virgin herself, represented by her image, who is doing the visiting accompanied by the faithful who make the *romerías* with her.

A characteristic which the *romerías* in Llano Grande share with the other three pilgrimages is the fact that they consist essentially in 'the going' portion of the event. As I learned when I participated in the twenty days of *romerías* in 1987, 'the going' is a rigorous trek mostly on foot or in the back of a pick-up truck hastening from one area of this large agricultural zone to another. Core companions of the Virgin for the trip include the commission of laymen responsible for the organization, preparation, and carrying out of the *romerías* and the care of the image during them; musicians, prayer leaders, and at least one member of the Rural Guard who is responsible for the security of the image. This group is usually joined by boys who carry candles, firecrackers, umbrellas for the commission, and rain gear for the Virgin; plus some local people and visitors.

Each day of the pilgrimages, after the morning Mass, Commissioners place the image in the wooden box (*camarin*) in which it is carried, taking care to use a handkerchief to touch the image. Then the *romería* begins with prayer and hymns. People in the sector to be visited have been notified in advance and ideally have arranged "to receive the Virgin"—an act meaning to welcome her into the home and into the heart. Material provisions for this reception range from very elaborate to quite simple; but regardless of the amount of financial expenditure, prayers and hymns are offered. At the end of the day, a feast is served at the home of a family of sufficient economic means (the *Posada*), to all who come. Most guests enjoy their meal out of doors; but the core group is served at the host's table, the musicians eating first so that they can begin a serenade. After this visit, the Negrita and companions join children who have been waiting near the church to escort the Virgin to her house in a candle-light procession.

These *romerías* have been carried out in Llano Grande without interruption since 1877. In that year, according to tradition, a plague of grasshoppers (*chapulines*) threatened to devour the crops planted in Llano Grande which was then an isolated farming hamlet (*caserío*) which at that time was part of the district of El Carmen within the parish of Cartago. The grasshoppers were concentrated in the holdings of Pbro. Echevarría y Carazo, located in that part of the hemlet now called Barrio Los Angeles. In great alarm, the farmers organized a delegation to go down to the city of Cartago in the valley ten kilometres below to ask the parish priest, Pbro. Juan R. Acuña, and the Governor, Vicente Villavicencio, to permit a pilgrim image of Our Lady of the Angels to visit the afflicted area. Permission was granted. On June 6, the image was carried up by the priest and placed on a boulder in Father Echevarría's terrain. Following prayer, the grasshoppers disappeared—as did eggs deposited beneath the soil and larvae.

To commemorate this 'miracle', a special *romería* takes place within the *romerías* : On Ascension Thursday, pilgrims either go directly, or accompany the Virgin, to the shrine in the fields of Barrio Los Angeles which encloses the stone on which the image of Our Lady of the Angels was placed in 1877—an event symbolized by an image of the Negrita which remains on the boulder in a glass *camarín*. At the site, the parish priest carries the pilgrim image into the shrine in procession; Mass is celebrated; and the fields, which have been distributed among a number of families, are blessed by the visit of the Virgin with prayer and song. Then, the majority of pilgrims have their meal in the environs of the shrine while the core group enjoys a *Posada* nearby.

On the part of the community of Llano Grande, gratitude to the Virgin is the motive prompting the enormous outpouring of energy and personal sacrifice associated with the *romerías*. However, petition is also very much in evidence. The *romerías* are believed to bring to the community spiritual and material blessing, and deliverance from all kinds of evil. They afford another kind of benefit as well. In this mountain district which can be reached by paved road only since about 1977, even the most isolated families can bask in the warmth which the Virgin's visit, the company of pilgrims, the burst of firecrackers, and the sound of music, bring.

## Formal Replication in the Pilgrimage Tradition of our Lady of the Angels

Differences among the four expressions of the pilgrimage tradition Our Lady of the Angels have been made clear and so have similarities, the latter being the major concern in this chapter. When Prof. Evon Z. Vogt, was struck by the similarities within the culture of Zinacantan, the community which he was studying in the Chiapas Highlands of Mexico, he chose the term, 'replication', meaning 'the action or process of reproducing' (Webster 1976 : 981), to express most precisely the patterning of that characteristic of the culture. He wrote (1969 : 571),

> Like all cultures, Zinacantan has evolved a network of beliefs, symbols, structural forms, and behavioural sequences that, taken together, form a consistent system. The patterned aspect of Zinacanteco culture that impresses me most is the systematic manner in which structural forms and ritual behaviours are replicated at various levels in the society, and certain key concepts, expressed explicitly in Zotzil, are replicated in various domains of the culture. . .

In Evon Vogt's analysis of replication in Zinacanteco culture, reproduction of a trait or pattern was horizontal, that is, found in various domains of the culture, or vertical, that is found at different levels of the society. As such, the construct, 'replication', was appropriate for my use in bringing order into data which revealed both vertical reproduction of structural and conceptual elements in pilgrimages on the local, regional, and national levels; and horizontal duplication of those same elements when identified in the various expressions of the same pilgrimage tradition viewed parallel. It also served well to designate the constituent elements which unify and bring consistency to the multiple expressions of that tradition.

Among such unifying elements is the presence of an image of the Virgin Mary under the special advocation treasured in Costa Rica. To study the Image and copies of it in this context, I apply the construct, 'replication', in a fashion analogous to that used by Prof. Vogt. He employed it to analyze structure and concept : I employ it to analyze something which incorporates them both, namely, iconographic form.

'Form' has three meanings : (1) the shape and structure of something as distinguished from its material; (2) the component of a thing that determines its kind and (3) the essential nature of a thing as distinguished from its matter (Webster 1976 : 451). The first two definitions pertain here and prompt two questions. What is the shape and structure of the Image of Our Lady of the Angels, Patroness of Costa Rica ? What component in a replica of the Image determines that it is what it purports to be ?

In response to the first question, the shape and structure of the Image can be described as follows. The figure measures approximately eighteen and one-half centimetres in height. Though the Virgin's hands are crudely sculpted, the nose and mouth are delicately formed, as are the eyes which are oriental in shape. A roughly hewn mantle veils the top of her head and falls, in just the suggestion of folds, over her shoulders almost to the hem of a pleated tunic extending to the base of the Image which rests flat on a surface, the feet having been excluded from the sculpture. The mantle is gathered up in front in such a way that much of the figure of the Virgin, clothed in the long-sleeve, jewel-neck tunic, is visible as is her hair which is parted in the middle and falls in front of her shoulders almost to her waist. Her right forearm is folded over her waist. Her left forearm supports against her body the Child Jesus who is clothed in an identically designed tunic. The Child's hair is short, parted in the middle, and combed back behind His ear. One of the Child's feet is visible. His left arm is drawn across His waist; and His right one is raised so that His hand reaches up over his Mother's breast toward her face.

As early as 1638, the Image of the Negrita was clothed in a cloth garment called a *manto*, topped by a small crown, which garment covered the figure except for the portion of the Virgin holding the Child. At present, the Image is clothed in a garment of fine material worn under a roughly-triangular-shaped *manto* fashioned of gold, which has an opening disclosing the ruffle of the garment around the Virgin's head and shoulders and permitting the figures of Mother and Child to be seen to just below the Virgin's waist. A gold crown which is part of the *manto* and a delicate halo studded with six stars made of gold and gems which is attached to the latter, complete the ensemble.

Outlining the shape of the *manto* and halo, is an elaborately worked, aura-like ornamentation called a *resplandor*, which symbolizes the immensity of the sky illuminated by the rays of the sun. The rays in *resplandor* are made of strips of gold studded with rosettes of gold and precious stones. Every other ray is tipped with a star made of gold and a gem. Below the *manto* there is a figure of an angel worked in gold and silver. Curving upwards to the *manto* at the top of the pedestal on which the whole assemblage rests, is a silver half-moon; and just below the half-moon, six petals of a silver lily, each holding an angel. On the heavy base of the pedestal, are tiny replicas of flowers and the shield of Costa Rica.

Ordinarily, the stone Image is viewed by the public only once a year, on 1 August, when the *manto* is removed to permit the undergarment to be changed and the Image to be dusted. This ceremony, known as the Vestition (*Vesticion*), formerly took place in the Sacristy of the Basilica; and did not become a public ceremony until 1979, when the Pastor of the Basilica parish, Pbro. Walter Sandı Solano, decided to perform it in the sanctuary of the church in order to show the sacred Image to parishioners, pilgrims, and visitors alike. Apart from this presentation, the majority of Costa Ricans have not had the opportunity to see the stone Image itself, except, perhaps, in photographs which have been permitted to be published only since about 1979. Ths majority knows only the form incorporating the *manto*, *resplandor*, lily petals with the angels, and the pedestal; and, if they view that form from a distance, perceive the visible portion of the Mother and Child only as a dark spot. As a result, it can be said that there really are two forms of the Image of the Negrita. One is that of the stone Image itself. The other is that of the whole assemblage which I call, for the sake of economy of expression, the augmented Image.

In response to the second question concerning the essential components in replicas of the Image of Our Lady of the Angels, to which Costa Ricans refer as 'the authentic', 'the real', or 'the legitimate' one, it is first noted that in the workshops of the Del Valle family to whom the care of the Image and commissions to reproduce it have been entrusted over the years, the mode of making a replica reflects the dual perception of the form of the Image. Moulds of various sizes are used ranging in measurement from one inch to the one metre height which is that of the augmented Image. When the perspective buyer orders a replica which will be at least twelve inches high, there is a choice to be made between a mould of the augmented Image which includes the figure of Virgin and Child enclosed within a removable *manto* and a mould which produces an image of one solid piece of bronze or silver, which can be made either with a *resplandor* which is not solid and not part of the piece, or, without a *resplandor*. If an order is placed for a replica in stone of the small Image of the Virgin with her Child, it is understood that a separate *manto* is required. If the replica is to be made of bronze, in one piece, the *manto* determines the form and only the face of the Mother and the face of the Child appear as part of the image.

The images carried in the *romerias* in Llano Grande and borne from San Ramon Centro to Barrio Los Angeles are replicas made in the Del Valle workshops. Both are made to include a reproduction of the stone image of the Negrita within a removable *manto*.

The only departure from the appearance of the authentic stone image permitted in replicas is the addition of paint—a feature which technically is not an element of structure unless so determined by tradition. However, no such regulation governs reproduction of the *resplandor*, as the pilgrim image in Llano Grande illustrates. In 1932, metal replicas of four large grasshoppers were attached to the *resplandor*. At a later date, the four were replaced by others : two grasshoppers and to larval forms of the grasshoppers. These figures interpreted on the exegetic level represent the insects which threatened the crops in Llano Grande in 1877. On the positional level, through being fastened to the augmented image of Our Lady of the Angels, they attest to her intercessory power under this advocation. On the operational level, the figures remind the inhabitants of the district of the miracle performed for their ancestors (Turner and Turner 1978 : 247-248). While the innovation which the attachment of the grasshoppers and larvae represents does not affect the shape and structure of the *resplandor* itself, it does modify the form of the augmented image, enlarges its symbolic content, and serves to make the image of Our Lady of the Angels in Llano Grande de Cartago special to the inhabitants and unique in Costa Rica.

The image of the Negrita in Jaunilama is unique and special to that locale for different reasons. First, it was not made in the Del Valle workshops : No one knows where Manuel Porres, the original owner, got it. It was carved from wood with a knife, and is about one hundred years old. The image is one solid piece, roughly triangular in shape, with a crown at the top. It is designed with simple lines to include a large *manto* which has an opening of adequate size to reveal the Virgin and Child— but only to the waist. As in the other replicas associated with pilgrimages described in this chapter, the mantle worn by the Virgin frames the inner proportion of the opening. However, the posture of the Mother and Child is unlike that of the authentic image or any of the replicas made by the Del Valle family. In Juanilama, the Child is positioned looking forward instead of to the side; his left arm and hand rest against his breast; his lower right arm is raised; and his right hand is carved so that the thumb is up and fingers are folded into the palm in what appears to be a gesture of blessing, rather than of caress. The Mother's right arm and hand are drawn across the Child's body at the waist, holding him securely. The faces are expressionless; the features, stiff.

The *manto* rests on an oval part from which the two horns of a half-moon extend on either side to touch the lower edge of the *manto* at its widest point. This part is screwed to a plain wooden block. When in the niche above the altar, the ensemble rests on a wooden pedestal which repeats twice the design of half-moon with its horns extending out from a central core.

It is probable that the rural carver, working at least a century ago, never saw the authentic stone Image, or an accurate representation of it; and so, may have used to models for the copy. One model would have been the form of the Image in its *manto* and crown as it looked in 1638, except for the posture of the Mother and Child. The other model might have been the form of another image of the Virgin and Child familiar to him or to her, and most likely made in Spain or in Guatemala.

In view of the departure of the Juanilama Negrita from the shape and structure of the authentic image with regard to posture of the Mother and Child, and from the concept embedded in the form of the authentic image which interprets the Child's position as lovingly oriented to the Mother, it is clear that one must seek further the essential element in the iconographic form of the image of the Virgin of the Angels who is Patroness of Costa Rica. Through a process of reduction from the most complex unit to the most simple and basic feature, Don José María del Valle Alarcon, the member of the Del Valle family who is now the official goldsmith for the Negrita, identified the element. His immediate predecessor had indicated that it was the little stone image, painted or unpainted—and nothing else—which was considered essential. Don José Mariã specified further that replicas were to be made of cement and, so far as possible, were to be exact copies of the original. Then, reflecting on the reproductions of the augmented image which were solid piece made of various materials, he concluded that what was essential was the representation of the face of the Mother and the face of the Child a criterion met by all of the replicas described above.

## Conclusion

Three sets of observations will conclude this chapter. First, Evon Vogt's construct, 'replications', has proven useful in addressing the question raised in the introduction to this chapter : Given the diversity found among pilgrimages in Costa Rica, what components of these pilgrimages provide consistency or unity among the various pilgrimages in the Republic or among various expressions of a single pilgrimage tradition which differ according to locale ? In these pages, the focus has been upon the second half of the question. It has been shown that the replication of iconographic form in images venerated in expressions of the Costa Rica pilgrimage tradition of Our Lady of the Angels, provides unity and consistency among those expressions. Study of iconographic replication would be equally fruitful in an investigation of expressions of other complex pilgrimage traditions in Costa Rica and elsewhere. With regard to the first half of the question, I suggest that examination of other types of structural or conceptual replication, such as specific facets of ritual in pilgrimages, or the notion of what constitutes a *romería* as distinct from a *peregrinacion*, would be productive in seeking consistency among pilgrimages representing a variety of devotions.

Second, it is worth emphasizing that it is not the pilgrims who are concerned about the iconography of the image of the Negrita. They rarely refer to the image as such, but rather speak about the Virgin Mary whom the image represents and makes present to them, and pay attention to the images in the *romerías* for reasons other than those regarding elements of form and authenticity which interest the Anthropologist and official goldsmith.

Third, recognition on the part of the Anthropologist of the central unifying position of the image among expressions of the pilgrimage tradition, insures examination of those 'other reasons' and what they reveal of beliefs, values, and character of relationships binding pilgrims to one another and the wider religious and secular society as well as to the Virgin under her special advocation as Patroness of the Republic. Such recognition combined with awareness that an image is called 'legitimate', 'authentic' or 'real', also assures inquiry into the fact that pilgrims do distinguish the authentic image from any replica. However, given the confines of this chapter, while such an examination and inquiry have been made, the data on the social and religious bonds rooted in the symbol of the image and the implications of distinguishing an authentic image from replicas must be treated elsewhere; as must the data on two matters closely related to the former, namely, (1) the concepts in both formal Roman Catholic doctrine and folk traditions found in Costa Rica, of what an image and its function within religious practice are and (2) the phenomenon in itself of the attraction which certain images have for pilgrims who make the arduous journey 'through the fields' to be in their presence.

## REFERENCES

1. The field research in 1934 and 1985 was supported in part by the Penrose Fund of the American Philosophical Society and the Committee on Aid to Faculty Research, Providence College. That in 1987, was supported by a Fulbright Scholars Programme Central American Regional Research Award. This funding is gratefully acknowledged.

2. The Image found in La Gotera particularizes the 'general advocation (Christian 1972 : 46) "Our Lady of the Angels", familiar in the Church, and transforms it into a special advocation "Our Lady of the Angels" who is the Negrita, the Patroness of the Republic of Costa Rica. Among Costa Ricans, this special advocation and the Image which gives it concrete expression are virtually inseparable.

## NOTES

Christian, William A., Jr., 1972, *Person and God in a Spanish Valley*. New York and London : Seminar Press.

Sanabria M., Victor, 1945, *Documenta Historica Beatae Mariae Virginis Angelorum Reipublica de Costa Rica Principalis Patronae*. San Jose, Costa Rica : n.p.

Straub, Leslie Ellen, 1985, "La romeria camo modelo de peregrinaciones en las tradiciones centroamericanas", *Mesoamerica* 6, 9 : 104-132.

Turner, Victor and Edith Turner, 1978, *Image and Pilgrimage in Christian Culture. Anthropological Perspectives*. New York : Columbia University Press.

Vogt, Evon Z., 1969, *Zinacantan : A Maya Community in the Highlands of Chiapas*. Cambridge, Massachusetts : The Belknap Press of Harvard University Press.

Webster's New Collegiate Dictionary, 1976, *Webster's New Collegiate Dictionary*. 7th ed. Springfield, Massachusetts : G. and C. Merriam Co.

# 18

# The Progress of Pilgrimage on the Holy Mountain of Athos

## RENE GOTHONI

## Background

A considerable amount has been written recently about the revival of monastic life on the Holy Mountain of Athos. The majority of the literature deals with this revival from the viewpoint of monastic life and the increase in the number of monks since 1972. The increasing number of visitors or pilgrims to the Holy Mountain has, however, mostly been regarded as an influx of tourism and therefore described in negative terms.[1]

In this chapter, which is based on fieldwork conducted during two one-month sojourns on Athos in September 1984 and 1985, and during a fortnight in August/September 1987. I have, therefore, chosen to deal with pilgrimage on the Holy Mountain of Athos. I will deal with the following questions : how should the word pilgrim be understood in the Athonite context ? Are those who go there merely tourists or are they pilgrims ? What kind or type of pilgrimage do we meet on Mount Athos ? What was the purpose of the visitor's journey to Athos ?

## The Meanings of the Words "Pilgrim" and "Pilgrimage"

The word "pilgrim" is a Middle English word that comes from Old French peligrin, derived from Late Latin pelegrinus, a form of the Latin peregrinus meaning "foreigner", from peregre "abroad", from perger "being abroad", from per "through" and agr, ager "land", "field".

Originally the word "pilgrim" (*peregrinus*) denoted a foreigner who stayed in an alien land, outside the territory of Rome (*ager Romanus*), and who was travelling or walking around. It was more or less synonymous with traveller or way-farer, who passes through life as if in exile from a heavenly homeland, or in search of one or of some high goal, such as truth. Thereafter it came to refer to one who travels to visit a shrine or holy place as a devotee, one who realizes the ideal of every devout pilgrim, and especially a person who travelled to the Holy Land. Later, the meaning was broadened to denote those who travelled to Rome, for example, as well; later still it came to apply to everyone, who travelled to a shrine or a sacred place, a centre of religious worship. A pilgrimage, then, simply means the "journey of a pilgrim", especially a journey to a shrine or a sacred place. In a broader sense, it means the course of life on earth.[2]

The Greek word for pilgrim, *proskinitis*, meaning "worshipper", from the verb *proskino*, "to fall down and worship", "to do obeisance to the gods or their images", "to avert divine wrath etc., has, however, a different connotation from the word "pilgrim".[3] Greeks go to shrines and sacred places to venerate the relics, to kiss the icons, to make confession and to discuss matters with their spiritual fathers. The emphasis of the meaning of the word is on worship, which originally referred to the Oriental fashion of prostrating oneself before kings and superiors. The word "pilgrim", on the contrary, emphasizes the aspect of travelling, the journey. This is natural, since the journey to Jerusalem was quite long and demanding, while for the Greeks, the shrines were very close. Since shrines were everywhere, the Greeks have never had any great interest in going to Jerusalem.

## The Pilgrimage Ellipse on the Holy Mountain of Athos

Every pilgrimage begins in a familiar place, goes to a far off place, and returns to a familiar place. This led Turner (1920-1983) to picture the routes of pilgrimage as forming an *ellipse*. Pilgrims may return by the way they came, yet the ellipse is still an apt mataphore for the total journey because "the return road is, psychologically, different from the approach road".[4]

Nowadays, travel to the Holy Mountain of Athos presupposes quite specific preparations. Generally speaking, entry is easier for Greeks than for foreigners, because there is no limitation to the number of Greeks who are allowed to enter the monastic republic. Foreigners must cross an additional "threshold" since a permit is needed to gain entry to Athos. This can be obtained either in Athens from the Greek Ministry of Foreign Affairs or in Thessalonica from the Ministry of Northern Greece. However, these ministries require a letter of introduction from the Greek-based consulate of the visitor's country of origin. In order to get this letter without complications, it is advisable to carry a letter of recommendation from one of the orthodox bishops, metropolitans or the archbishop, of one's own country. As the number of entry permits given to foreigners is limited to twenty a day—ten from Athens and ten from Thessalonica—it is best to make a reservation in advance if the intention is to take the boat to Athos on a particular day. There is usually a fortnight's wait for a vacancy on board, a delay deliberately aimed at reducing the number of foreign visitors.

## Departure as Separation from the World

On the basis of the structure of the journey Turner formed the concept of a pilgrimage as a *liminoid* phenomenon *i.e.*, as having some of the attributes of liminality in passage rites. Van Gennep (1873-1957), the originator of the theory of rites of passage, distinguished three phases : separation, margin or limen, and reaggregation.[5] By utilizing the Latin word for "threshold", *limen*. Turner adopts a metaphor that emphasizes the threshold nature of the phenomenon. From the standpoint of the believing actor, a pilgrimage centre represents a threshold, "a place and moment 'in and out of time', and such an actor hopes to have there direct experience of the sacred, invisible, or supranatural order, either in the material aspect of miraculous healing or in the immaterial aspect of inward transformation of spirit or personality".[6] In this liminal phase, the "passenger" or "liminar", passes through a realm that has few or none of the attributes of the past or coming state. He is betwixt and between all familiar lines of classification and his state becomes ambiguous.

*Social Separation* : Departure from the harbour of Ouranou-

polis can indeed be seen as a *separation* : "preliminal" routines
have been performed *i.e.*, travellers have disengaged themselves
from their duties, family and wives; they are free from involve-
ments, demands and social pressure; the permit has been
received from one of the ministries, and, once on board, surren-
dered together with the passport to the local authorities—to be
returned only in Karyes, the administrative centre of the peninsula, where the visa is obtained.

Therefore, when the boat releases its ropes and the two-
hour voyage begins, and the traveller is finally on the sea,
there is no immediate return. There is a real feeling of
having crossed a "threshold" and of being on the way
towards the sacred centre. No one I met seemed to be
totally indifferent. Some people openly discussed their atheist
feelings and explained that they came to Athos only out
of curiosity. A defence I think Freud would call it. Most of
the travellers I interviewed, however, felt expectant during the
voyage and were very eager to see what the sacred place, about
which they had read and heard so much, really would be like.
One traveller said in fact : "I was very tense, the feeling was
very expectant and tense."[7] Another said with a humorous
smile: "I feel like a man who is going to the moon".[8] These
interpretations of the feeling on board were very illuminating,
because after about one hour on the sea, when the first principal
monastery was seen from the port side of the boat, a long,
exciting outburst, "look", spread like wildfire on board and
every first-time visitor made for the left-hand side of the boat
to take a look at the wonder. A release of tension indeed !

The voyage from Ouranoupolis, the last outpost of the
"world", to Daphni, the main port on the Holy Mountain of
Athos, makes the feeling of physical separation from the
"world" total. The transition from a profane to a sacred area
is marked by the fact that the peninsula, which the visitors are
to approach, is regarded by the monks as the Garden of the
Virgin, one of the outer signs of which is that no woman is
allowed to enter the area. This prescription is sanctified both
by legend and by the advice of the holy fathers of the Orthodox
tradition. Therefore, there are no women on board. When
approaching Daphni hardly anyone, however, reflects on this
matter, since the natural scenery of the peninsula is so absorbing.

Moreover, separation from the world is marked by the fact
that the monks use the Julian calendar, a calendar thirteen days
behind the Gregorian one. If it was September 9th when the
traveller's foot left the boat at Daphni —as it was in my case—
the leg would land on the dock side on August 28th. Moreover,
the clocks at most of the monasteries point to twelve at sunset,
when it is no more than eight o'clock Greek time, the time on
the Holy Mountain of Athos being about four hours ahead.[9]

*Separation : Corresponding to a "threshold" in the Life Cycle :*
The age of the pilgrims varied from about twenty to about
sixty. When I asked what particular reason the pilgrims had
for coming to Mount Athos, what was the purpose of their
travel, what did they search for and what did they hope to find,
the moment of travel proved to correspond with the life cycle
"thresholds" of the individuals concerned. Those who had
come to Mount Athos for the first time had usually heard about
the place from their close friends who had been there the year,
or some years before. They had prepared themselves by reading
some books written by other visitors or pilgrims.

The young Greek students who came there were usually in
their early twenties or approaching thirty. They had already
made preliminary steps in adulthood, explored some possibilities of adult living : studying, temporary work and life in the
great cities of Athens and Thessalonica. They were somewhat
confused by the options in the city and by city life. Therefore,
one of the young Greeks, a student of archeology, for example,
said : "I wanted to get away from cars, machines, towns,
village, you know, to meet nature in the wild, I like the woods
very much . . . to spend a little time far away from civilization,
if you can call all this civilization . . . to relax in a very quiet
and peaceful place and to see the life of the monks and to meet
something strange, something natural."[10] Another of the young
Greeks, a student of medicine, said that he would also like to
come to Mount Athos next year "not only to relax and for
peace, but for about a month or two months . . . it would be
very good if I got the opportunity to build a little house there,
you know, by the sea, to live there three months of the year . . .
that is why I would like to live there, not for the purpose of
praying to God. .."[11] These students were indeed experiencing
life as confusing and the wish to build a hut by the sea on the

Holy Mountain certainly expressed a fear of, or at least confusion about entering the adult world. Not a few young Greek students have chosen novicehood on Mount Athos, as this has seemed to be a better option than entering adult life and taking on responsibilities.

Among the foreigners who came to Mount Athos for the first time were :

(a)  young students of architecture, archeology, Byzantine art and history, comparative religion, computer science, medieval history, journalism, philosophy, psychology, Slavonic languages, sociology and theology, who said that they came there mainly for scholarly reasons. One Yugoslavian student of architecture, for example, said that "some elders at college had lectured about Mount Athos and its medieval architecture". Being an atheist, he stressed at the beginning of the interview that the sole criterion for his travel was his interest in the architecture. Later on, when we were discussing his experiences of walking on Mount Athos and how exhausting it was, he said, however : "Anyway, I expected it, because I wanted to live and to see Athos as the monks did". Another young Austrian student of journalism said that he wanted to visit Athos, because he had heard so much about it from one of his friends. While waiting for the boat to leave, he told me at one of the taverns : "I expect so much, and here in Ouranoupolis, I sometimes wonder while waiting, if this will be all I expect."[12]

Some of the students had been converted to orthodoxy out of love of the Byzantine art, music and history. These were of a romantic mind. A French art student said that he was converted five years ago when he discovered Byzantine art : "At first I did not understand why Byzantine art was so different from Roman Catholic art. Then I understood it was because the church was not the same. I liked Byzantine art very much, the icons, and I wanted to know about the church that produced this art." When I first met him in 1984 he had stayed four weeks in one of the monasteries. When I met him again a year later, it took some time before I even recognized him. He had let his hair grow long and it was tied in a knot on the back of his head; he had grown a scrubby beard and wore black monastic clothes. Only the glasses were old, and it was in fact by his glasses that I recognized him. He told me that he had been baptized in the same monastery on Eastern and that he now had lived there for three months practising to become a novice;

(b) middle-aged school teachers, priests, lawers and others with an academic education who, in their mid-life crisis, wanted to get away from the world for a while. They felt that, if they were ever going to see Mount Athos, they had to do it now, because soon they would be too old and it would be too late. One German senior history master told me that he was interested in monastic life and in experiencing the medieval atmos phere, for which Mount Athos is so famous. He was a very religious man and he said : "erstens mal das Intresse am Leben dort, auch das Historische und Kunst-Geschichtliche . . . ich wollte schon miterleben diese Frömmigkeit, die Frömmigkeit der Mönche."[13] A Swedish priest said that he came to Mount Athos mainly to take part in the liturgy and to listen to the beautiful singing in the church;

(c) athletes, whose main aim was to climb to the peak of Mount Athos. They were easily recognizable by their huge rucksacks, their climbing boots and so on; and finally;

(d) the curious ones, who just came there to take a look at the place, to see what it was all about.

Foreigners who came to Mount Athos for the second, third, fourth or eleventh time usually came to see some particular Father, whom they had met on their earlier visits. Some went to buy an icon. Others, who had already visited all the principal monasteries, intended to visit the hermitages to meet the hermits, who are generally considered to be of higher status than those living in the larger monasteries.

To sum up : these people went for a specific purpose.

Finally, we meet on Mount Athos middle-aged Greeks, who travel either alone or with their 10 to 15-year old sons to visit their spiritual father. They tend to go there every year. Some of these Greeks were living abroad and returned every year to Mount Athos for confession and/or discussion. These men were very religious and they usually participated in every service. They were very helpful and gladly played the role of guide and interpreter when foreigners wanted to talk to some of the fathers.

The fact that travel to Mount Athos was a "threshold", a turning-point, in one way or another, in the life cycle of the visitors or pilgrims, was nicely and explicitly expressed by a middle-aged German Lawyer, who said that he finds himself confronted with the questions : "am I living for my work, am I living for my parents, am I living for my children, am I living for my wife, why am I living, what is the point ? Somewhat later he expressed the agony even more movingly : "there is no point, there is no point, I am just eating, drinking, joking, thinking, going to work, earning money, just to make money, there is no point. When the children were young, there was a point in working. Now, when they have grown up and left me, there is no point, there is no point, may be it would be better to become a monk !"[14]

When I asked what it was in orthodoxy that was so appealing, the common answer was : the liturgy, the mysticism. "When I take part in the liturgy and listen to the singing, I feel as if I were in heaven, it really absorbs me",[15] a Swedish priest said. Therefore, the departure also marks separation from intellectualism, which so eagerly tries to solve all questions, the ultimate questions and concerns of life which cannot, however, be solved intellectually, but only through experience of divine grace. That is why the unceasing praying for the mercy of God during the liturgy moves participants struggling in an overintellectualized world, a cosmos, so deeply.

## The Liminoid Phase

The receiving of the visa, *diamonitirion*, at Karyes from the Holy Community, *Epistasia*, which permits the travellers to visit any of the twenty monasteries on the peninsula and to stay at the Holy Mountain for either four days (foreigners) or eight days (Greeks), marks the end of the process of departure and the beginning of the liminoid phase. It usually requires about an hour's wait before the visa at Karyes is obtained. During this time, the travellers talk to each other and discuss the routes they are going to take. Some decide to walk together, others prefer to walk by themselves. Everyone is free to do whatever they choose.

*Walking—A Means to Inner Change* : It has been said that a journey to the Holy Mountain of Athos is a journey back to medieval times, a journey of which walking is an essential part. This interpretation had been followed by the Yugoslavian architect, who said that, while walking, he was "comparing Athos with our European country. Monasteries were cities and the paths were roads which connected the cities. I wondered if monks from different monasteries had any contact and how often they visited each other ... Athos was another kind of world. The medieval world. It was good to walk because the monks walked as well. Thus it was possible to experience medieval times. More fully walking was, however, very difficult with a heavy rucksack, I was not prepared.[16]

An English lecturer in medieval history had been robbed of his Greek money and, reflecting on the matter, he said to me : "it was a real pilgrimage, as in medieval times there was always an element of robbery and things like that."[17]

Walking almost always nowadays starts from Karyas, since travellers are herded into a bus in Daphni, which takes them to Karyes, where the visa is given. Usually everyone walks to whatever monastery they have chosen as the starting point. From then on they continue the journey from monastery to monastery, or to a *skete* or to a *kelli*, mostly on foot; nowadays some people travel by boat if the goal is, for example, the remote monastery Megisti Lavra at the end of the peninsula, or by jeep, if some monks happen to turn up on the road and a lift is forthcoming. The road or path from one monastery to another is never calculated in kilometres or miles, but in length of hours of walking. Experiences of walking were described as follows :

(a) A middle-aged French teacher of mathematics : "I walked the whole morning and the afternoon together with a Greek and a Canadian. It was difficult to talk because it was tiring."[18]

(b) A middle-aged German teacher of history : "I found walking very nice, but tiring because of the heat. Nice in the shadows of the trees though. Walking makes you completely tired, but you are nevertheless impressed by the scenery and by nature and by the acquaintances you make. Mostly I walked together with Greeks. You always seem to meet the same people again, you greet each other warmly and talk about the places and monasteries you have seen. It was about a two-and-a-half-hour path from Stavronikita to Vatopedi."[19]

(c) A middle-aged Swedish priest and a middle-aged Swedish Lawyer : "We walked together from Vatopedi Karyes with 12 Greeks. When someone felt tired everyone rested. There was one fellow who had a mania for changing shirt and he changed at least six times and as soon as we stopped he dried the sweat off his shirts on a stone in the sun. We had several rests. It was a nice feeling and everyone talked to each other. We walked for about three and a half hours. We started in the early morning, because then it was not so hot. We had good hats. Nature was very beautiful, we experienced the beauty of nature, a nice smell from some flower we didn't recognize what flower it was, but every now and then we recognized the penetrating smell. While we were walking we wondered how many had walked on these same flat stones before us, how many monks and mules had felt the same stones."[20]

(d) A Greek student of medicine : "walking was incredible, first of all tiring, physically very tiring. We walked from Megisti Lavra to Karakalou for about twelve hours. The eye could see a very long distance, the eye could see the sky, virgin nature, the mountain, the valleys, the spirit flies, you get a good feeling, we had many breaks, rests. Drank only water. We climbed about 1,000 metres, Athos was right over our heads and then from 1,000 metres down to the sea and then from the sea up about 200 metres to Karakallou. I felt there at 1,000 metres on Athos, between the trees—It is

impossible for me to translate my thoughts into words,
it was the kind of experience you can live, not
explain—I found myself there, I returned to my roots as
a human being, my mind became peaceful, I found
myself as a human being."[21]

According to Sherrard "a pilgrimage is not simply a matter of
getting to a particular shrine or holy place. It is a deliberate
sundering and surrender of one's habitual conditions of comfort, routine, safety and convenience. Unlike the tourist,
whose aim is to see things and to travel around in conditions
which are as comfortable, secure, familiar, convenient and
unchallenging as possible, the pilgrim breaks with his material
servitude, puts his trust in God and sets out on a quest which
is inward as much as outward, and which is, in varying degrees,
into the unknown. In this sense he becomes the image of the
spiritual seeker. He removes himself as far as possible from the
artificiality within which he is enclosed by his life in society.
Of this spiritual exploration, inward and outward, *walking* is an
essential part. His feet tread the earth—the earth from which
he is made and from which he is usually so cut off, especially
in the more or less totally urbanized conditions of modern life.
Through his eyes, ears, nose, he renews his sense of natural
beauty—the beauty of God's creation. He watches the flight of
bird or insect, the ripple of light on leaves, the timeless vistas
of the sea; he listens to the song of water, the calls of God's
creatures; he breathes in the scent of tree and flower and soil.
His feet tire, his body aches, sweat drips from his head and
trickles into his eyes and down his neck. He tastes rigour and
hardship. But through all this—and only through all this, and
through his prayer and dedication and confidence—slowly an
inner change is wrought, a new *rhythm* grows, a deeper
harmony. The pilgrimage is at work."
    "The pilgrimage is also a process which must not be hurried.
The bonds of routine, dependence on material comforts, on the
familiar and the settled, have a far stronger hold on one than
one is aware of. The conditions of modern life have so blunted
the senses that it may take days, weeks even, until they begin
to respond truly to the beauty about them. If the aspiring
pilgrim attempts to speed this process up, or refuses to face the

conditions, including the hardships, which are essential for the development of the pilgrimage, then he becomes a mere tourist."[22]

*At the Monastery* : For a pilgrim the important thing is not the goal, but the path. The pilgrims take various routes but the main thing is, above all, treading the path.

Having done the path and reached the monastery, the traveller is usually warmly welcomed by the "guestmaster" (*archontaris*) monk, who in no time at all brings a tray with a glass of water, Greek coffee, *raki* and a piece of *loukoumi* to each visitor. Thereafter (sometimes before) he takes the visitors first to the church and then to the guesthouse, where, nowadays, they are expected to stay only one night.

The daily routine varies somewhat in every monastery. There is, however, no need to worry about the programme, because the monks carry on with their duties and visitors are expected to participate in vespers, morning service, liturgy and meals only. Many foreigners visit monasteries and talk with only one or two monks. This is how the travellers explained their stay in the monastery :

(a) The middle-aged Swedish priest and the middle-aged Swedish Lawer : After we had climbed up to the monastery of Simonopetra we were completely exhausted. The host welcomed us and gave us coffee, raki, water and loukoumi, we were saved. Then we were shown to the guestroom. There were eight beds, but at that time there was only one young Greek man who was visiting his brother, a hieromonk at the monastery. We changed our shirts, which were wet with sweat and then we rested until vespers . . . Then we went to vespers. First we stood in a stall in the narthex of the church and then we went to the nave. We did not kiss the icons, because we were not orthodox . . . Thereafter we were allowed to participate in the communal dinner. It was interesting to see how all monks moved to the refectory for the meal. There the service was continued by means of reading from the legend of a saint and then everyone went back to the church for prayer. It was a fantastic experience.[23]

They described their participation in morning service even more vividly : We went down to morning service. It was completely dark and dawn came very gradually. Candles were moved around and the monks passed by more or less like shadows, it was attractive. Somehow there was a mystical tune that attracted us . . . And when dawn began to break, the monks sort of flapped about and gradually the features of their faces was recognizable and, in my opinion, the most beautiful moment was somewhere between night and day, in the break of dawn, when the monks could be seen with their great skouphos and veils, which really had a function then, at least I thought so, yes, it was really beautiful !24

(b)  The Yugoslavian architect described entering the monasteries as follows : On our way to Daphni, the ship stopped a few times at small ports belonging to the monasteries. It was a strange feeling for me, as if I was entering the Middle Ages. Everything was, for me, almost a world of fairy tales. But it was reality.25

(c)  The Greek student of medicine described the meals as follows : Eating in the Great Lavra is like a ceremony. Before the meal, the Higoumenos asks Jesus to bless the food. Then a monk stands in a high place and reads the life of some saint while the monks and visitors are eating their meal. This is because the monks do not want their spirit to be in the food.26

(d)  The middle-aged German teacher of history felt the services were too long : I was, however, tired, for example, during morning service and vespers. One is certainly tired at three o'clock in the morning and the service lasts very long, for ever, they read again and again : "Halleluja", "Halleluja" (by this he meant *Kyrie eleison*), monotonously; for us this is strange.27

## The Return

According to Turner, "the return road is, psychologically, different from the approach road." While approaching the sacred goal, the pilgrim is burdened by stress, uneasiness, anxiety and nagging feelings of guilt piled up in the course of time. On the road back, the pilgrim wants to come home as swiftly as possible. The sins have been forgiven, and the pilgrim can, due to the transformative and curative effect of the pilgrimage, relax and enjoy himself, while looking forward to a warm and admiring welcome at home.[28]

To some extent, my own field material from Athos supports Turner's interpretation of the return from pilgrimage. The travellers indeed experience a feeling of relief after having returned to the world. But, the picture of a black and white process, *i.e.* a sinful phase and a sinless phase, is more idealistic than real. Many of the visitors felt their days on Athos to be somewhat strenuous and were therefore relieved not to have to live there for ever. After the visit to Athos the world was, in fact, seen with newly opened eyes. The first remark almost every visitor made was : women ! The Jugoslavian architect said that these few days had been his first days without seeing women.

The difference between the two worlds, Athos and this world, was nicely described by the Greek student of medicine : the difference between these two worlds are : peace and war. There is peace on Athos, and war in society. Moreover : rich and poor. Athos is rich in mentality, rich in mind, psychologically rich, rich in peace, the monks live in peace, we live at war, noises and stress. Here we are made animals, but the monks very human, very human.[29]

## Discussion : Pilgrimage Rediscovered

*The Increase of Visitors* : When I collected statistical data on the amount of visitors, pilgrims and tourists and the number of lorries, cars, etc. coming to Athos, I was surprised by the rapid increase. The majority of the traffic to Daphni, the main port of Athos, goes through the little village of Ouranoupolis on the border of the monastic peninsula. The other port of departure is in Ierissos on the east side of the peninsula.[30] (See Table on next page).

From Ierissos, traffic consists only of passengers, no lorries, cars etc. The statistics are given on next page.

At the beginning of 1970's, only about 3,000 visitors entered the Holy Mountain. A simple calculation of the numbers of visitors to Athos reveals that, nowadays, nearly 35 000 visitors enter the Holy Mountain every year. Moreover, there is a rapid

| | Ouranoupolis—Daphni | | | | Daphni—Ouranoupolis | | | |
|---|---|---|---|---|---|---|---|---|
| | V | L | C | P | V | L | C | P |
| 1984 | 19,688 | 233 | 63 | 56 | 20,347 | 171 | 44 | 60 |
| 1985 | 25,944 | 153 | 128 | 106 | 26,966 | 143 | 125 | 59 |
| 1986 | 28,212 | 207 | 116 | 169 | 31,674 | 182 | 125 | 144 |
| 1987 January-June | 13,375 | 259 | 1,113 | 79 | 10,782 | 188 | 909 | 38 |

V=visitors; L=lorries; C=cars; P=pickups, trucks, tractors

| Ierissos—the Holy Mountain | |
|---|---|
| 1985 | 4,186 |
| 1986 | 4,623 |
| 1987 (January-June) | 1,892 |

increase in lorries, cars and tractors. The statistics for the first half of this year (1987) show an impressive increase in cars. Since July, August and September are months when many visitors come to Athos, there will most probably be an overall increase for the year.

*Are the Visitors Tourists or Pilgrims* ? According to Sherrad "at least ninety per cent of the visitors to Athos today are not pilgrims. "They are tourists however much they may like to think they are not . . . They do not walk the long, steep, often relentless paths, and so that inner change, to the production of which walking is an essential element, cannot take place in them."[31] I do not agree with this statement. Neither do I agree with the statement so often heard that the foreigners are tourists and the Greeks are pilgrims. There is indeed enough walking to produce a change, as my example of the Greek student of medicine clearly indicates : I found myself there, I returned to my roots as a human being, my mind became peaceful, I found myself as a human being.

Moreover, as my fieldwork interviews show, when asked before the journey, the visitors generally said that they were just going to visit the place because they had heard and read so much about it. Having returned to the world, to the little village of Ouranoupolis, most of the visitors clearly stated that they now realized that they had made a pilgrimage. They were indeed very deeply impressed with what they had seen and what they had experienced and they were very moved. Some of the visitors felt they had been reborn, some that they now looked at the world and at society with new eyes.

It must be stressed, however, that foreigners had difficulties in achieving closer contact with monastic life (1) due to the fact that they didn't speek Greek and (2) because most of them were not orthodox and, therefore, in most of the monasteries, were not allowed to participate in the liturgy or to eat together with the monks. The Greeks usually went to meet some monk friend, but neither did they participate in all services. Most of them, however, participated in the vespers.

My field material, therefore, suggests that the laity is about to rediscover pilgrimage as a means of distancing themselves from everyday life and the life situation, of self-renewal and of gaining a fresh point of view about worldly difficulties. This type of pilgrimage provides a cooling-off period and enables the traveller to reorientate himself into his worldly situation afterwards. Moreover, it seems that this type of pilgrimage, where the travellers only realize afterwards that they have made a pilgrimage, is connected with a religious search, a search for a direction in life. During their journey, many of the visitors deal with the tension between what their life is and what they would like it to be. In this sense, a pilgrimage really sets the traveller free.

## REFERENCES

1. See Rene Gothoni. The Revival on the Holy Mountain of Athos Reconsidered. *Byzantium and the North. Acta Byzantina Fennica*, III. He'sinki 1987 (in press).
2. See Webster's Third New International Dictionary. See also Ludwig Schmugge Pilgerfahrt macht frei"—Eine These zur Bedeutung des mittelalterichen Pilgerwesens—*Romische Quartalschrift* 74, 1-2, Freiburg 1979.
3. See Greek-English Lexicon, ed. by Liddell and Scott, 7th edition, Oxford 1972.
4. Victor Turner. Image and Pilgrimage in Christian Culture. Anthropological Perspectives. New York 1978, 22-23. Turner has dealt with pilgrimages in several articles and books, both as the phenomenon appears in historical religions in general and in Roman Catholicism in particular, but he has not even mentioned the Holy Mountain of Athos, although it has rightly been considered the main oasis of pilgrimages among the orthodox.
5. Van Gennep distinguished three successive phases in those (ritual) processes where the individual is transferred from one social status to another during his life time. The rites that are performed when the individual is detached from his previous position (separation) he called *preliminal*, those performed during the intermediary phase between the two positions (marge) he called *liminal* (or threshold) and those rites where the individual is taken up into the new circle

(aggregation) he called *postliminal*. Arnold Van Gennep. The Rites of Passage. Chicago 1960, 10-11; 21.

6. Victor Turner, Dramas, Fields, and Metaphors. Symbolic Action in Human Society. Ithaca and London 1974, p. 197.
7. Interview Dairy 1985, VI, 5-6. Preserved at the Department of Comparative Religion, University of Helsinki.
8. Interview Diary 1985, VII, 2.
9. See Rene Gothoni, Monastic Life on Mount Athos : a Reflection of Cosmic Order—Mythology and Cosmic Order, ed. by Rene Gothoni and Juha Pentikainen. *Studia Fennica* 32. Helsinki 1987.
10. Interview Diary 1985, VIII, 2-3.
11. Interview Diary 1985, VII, 1; 8-9.
12. Interview Diary 1985, IX, 3.
13. Interview Diary 1985, VI, 7.
14. Interview Diary 1985, XI, 2-3.
15. Interview Diary 1985, VI, 5-6.
16. Interview Diary 1985, XII, 4.
17. Fieldwork Diary 1985.
18. Interview Diary 1985, III, 6.
19. Interview Diary 1985, VI, 11.
20. Interview Diary 1985, IV, 8-9.
21. Interview Diary 1985, VII, 4-5; 7-8.
22. Phillip Sherrard. The Paths of Athos. *Eastern Churches Review* IX, 1-2. Oxford 1977, 101-102.
23. Interview Diary 1985, IV, 7.
24. Interview Diary 1985, IV, 2.
25. Interview Diary 1985, XII, 2.
26. Interview Diary 1985, VII, 6.
27. Interview Diary 1985, VI, 9.
28. Turner 1978, *op. cit.*, 22-23.
29. Interview Diary 1985, VI, 8.
30. The statistical details were received from Thessalonici, the Head Office of the port authorities of Ierissos and Ouranoupolis.
31. Sherrard 1977, *op. cit.*, 102.

# 19

# Pilgrimage in Mormon Culture

## D.J. DAVIES

THE prime purpose of this chapter is to explore the dynamics of pilgrimage within Mormon cultural groups. A secondary goal integrates aspects of this Mormon case with the general theoretical interests presented throughout this volume.

For analytical purposes I define pilgrimage as *corporate soteriological movement*. While all three elements of corporateness, soteriology, and movement, are inextricably linked they merit the separate consideration given to them home. For clarity's sake I must point out that in this chapter Mormonism refers to the culture of the Church of Jesus Christ of Latter Day Saints centred in Utah, focused in Salt Lake City, and with many smaller groups of members spread across the world.

While the process of movement embraces the fact of a destination some pilgrimages stress the journeying as much as its goal. This is especially the case in metaphorical uses of the pilgrim motif espoused in loose existential contexts and applies in one particular sense to the Mormon material considered below. The concept of salvation will be interpreted broadly to express a popular wish to gain access to greater sources of what can usefully be called 'power' following Gerardus Van der Leeuw's phenomenological scheme, (1967 : 3; 2). This general category could be explored more specifically in terms of search for supernatural salvation, for merit, for healing, or some other goal. In the Mormon case it included the desire for economic benefit as well as more traditional expressions of salvation. The corporate dimension not only needs to be included but also needs to be extended to embrace ideals of groups long gone. In Mormon terms this means that living members engaged in pilgrimage see themselves as part of a long religious tradition of people moving under divine command, a concept closely related to that of 'pokhod' as explored by N.M. Olson elsewhere in this volume.

## The Question of Models

Mormons themselves do not normally speak of pilgrimage. So to talk of the dynamics of pilgrimage in a group which does not explicitly employ the category raises the question of interpretation. The issue thrown into starkest relief is the relationship between folk-models and models of anthropological analysis, (*Cf.* L. Holy, and M. Stuchlik, 1988 : 1 ff.). As far as the material presented in this chapter is concerned I simply suggest that theoretical analysis of endemic features involves specific advantages when there is a perceived distance between emic categories and etic analysis. The anthropologist is left more free to explore the logical possibilities of the symbolic universe of the culture concerned. In this sense the present chapter is an exercise in the symbolics of Mormon theology and praxis. It is not an attempt to force alien categories upon recalcitrant material.

The issue of appropriate models makes it inevitable that we mention Victor Turner's work on pilgrimage. In particular his suggestion that anthropology, like history, should focus on drama rather than on culture or archieve in seeking its unit of analysis, (1985 : 190). Turner's discussion of pilgrimage was a peculiarly appropriate subject for some of his later work since it availed itself of an integrated study of symbolism, social process, and the ultimate values of life. Above all it facilitated a multifaceted consideration of man as a symbolic animal whether in preliterate or post-modern societies. The last point on Turner will be my point of departure in analysing Mormon pilgrimage, for I wish to disagree with his gloss that 'if mysticism is an interior pilgrimage, pilgrimage is exteriorized mysticism', (1978 : 7).

While there may be some cases where that is an appropriate interpretation the complexity of Mormon spirituality is such as to belie this neat inversion of internal and external experience. This is particularly obvious when historical factors are brought to bear and show how interior and exterior dimensions are mutually united.

## Major and Minor Themes

My argument identifies two major and two minor themes underlying what I construe to be pilgrimage in Mormonism. All four are influenced by time, by experience of a personal nature, as well as by the formal history and theology of the Mormon Church. The major themes are, firstly, the extensive emigrations of nineteenth century converts and, secondly, the missionary journeys of twentieth century missionaries. The minor themes represent ritual participation in contemporary Temple ceremonies and life itself interpreted as a journey to heaven. For the sake of completeness an additional phenomenon will be included dealing with visits some Latter Day Saints make to sites of Mormon historical interest. This will also enable some discussion of the difficult theoretical distinction between pilgrimage and tourism.

## Emigration as Pilgrimage

Nineteenth century Mormonism offers to anthropological analysis an interesting example of the complexity which literate cultures bring to pilgrimage. In this case it is the Bible which furnishes a ready source of images of pilgrim movement. The Old Testament in particular added layers of significance to the migrations of converts as they identified themselves with ancient Israel, a people believed to be called by God as a chosen people destined for a promised land. The Biblical accounts of an exodus from Egypt combined with the return from Babylonian captivity to yield a charter of pilgrim response. Throughout the period 1830-1890 the earliest missionaries travelled widely in both the United States of America and in Europe preaching a message of Christ's imminent return and the establishment of his millennial kingdom in America.

Geographical locations were qualitatively evaluated as the centre of this earthly kingdom and were called Zion; by contrast the convert's land of origin was deemed to be evil Babylon. The movement from Babylon to Zion was the pilgrim journey. This mythical geography was superimposed upon actual physical geography within Mormon spirituality and experience. Self and group identity were grounded in these Biblical motifs pregnant as they were with ideas of divine wrath and blessing. Inherent in the journey was the hardship betokening the seriousness of the convert's response. This pilgrimage too involved both considerable distance and much hardship : features characteristic of ideal typical pilgrimage.

**Tribulation and Values**

The fact that pilgrims gladly embrace trials and tribulations ought not to be passed over without analytical comment. In particular I want to suggest that itinerary burdens underpin pilgrimage as a process of moral development. Here I invoke the full force of Durkheimian orthodoxy to relate religious factors with the intrinsic social forces which comprise the corporate substratum of human religiosity. Through emigration early Mormons set themselves firmly within the ethical life of their new religion. And this not only in the sense of embracing a new creed, but also in terms of living very closely with fellow converts within the emergent community. They were encouraged to learn and speak English when it was not already their mother tongue. They were also taught quite explicitly to see the very organization of their new society as being of divine origin, an earthly pattern of a heavenly reality. In Durkheimian terms they were socialized into a moral community which saw itself as distinct from other communities in the profane world. There was power in this process : a sense of new purpose and fellowship. Above all there emerged an inward knowledge that all these experiences and doctrines were divine, an awareness the saints called a 'testimony'. This feature along with many other aspects of Mormon history and spirituality I have dealt with in detail elsewhere and can only sketch in this chapter insofar as it furthers our discussion of pilgrim themes, (Davies, D.J. 1984 : 131 ff).

Nineteenth century Mormon emigration thus constituted a kind of elementary form of Latter Day Saint religious life. The perils of pilgrimage, especially from Europe across land and sea to America and then through conflict and persecution to the final goal fostered Mormon pilgrimage through a complex rite of passage. From the profanity and geographical distance of evil Babylon they crossed the liminal wastes before entering Zion. The moral power engendered by this pilgrim-migration resembles the power generated in many if not all pilgrimages even though it may be described in a variety of ways depending upon the dominant ideology or theology involved. It is a power which is intrinsically soteriological though the precise connotation of salvation will similarly vary. Very often it involves the idea of merit, a concept as radically significant in the anthropology of religion as in many formal theologies. Merit involves access to or possession of that moral power which is constitutive of the religious group as such. It can be utilized to foster the ultimate salvation of individuals and to benefit them in the more immediate short term through healing, some material benefit, or a sense of wellbeing. In the Mormon case the emigration of converts not only helped prepare for the coming of Christ but also substantially improved the standard of living of many.

In rather direct Durkheimian terms it is possible to interpret the notion of merit as one example of moral power gained by individuals as a result of fully engaging in the ideal expectation of their social group. In a similarly direct way the notion of salvation can be viewed as the benefit accruing to one who participates fully in central social rites. Merit might thus resemble 'mana' in expressing moral harmony, increased energy in social endeavour, and a renewed confidence in life activities and social goals.

Anthropologically speaking merit enshrines the social and hence moral nature of socially prized goal directed activity. Once we divorce the concept of merit from any theological scheme and use it sociologically it becomes a significant hermeneutical concept whether in analysing western groups like the Mormons or the more usual contexts of Buddhist popular piety. So it is I suggest that migration be deemed a pilgrimage activity involving as it did a collective moment to a physical goal in the expectation of soteriological benefit.

## Boundaries through Pilgrimage Drama

Not only so, but this pilgrim-migration was one means of asserting a distinctive boundary between Mormons and all outsiders who, consistent with Biblical motifs, were called Gentiles. This particular form of pilgrimage as a form of boundary maintenance was enhanced by the physical fact of leaving and then passing through originally familiar groups of kinsfolk and compatriots. It is as though the maintenance of boundaries by a group on the move demonstrates greater religious power than does the boundary maintenance of static populations.

This is precisely where Turner's notion of drama becomes instructive. To Mormon perception at least two potential 'audiences' were involved. On the one hand there was God who witnessed their obedience to the divine call to emigrate and who was also in the position to compare their obedience with the disobedience of ancient Israel. On the other hand stood the nations of the world from whose corrupting presence the saints could be seen to depart. In what can only be described as self-conscious metacommentaries on their own activity the Mormons gained an even greater sense of corporate purpose. In their migratory witness to the world the saints enacted a drama expressing their own faithfulness amidst gentile unbelief. It was a drama destined to comprise another chapter in the book of God's dealing with mankind, not only so, but it would help initiate the next phase of God's saving work.

## Missionary Journeys as Pilgrimage

It so happened that no catastrophic divine intervention came as the next phase of salvation. Instead the Mormon Church grew into a highly organized set of institutions centralized largely in Utah. Over the turn of the century the message changes telling converts in other parts of the world not to emigrate nor even to think of emigration as a divine vocation. Their duty is now to remain in their native lands and establish the church organization there. This was a major theological shift of emphasis with significant consequences for the general hypothesis of this chapter which, so far, has stressed only nineteenth century migration-pilgrimage within Mormon spirituality.

When a movement or, more importantly an emergent sub-culture, finds that its adopted motif of identity is undergoing change the consequences for future corporate identity cannot be ignored. A sense of cognitive dissonance was avoided by Mormons over this transition period because of changes in missionaries activity. Hundreds and then thousands of young Mormons were encouraged to leave Utah to serve as missionaries for some two years in other parts of the world. After the second world war this practice has gained recognition as a vital part of the church's life. In this chapter I accentuate such missionary work to see in its aspects of the dynamics of pilgrimage.

It is a complex picture that emerges. Many late teenage men and women born and bred in Utah left to work in far flung areas of the church. Sometimes this involved learning a new language, a task which is today professionally undertaken by the church. That language might be the tongue of earlier migrant ancestors, when that is the case the missionary goes to serve in the land of his forebears. This I interpret as a form of reverse migration, a pious retracing of family steps. This, I suggest, can be viewed symbolically as a pilgrimage. Not inspired simply by a curiosity but by a desire to take back the message which had originally brought their people from their native heath.

In other cases the missionary travels to areas without any historic family connections. Where this is the case the journey is certainly not in vain but is similarly believed to be undertaken in response to divine call through a local church leader. In this the contemporary missionary may legitimately see himself as resembling his migrant ancestors who themselves journeyed in response to a divine vocation. In essence Utah Mormons retained a sense of obedient movement as intrinsic to their religion. This, too, may have helped avoid dissonance between nineteenth and twentieth century patterns of religiosity.

## Travel and Commitment

A further feature of missionary travel adds significance to the Mormon evaluation of mission work and also touches our anthropological analysis of pilgrimage. It is that many missionaries become more deeply attached to their religion as a result of their endeavour to convert others. This form of reflexive conversion is interesting for it too allows contemporary Mormons to identify with nineteenth century migrants.

Though Mormons are not 'conversionist' in terms of their religious behaviour and expect no momentary relief from guilt in regenerated hearts they do stress the place of insight and emotion in arriving at the 'testimony' to the truth of their religion. 'Testimonies' are either gained or strengthened during the missionary period. This reinforces the place of movement and faith within the total symbolic scheme of Mormonism. For it is in having actually taken a physical journey that missionaries progress within their faith.

Another influential dimension of the mission period is the disciplined life-style followed. This involves supervision of life and friends by senior missionaries and leaders and an extensive study of the Mormon scriptures. Such control expresses something of that ascetic withdrawal from the everyday life world which E.J. Jay considers elsewhere in this volume as a significant element in pilgrimage.

The disciplined life is indicative of the mission period as a rite of passage. The separation from home, the liminal phase in the mission field, and the reincorporation of the returned missionary express a classic formulation of transition ritual. The liminal phase is certainly one when learning occurs though the sense of being distanced from ordinary life whilst devoted to the ideals which that life intrinsically seeks. The mission period is itself interpretable as a polysemic symbol whose multivocality embraces nineteenth century movement, the contemporary missionary's movement, and the more general movement, through life itself. Such life-pilgrimage constitutes one of our two minor themes to which we now turn.

**Temple Visiting and the Journey to Heaven**
These two themes are closely linked and gain part of their rationale from the dominant and obvious motifs of pilgrimage already outlined. If pilgrimage is grounded in the process of movement towards a sacred space for soteriological ends then it is perfectly legitimate to approach the Mormon practice of temple visiting and the idea of life as a journey to heaven as aspects of pilgrimage. One theoretical problem concerns the

aspect of 'the return journey' both in the general category of pilgrimage and in these Mormon cases and will be considered below.

## The Temple as Pilgrimage Centre

From the eighteen seventies until the close of the century Mormonism witnessed a steady growth in the idea of temples both in its broad conception of salvation and in a parallel stress upon temples in the explicit teaching of the church. Over the turn of the century as it came to be appreciated that no dramatic second advent of Christ was likely in the near future a new significance was added to temples. The first stage in this affected the entire geography of Utah, at least within Mormon perceptual geography. Whereas Utah had been seen as the promised land it became increasingly apparent that evil and wickedness were to be found there as anywhere else in the world. What had been thought of as a geographical Zion of the pure in heart was reclassified so as to restrict the purity of Zion to the temples as sacred spaces amidst the geographical Zion. Temples now comprised Zion within Zion (D.J. Davies, 1973).

One major consequence of this changed symbolic ordering was that migrant-pilgrimage was replaced by temple attendance. Though not involving the same distance as far as most Utah residents were concerned dedication was still required. Indeed as time went on it became a matter of a religious test as to whether members were worthy to attend the temples to perform rituals there. As for Mormons living far from temples who were now explicitly told not to contemplate emigration, there still remained the possibility of a short duration journey from, say, Britain to America. Although this was not an emigration it exhibited features of pilgrimage.

In fact it is easier to interpret these ventures as pilgrimages than the nineteenth century migrations simply because they correspond more easily with the popular idea of pilgrimage as a visit to a sacred place of power with a corresponding return to the home base benefited by the journey.

As temples came to be built in other parts of the world it became relatively easy to visit them for ritual purposes. Some personal dedication was still involved. What might be suggested is that in the period when emigration was no longer favoured the possibility of a short temple visit enabled one form of pilgrimage to be replaced by another. This too may have helped overcome any doctrinal dissonance over the change of teaching in the decades bordering the turn of the century.

Though I do not intend discussing temple ritual in detail in this chapter I must explain that they served several purposes, not least the bonding of members of the Mormon extended family for the purposes of ultimate salvation. Temples were sacred places where the time dimension of earth touched and participated in the eternal dimension of the world beyond. In this sense temples were symbols of eternity and of the family as an eternal institution. Very definite soteriological ends were achieved in the rituals performed once the temple had been gained. Indeed Mormon ideology developed an extensive rationale of the temple as a place apart from which eternal goals could not be attained. Temple-going as a form of pilgrimage became an essential and not merely an optional practice for Mormons seriously committed to their religion.

Structurally speaking the temple itself was a liminal institution being located on the interstice between this world and the next. Rites performed in them were often rites of passage in and of themselves. Not least did they impress many Mormons with a sense of unity with their family members and with God. But part of the significance of temple-going lay in the long established Mormon idiom of behavioural obedience. Concrete things were to be done in response to the revealed truth. So it is that Mormons speak not simply of the truth of their religion but also of the 'ordinances of the gospel'. It is insufficient simply to believe, action is also necessary, action involving temple ritual. The fact that a theological distinction exists which qualitatively differentiates between temples and the ordinary weekly meeting places of Mormons makes the idea of travelling to a temple all the more significant.

As in the case of nineteenth century emigration which had its Biblical model as validation so too in the case of modern temples. The Latter Day Saints possessed the Old Testament background of the temple at Jerusalem along with earlier tabernacles as part of their contemporary spirituality. Mormons today could attend a temple as had characters in ancient Israel and in the time of Christ. Layer upon layer of meaning made temple going an increasingly profound experience.

## Life as Pilgrimage Heavenwards

If emigration and temple-going together constitute distinctive Mormon features this last theme is one more commonly shared with other religious traditions as in the widely known example of John Bunyan's *Pilgrim's Progress*.

As Mormon theology developed ideas about temples as centres for eternally significant rites it also came increasingly to view life on earth as an experiential means of journeying towards those eternal realms. Earthly life flowed into the next life and laid a firm foundation for it. More significantly still Mormons interpreted earthly life as itself having started in a pre-existent stage in 'heaven'. Earthly life was an embodied phase for spirits which had pre-existed with God prior to their birth. Birth itself was but part of the total journey of existence. This being the case it was easy for Mormons to speak of earthly life as a journey of obedient testing.

This raises an important theoretical point in the dynamics and structure of pilgrimage as an analytical category. The ideal type pilgrimage starts from a home base, passes through dangerous or arduous environs, reaches a sacred phenomenon, returns to home base in a somewhat changed state. But the ideal type is ever subject to particular interpretation in the light of specific cultural values, not least theological beliefs.

## Pilgrimage, Eschatology and Matter

In this connection I would draw a distinction between religions of a more catholic and sacramental tradition on the one hand, and the more protestantly inclined on the other.

Sacramental traditions easily accept the sacredness of matter, whether in the phenomena of sacred persons or sacred spaces. It is no accident that pilgrimages are widespread in Roman Catholic and Orthodox traditions. Regular pilgrimage expresses a kind of 'eternal return' in Mircea Eliade's sense of human participation in the regenerative power of theophanies, (1970: 123ff.). The practice of the Mass itself fostered such an outlook. But in the literary world of Protestant theology and practice this was not so. Protestantism was iconoclastic towards sacramentalism when it encouraged veneration of sacred persons or places. Protestant theology espoused a theory of time and providence which was more linear than ritually repetitive. The eschatological dimension replaced sacramental motifs. Christian worship and ethics were to press on to a future reign of God rather than dwell upon contemporary mystery in God. The word of a future kingdom replaced the sacramentality of an eternal return. This theological point, stark and unqualified as it is, helps make sense of the Mormon material. This pattern of religiosity has occurred in numerous contexts where long established traditions have undergone reformation or prophetic revitalization.

For Mormons life as a pilgrimage fits the ideal type in a reversed way with a spiritual journey from God in heaven through an earthly body enhanced by temple ritual back to heavenly realities. This pilgrimage is one of testing. It may, in fact, elucidate the endeavour-factor in pilgrimage. Life is a period of testing. The home base is heaven itself. The goal is 'away' from God rather than being a relatively more sacred arena than the home base. But and this is an important qualification, the Biblical background of Morminism coupled with a fundamentally protestant hermeneutic meant that the return to God was the aspect most stressed for practical purposes. Nor can the historical dimension of pilgrimage be ignored, for the nineteenth century migration pilgrimage was validated by Biblical and Mormon scriptures as they referred to the divine guidance journeying peoples. It was only after the nineteenth century migratory phase has ceased that any stress came to be placed upon a more metaphorical interpretation of life itself as a journey from God and back to God through the mediating ritual benefit of temples.

## Conclusion

If Biblical influences cannot be ignored neither can other cultural idioms which helped form early Mormon attitudes. One such was the idea of the pioneer and frontiersman. This is clearly evident in Mormon hymnody where the pilgrim motif appears more starkly in the guise of the pioneer. Only after the Utah settlement and change in millennial doctrine did what might be seen as a pilgrim ethos emerge. A hymn by Joseph

Fielding Smith, one of the church's prophet leaders, and which belongs to the early twentieth century asks the question, 'Does the journey seem long?' It goes on to encourage the saint experiencing hardship to be strengthened by the beckoning hand of one who has already gone ahead to the pure land where all troubles end.

So we see that Mormon spirituality cannot be interpreted without some idiom of pilgrimage. Its entire notion of faith is grounded in movement, and in a corresponding belief that God will reward the venture. At the beginning of this chapter I dissented from Victor Turner's aside that, 'if mysticism is an interior pilgrimage, pilgrimage is exteriorized mysticism'. While my reasons for this will already be obvious I wish, in concluding, to make them even more explicit.

The obvious criticism of Turner's gloss is one he himself would probably not have denied, namely, that religious experience is as much a reality to the person engaged in physical pilgrimage as in one set immobile in meditation. Whilst the nature of the experience probably differs and its accentuation varies it is likely that commitment to religious action would not exist unless some experiential outcome occurred. While in migrant-pilgrimage and missionary-pilgrimage it was the very process of movement which occasioned a sense of religious benefit it was still the practice of prayer within these events which allowed it to be focused. Whatever faith existed prior to movement it was enhanced through the process of religious activity.

A subtler criticism concerns the popular idea of mysticism. Here, for the sake of argument and to clarify categories, I press Turner's point further than might properly be warranted. The pragmatic mysticism of Mormon pilgrimage involves a shared and corporate dimension. Mysticism is often said to be ineffable, and because of that to draw away from the social dimension for which communicability is essential. The emphatic point of the Mormon example is that while religious experience possesses an intimately personal pole of significance there also exists a prized communal pole. This is expressed in hymns, in the practice of family temple-rites, in folk-histories of migration and of missionary work. In Mormon culture activity itself is prized and is said to be intrinsic to priesthood, the ontological category shared by God and priests of the church. Experience is not left unexplored and unvalued.

At a more abstract level the temple affords and elaborate example of symbolic polysemy depicting mystic pilgrimage. It is a sacred space where some Mormons find and experience of deity beyond that of the everyday life world. It is the temple itself along with its ritual which could best be described as the exteriorization of Mormon spirituality. To enter the temple is, metaphorically speaking, to enter the heart of Mormon practice. But, and here the polysemy continues, the temple is a transformation and a materialization of the historical Mormon ideal of Zion. The location which would be the focus of divine revelation, world-reorganization, and which was set as the goal of migrant pilgrims. The condensation of faith and historical events is clearly seen. As such the temple serves as the final unifying focus both of historical patterns of pilgrimage, of missionary pilgrimage, and of life itself as pilgrimage.

### TOURIST PILGRIMS

Temples also stand as historic monuments to Mormons. Some mark stages in the march westwards under persecution, these along with other sites of historical interest are sometimes visited by groups of Mormons raising the question as to whether such visitors count as pilgrims or tourists ? In Great Britain in 1987, for example, many American Mormons with British origins visited numerous sites where Mormon activity was strong in the past. That year celebrated a hundred and fifty years of Mormon life in Britain and witnessed numerous such visit-pilgrimages. For many of these people the religious significance of places renders them more than bare monuments. As a final comment on this particular theme it must be said that where some sites stand as radically significant in a historical and spiritual sense, as in the major Utah temples, it is not easy for any other historical monument with a religious connotation to fail to participate in that prevailing ethos.

Given this variety of locations and of historical manifestations of religious movement for religious ends the issue of whether or not a single category of pilgrimage is justified in anthropology remains questionable. What is vital is that each cultural case be given its full ideological, historical, and social weight. The historical perspective is particularly valuable within the comparative method. D.J. Hall's historical analysis of English medieval pilgrimage affords one good example of such benefit. His focus on people's 'struggle against circumstance' is instructive for the Mormon case, (1965 : 9). For pilgrimage in its nineteenth century migrant form involved a major struggle against adverse economic and social conditions as well as a positive search for those better things which may be interpreted as belonging to salvation. And that is without mentioning the adverse nature of the natural elements.

The modern pilgrimage variants in missionary and temple work, as I have interpreted them above, also express something of that *peregrinatio* which has been part of the dynamics of broader Christian tradition from its earliest period, (*cf*. R.C. Finucane 1977:39). The 'Lure of a Holy Land' which E.D. Hunt (1982) documented so well for fourth and fifth century Christians has itself hauntingly revisited many subsequent Christian generations. In the Mormon case it was initially viewed as a geographical location and occasioned migrant-pilgrimage then later, as we have shown, a more metaphorical and existential interpretation set Zion as a goal of qualitative life to be attained in the future even though it might be occasionally sensed on earth. This more recent Mormon sense of life as pilgrimage is very much in tune with wider Christian thinking since the nineteen fifties. It accords particularly well with that style of theology called 'narrative theology' which sets the believer within the contemporary group of God's people and then sets that group within the historical flow of the chosen people down the ages, (*cf*. J. Navonne, 1977, and G.W. Stroup, 1981). In this modern tradition self-reflection is supported by a strong literary sense of sacred texts and sacred history. It easily involves an explicit tendency to mythologize and assumes canons of validity drawn more from literary criticism than from philosophical logic.

As a conclusion we review this Latter Day Saint case of pilgrimage as a sweep of interpretative change. Beginning with the general Christian ideal of pilgrimage to the promised land interpreted as a heavenly realm the Mormons turned heaven into an earthly and American Jerusalem. From its accompanying stress on emigration-pilgrimage to that locale the church message shifted making missionary work to be a pilgrim endeavour appropriately fitting the dawning realization that no single geographical Zion was materializing. Then temple-work and finally life itself as pilgrimage. Better than taking this process of change to be an interiorization of an external act as might Victor Turner, I would set it in the different interpretative scheme of a more hermeneutical kind. The shift through history was one in which literalism gave way to metaphor, a switch which might be taken as the formula of transition from tradition to modernity and beyond.

All these phases display pilgrimage as a corporate soteriological movement with the history of Mormon religiosity being a drama in which successive generations explore and subtly rewrite their parts in the light of a folk-knowledge of earlier performances.

## NOTES

Davies, D.J. (1973). 'Aspects of Latter Day Saint Eschatology'. *Sociological Yearbook of Religion in Britain*. No. 6. Ed. Michael Hill. London. S.C.M. Press.

Davies, D.J. (1984). *Mormon Spirituality : Latter Day Saints in Wales and Zion*. Nottingham University Series in Theology No. 1. University of Utah Press.

Eliade, M. (1970). *Myths Dreams and Mysteries*. New York, Fontana.

Finucane, R.C. (1977). *Miracles and Pilgrims*, London, J.M. Dent.

Hall, D.J. (1965). *English Mediaeval Pilgrimage*. London. Routledge and Kegan Paul.

Holy, L. and M. Stuchlík. (1981). *The Structure of Folk Models*. London. Academic Press.

Hunt, E.D. (1982). *Holy Land Pilgrimage in the Later Roman Empire A.D. 312-460*. Oxford. Clarendon Press.

Leeuw, G. van der. (1967). *Religion in Essence and Manifestation*. Gloucester. Mass. Peter Smith.

Navone, J. (1977). *Towards a Theology of Story*. Slough, England. St. Paul Publications.

Stroup, G.W. (1981). *The Promise of Narrative Theology*. London. S.C.M. Press.

Turner, V.W. and Edith Turner. (1978). *Image and Pilgrimage in Christian Experience*. Oxford. Blackwell.

Turner, Victor Edited by E.L.B. Turner (1985). *On the Edge of the Bush*. University of Arizona Press.

# 20

# Intensification Rituals of Revitalization of Sacred Stages in Northwest Mexico and Northwest Peru

N. ROSS CRUMRINE

So great is the incompatibility between the profane and the sacred worlds that a man cannot pass from one to the other without going through an intermediate stage." In this quotation Van Gennep (1960) suggests the hypothesis that forms the basis of this article, which refines and tests it in terms of Mayo and Catacaos field data.[1] In order to analyze the dual processes of individual transformation and sacred centre revitalization, I will focus upon Latin American examples especially those drawn from Mayo pilgrimage "visits" in Sonora, Northwest Mexico and Catacaos ones in the Department of Piura on the far North Coast of Peru. In these examples humans communicate with their sacred worlds by means of a dual process of mediation of the separation or opposition between the human secular world and the sacred realm of the gods and saints. In these cases, as well as others from Latin America, both human beings and the supernaturals, often objectified as saints, achieve communication by means of a process in which both move through intermediate stages. While humans move toward the sacred earthbound home of the supernaturals, the latter's presence and power descend to fill their residences and images with their spirit. Thus both ends of the secular-sacred or human-super-natural continuum, moving through intermediate stages, achieve a final unification during the sacred period of the fiesta or celebration of the saint's special day or days.

### INTRODUCTION : PILGRIMAGE ? A STAGE IN SPECIAL TIME AND SPACE

The heightened complexity of the historical processes and syncretism in Latin America and increased informality challenges a clear conception of *pilgrimage*. One classic dictionary definition might be that of the *Encyclopaedia Britannica* [(1973) (17) : 1076)] :

> Pilgrimage, a journey to a saint's shrine or other sacred place, undertaken for a variety of motives : with the object of gaining supernatural help; as an act of thanks giving or of penance; for the sake of devotion. Pilgrimages are charac-teristic of most of the higher religions.

*Webster's Third New International Dictionary*, unabridged, (1971 : 1715) suggests a broader fan of meaning for the terms *pilgrim* and *pilgrimage* :

> *Pilgrim* . . .1a : one who journeys esp. in alien lands : TRAVELER, WAYFARER b : a person who passes through life as if in exile from a heavenly homeland or in search of it or of some high goal (as truth) 2 : one who travels to visit a shrine or holy place as a devotee. . . 3 : Pilgrim Father. . . 4 : recent immigrant. . . . 5 : (colour) 6 : (breed of domestic geese). Pilgrimage. . . 1a : a journey of a pilgrim; esp : one to a shrine or a sacred place. . . b : the act of making such a journey. . . 2 : a trip taken to visit a place of historic or sentimental interest or to participate in a specific event or for a definite purpose. . . 3a : the course of life on earth. . . b : a particular part of the life course of an individual. . . 4 : a search for mental and spiritual values. . .

In the Mayo region of Northwest Mexico, a clear *pilgrimage*

in the classic sense of the term, to a neighbouring church centre
is called a "bisita" (visit) and the terms "peregrinacion" or
"romeria" are not used. In the Catacaos region of Piura, far
Northwest Peru, the travels and arrival of the Three Kings on
January 6th is seen by some of the people as "the pilgrimage
of the Reyes." Many others see the action of the Kings as
simply an announcement of the fiesta celebration to take place
in Nariwalā, whereas they point out that the long procession
with the Niño (Christ Child) the preceding evening is the
"pilgrimage of the Niño." Nearly all of the descriptive articles
in the forthcoming book, "Pilgrimage in Latin America",
(Crumrine and Morinis nd)[2] examine pilgrimage as part of the
fiesta ceremony complex or as pilgrimage fiestas. The fact is
that pilgrimage does not have to include a long or complex
physical journey nor actual physical death in contrast to Victor
Turner's argument. "But it is only death on the way to or at
the shrine that makes a pilgrimage a true rite of passage. . ."
(1975 : 107). One might not even leave his or her community
but still be a very important part of the pilgrimage action.
These cases, and numerous others mentioned by Smith (1975)
etc., are unified in a *pilgrimage process of mediation*. In this
rite of passage it would seem that individuals pass from one
world to the other, a passage ritually dramatized, without
actually physically dying in the process. Thus the classic
concept of pilgrimage must be either discarded or re-examined
in terms of this new data and different perspective.

YOREM PAKHO AND GOH NAIKI PUEBLO IDEOLOGY : FIESTAS AND
EXCHANGE PILGRIMAGES IN MAYO INDIAN IDENTITY, SONORA,
                        NORTHWEST MEXICO

Yearly, Mayo Indians of the lower Mayo River valley, Sonora,
Northwest Mexico, engage in two large exchange pilgrimages
(*pasom*) which involve ritual visiting (*bisitam*) of church based
sodalities, their patron saints, and church centre membership.
Although numerous smaller visits link church centres into an
integrated network, the major exchange pilgrimages focus upon
the Sundays of the Espiritu Santo (Holy Spirit) or Itom Aye
(Our Mother) and of the Santisima Tiniran (Holy Trinity) or
Itom Achai (Our Father) which are movable and usually fall

towards the end of the month of May. The smaller church centres and their exchange *bisitam* usually do not cut across *municipio* (municipal) or "pueblo" boundaries, however the Holy Spirit Holy Trinity exchanges unify the two "pueblos" of the lower river valley, Etchojoa (Etchojoa) and Santa Cruz (Huatabampo). Since Mayos perceive both of these rituals as *yorem paskom* or *yorem kastumbre* and also of each centre, Etchojoa (Espíritu Santo) and Santa Cruz, now Júpare (Santíisima Tiniran), as representing one of the "Eight Mission Pueblos Jurisdictions", this pattern of exchange pilgrimages restates the Mayo Goh Naike Pueblo Hurasionim ideology and reinforces their image of Yoremes (Mayos) as a separate and unique people.

In a very general sense, my research suggests modern Mayos exhibit a transitional stage in their development from an autonomous tribal society to either a well-defined ethnic enclave or a fully assimilated condition, at which time Mayos as such would cease to exist. Today Mayos are neither completely autonomous nor have they lost that unique set of common understandings and shared system of symbols which we call the enduring identity symbol system or, more generally, the Mayo way of life. They are "betwixt and between," a part society characterized by a rather highly integrated symbolic and ritual system. This cultural system is maintained by a rather mobile, rather heterogeneous group of people, whom we call the Mayos. The facts that Mayo peasant farming and their more modern irrigated commercial agriculture must be supplemented by wage labour and that their identity symbol system must be supported by cycles of ceremonials require some mobility within the river valley and even between river valleys. This state of transition and mobility makes it difficult to draw clear boundaries between Mayos and Mestizos as many aspect of mestizo culture and society are shared by Mayos. In certain cultural aspects Mayos seem quite assimilated, whereas in others, especially the *pahko* complex, they appear quite different from Mestizos.

## Mayo Cultural Ecology

The ecological limitations in terms of which Mayo ceremonialism must be adapted prove to be extremely complex. Living in a zone of high production irrigation agriculture on the coastal plane of southern Sonora and northern Sinaloa, the modern Mayos are characterized by almost complete technico-economic assimilation (*see* Crumrin 1977). Depending upon the figures which one wishes to accept, the modern Mayo population is placed somewhere between 20,000 and 60,000 individuals. The region receives an average of 40 to 80 cm of rain per year and is characterized by two principle seasons, a cold time (*sebe tiempo*) with temperatures which drop almost to zero degrees Celsius during the coldest nights of winter and a hot season (*tata tiempo*) with occasional summer temperatures which reach 45 degrees or more during the hottest days of summer.

Many Mayos farm small plots of land, around four to six hectares, as members of *ejidos* (governmentally established land holding societies) or as small property owners. By far the majority of Mayos identify themselves as farmers although most must supplement their meager income through wage labour. A few are fishermen and others hold traditional specializations such as fireworks makers, mat makers, *maso* (deer) and *paskola* professional dancers and musicians, and maestrom (lay ministers). However these represent only part-time specializations and these individuals also perceive of themselves as farmers. Although most of the farming in the lower Mayo River Valley involves irrigation, two types exist, both rainfall farming and irrigation agriculture. As farmers, Mayos are little different from many poor undereducated mestizo Mexican peasants living in the river valley. Charles Erasmus (1967) describes this Mayo-mestizo peasant farming and discusses the problems of reform and rural poverty. As members (socios) of *ejidos*, Mayos possess their own lands which they must work themselves at least every two years and legally must not rent nor sell. Most rural peasants in the Mayo River valley do not own sufficient lands to make an adequate living and some hold very little or no lands at all. Thus they must supplement their crop income.

In order to pay for water, seed, land improvements, and insecticides, etc. farmers must seek loans from *ejido* agrarian banks or from private moneylenders, or must rent their lands to other farmers, often non-Mayos. Mayo farmers would prefer to plant food crops such as corn, beans, squash, and water-melons, however if they seek a loan from the local banks they must plant what the bank recommends and the crop the hydraulic commission is willing to provide irrigation water to support. In spite of this commercialization, corn is still a popular winter crop. In contrast to corn, which is eaten in all rural households, sesame has been and still is a popular winter cash crop especially in some of the non-irrigated or more marginal areas, although it is not eaten in peasant households. Cotton has been a popular summer crop, although wheat, cartamo (safflower) and soyabeans have essentially replaced cotton. Cartamo requires only one irrigation and rather little care as it is covered with little spines and one cannot work in the field after it is well established, in contrast to cotton which is quite difficult and costly to raise requiring a great deal of irrigation water, fertilizer, and insecticides. Wheat, a crop introduced by the early missionaries in the sixteen hundreds, is also very popular, grows very well in the area, and receives governmental encouragement and financial support. Most peasant farmers do not own draft animals and must rent a tractor and operator to work their fields, although many *ejidos* own tractors and other farm equipment. Thus in recent years peasant farming has become more complex, costly, and cash crop oriented. Other Mayos, of course, have no lands and must work as day farm labourers, wage labourers, fishermen, etc. But modern technology such as insecticides, fertilizers, hybrid seed, tractors and complex levelling equipment, and even small airplanes which spray insecticides, fertilizers and even chemicals on the clouds to produce rain is a daily part of the life of all Mayos.

Many Mayos still utilize the rapidly disappearing thorn forest and desert areas for firewood, construction materials, and cactus fruit. Most families keep some domestic animals, such as chickens and pigs. Although the pigs are often sold, chicken eggs which are eaten almost daily provide an important source of protein and if guests arrive a chicken can be cooked in a stew to provide a quick meal. Much of the material culture of the river valley is shared by both Mayos and mestizo Mexicans. Everyone purchases prepared foods, tools, most clothing, and manufactured items in the local markets of Huatabampo and Navojoa or in small local stores. Mayos buy foods such as sugar, coffee, lard, and fruit and even wheat flour and cornmeal, if their own supply is exhausted. Some Mayo women still grind their own cornmeal and home roasted coffee beans with a small hand grinder although most households buy machine made tortillas at least occasionally while others rely upon these commercial tortillas. All Mayo clothing is purchased in the market and reflects a typical western farm labourer's costume. Home furnishings are simple and often purchased although the home construction is more traditional, and characteristic of both Mayo and the poorer mestizo farmers. Families living in small clusters of households beside irrigation canals or at the edges of their fields must carry water from a canal or well and rely upon kerosene torches for light, while families in larger rural hamlets, villages, and towns have a running water tap in their yards and electric power usually for one or several light bulbs. In their sleeping rooms most Mayo families have a small table altar with pictures and images of selected saints, and perhaps a wooden cross or metal crucifix, while a wooden cross stands in the tabat (patio) of many Mayo families especially during Lent or at the time of funeral rituals for a death in the family. Thus with the exception of this *tebatpo kuru* (patio cross) Mayo material culture is quite identical to that of the poorer mestizo Mexican farmers of the Mayo River Valley.

However, modern Mayo ceremonialism and the use of the Mayo language provides a complete contrast with this pattern of technico-economic assimilation. Mayo identity, insofar as it represents a system apart from that of mestizo Mexico, is crucially linked with the Mayo mythico-ritual system and with the sacred societies or sodalities which produce Mayo ceremonials. Within this Mayo symbolico-ritual system, the ceremonials of Lent and Holy Week, of the Santa Kuru (Holy Cross) on the third of May, of the dead the first and second of November, and of Espíritu Santo and Santīsima Tiniran in late May or early June represent the most complex and important ritual events in the Mayo ceremonial cycle of the lower river valley. This present ceremonial system is the result of a number of structural and historical processes : a marginal position combined with early Jesuit missionary activities before their expulsion from the New World, followed by years of relative autonomy leading to recent pacification and present embedding within modern Mexico (see Crumrine 1977 and n.d.). In the production of the cycle of Mayo *pahkom* and *bisitam* or pilgrimages, the Mayo ceremonial sodalities or *cofradias* such as the Paskome. Pariserom, Matachinim and *paskola* and *maso* dancers and musicians, socially maintain, produce, and adapt this symbolico-ritual system.

Within the modern river valley, Mayo families live in four different settlement patterns : (1) the rancheria type or scattered rural household clusters often of related Mayo families, a pre-hispanic pattern, for example Pueblo'ora which was a former ceremonial village centre but now is reduced to a large rancheria, (2) the modified Spanish village ceremonial centre type, a Spanish mission type of pattern, for example Jūpare with a church-cemetery area or Etchoropo, (3) the modern northwest Mexican urban market centre type for example Huatabampo, Etchojoa, or Navojoa, (4) the more recent *ejido* community type, for exmple Pozo Dulce. In all these settlement patterns Mayos and mestizo Mexicans live as neighbours although the rancheria and village types provide the most privacy and isolation from the outside world. Located on the sand hills adjacent to the beach, a number of fishing communities are characterized by a combination of grid and random patterning depending upon the shape of existing relatively flat lands. In summary, in spite of this broad variety of settlement patterns, Mayos generally live dispersed among mestizo Mexicans without special regard to Indian or non-Indian identification.

Modern Mayo social organization is rather simple, consisting of four levels : the family, the household, the ceremonial kindred, and the ceremonial centre consisting of the ritual sodalities, church, and church officials. Although a more complex kinship system existed in the past, within the modern Mayo family the major emphasis is placed upon the nuclear family itself, of mother, father, and children. Most modern households consist of nuclear families although many include additional relatives such as one or several old parents or one or more siblings with their own families. During the typical times of the rites of passage, a traditional extended household will co-operate and new alliances will be established through the selection of godparents for the newborn, the marrying couple, or the initiate into a ritual sodality. When an individual sponsors a ceremonial, his or her household and group of relatives and

compadres become an important cooperative unit. Recovery
from an illness or escape from a life threatening situation after
making a promise (*manda*) to God or one of the Saints which
means that one must repay the supernatural by helping produce
a ceremonial (*pahko*) or a cycle of *pahkom* in the Saint's honour.
Modern Mayo public ceremonials reveal a fusion of aboriginal
and early Jesuit traditions modified by several hundred years of
dynamic adjustment with first Spanish and later Mexican
society and culture. Many pre-hispanic elements, such as the
use of masks, fermented drinks, a hierarchy of officers, and a
formal initiation with a ritual sponsor, still appear in modern
Mayo ceremonialism. Certainly the Jesuits enriched the Mayo
ceremonial system introducing new ceremonials and new supernaturals such as the Virgin of Guadalupe, Jesus, and a number
of other Christian Saints and re-interpreting other indigenous
rituals and ceremonials. The highly integrated modern Mayo
folk culture as well as the modern church-pueblo ceremonial
organization remain intact as a kind of living history of Mayo
contact with the world beyond the river valley. The modern
church-pueblo organization includes (*1*) the five church gover-
nors and five helpers, generally elected by the pueblo for extended terms, (*2*) the Maestrom (lay ministers), (*3*) Matachini
dance sodality (church dancers), (*4*) the Parisero sodality (the
Lenten masked society), and (*5*) the Pahkome (fiesteros). The
Pahkome pay their promise (*manda*) for a cure by praying each
Sunday at the church, producing the Saint's day ceremony
(*pahko*), and providing the fireworks, food, entertainment in the
form of Pahkola and *Maso* (deer) dancers and musicians during
the period of the *pahko*. In the lower river valley ceremonial
centres, the Pahkome must make two major ceremonials for
their Saint's *pahkom* as well as participate in certain funerals
and remembrance rituals. Assisted by the Pahkome the
Pariserom enact the life, death, and resurrection of Christ from
the first of the year through Easter week. The *pahkom* for the
Holy Cross (Santa Kuru) take place in early May and September, for the Espíritu Santo and Santísima Tiniran late in May
or early in June, for San Juan late in June, and for Guadalupe
early in December. All of these *pahkom* involve ritual exchange
and *bisitam* of neighbouring Pahkome although the *pahkom* of

Espīritu Santo and Santīsima Tiniran represent the most elaborate examples of this ritual pattern.

Dedicated to their specific patron Saint the Pahkome consist of twelve ranked *personasim* (persons) : four Parinam, four Alperesim, and four Alawasim. These individuals generally have made a promise to serve the Saint for three years, however, they usually are able to work only a year at a time and rest for several years before taking on the cargo for another year of service. During the majority days of the *pahko* the Pahkome must kill a bull for meat and provide the bread, coffee, tortillas, and meat stew to be eaten by the participants. Nevertheless, much of the meat is given to relatives, compadres, and close friends as repayment for their assistance or in order to establish debts to ensure future aid for following *pahkom*. In this sense the Mayo Pahkome distributes food and in doing so reinforces social ties producing a cooperative group which through its return support of the Pahkome makes possible the *pahko*. Thus Mayo social ties and group identity are reinforced by means of the *pahko* institution and an equality amongst the "poor" is established.

On a more general symbolic level the Mayo set of exchange *pahkom* in honour of the Espīritu Santo and the Santīsima Tiniran presents and mediates the inner-outer, the we-they, opposition. Members of each ceremonial centre participate in and thus actualize two ritual structures : (1) *paso* (pilgrimage), *pahko* (fiesta), *paso* (return pilgrimage); (2) *komchepte* (descent of the Saint), *nobena* (nine days of prayers), *pahko* (fiesta). From one weekend to the next the human visitor-host relationship flips over while Itom Aye (Our Mother, Espīritu Santo) first hosts Itom Achai (Our Father, Santīsima Tiniran) and then is hosted by Him as the supernatural roles also reverse. In the *pahko* context the unity of visitor and host also creates a mediation of the human-deity opposition as the saints also participate in and enjoy the ritual. In this article both the Mayo status as an embedded enduring peoples as well as the unifying and mediating powers of the exchange *pasko* will be described and analyzed.

## The Santīsima Tiniran Komchepte

The first important rituals associated with the Santīsima Tiniran role in the exchange pilgrimage actualize the *komchepte*, the coming down of the power of the Santīsima Tiniran, and initiate the nine days of prayer (*nobena*) preceding the Santīsima Tiniran *pasko*. The *komchepte* takes place during the noon hours nine days before the Holy Trinity Sunday, for in 1983 the *komchepte* occurred on Thursday May 19th and Holy Trinity Sunday, May 29th.

When I arrived in Jūpare on the morning of May 19th and entered the church, I immediately noticed that the main altar was different. The Santīsima Tiniran was gone and placed on the top of the altar were two crucifixes. As usual the big crucifix was in the left-hand corner with the flags of the Pahkome (fiesteros). There were chiefly a number of big vases full of flowers on the altar, a few yellow ones, but mainly white lilies. The donation box was in the lower centre of the altar and the large Santīsima Tiniran in the ante room to the left of the altar. It was practically impossible to get inside the little ante room as it was jammed with worshippers. The Santīsima Tiniran was resting on a table just as you went in to your right, against that right hand wall.

As I left the church through the side door I discovered the Pahkome kontiing (encircling) the church carrying the *bera castillos* (fireworks). These were not the large *castillos* (fireworks displays), but a smaller single flat type of *castillo* which they stuck in the ground and shot off during the *komchepte*.

Led by a Mo'oro (ritual advisor) all the Alawasim (lowest ranking Pahkome) moved around the church in a counter-clockwise direction, while appearing from the other direction I say the Parinam and the Alparesim (higher ranking Pahkome). The Parinam and Alparesim were followed by eleven men carrying these *bera castillos* and the Alawasim were followed by seven men also carrying *bera castillos*. The lines contied (surrounded) around the church three times. They formed two lines in front of the church and then carried these *bera castillos* up one by one and dipped them in front of the church. Then they carried them out to an area just beyond the church bells and cross to set them up in the ground.

I returned to the church which was beginning to fill up. They had put down mats directly in front of the altar and in front of the two side altars to the worshippers' left where the other two images of the Santisima Tiniran rested, and then threw flower petals and a lot of lilies down on the mats. The Matachinim (church dancers) had danced earlier and the Paskolas and Maso dancers (professional *pahko* dancer-entertainers) were dancing in their ramada out beyond the church at this time. As the Pahkome returned to the church, I noticed the four flags of the four different sets of Paskhome, from Navowaxia, Pozo Dulce, Pueblo'ora and Jūpare.

The Mo'oro lit several candles that stood by a kneeling rail in front of the altar. They brought a chair for the old Cantora (church singer) and she sat down as the Maestrom (lay ministers) knelt and began to chant and pray. As this happened inside, outside the church *kamaram* (large fire crackers) and the little *bera castillos* began going off and I assumed the *maso* and *paskola* dancers and the Matachins began dancing in front of the church. Then assisted by the Mo'oro and a couple of the Paskome wearing the kerchiefs over their heads, they carried the Santīsima Tiniran into the church emerging from the door of the little anteroom. They held it way up high and lowered it clear down to the floor of the church. Then they held it up again and lowered it down again, however when they had it part way down, they turned it, first to the right hand side of the church and then to the left hand side of the church. Thus in its descent the Santīsima Tiniran swung in front of the worshippers as they brought it to the centre and dropped it clear down to the floor. Then they lifted it up again, drew it down part way, did these turns and lowered it to the floor again. Afterwards, the Mo'oro told me that it should descend 12 times, although in the excitement I lost count as they were doing it reasonably fast. At the same time other individuals did the *komchepte* with the side altar images of the Santīsima Tiniran.

When they finished lowering them, and as the Maestros went into another set of prayers, they rested the three images on the mats at the foot of the altars. Then individually the Pahkome began to come up, were given a cloth, crossed themselves, and wiped and dusted the main image as they knelt in front of it, which took quite awhile. During this time the Mo'oro was constantly ringing a small hand bell, the Maestros and the Cantora were singing and praying, and many people were holding candles which they lit just before the descent. Outside there was a great din as the fireworks were set off, the large church bells were rung, and the dancers were dancing. Inside, the church was completely filled with people who seemed very excited even though it was extremely hot and many were sweating, complaining and fanning themselves.

As the Pahkome finished greeting the Santīsima Tiniran other individuals in the church went up to cross themselves: kneel, and pray. Soon the Paskome returned with the *maso* and *paskola* dancers and musicians who also greeted the image. Then the dancers did the *hinangkiwa* (a procession form in which the dancers move to and fro as the procession advances) with all these different Pahkome and their flags escorting the Paskolas and Maso back to the *paskola* ramada. The Matachins were dancing in two long lines also accompanying the *hinangkiwa*.

After the *hinangkiwa* was over, and the Maestros, Cantora, and head Paskola prayed at the ramada cross and the *maso* and *paskola* dancers danced for a short while. Someone said that there would be three songs, but it seemed like they danced more than that. The Fiesteros did their *ehersisio* (ritual) at the ramada cross which took quite a long while as there were four different groups of Pahkome taking part.

As they finished the ritual and the Jūpare Pahkome tied their flag to the cross, I returned to the church. Most people had left the church although the images were still resting on their mats and had not been replaced on the altars. The visiting Pahkome then entered the church, rolled up their flags and placed them to the left of the main altar, and left the church going in the direction of the Jūpare cooking ramadas for their lunch. By this time it was around 1 : 30 p.m., since the *komchepte* had taken place at noon. After more *paskola* and *maso* dancing and additional feasting the Visiting Pahkome bid goodbye in a brief ritual and left, although by this time most people were already on their way home and the Santīsima Tiniran *komchepte* was concluded for another year. Nine days of rather brief prayers and chants, the *nobena*, would follow leading to the *pahko* which would take place the next Saturday-Sunday in slightly over a week.

## The Santisima Tiniran Bisita and Espiritu Santo Pahko

A week earlier the Espíritu Santo *komchepte* had taken place
and now Her Pahkome were organizing the *pahko* in Her honour
in Etchojoa. On Saturday, May 21st slightly before 3.00 a.m.
I arrived at the church in Jūpare. The Matachins were dancing
in front of the church and there were quite a few people standing around. I was a bit surprised since it was very early. I went
directly into the church. Just a little while after I had arrived
the Pahkome lined up with the visitors from Pozo Dulce,
Pueblo'ora and Navowaxia, as well as the locals from Jūpare,
all present. The Maestro knelt on the kneeling bench and he
gave the *nobena* prayers for the second Santīsima Tiniran *nobena*
which did not last very long.

As the *nobena* concluded, they removed the image from the
altar and brought up a *heeka* (small canopy to shade an image).
The Matachins who had been dancing since I arrived, preceded
the main body of the procession as they would for the entire
*bisita* and return. The Pahkome left the church first with the
image, the Maestros and Cantora singing and the people
following. The procession moved around the west side of the
church out to the main highway, across a drainage canal, and
along that canal to the Mayo river banks. Many people had
large candles which they were burning. Also a few people had
flashlights, so there was enough light to see what was taking
place.

We went down and crossed the Mayo river, stopping just
along its bank. There was a little prayer service there and they
wrapped the image, carefully, for the road. The Matachins had
gone on ahead. We followed them with the Paskome and then
finally came the image and the Maestros. We left the river bank
about 4.00 a.m. Someone said something about the Cross as
we went by the Cruzasitas which was decorated with flowers.
We went on in the road that goes past the penitentiary and
arrived at the edge of Huatabampo about 5.00 a.m. as it was
beginning to get light. Just before we crossed the canal bridge,
as you enter Huatabampo the Pahkome unrolled their flags and
we enjoyed two short rest stops as they set the image on a
little table. After we crossed the canal, they made another rest
stop. During all the rest stops, the Pahkome stood in their

typical formal pattern, out in the street facing the image. In this characteristic pattern, the Parinam and the Alperesim stand in a line across and directly face the image and the line of Alawasim are directly to their right and vertical to the image with the Mo'oro at their head. Then at the third rest stop just as we entered town they unwrapped the image. As we moved through Huatabampo toward the church the procession continued making several more rest stops as it was joined by many towns people. Finally there was a fifth rest stop, before we turned and went down the road that goes into the square of Huatabampo. Hurrying ahead of the procession I went in the side door of the Huatabampo church. There was a brass band in front of the church that was playing as the image approached and entered the main church door.

Our Pahkome entered while I observed that the Pahkome and their Santīsima Tiniran image from Etchoropo, a neighbouring village, had already arrived. The Parinam and the Alperesim sat on the left hand side of the church while the Alawasim sat on the worshipper's right hand side. They simply sat down in the centre of the church where they could find room amongst the other non-Mayo people that had begun together. The image was carried directly down the main aisle. When they approached the front rail, they dipped the image a number of times to the big Santīsima Tinīran above the altar that is the patron saint of the Huatabampo church. Then they dipped it to their left side and to their right side. Finally they carried it over to the side altar on the far right. They put the Jūpare image on the worshippers' far left where it joined the Etchoropo image and an image of Guadalupe which was positioned in the centre. As they had at all these rest stops towns people also went up now and muhtied (crossed themselves, knelt, prayed, touched the image, touched themselves and crossed themselves again). At 6.30 a.m. the lights were turned on and the local priest came out, recited the mass, and talked a little about the fiesta. Very few people and none of the Pahkome or Mayos went up the rail to receive communion. Most of the Matachins stayed outside and there appeared to be rather few Mayos inside the church although it was very crowded. The few Mayos I saw were just sitting in amongst everyone else on the benches, or standing along the walls beyond the seating area. After the mass was over and the priest left the altar area, the Pahkome with their flags and regalia moved out of the church and the two images were picked up. There was no greeting at all between the Etchoropo and the Jūpare Pahkome.

The procession came out of the front door of the church, turned left and went on around the park where we had entered and continued to the Etchojoa edge of town, making three brief stops in route. At the corner of Huatabampo inside the railroad tracks they rested the images up against a wall and wrapped them and rolled the flags for travelling at about 7.30 a.m. Approximately halfway down the highway to Etchojoa the procession made a rest stop at La Liña. I noted that there were several ambulances following along behind the procession which had become very large as we were picking up people standing along the highway as well as a large number of individuals who had joined in Huatabampo.

On the procession to the edge of Etchojoa a woman approached with several doves that she released in front of the covered images, many people came with donations which they placed in money boxes carried just in front of the images, and at least two people began walking on their knees as the procession neared them. The procession would open and the images would move up to these people and then stop as they prayed and made their contributions. Thus as we approached Etchojoa, the procession proceeded much more slowly. The weather was cool and clear early this morning, a nice temperature for a fast walk, although it would have been cold just in shirt sleeves, had one not been walking hard. After dawn it remained cool, although from La Liña on it began to warm up and by the time we got to Etchojoa it was extremely warm. People were perspiring and were very hot.

A number of people asked me if I was tired which was a major topic of conversation on the pilgrimage. Clearly the value here involves a fast tiring walk as part of the repayment to the Santisima Tiniran for his intervention in a previous cure. The Matachins also dance in compensation for a cure, good health, or a favour. In Etchojoa I noticed a non-Mayo woman who must have been in her 60s who was dancing Matachin, however most of them, are young girls and boys, between seven and fourteen years of age. As we reached the edge of Huatabampo, I counted around 50 girls directly in front of the Pahkome and then two long lines of boys with perhaps 100 in each line. Certainly the Matachins surpassed 200 individuals and there may have been more than 300 including those not dancing and scattered in the crowd.

Around 10.00 a.m. we arrived at the outskirts of Etchojoa, were met by masses of people everywhere and proceeded directly to an open area in a relatively new children's park where one line of Alawasim and a second one of Alperesim and Parinam from Etchojoa, Seaba'a, and Wichaka ritual centres awaited the formal greeting of Pahkome. This greeting would link the ritual centres of Jūpare, Etchoropo, Pozo Dulce, Pueblo'ora and Nabowaxia all from *Santa Kuru Pueblo*, Huata-bampo Municipio, with Etchojoa, Seaba'a, and Wichaka from *Etchojoa Pueblo*, Etchojoa Municipio. As we approached, our Alawasim and Alperesim-Parinam filled the two remaining open sides of a square. The visitors' Mo'oro, that is our Mo'oro, followed by all our Pahkome began shaking hands and greeting the host Pahkome moving from right to left down the Alperesim-Parinam line and then from left to right down the Alawasim line. After this greeting when everyone had returned to their places, our head Mo'oro stepped out from his line and called out "dios em chania" (Hello) and their Mo'oro respond-ed, "dios em chania." The two groups of Pahkome came together and led the image and procession over to two covered niches which are on top of a round flat brick platform. The images were carried up onto the platform, turned around, placed underneath those arch niches and uncovered. The masked *paskola* dancers, who arrived with the Etchojoa person-nel, began to perform down in front of the Pahkome who were lined up on the ground in front of this little platform. Beyond the crowd at the platform a brass band also was playing. The Paskolas moved up on the platform, crossed themselves, prayed, and danced directly in front of the images. Preceded by the Matachins, with the Paskolas dancing the *hinangkiwa* between the images and the Pahkome, and followed by the Maestros and the brass band, the images were carried into Etchojoa and to a home where they rested. There the Maestros prayed, the visit-ing Pahkome did their ritual *ehersisio* (exercise), the Matachins danced, and everyone also rested and ate. This ritual resting is called the *kopana* or *kopanake,* and also gives people in the host community a chance to greet and pray before the visiting images.

Around 4.00 p.m. the procession left the resting home and moved through town to the area in front of the Etchojoa church. The Matachins were dancing at the front followed by the Pahkome, the images and the band playing a processional tune. We went right, then directly across the highway, down one block, turned to our right and went directly down to the church. The procession made several brief stops for worshippers who came up to donate money and pray before the images. As the line of Alperesim-Parinam moved to the far side of the street, we stopped on the street corner nearest the church and watched the approach of the Holy Spirit procession moving down this street in front of the church. The Holy Spirit came up ripidly to meet the Holy Trinities. As the images moved closer together and when they were a metre or so apart, they bowed them, going first to the Jupare Santisima Tiniran and bowing both images. Then they pushed the images right up close together, just a few centimetres apart. I don't know if they actually touched but the Santisima Tiniran and the Espíritu Santo were very close, as though they were embracing and then they were both bowed up and down a number of times together, very close together. Then they backed off the Holy Spirit and moved Her over and bowed Her also to the Etchoropo Santisima Tiniran, again bringing the Holy Spirit right up close so it was practically, if not actually touching the Santisima Tiniran. Finally, they turned Her around and walked behind the image of Etchoropo. Thus the three images did not walk abreast, but the Holy Spirit walked behind the other two. Again the Pahkome fell into their proper formation and the procession moved on past the church and down to the area where the church bells and cross are located, where we turned to our left twice and entered the side church door, the front door being rather high and a more difficult access. As we entered the door there was a great crush of people with this large crowd all jamming inside. However, they were able to return the Espíritu Santo to Her place rather high above the centre altar. On a table in the back right hand corner of the altar area they placed the Etchoropo Santisima Tiniran and in

Social Anthropology of Pilgrimage

the back left hand corner they put the Holy Trinity from Júpare. As they were arranging the images the Pahkome left the church and set up in the area between the cross and bells and the church. They were preparing to exchange the bead rosaries, the *panim kokam*, which consisted of tied strings of buns and oranges instead of beads.

The Pahkome lined up, the *Etchojoa Pueblo* Alperesim-Parinam with their backs to the cross and bells and the *Santa Kuru* Pueblo Alperesim-Parinam directly across from them and facing them with their backs to the church and the Alowasim on both remaining sides, forming a square with an open centre. They put down mats which they covered with their bead rosaries. Standing in the centre area, the Mo'orom from the different church centres organized and directed the exchange. First the Alawasim exchanged their bastons, little wooden sticks with the ribbons attached to one end, and then the Alperesim-Parinam exchanged their flags. The Mo'orom called a pair of individuals from different church centres into the open centre of the square. They crossed themselves while they were standing up, knelt and crossed themselves, then circled each other's head with the baston or flag and exchanged them, crossed themselves, stood up again, crossed themselves and then walked back to the lines.

It was after 5.00 p.m. when they began to exchange the bead rosaries. The Mo'orom pointed to two Pahkome from different *Pueblos* who picked up a bead rosary which they held first in their left hand because they had their usual rosary in their right hand. They carried the bead rosaries into the centre, stood up first facing each other, crossed themselves, and then they knelt and crossed themselves. They were holding the bead rosary in their left hand. Some switched it over to their right hand and put it on the shoulder of the person directly across from their right hand. Others continued to use their left hand and put it on the other shoulder of the person across from them. Thus there didn't seem to be any definite pattern whether they moved it from one hand to the other and which shoulder they placed it on. After they had both exchanged, and the other person held it on his or her shoulder, they stood up, crossed themselves again, and went back to their positions behind the mats. A few Pahkome did try and throw the *panim kokam* over the other person's head. There was some laughter in the crowd especially when this was successful. Towards the end there were a few *panim kokam* left and the Pahkome gave these to their Mo'oro, and the Mo'oro took them then and simply gave them without any ritual to some of the other Mo'oro. Our head Mo'oro was able to throw one or two over the heads of some of the other Mo'orom that were not watching, which produced laughter among the Pahkome and in the crowd. Thus the Mo'orom finalized the exchanges of the bead rosaries while people put them in boxes to carry away. The Pahkome returned to the church, rolled up their flags, put some in the upper left hand corner and others in the upper right hand corner of the church, and disappeared out the side door of the church. *Paskola* and *maso* dancing and entertainment, eating, drinking, social dancing, and a large fireworks (*kastiom*) display followed during the night and early Sunday morning.

Sunday morning the Matachins danced in the church and a white wooden table with an altar cloth and a chalice, etc. were placed in the front altar area of the church. The local Etchojoa priest arrived, heard about two dozen confessions from non-Mayo appearing individuals at the table-altar, passed out a little newspaper with a responsive reading, read from that responsive reading, and went into the sermon. During the sermon the Pahkome began to drift into the church and to go up to the altar area to obtain their flags, etc. He discussed love, especially love for God and love for the Holy Spirit and stressed that true love is first one's love for God. Thus one cannot know how to love unless you love God. While they passed out a dish for a collection and most of the Pahkome had entered the church, the priest said mass and offered the host to a few non-Mayo looking persons who moved through the crowd up to the altar area. When the mass was over he came right down immediately and started changing the Etchojoa Pahkomes' rosaries from the present Pahkome to those entering the position for the coming year. He began with the high ranking Pahkome, the Parinam and the Alperesim, and changed them going right down the line in the same order as the greeting handshake which had characterized our initial entry into Etchojoa yesterday. Then he moved to the head of the Alawasim and back down that line exchanging their rosaries. This all happened very quickly. When it was completed the Pahkome went up to the altar area, wrapped up their flags again, put them up by their images and then disappeared out the side door of the church.

The Matachin dancing, confessions, mass, and changing of the rosaries took place around 10 a.m. to 11 a.m. Afterwards I wandered by the *paskola* ramada where there was very little dancing and more drinking, chatting and sleeping. Then a lot of *kamaram* bombs were set off at the Pahkome kitchen ramadas indicating the *mabedwa* was in progress. In the *mabedwa*, the Etchoja Pahkome, old and new, were giving out large baskets of food, bread, and small rockets to selected families. These *gifts* represented either repayment for assistance or obligated the recipient to return the food two-fold to the Pahkome at the time of the next *pahko* thus establishing a debt. After the *mabedwa* around 2.30 p.m. the Pahkome drifted back into the church as the visitors were getting anxious to go. Some visitors started out the side door of the church, but then they came quickly back in. The Paskolas, Maso and their musicians were being brought into the church by the local Pahkome. They danced in front of the altar, in front of the Holy Spirit. The Mo'oro climbed up on the altar and took the wire down that holds up the Espíritu Santo. He dropped Her down, and set Her on the altar while the Paskolas danced up to Her a number of times, dancing right in front of the altar for a short while. Then they began the *konti* (procession around the church) doing the *hinangkiwa*. We went out the side church door. The Matachins were already dancing outside. They were followed by the Pahkome with Maso and Paskolas and their musicians playing and dancing back and forth, *hinangkiwa*, between them and the images, with the two Holy Trinities first and the Holy Spirit following. The procession moved counter-clockwise in a decorated aisle, which ran towards the *paskola* ramada and around to the front of the church. But when we reached the front of the church, instead of going back in, the procession stopped in the street and Itom Aye said goodbye to Itom Achai. They dipped both sets of images and brought the Espíritu Santo right up close to both the Santisima Tinirans of Júpare and of Etchoropo. As the Espíritu Santo turned back toward the church, we moved down this street clear to the end of town, turned left and crossed the Huatabampo highway. Just across the highway they rested the Santisima Tiniram images up against a tree and wrapped them for the road. The Pahkome formed their square, and re-exchanged or returned their paraphernalia. The visitors, the *Santa Kuru Pueblo* Pahkome, shook hands with the *Etchojoa Pueblo* Pahkome and the head Mo'oro of the visitors made a little speech saying that they would welcome them next week in Jūpare for the Santisima Tiniram Pahko and goodby for now. The visitors then took to the road.

We walked directly down the highway making only a short stop at La Liña and directly on until we hit the outskirts of Huatabampo. As we entered Huatabampo the procession stopped to uncover the images. There were four additional stops before reaching the Huatabampo church a little after 5.00 p.m. The *konti* around the church in Etchojoa took place before 3.00 p.m. By about 3.15 the visitors were on the road back to Huatabampo. We arrived back in Huatabampo around 4.30 and a little after 5.00 p.m. were in the Huatabampo church ready for the evening mass. This return walk seemed faster and considerably more tiring than the preceding day since there were not so many stops.

The images were carried into the church, bowed, and placed on the side altar. After a series of prayers the priest explained that this was the Sunday for the Holy Spirit and next Sunday it would be the Holy Trinity celebration in Jūpare. The mass was somewhat more formal than the one the preceding day. After 6.00 p.m. we were on the road again to Jūpare.

After leaving the church and starting around the central plaza of Huatabampo, the Pahkome from Etchoropo continued straight ahead down the street that parallels the side of the church, whereas the Pahkome from the Jūpare area turned and went on around the park. Some of them waved to each other as they split, however there was no hand shaking ritual. They turned the two Santisima Tiniran images so they faced each other and brought the Etchoropo image up to the Jūpare one. The images were bowed in front of each other, moved very close together as though they were embracing, bowed again, backed off, turned, and as the Jūpare Santisima Tiniran went on around the plaza, the Etchoropo Santisima Tiniran moved on straight down the road leading to Etchoropo. Accompanied by a huge

mass of townspeople, our procession observed the same brief
stops which we had made entering town the preceding day. At
the fifth stop the image was covered while the last stop took
place across the little drainage canal. During the fast march to
the Mayo river bank it was getting dark, as the procession left
Huatabampo a little before 7.00 p.m.

Several *cohetes* (small rockets) were shot when the procession reached the river and the image was uncovered. Then we
marched directly into Jūpare arriving around 8.00 p.m. They
brought the Santisima Tiniran right on the church and rested
Him in front of the altar. There were a lot of people in Jūpare,
some candles were set out on the far side of the canal to greet
the image and many Matachins were dancing in front of the
church. Everyone seemed to be waiting for the procession to
arrive. The Pahkome quickly rolled up their flags and left
them all up in the front corner and disappeared out of the
church door. As local people drifted into the church crossing
themselves and praying to the image and the Matachins continued dancing out front, worshippers placed a large cluster of lit
candles just in front of the church cross. Thus the *bisita* to the
*pahko* of the Espiritu Santo in Etchojoa was complete for
another year.

As we returned to Huatabampo an older Mayo who had
walked from Huatabampo to Jūpare with me said "we will all
certainly sleep very well tonight, and in a day or two the sores
of the *bisita* will be gone."

**The Santisima Tiniran Pahko**

For the next *pahko* the Jūpare visitors now became hosts. Each
day the *nobena* prayers continued in the Jūpare church as small
commercial stands and numerous games and carnival rides were
set up in the open area in front of the church. Although larger
numbers of persons attended the Santisima Tiniran Pahko as it
is believed to be more miraculous, the visiting Pahkome are
fewer because a completing *pahko* in honour of the Santisima
Tiniran was taking place in Etchoropo. The events which we
have described for the *bisita* and *pahko* in Etchojoa in honour
of the Espiritu Santo are repeated for the Santisima Tiniran.
Thursday evening and Friday night the Maso and Paskolas
danced and entertained the worshippers. Saturday morning the

arriving Espíritu Santo and Her Pahkome were met at the river bank and escorted to a home in Júpare where the image was rested until late afternoon. Saturday afternoon the two images, Santisima Tiniran and Espíritu Santo met and the Espíritu Santo was accompanied into the Júpare church where She remained until the *konti* procession and Her leave-taking late Sunday afternoon. The Paskolas and Maso and Matachinis danced, several *castillos* (fireworks displays) were shot off Saturday night, a mass and the exchange of the rosaries took place within the church, the bead rosaries and flags were exchanged and returned in front of the church by the Pahkome, the *mabedwa* took place Sunday afternoon, and the Espíritu Santo was sent on Her way back to Etchojoa after saying goodbye Sunday afternoon. During the *bisita* the church was jammed with people entering to cross themselves and pray to the image. Thus a very similar pattern was enacted during the second half of this set of exchange *pahkom*.

## The History of the Pahko and of Santa Kuru Pueblo

Before the Spanish conquest, the Mayos likely lived in rancherias of less than 300 inhabitants who were small scale farmers, hunters, and fishermen. In 1533 the Spaniard Diego de Guzman made the first contacts with the Mayos and in 1609 Captain Diego de Hurdaide established a peace treaty with the Mayos who requested missionaries. By 1614 several Jesuits had appeared in the Mayo region. They were welcomed by large groups of Mayos and initiated their conversion activities. The Jusuits concentrated the Mayos into a chain of mission pueblos extending from the coast into the foothills of the Sierra Madre mountains. Although it depends upon how far one considers Jesuit settlements into the foothills of the mountains as actually Mayo and what one counts as a *Pueblo*, modern Mayo ideology claims eight original mission-pueblos, *Goh Naike Pueblo Huracionim*. In addition to initiating a programme of concentration, the Jesuits taught in the Mayo language, cooperated and worked through the Mayo leadership, and lived among the Mayos without the support or overt threat of the Spanish military. Their programme produced far-reaching changes in the Mayo socio-cultural system, both in the technico-economic and

social system as well as in Mayo ritual and ceremonialism.
They most likely modified Mayo war societies, founding sacred
sodalities or *cofradias* such as the Pariserom and the Pakhome.
In 1767 the Jesuits were expelled from the New World and
thereafter the Mayos took more or less complete control of
their ceremonies, churches, and chapels.

The 1800s were years of autonomy and of turmoil with
gradual increase of mestizo Mexican military and political
power, or encroaching colonization, and of land loss to mestizo
colonists. Years of both peace and of rebellion characterized
this autonomous period which closed with the final pacification
of the Mayos in the 1880s.

Although the town of Etchojoa has remained the ceremonial centre of the original Mayo *Etchojoa Pueblo*, the history of
*Santa Kuru Pueblo* appears more complex yet more integrally
Mayo. One comes to realize that the Mayo concept of *Pueblo*
includes not only the *village* itself but also the general region
under the control of the ceremonial centre. Thus the modern
*Santa Kuru Pueblo* as a region of Mayo identity is essentially
identical to the Huatabampo Municipio and *Etchojoa Pueblo* to
Etchojoa Municipio. Until the 1880s the Santa Kuru mission-
village (the modern Pueblo'ora) remained the ceremonial centre
of *Santa Kuru Pueblo*, after which time it was gradually de-
populated and the church-ceremonial centres shifted to Hauta-
bampo. In the early nineteen hundreds, as Mayos gradually
lost control of Huatabampo, they established a new church-
ceremonial centre in Jūpare. Gradually tensions grew in Jūpare
and during a flood an unfriendly split took place. The dissent-
ing group formed the Etchoropo church centre also with the
Santisima Tiniran as their patron saint, thus competing with
Jūpare. Closer to Huatabampo a church dedicated to the Santa
Kuru was constructed at Nabowaxia, a friendly church centre
which for years has supported a full set of Pahkome, very
recently has established its own Easter ceremonial, and maintains a pattern of *bisitam* with the Jūpare Pahkome.

Through a process of incorporation of and adaptation to
recent historical events, traditional Mayo symbolism, mythology,
and ceremonialism provides a dynamic basis for ceremonial
revitalization and new cult development. Existing records
suggest that this process has intensified since the Mayo pacifi-

cation and loss of autonomy, which took place during the late 1880s. A number of Mayo prophets, among them the celebrated "Santa" Teresa (see Crumrine 1977 and Macklin and Crumrine 1973) appeared in the later 1880s and in September 1890 many were sent to the mines in Baja California. Several years later "Santa" Teresa was deported to Arizona where she continued curing, becoming famous as a folk doctor. Modern Mayos still recognize her name and know that she was a powerful Mayo curer, although they tend to be much more concerned with more recent events in the lower river valley.

In 1926, President Calles enforced both established and new anti-church legislation which resulted in the burning of Mayo churches in the river valley, including the Jūpare church. Although such church burnings took place in other areas of Mexico, Mayos believe that the local mestizo power structure took this occasion as a chance for revenge against Mayos. They argue that only Mayo churches were burned and not those of the rich and powerful mestizos. These events and especially the burning of the Jūpare church images at Crusacitas, still marked with several decorated crosses by which the procession to Etchojoa passes, are clearly remembered by *Santa Kuru Pueblo* Mayos. In the late 1920s and the early 1930s lands were redistributed in the form of *ejido* society memberships and by the late 1930s the Jūpare church had been rebuilt and Mayo ceremonialism revived. Since that time Mayos have been rebuilding their churches and reviving and adjusting their *traditional* way of life (see Crumrine 1977).

In the late 1950s and early 1960s a very powerful new religious cult developed in the area and many Mayo families made home *pakhom* as gifts to God. A young man had seen and talked with God and proceeded to make speeches informing Mayos that God was very angry and He would destroy mankind if ceremonials were not made. For several years his message was generally accepted by traditional Mayos. Even though the cult eventually died out, the Santa Kuru church in Pozo Dulce resulted from the excitement and home rituals which the cult generated in this predominantly Mayo *ejido* community. Thus, the Pozo Dulce church and its Pahkome organization was established as recently as the mid 1960s.

Pueblo'ora, with a small home chapel housing an image of

the Santa Kuru, customarily hosted a social dance for the May celebration of the Santa Kuru. However, only some very few years ago a formal group of Pahkome was established and now a full *pahko* is offered to the Santa Kuru. Several of my Mayo friends remarked when I recently left the Mayo valley, "when you next return we will have built a proper church in Pueblo-'ora." Although at that time I remained somewhat skeptical concerning the immediate construction of a church, they clearly perceive this reestablishment of the Santa Kuru ceremonial centre as a movement towards the return to the "Goh Naike Pueblo Hurasionim." In fact by 1986 a brick church was under construction and gradually nearing completion in 1988.

### EASTER WEEK RITUAL AT CATACAOS, PIURA, PERU: A PILGRIMAGE FIESTA

During each Holy Week an elaborate ceremonial takes place in Catacaos, Piura, northern coastal Peru. Many pilgrims as well as local participants and visitors crowd the main plaza beside the church of Saint John taking part in the processions and events described in this article. Numerous booths presenting foods, clothes, religious artifacts, and crafts have been set up in order to attract pilgrims and visitors and encourage them to make purchases. This ceremonial, a kind of folk and ritual drama, portrays the passion of Christ through the use of images, events, processions, and specific rituals. Numerous Peruvian fiestas attract many pilgrims who have made promises to attend and take part in the ritual events. This article focuses upon an understanding of the structure and organization of the ritual drama in which the pilgrims and visitors participate. Thus it examines the typical local organization necessary to maintain pilgrimage fiestas.

Yet this type of pilgrimage fiesta is not unusual along the Peruvian coast. James Vreeland (nd), in "Pilgrim's Progress: The Emergence of Secular Authority in a Traditional Andean Pilgrimage", discusses the pilgrimage fiesta for the Cross of Chalpon in the town of Motupe just to the south of the Department of Piura, where Catacaos is located. Further south on the North Central coast at Otuzco in the Department of La Libertad, Robert Smith described and analyzed the fiesta for the La Virgen de la Puerta (the Virgin of the Door). In 1966, the year of his study, the band of Santa Cecilia of Catacaos made a devotional trip to attend and perform at the fiesta in Otuzco. Their trip expenses were paid by a local fiesta sponsor, however their performance was a gift to the Virgin (Smith 1975:58). Considerably further south in the coastal Department of Ica, both Helaine Silverman (nd), in "The Ethnography and Archaeology of Two Andean Pilgrimage Centres", and I (Crumrine 1977, 1978) have described three major pilgrimage centres located in three of the main river valleys running from the mountains out toward the coast and the Pacific Ocean; the Sanctuary at Yauca for the Virgin of the Rosary in the Ica valley, the House of Melchorita in the Chincha valley, and the village of Humay, the centre of the cult of the Beatita de Humay in the Pisco valley. The latter two, like the pilgrimage centre of Sarita Colonia in the cemetery of Callao just outside of Lima, are dedicated to recent historical individuals and are ritually considerably less complex than the pilgrimage fiestas of the far north coast. These pilgrimage centres and fiestas only cover several of the numerous coastal Departments of Peru. I would expect other such centres in these additional Departments as well. Thus the Peruvian coastal pilgrimage fiesta complex is extremely popular and still very dynamic.

Within the Department of Piura itself, in addition to Holy Week in Catacaos, there are numerous pilgrimage fiestas spread throughout the yearly cycle. Richard Schaedel, in "The Fiesta de los Reyes o del Niño in Northern Peru: Locational Symbolism, discusses and analyzes the fiesta of los Reyes or del Niño of the village of Nariguala which lies just beyond the outskirts of Catacaos. Several other pilgrimage fiestas also are celebrated within this department, that of El Señor Cautivo in Ayabaca, of El Señor de Chocan in the province of Sullana, and of El Señor de la Piedad de Yapatera near Chulucanas in the province of Morropon. Manuel Marzal (1977:225-26) mentions the following sacred images located in "regional" sanctuaries, el Señor Cautivo de Ayabaca, Nuestra Señora de la Merced de Paita, Nuestra Señora de Perpetuo Socorro de Piura and the Santa Cruz de Motupe. However, he continues his discussion of regional saints and centres by focusing upon the Santa Cruz of Chalpon or Motupe. My experience suggests that the pilgrimage to Ayabaca for the fiesta of Señor Cautivo is equally popular among Piura valley people as is that for the Santa Cruz of Chalpon.

Ayabaca, with only some 10,000 permanent inhabitants (Cortázar 1975:7), is located high in the Andes above the Piura desert region. Receiving considerable rainfall this very mountainous region is heavily forested. Leaving extremely early in the morning from Piura, local pilgrims can drive up to Ayabaca for a brief visit to Señor Cautivo and his sanctuary and return the same day, arriving in Piura very late that night. However, the road is very difficult and most serious pilgrims plan to stay several days, sleeping in buses or trucks as there are no hotels in Ayabaca. Many, of course, walk rather than ride and remain for the entire week of festivities, which reach a climax on October 12th, the feast day of Señor Cautivo. The walk requires some four days in each direction. The pilgrims pray to Señor Cautivo, either, thanking him for a cure, or requesting a favour or personal miracle, participate in processions and other rituals, and take part in the large diverse market which is associated with the fiesta. Woven cloth, candies, famous Ayabaca hams, and numerous other dishes, foods, and articles are sold. Numerous tradesmen, pilgrims, and returning native sons and daughters arrive from all regions of the Department of Piura, from neighbouring Ecuador, and from as far as Lima and other regions of Peru. Having been established more than 200 hundred years ago, this pilgrimage fiesta is one of the most ancient and most humble in Piura. In addition to this pilgrimage fiesta, a new church has been constructed in Querecotillo as the shrine of El Señor de Chocan whose feast day is celebrated in February. And a recently discovered image, El Señor de la Piedad de Yapatera has become the focus of a pilgrimage fiesta in Chulucanas which takes place in the middle of September. The image, which is kept in a little chapel in Yapatera, is carried to nearby Chulucanas for the festival and is reputed to be very powerful as a curer. Thus a similar general north coastal Peruvian pilgrimage fiesta pattern emerges. However, in this article I shall concentrate upon a description of the Easter Week festival of Catacaos.

## Catacaos

Catacaos is located near the city of Piura, the capital of the Departamento de Piura (State of Piura). Acting as a ceremonial and an economic capital of the Bajo Piura region which extends west of Catacaos down the Piura River valley to the Pacific Ocean, Catacaos and its other ten related districts include some 100 thousand persons according to the 1972 census, with 20 thousand in Catacaos and 40 thousand in Catacaos district (Cortāzar 1975:7). The area consists of hot, dry coastal plains broken by green irrigated river valleys such as the region of the Bazo Piura. In contrast with the rainless coastal deserts to the south, some rain usually falls during the "rain season" from around January to May and the weather is warm the entire year, peaking with days from 35 to 38 degrees Celsius in January and February to cooler in June, July and August; however it is never unpleasantly cold nor extremely hot. The area represents a prime agricultural region with cotton ranking as the major crop and food crops grown in smaller garden areas (Orlove nd.). Most people work as small-scale farmers, wage labour, craftsmen, or fishermen. The town of Catacaos also acts as a craft centre with numerous small craft stores located just off the central plaza. In terms of the general ecology, the region is densely populated with a high percentage of under- or unemployment.

Since the time of Spanish conquest, the area has experienced intense contact resulting in the loss of the indigenous languages and the disappearance of the two aboriginal groups, the Sechura Indians living in the lower Bajo Piura and on the coast, and the Catacaos Indians living in the upper Bajo Piura around and below Catacaos. After Spanish contact, during the early Colonial times, the Catacaos area fell under the *encomienda* system and la Comunidad de Indigenas was created on January 10, 1533, and given the name San Juan de Catacaos: On July 20, 1645, the parish priest, Juan de Mori y Alvarado, bought the Indian lands from the Spanish crown and gave them to la Comunidad de Indigenas de San Juan de Catacaos. This event, commemorated with a plaque in the Plaza de Armas, provided the basis for modern communal land holdings in Catacaos and is proudly pointed out to strangers. Growing, Catacaos became

a Parroquia and on January 11, 1828, it was made a Distrito.
Catacaos cemetery dates to 1843; the telegraph, mail service,
and telephone to 1890; the paved Piura-Catacaos highway to
1924; the railroad service which was opened in 1887 in Piura
also had an extension to Catacaos; and public lighting to 1934.
However, the major church of Catacaos does not date to the
colonial epoch as does the one of Sechura near the mouth of
the Piura river. The colonial temple of Catacaos was damaged
by flooding and finally destroyed by the earthquake of 1912,
after which the present church was constructed. Although the
area is recognized as an "Indian" one in the guide books, the
present cultural tradition reflects years of fusion or syncretism
between indigenous and foreign elements. Chicha, the very
popular fermented corn drink and staff of life, the use of a
three-log balsa raft for ocean fishing, pottery making, and
cotton agriculture to name only a few, are aboriginal and
contrast with electricity, running water, and TV which exist in
many homes in Catacaos. Concerning the Easter pilgrimage
ceremonial itself, we shall point out several suggestive implications of fusion in specific rituals and ritual symbols as we
examine the events of Semana Santa in Catacaos. What is
unique and special is a certain type of syncretism which has
produced a ritual complex unique in its fusion of ritual fervour
and intense labour with a ritual massiveness and a ritual complexity. This complexity which the pilgrim experiences is a
phenomena, not of finicky details, although details are of some
importance, but one of massing ritual upon ritual. For example,
the main church in Catacaos houses some 45 images, many of
which are statues, life-sized or even larger and take part in the
Easter week ritual. Holy Week simply compacts a pattern of
saints' day rituals within one week. Many of these rituals reveal
the same forms and symbols as the North Coastal pilgrimage
fiestas mentioned earlier. Usually the ritual for each saint is
not extremely complex but with such a large number being
worshipped, decorated, and carried in procession, during Holy
Week, the overall picture is impressive. It is especially impressive when one considers that the church in Catacaos is only one
of the numerous churches in the Bajo Piura, all with their own
special set of saints and ceremonies, although the Catacaos
Easter Week is the one attended by the major number of pil-

grims. I was also told numerous times that "Catacaos is a very religious pueblo, probably the most religious in the world." This general belief and attitude, coupled with the massiveness of the images, length of procession, numbers of pilgrims and locals attending and this specific massing type of complexity represents a general ritual orientation and ritual symbol which is extremely characteristic of and may be unique to this "Indian" region of the Bajo Piura. During Easter week, I have observed individuals wearing narrow banners across their chests from as far away as Talara, north of Catacaos, walking toward the Catacaos church, although most individuals attending Holy Week rituals in Catacaos do not wear such symbols of their pilgrim status. Even though these pilgrims purchases and carry photographs of the Catacaos image of Christ in his coffin, yet they are soon lost in the huge amorphous crowds that participate especially in the Good Friday and Easter Sunday rituals.

In order to present what the pilgrim experiences and to examine the ritual orientation of Catacaos, we turn to a description of Semana Santa. After discussion with Richard Schaedel who suggested that very little research had been done in the area and that the ritual system was complex and still well integrated, I visited the area that summer (1977), for several weeks during Holy week (1978, 1979, 1980 and 1981), and for the latter weeks of June 1979 and 1985. Besides several tourist guides such as the *Documental del Peru, Departamento de Piura* (Cortăzar 1975) and the printed programme for Semana Santa, the published material has been very scanty. The only exception is the study by Manual M. Marzal (1977 : 215-302), published as a very long chapter "El Sistema Religioso del Campesino Bajopiurano," in his book, *Estudios sobre Religion Campesina*. In his excellent survey of the religious life in the Bajo Piura, Marzal discusses the belief, ritual, and ceremonial systems and their social organization. Although his data are excellent, Marzal does not include much specific information concerning and describing individual ceremonies or specific ritual symbols and devotes essentially no space to the Holy week of Catacaos. Thus the following main section of this chapter will provide a description of the Semana Santa ritual and symbolism, of Catacaos. The final concluding section will discuss the social and symbolic organization of Semana Santa in Catacaos, develop a broader understanding of the *cofradias* and societies which produce the Easter ceremonial and provide the more general ritual context as experienced by the pilgrims.

## Semana Santa in Catacaos

After the Fridays of Lent, Semana Santa in Catacaos begins with Palm Sunday and its morning mass and blessing of the palms in the Catacaos church. Under the direction of the Society del Señor de Ramos, a small white donkey, the image of Señor Triunfante, the Catacaos priest (Vicario Cooperador), certain members of the *cofradias*, the Depositario and the Doliente gather in the afternoon in the church of Carmen located in the Monte Sullon section of greater Catacaos, a number of blocks down Calle Comercio from the main Catacaos church. The *cofradias* of la Virgen de Dolores and of San Juan Bautista bring the images of Dolores and of San Juan Evangelista down Calle Comercio to the plaza in front of the church of Carmen. Late in the afternoon the procession takes place with Señor Triunfate mounted on the white donkey and the officials moving past Dolores and San Juan who bow and then join the procession with San Juan following the little donkey and Dolores at the end. They proceed up Calle Comercio with residents throwing flowers from their second story windows and roof tops and triumphantly enter the front door of the Catacaos church. This early in Holy week rather few pilgrims or visitors would yet have arrived. Thus this procession is attended chiefly by local people.

Monday, Tuesday, and Wednesday *cofradia* and *sociedad* members gather in the church to mount their images on the *andas* (carrying frames), decorate them with lights, gold, and silver ornaments, and flowers, and carry them in the processions which last around six hours. To power its lights, each image has its own rented generator which follows behind on a three-wheeled bicycle, and many also have their own bands which play in their honour, following behind the image or behind the members of the *cofradia* or *sociedad* when they go on official errands. Late Monday afternoon the image of Señor Cautivo is highlighted in the procession and followed by San Juan Evangelista and Dolores. This image, a replica of the Ayabaca

one, is owned by a local society and represents the Ayabaca centre. On Tuesday the image of El Señor del Prehendimiento appears, followed by the others. Wednesday the Gran Despedimiento takes place with the image of El Señor Jesus Nazareno making its appearance. In the procession the images of Jesus leave the front door of the church whereas the images of San Juan Evangelista, Veronica, and Dolores leave the side door, the one through which images usually return to the church. The latter images circle the Plaza de Armas in a clockwise direction and meet the images of Jesus on the far side of the plaza. When they meet, each approaching image is brought up in turn and bowed to the image of El Señor Jesus Nazareno. Then the procession with all the images, the others following those of Jesus, leaves the Plaza, moves around the town, and returns to the church later that night.

The *Cofradia Jurada* del Santisimo Sacramento takes charge of the preparation and ritual symbols on Thursday. With wooden figures, a table, and real fruit and bread they construct a replica of the Last Dinner in the centre of the altar area. To the far right of the major altar area, they erect a diorama of Abraham preparing to sacrifice Isaac when the angel stops him and on the far left a monument of angels and on top la Custodia, an image enclosed in a glass faced elaborate wooden box. In the morning the officials of the *cofradia* gather and visit both the home of the Depositario, who hosts the Thursday banquet, and also the office building of the town Concejo (council), collecting the Depositario and the town, department and military officials and proceeding to the church. In front of the main altar, the priest places the gold Llaves Sagradas de la Custodia del Santisimo Monumento (the keys to the Custodia) over the head of the Depositario. Then all the officials retire to the home of the Depositario for the Gran Almuerzo (lunch), el banquete de "los siete potajes" (the banquet the seven traditional dishes). It is said that over one thousand persons are served at this banquet. On Good Friday, the *cofradia jurada* del Santo Cristo takes over the ritual, constructs three huge crosses at the front of the church, and places the images of Nuestro Señor Jesucristo del Calvario on the centre cross and, on the worshipper's left and right hand crosses, San Dimas and Alejandro. The photographs of the

centre image, Jesucristo del Calvario, are the ones often carried
by the pilgrims. On Good Friday the Doliente replaces the
Depositario. In front of all the officials, the priest places La
Insignia de Duelo por la Muerte de Nuestro Señor Jesucristo
(the Insignia of the Mourning for the Death of Jesus) around
the neck of the Doliente and he in turn is responsible for the
Gran Almuerzo (a banquet completely of fish and shellfish
dishes). After the banquet the sermon of three hours takes
place and Los Santos Varones, men dressed in white gowns,
remove Christ from the cross and place him in the Santo
Sepulcro (sacred coffin). These events also are photographed by
a local photographer. In a few hours the photographs are
available for sale. While many in the huge crowd of worshippers
try and throw perfume on the body of Christ as it is moved
toward and lifted into the Sepulcro, one of the emotional peaks
of the ceremonial is attained. His Sepulcro is decorated and
carried in a huge procession which lasts all night and only
returns to the church early Saturday morning. It is estimated
that four thousand worshippers take part in this Good Friday
and Saturday of Gloria ritual.

The Cofradía Jurada del Santo Cristo also organizes the
preparations and ritual symbols utilized on Easter Sunday.
After the return of the procession Saturday morning, the Santo
Sepulcro is taken apart and the image of Christ is returned to
the Cross standing in the case on the left hand front wall of the
church. His gold adornments are stored by the *procurador*
(head) of the *cofradía*. The former Sepulcro is made to
symbolize the resurrection by placing the image of the Señor de
la Resurreccion on top of the decorated *anda*. After the Misa
de Resurreccion at 4 a.m. Sunday, the last Semana Santa
procession and the Gran Despedimiento takes place. The
images of la Santisima Cruz and el Señor de la Resurreccion
leave the front door of the church and proceed around the
Plaza de Armas in a counter-clockwise direction, moving quickly.
The images of San Juan Bautista, la Veronica, la Virgen del
Transito, and la Virgen de La Luz emerge from the side door
of the church and move around the Plaza in a clockwise direction. Half way around the Plaza the image of el Señor de la
Resurreccion stops and the ones of the approaching procession,
San Juan, Veronica, and the Virgin of Transito, are carried up

one by one and bowed in front of Christ. When, at last, the Virgin of la Luz is carried up, both the Virgin and the huge *anda* with the image of Christ are bowed. At this same instant while the first rays of the rising sun are striking the figure of Christ standing high above the former Sepulcro, numerous white doves are released from beneath the image, the church bells are rung, and the *castillo* (fireworks) is lit. Then several hours pass as the Holy Cross and Christ lead the procession on around the plaza in a counter-clockwise direction and the other images, San Juan, Veronica, the Virgin of Transito, and the Virgin of la Luz, follow behind. Returning through the side doors, the images are left on display for the remainder of the morning and early afternoon. However the members of the *cofradias* and *sociedades* are first busy removing the gold and silver adornments from the images and returning some of them to the glass cases which line the walls of the church and then occupied in feasting next year's new members, visitors, and pilgrim relatives. Semana Santa in Catacaos is over for another year and many pilgrims and visitors are on their way home, yet many of the *cofradias* and *sociedades* remain active, especially during certain times of the coming year when they will celebrate their patron saint's day.

## The Organization of Semana Santa

In addition to the above events, experienced by pilgrims and participants in general, which present the meaning of the Easter Week, the organization of the *cofradias* and *sociedades* provides the human cooperative basis for the action observation by the pilgrims. The societies maintain their own *locales* which often are chapels housing their patron saint. They maintain much the same membership through the years and hold a proper charter which provides for officers such as president, vice-president, secretary, treasurer, etc. Society members pay dues and ideally the *sociedad* will aid members who are sick, in trouble, or have died and require funeral ritual. On the other hand, the *cofradias juradas* are organized through the church and change in membership each year. Ideally, each *cofradia* consists of 14 members; the *procurador* and the *secretario* who are the heads of the first and second *fila* (file), a first and second *mayor* (a *mayor* for each *fila*) and 10 *mayordomos* (five in each *fila*).

The *procurador* keeps the adornments of the saint, a small image of the saint, two angels, etc. in his home which is open to the public for worship. The home of San Dimas, that of the *procurador* of the *cofradia* of Santo Cristo, is very popular throughout the year with worshippers who drop in all day long to burn candles and make donations to Christ or San Dimas. Many of these individuals arrive from some distance and thus are pilgrims to the shrine of San Dimas. In fact, each *mayordomo* of this *cofradia* must spend a week in turn at the home of the *procurador* making sure that the worshippers have candles and taking care of the images. The home of the *procurador* of the *cofradia* of the Santisimo Sacramento houses three images of the Custodia (one of which is used during Easter Week and another during Corpus Cristi and the Octavo processions) and also an image of Cristo Niño which is worshipped at Christmas time. The third and fourth most important *cofradias* are Animas Benditas and San Juan Bautista. The former is active during funeral services and plays little, if any, role in the Easter ritual, while the latter carries both images in Easter Week processions, San Juan Evangelista and San Juan Bautista, and celebrates the fiesta of San Juan Bautista. Several days after the celebration of the *cofradia* fiesta, the outgoing members and the incoming members meet with the priest in the church. The old secretary presents the books and accounts of the *cofradia* and the gold and silver adornments of the saint are examined, weighed passed on to the incoming *procurador* and his *secretario, mayores,* and *mayordomos.* In summary, in addition to the pilgrims and participants in general, the Semana Santa ritual is supported by these two sets of organizations, the *sociedades* and the *cofradias,* who work together to produce a most complex and extremely powerful ceremonial.

### CONCLUSION : THE STRUCTURE AND FUNCTION OF MEDIATION OF SAINTS *vs* HUMANS

## The Structure and Meaning of Semana Santa in Catacaos

Similar in structure to other North Coast pilgrimage fiestas yet different in specific meanings, the Easter ritual in Catacaos develops toward two major events or dramatic climaxes; the *crucifixion* and *funeral procession* of Jesus and the *resurrection* and *farewell* of Christ on Easter Sunday. Beyond a doubt, the Sunday ritual is timed to take place just as the sun rises is located at the only position in the Plaza de Armas where the first rays of the rising sun shine on the face of the risen Christ. This image of Christ dressed in a gold kilt with a gold sunburst behind him and gold rays around his head, looks more like a young Greek athlete than Jesus Christ. It is as if Good Friday's ritual represents the death of the sun god, perhaps the Inca or pre-Inca deity, and the Easter Sunday ritual the return of the sun as a young deity. Clearly the Good Friday afternoon ritual enacts the descent of the Deity as Christ is removed from the cross, lifted and carried to his coffin, and borne throughout the town during the hours of darkness.

Structurally this Good Friday descent-crucifixion parallels the descent of El Niño in Narigualá (see Schaedel nd), the descent of the Cross of Chalpon from its sacred hillside shrine and pilgrimage—procession to Motupe (see Vreeland nd), la Bajada of the Virgin of the Door in Otuzco, and the dual removal from the mountains to the chapel in Yapatera which is now a legend, and procession-pilgrimage to Chulucanas of El Señor de la Piedad for his fiesta. The second climax, the return and Despedimiento (farewell) of Christ in the Easter Sunday procession and feasting also is structurally identical with the second climax of the other pilgrimage fiestas of the North Coast, for example La Salida of the Virgin of the Door as described by Smith (1975). Thus the pilgrims and participants experience two major climax events before returning to their homes.

The meaning and symbolism of these dual set of events suggests that the pilgrimage on the North Coast of Peru is on another level a dual process, as the individual moves to greet, honour, worship, and absorb health and power from the supernatural the Saint or Christ also move in the opposite direction, descending, so an encounter, a mediation, can take place. At the place of mediation, communication, and encounter, pilgrims give gifts to the deity and the supernatural reciprocates. Feasting, processions, and ritual leave-taking provide the second climax event and symbolize both the return of human and supernatural personages to their permanent homes and the rupture of the encounter, reduced communications, and the lack of mediation. Thus the ritual pattern is one of reciprocity with both humans and supernatural power moving to an encounter which mediates the life *vs.* death and this world *vs.* other world opposition. The place of encounter and mediation, the shrine or church centre, therefore, becomes crucial in this power exchange and transformation of individuals and supernaturals. The pilgrimage fiesta also takes place not only at a specific location in space but also at the point in time in the ceremonial cycle when the supernatural power descends, the images are "alive", and thus the transformational mediation becomes possible.

## The Function of Mediation among the Mayo

I have argued that modern Mayos are in a transitional stage at some point between a pre-contact tribal society and a modern ethnic or fully assimilated status (see Crumrine 1964, 1977, 1981). Today I would hesitate to predict whether Mayos will become a more deeply entrenched ethnic enclave, embedded in modern mestizo Mexico or move toward more assimilated status. Clearly, at this point in time, Mayos are maintaining and reviving their *traditional* way of life and dynamically adapting their key symbols, values, and rituals to the cultural ecology of the modern Mayo River Valley. In an important socio-political sense the exchange *pahkom* in honour of the Espíritu Santo and the Santísima Tiniran unify Mayos at the *Pueblo* or intermunicipio level and contribute to the maintenance of their social group and cultural traditions as separate from those of non-Mayos. For example at the Espíritu Santo Pahko, numerous Mayos pointed out to me that these were the *Goh Naiki Pueblo Hurasionim* as well as discussing this ceremonial and political unit among other attending Mayos. Calling my attention to the eight flags of the Pahkome groups, they argued that each flag represented a *Pueblo*, which symbolically is very powerful although in reality each flag is from a church centre, all within only two of the eight original *Pueblo Hurasion'm.* It would seem to be a fortunate accident that the flags total eight, an increase over the five church centres that we observed participating in the *bisita* of 1959 (Crumrine 1969). Thus the *bisita* and *pahko* ritual pattern is extremely dynamic and capable of reflecting and adapting to recent historical and cultural ecological processes. In addition a number of Mayos participating in or attending the Espíritu Santo Pahko argued that this was a Mayo ceremony, the people attending were all Mayos, all Yoremes, and that the land was Mayo *bwiya* (land). Clearly all this discourse carries messianic implications, a messianic symbolism which characterizes other levels of Mayo ritual as well as the exchange *pahkom*. In summary, the exchange *bisitam* represent and symbolize Mayo unity and their shared historical experiences and also contribute to Mayo continued existence as an enduring people.

At a more general symbolic level, these exchange *pahkom* provide two structural patterns, the *bisita* and the *pahko* in which the roles of the participants and of the ritual patterns are reversed from one weekend to the next. The visiting *Pueblo* moves across the *Pueblo* boundary, passing through space, in order to meet the hosting Pahkome at their sacred church centre and to celebrate the special feast day of the patron saint. In doing so they not only unify the *Pueblos* but also establish contact with the saint through the *nobena* and *pahko* rituals. As Pueblo oppositions are unified into the "*Goh Naike Pueblo Hurasionim*, the human-deity oppositions are also mediated and Mayos communicate not only amongst each other but also with their shared past and with God and the saints.

## What is Pilgrimage ?

Pilgrimage, in the cases presented here, is a dramatic mediation of two worlds or opposed poles through the ritual process of reduction of the opposition and the establishment of communication between two sets of reduced or transformed personages or terms. The special pilgrimage ritual process places emphasis upon the descent of one set of God/Saints and the ascent and transformation of the other set, the participant/pilgrims. The pilgrimage process can function not only to mediate ethnic, class, differences and but also to set participant/believers apart from outsiders and to reinforce ethnic, tribal, and/or group identity.

## REFERENCES

1. The field work, upon which this chapter is based, was financed in part by grants from The Canada Council, The Social Sciences and Humanities Research Council of Canada, and the University of Victoria. I wish to thank these institutions for their kind financial help. Professors Richard Schaedel, Juan Ossio, Antonio Rodrigues Suy Suy, and Manuel Marzal and Mr. Edward Franco Temple were most kind in their encouragement and assistance and in their open exchange of ideas and information. I wish to thank them all for their most considerate interest and aid. Especially I wish to thank the Mayos and the people of Catacaos and the Bajo Piura for their warm hospitality and generosity. Besides being the "most religious pueblo in the world," the people of the Bajo Piura are some of the most hospitable peoples in the world.

2. The data reviewed here are drawn from my two chapters in "Pilgrimage in Latin America" (Crumrine and Morinis n.d.).

## NOTES

Cortazar, Pedro Felipe, 1975, Informe del Peru, Departmento de Pilura. Volumen IV. Lima, Peru : Promotora Editorial Latinoamericana Newton-Cortazar, S.R.L.

Crumrine, N. Ross, 1964, The House Cross of the Mayo Indians of Sonora Mexico : A Symbol of Ethnic Identity. Anthropological Papers of the University of Arizona, Number 8. Tucson, Arizona : University of Arizona Press.

Crumrine, N. Ross, 1977, Three coastal Peruvian pilgrimages. El Dorado 2(1) : 76-86.

Crumrine, N. Ross, 1977a, The Mayo Indians of Sonora, Mexico : A People Who Refuse to Die. Tucson, Arizona : University of Arizona Press. Reprinted in 1988 by Waveland Press, Prospect Heights, Illinois.

Crumrine, N. Ross, 1978, Romerias en el Campo Peruano. Americas 30(8) : 28-34. (Published in the Ehglish edition as The Peruvian Pilgrimage).

Crumrine, N. Ross, 1981, The Ritual of the Cultural Enclavement Process : The Dramatization of Oppositions Among the Mayo Indians of Northwest Maxico. In George P. Castile and Gilbert Kushner, eds., Persistent Peoples, pp. 109-131. Tucson, Arizona : University of Arizona Press.

Crumrine, N. Ross and Alan Morinis, editors. (n.d.), La Peregrinacion : Pilgrimage in Latin America. In press, Greenwood Press.

Crumrine, N. Ross and Phil C. Weigand, editors 1987, Ejidos and Regions of Refuge in Northwestern Mexico. Anthropological Paper of the University of Arizona Number 46, pp. 125. Tucson : University of Arizona Press.

Erasmus, Charles J., 1967, Culture Change in Northwest Mexico. In Julian H. Steward, ed., Contemporary Change in Traditional Societies, Mexican and Peruvian Communities, Volume 3, pp. 3-131. Urbana, Illinois : University of Illinois Press.

Macklin, B. June and N. Ross Crumrine 1973, Three North Mexican Folk Saint Movements. Comparative Studies in Society and History 15(1) : 89-105.

Marzal, Manuel M., 1977, El Sistema Religioso del Campesino Bajo-piurano. In : Estudios sobre Religion Campesina, pp. 215-302. Lima, Peru : Pontifica Universidad Catolica del Peru.

Orlove, Benjamin S. (n.d.), Some Interactions of Production Scale, Natural Environments, and Socio-economic Impacts on Food Production Strategies in Latin America. Paper presented at the Annual Meeting of the American Association for the Advancement of Science. Washington, D.C., February 1978.

Schaedel, Richard P., (n.d.), The Fiesta de los Reyes o del Nino in Northern Peru : Locational Symbolism. In N. Ross Crumrine and Alan Morinis, edited, la Peregrinacion : Pilgrimage in Latin America.

Silverman, Helaine, (n.d.) The Ethnography and Archaeology of Two Andean Pilgrimage Centres. In N. Ross Crumrine and Alan Morinis, edited, la Peregrinacion : Pilgrimage in Latin America.

Smith, Robert J., 1975, The Art of the Festival. University of Kansas Publications in Anthropology 6. Lawrence, Kansas.

Van Gennep, Arnold, 1960, The Rites of Passage. Chicago : Phoenix Books, University of Chicago Press.

Vreeland, James, (n.d) Pilgrim's Progress : The Emergence of Secular Authority in a Traditional Andean Pilgrimage. In N. Ross Crumrine and Alan Morinis, edited, la Peregrinacion : Pilgrimage in Latin America.

# Index

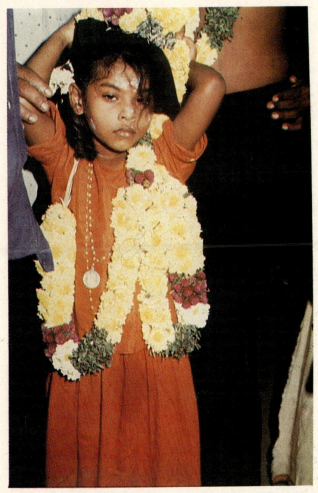

*Illus. 1*  :  Girl with irumudi at start of journey for Sabari
                Malai

*Illus.* 2   :   An Aiyappan altar

*Illus. 3* : Main entrance - Kamakhya Temple, Assam

*Illus. 4* : Goat Sacrifice - Kamakhya Temple, Assam

*Illus.* 5   :   A distant view of Badridham

*Illus.* 6  :  Author  with  the  Kaulacharya  of  Kamakhya
Temple

*Illus. 7* : Indian delegates at the 12th ICAES at Zagreb

*Illus. 8* : Indian participants at the symposium

*Illus. 9* : A session in progress

*Illus. 10* : Sathagoparamaniya group waiting to receive the Raja of Pandalam